Kitchen & Bath Source Book 1999/2000

Sweet's Group

McGraw·Hill Construction Information Group

A Division of The **McGraw·Hill** Companies

1221 Avenue of the Americas
New York, New York 10020-1095

Two Penn Plaza
New York, NY 10121-2298
Tel 212 904 2063
Fax 212 904 6214
norbert_young@mcgraw-hill.com

Norbert W. Young, Jr., AIA
President

**McGraw-Hill Construction
Information Group**

A Division of The **McGraw·Hill** Companies

April 1999

Welcome to the *Kitchen & Bath Source Book!*

As you create your new kitchen or bath, you'll be drawing on your own imagination and common sense. But you need more—you need product information and design guidelines to develop your ideas.

That's where Sweet's *Kitchen & Bath Source Book* comes in. It's brimming with product, color and design ideas all in one handy reference guide. Published by **McGraw-Hill**, this easy-to-use book is composed of manufacturers' catalogs offering all the information you need to plan your dream kitchen or bathroom.

Forget those piles of brochures and individual catalogs that are so easily misplaced. You'll find all the best information and ideas between the covers of the *Kitchen & Bath Source Book!*

For more than 90 years, Sweet's has provided designers, builders and consumers with the best resources for planning construction and renovation projects. The secret to our success is listening to our customers, and finding out what they need to help make the construction process go smoothly. I welcome your questions and suggestions on how to improve the *Kitchen & Bath Source Book* or other Sweet's products and services.

In the meantime, I hope you'll take full advantage of everything the *Kitchen & Bath Source Book* has to offer. Your new kitchen or bath should be everything you dreamed it would be. The *Kitchen & Bath Source Book* can help you make that happen.

Sincerely,

Sweet's Group
McGraw-Hill Construction Information Group

Contact our Customer Service Hotline if you are a construction professional with inquiries regarding Sweet's products and services:
1-800-442-2258 *or*
fax 212-904-2348

Contact our Sales Hotline if you are a building product manufacturer interested in participating in Sweet's:
1-800-421-9330 or
1-877-SO SWEET
(1-877-767-9338)

Look for Sweet's on the World Wide Web at http://www.sweets.com

Officers of The McGraw-Hill Companies

Chairman of the Board
Joseph L. Dionne
President & Chief Executive Officer
Harold W. McGraw III
Senior Vice President & General Counsel
Kenneth M. Vittor
Executive Vice President & Chief Financial Officer
Robert J. Bahash
Senior Vice President, Treasury Operations
Frank D. Penglase
President - Information & Media Services Group
Vasant Prabhu

President - Construction Information Group
Norbert W. Young, Jr., AIA
Senior Vice President - Sales & Marketing, CIG
Eric J. Cantor
Senior Vice President - Finance & Administration, CIG
Stephen L. Kessler
Vice President - Finance & Planning, CIG
Scott J. August
Vice President - Sales, Sweet's Group
Joseph J. Pepitone
Vice President - Sales Development & Support Programs, CIG
Craig B. Soderstrom
Vice President - Marketing, CIG
Daryl D. Brach
Vice President - Construction On-line, CIG, Product Development, Sweet's Group
Steve Y. Fan
Vice President - Infrastructure, CIG
Shirley M. Marshall
Director - Publishing Operations, Sweet's Group
Thomas H. Koster
Director - Product Management, Catalog Files, Sweet's Group
Douglas A. Lockhart
Director - Government Affairs, CIG
Mary E. Fenelon
Director - Residential Products, CIG
Gary C. Graziano, AIA
Director - Client Services, Sweet's Group
Brenda Griffin
Director - Sales Operations, Sweet's Group
William E. Keller
Director - Product Manager, Kitchen & Bath Source Book, Sweet's Group
Stanley Shapiro
Director - Direct Response Marketing, Sweet's Group
M. Louise Slater
Director - Market Research, Sweet's Group
Alma L. Weinstein

Sweet's Consultants

Cynthia Belisle, AIA, CSI
Robert C. Boettcher, AIA, CSI
Donna Burns, AIA, CSI
Robert C. Chandler, AIA
Dorothy H. Cox, AIA, CSI
John W. Embler, AIA, CSI
Raymond M. Hennig, AIA, CSI
Eugene M. Hollander, AIA
Richard J. Mazzuca, AIA, CSI
Wayne W. Puchkors, AIA, CSI
Barbara Ruppel, AIA, CSI
Peter G. Schramm, AIA
G. Robert Steiner, S.E., ASCE, CSI
Albert J. Thomas, AIA, CSI
John S. Vaci, AIA
William E. White, AIA, CSI

Regional Offices

Atlanta, GA 30319
4170 Ashford Dunwoody Road, Suite 275
404-843-4787 • 404-252-4056 - fax
Regional Director of Sales –
Christopher J. Noble

Chicago, IL 60601
Two Prudential Plaza
180 North Stetson Avenue, Suite 700
312-616-3210 • 312-616-4554 – fax
Regional Director of Sales –
Kevin J. Glynn

Dallas, TX 75247
1341 West Mockingbird, Suite 1103E
214-688-5155 • 214-688-5157 – fax
Regional Director of Sales –
Bret A. Ronk

Pittsburgh, PA 15222
600 Waterfront Drive
412-330-2225 • 412-231-6868 – fax
Regional Director of Sales – Elizabeth F. Hazle

San Francisco, CA 94105
1625 Van Ness Ave., 3rd Floor
415-447-7885 • 415-447-7896 – fax
Regional Director of Sales – Nancy E. Harmon

Canadian Offices

Montreal, QC H3G 2A5 Canada
3495 de la Montagne, Suite 11
514-842-9573 • 514-843-3166 – fax
Regional Manager – Pierre Savoie

North York, ON M2J 1R8 Canada
270 Yorkland Boulevard
416-496-3100 • 416-496-3104 – fax
Director of Manufacturing – Bruce Irish

Cover Photos:

Top left: Courtesy of Gerard Valentini.
Top right and bottom: Images © 1996 PhotoDisc, Inc.

Kitchen & Bath Source Book

Table of Contents

To Find Information Quickly

The *Kitchen & Bath Source Book* is organized in an easy-to-use format. Catalogs are grouped by similar product type to help you quickly locate information on manufacturers and products for your kitchen and bath projects.

Coding System

Catalogs are assigned a four-character code indicating their position in the *Kitchen & Bath Source Book.*

As an example: C123

In addition, each catalog displays a unique BuyLine® number for use when calling Sweet's BuyLine® service (see page 5). You will find a two-tiered code on Kitchen & Bath catalog covers:

C123

BuyLine 1234

Refer to the Indexes

The *Kitchen & Bath Source Book* contains complete Firms, Products and Trade Name indexes:

The **Firms** index is an alphabetical list of manufacturers and their catalog codes.

The **Products** index is an alphabetical list of all products within the book. Manufacturers and their catalog codes appear for each product heading.

The **Trade Names** index contains an alphabetical list of trade names accompanied by a brief product description and the catalog code.

Sweet's BuyLine is a service for kitchen & bath professionals. It does NOT provide information of use to consumers.

Attention Kitchen & Bath Professionals:
Need to contact the local sales representative for any manufacturer in Sweet's *Kitchen & Bath Source Book*? **Call Sweet's BuyLine®.**

Here's how to use BuyLine

1. Dial 1-888-280-9950. If you are using a touch-tone line, you will be greeted by an automated voice response from the Sweet's computer. If your telephone uses a rotary line, an operator will assist you (between 8 AM and 9 PM Eastern Time).

2. You will be asked to enter your telephone number using the numbers on your telephone keypad.

3. The system will then instruct you to enter the four-digit BuyLine code assigned to the manufacturer you have selected. The BuyLine code may be found on the front cover of the manufacturer's catalog (upper right-hand corner).

4. The BuyLine system will respond with the name, telephone and fax number (if provided by the manufacturer) of the manufacturer's sales representative serving your area.

   When you call the sales representative, let him or her know you found them through Sweet's BuyLine. It's the best way to make sure manufacturers continue to provide you with valuable information in Sweet's.

Sweet's Customer Service

Call 1-800-442-2258

Sweet's wants to provide you with the quickest and easiest access to the wealth of information within the *Kitchen & Bath Source Book*. This guide outlines several of the special services we offer.

To answer any questions you may have regarding the *Kitchen & Bath Source Book*, our Customer Service representatives are available Monday through Friday from 7:30 AM to 8:00 PM (Eastern Time). Use our toll-free number for any of the following.

Shipping Inquiries

Please call us if your book arrives damaged or if you have received a duplicate copy.

Qualification or Additional Orders

If you have any questions concerning your qualification for the *Kitchen & Bath Source Book*, or any of Sweet's Catalog Files, please call. You will be immediately directed to the proper individual for assistance.

Change of Address

Please let us know if you have moved recently or plan to move in the near future. We need to keep our address records current to make sure you continue to receive the *Kitchen & Bath Source Book*.

If you wish to contact Sweet's Group in writing, please send correspondence to:

Sweet's Group
A Division of The McGraw-Hill Companies
2 Penn Plaza, 10th floor
New York, New York 10121
USA
E-mail: sweet's_customerservice@mcgraw-hill.com

Visit our Web site at http://www.sweets.com

Selected Articles from the National Kitchen & Bath Association (NKBA)

If you're building or remodeling your home, the bathroom is one space you can't afford to overlook. When you consider how much time you spend in this room, you realize that this is one space you definitely want to be comfortable and functional, as well as good looking.

The bathroom is more than a space for three necessary fixtures; it's the place where you can relax after a long day, change your clothes, mend your wounds, apply your make up, comb your hair and take care of a multitude of other grooming and hygiene needs. It's probably the first room you visit in the morning, and the last room you visit at night.

But, how do you begin to make it the luxury room of your dreams? The National Kitchen & Bath Association (NKBA) recommends beginning by assessing your needs for the space.

"First, you must determine who will use the bathroom," says NKBA Director of Professional Programs John Spitz, CBD, CKD. "This will affect the mood of the space as well as the features included in it."

According to Spitz, bathrooms should be designed around the users - a family bathroom, a children's bathroom, an adult's or master suite bathroom, a powder room or guest bathroom.

Each of these types of spaces has its own specific needs and concerns.

The Family Bathroom

"Traditionally, all of the fixtures in the bathroom are placed in one open space," adds Spitz. "But, for a family of four or more who is sharing one bathroom, zoning the fixtures would work much better."

By separating the fixtures into individualized compartments, several family members can use the space together while retaining some privacy. For example, the tub/shower and toilet could be placed in one space and a single- or double-bowl vanity in a second area. This would allow one person to use the vanity area while someone else was using the tub/shower area. Dividing the space into three separate areas may be the best approach for a larger family - one long vanity with the toilet and tub/shower in their own nooks allows three people to use the space concurrently.

The Children's Bathroom

"Small children always pose unique concerns in the home," Spitz says. "They require more safety features and lower heights, but also adaptability as they grow."

According to Spitz, some features which should be included for children are safety latches on drawers and cabinets; door locks which can be opened from outside the space; above-floor storage for cleaning supplies; shower valves which balance water pressure and temperature; pull-out step under the vanity; and adjustable pole-mounted showerheads or hand-held shower-heads.

"Many of the safety features listed for a child's bath can and should be included in all bathrooms," notes Spitz.

The Adult's Bathroom or Master Bath Suite

When planning a bathroom for adults only, or a master bath suite, it is important to note the reasons for the space - privacy, relaxation, efficiency. Again, the reason will affect the fixtures, the lighting, etc.

"When space is limited, but you want a large private bathroom, the master bath suite is the answer," Spitz adds. "By 'stealing' space from the bedroom, the master bathroom can be enlarged creating a private retreat."

According to Spitz, adult baths may also incorporate added amenities such as whirlpool tubs, saunas and bidets, which increase the level of relaxation and luxury for the user. And for those who dream of a more efficient place to dress and groom, Spitz suggests improving the storage and closet area.

"Adequate cabinets with interior storage are a must in the adult bath," says Spitz. "Built-in drawers, racks, and hooks should be added for clothing storage, and divided, shallow drawers as well as deeper drawers and adjustable shelves should be added for grooming supplies in the bathroom area."

The Powder Room or Guest Bath

This specialized space is also known as the "half bath" because it does not include the tub/shower fixture. This is the bathroom that is typically used by guests.

"Obviously this type of bathroom requires less space than a full bath; however, comfort is still important and should not be overlooked," Spitz adds.

According to Spitz, the powder room should incorporate enough space for the fixtures as well as for storage, and enough room for the user to comfortably enter and exit the space.

It is also important that the room include proper soundproofing and ventilation.

As you can see, a bathroom remodel, no matter what style, is a major undertaking. Beyond planning the type of bathroom it will be and the users it will serve, there are electrical, plumbing and clearance considerations which must also be carefully planned. With all these things to consider, it's easy to see that this is not a do-it-yourself project. Spitz recommends working with a bathroom specialist, or a Certified Bathroom Designer (CBD). These are professionals who know the ins and outs of bathroom planning and can make your dreams become reality.

The National Kitchen & Bath Association offers consumers help when remodeling their bathroom. Visit NKBA's web site at www.nkba.org for more information.

The decision has been made! You've decided that the time has come to turn your dream kitchen or bathroom into a reality. Great! Now what?

The Beginning

Your first step should be locating and hiring a professional kitchen/bathroom designer. What can a professional do for you? Plenty!

A kitchen/bathroom specialist can guide you through every phase of your project — decorating, design, construction, and plumbing and electrical systems.

Specifically, kitchen/bathroom specialists are able to:

◆ work with contractors, electricians and plumbers

◆ answer any questions you have about design, products and colors, as well as anticipate and prevent problems that you may not have considered.

◆ create designs that reflect your individual personality through color, style and pattern selection

"To ensure a successful project, it is important to find a kitchen or bathroom professional who is right for you," explains Doris Lacroix, CKD, CBD, NKBA's 1997 President. "Similar to finding a doctor or dentist, you need to locate someone who is capable of completing the job, but who also meshes with your personality."

The National Kitchen & Bath Association (NKBA) provides a list of its retail members, including Certified Kitchen and Bathroom Designers (CKDs and CBDs), in your area who can help you with your project.

The Middle

"Once you have found the kitchen/bathroom planners near you, it is a good idea to visit them in person," says Lacroix. "This gives you the opportunity to see kitchens and bathrooms on display and to talk with designers about products, materials and colors. This will help you discover which designer is right for you."

Lacroix also suggests that you prepare for your visit. Here's how:

◆ Collect and clip photographs of kitchens or bathrooms that appeal to you. Examining these with the designers during your visits will give them a good idea of the styles to which you are attracted.

◆ Evaluate your current kitchen or bathroom to find out what works and what doesn't.

For example, is there enough cabinet shelf space? Is there enough counter space? Is there adequate task lighting above the countertop? In the bathroom, is the bathtub big enough? Is the showerhead at a comfortable height for all users? Is the bathroom safe — does it include grab bars and non-slip flooring?

◆ Write down the answers to these questions and bring them with you when you visit the kitchen/bathroom planners. They will play an important role in the design of your new space.

The Completion

After you choose a firm, a designer will visit your home to take precise measurements. He or she will also spend a great deal of time interviewing you to discover the exact type and style of kitchen or bathroom you desire. Then, a plan, which includes material costs, specifications and design details, will be prepared. When the design is approved and the budget is set, a payment schedule will be arranged. Typically, a schedule is set up where 50% of the total is paid at the signing of the contract, 40% upon start of installation and the remaining 10% when the job is completed. NKBA member firms will usually offer a contract that outlines project responsibilities and a payment schedule.

The time frame for completion of projects will vary. Generally, kitchen and bathroom projects take two weeks to several months to complete. Although living with construction is not easy, it will all seem worth it once your new kitchen or bathroom is complete.

To obtain a list of NKBA member firms in your area, visit their web site at www.nkba.org.

Universal Design: Planning Kitchens That Last a Lifetime

People come in all sizes, shapes and varieties. So do their kitchens. But this space should do more than just reflect personal tastes in regard to color and style. The kitchen must be functional, and it must be designed to suit the needs of all users throughout their lifecycles. This is the basis of universal design.

"When planning a new kitchen, it is just as important to consider who will use the space and how they will use it as it is to choose colors, appliances and styles," explains Mary Jo Peterson, CKD, CBD, Mary Jo Peterson Design Consultants, Brookfield, Conn.

For example, the kitchen is no longer the sole domain of the female of the household. According to the National Kitchen & Bath Association (NKBA), men, women and children are sharing in kitchen activities such as cooking, doing homework, paying the bills, entertaining, etc., and this has an effect on how the space is designed.

Another aspect to consider when conducting a kitchen project is aging. According to the American Association of Retired Persons (AARP), by the year 2020, over 20 percent of the population will be over 65 years old. A survey completed by the AARP shows that a majority of these people wish to stay in their homes and age in place.

"In order to achieve this, it is essential to plan kitchens that allow for independent living," Peterson says. "Although you may not currently need special features, it is a strong possibility that you will someday. So why not plan for it now?"

Planning a universally designed kitchen requires special consideration of every aspect of the space: countertops, cabinets, appliances, etc.

Countertops and Cabinets

Countertops, for example, must be designed within easy reach of the user. Therefore, countertop height must be carefully considered.

A standard countertop is 36″ high, but this height is often uncomfortable for children or adults who are shorter or taller than average or for those who prefer to work while seated. For a universally designed kitchen, NKBA recommends including some countertops that are 28″ - 32″ high. This height is appropriate for seated or shorter users and for use as a chopping or baking center. For taller users, countertops that are 42″ - 45″ high are suitable. This height will work well as a snack bar also. The space should also include some countertops at 36″ high for general use by standing users. In addition, adjustable countertops can be incorporated into the space. By doing so, the kitchen becomes functional for all who will use it, both now and in the future.

NKBA also offers the following suggestions for cabinets:

- Lowering wall cabinets via motorized or mechanical system
- Interior storage systems such as divider drawers, roll-out shelves and tray dividers to provide clear accessibility and easy retrieval of items
- Open shelves for quick detection of items and to eliminate the hazard of open doors
- Drawers instead of doors to eliminate the need to get around the open door
- Lever handles as opposed to knobs to allow easier opening of doors

Appliances

As more and more manufacturers become aware of universal design, more appliance options become available. This allows universally designed appliances to be incorporated into the space without sacrificing aesthetics.

Consider the following items when planning a universal kitchen:

- Side-by-side refrigerators or bottom freezer models provide ideal access for all users — young and old
- Separate cooktop and oven accommodate height differences
- Appliance controls placed at the front allow easy access
- Easy-to-read numbers and touch-pad controls rather than knobs are easier to see and use
- Microwave placement within reach and sight of the individuals who will use it

By including these items in the kitchen and considering carefully their placement in the design, you ensure that the space can be used by everyone, regardless of their abilities or stage of life.

Hiring a Professional

Peterson cautions that the above suggestions are just that — suggestions. And they only scratch the surface.

"Each kitchen is unique — a reflection of the person who uses it," she says.

To be certain that your kitchen suits your needs, it is a good idea to consult with a professional. NKBA provides a list of its retail members, including Certified Kitchen and Bathroom Designers (CKDs and CBDs), in your area who can help you with your project. These professionals will work with you to plan a space that is right for you.

"Your new kitchen should last a lifetime," Peterson says. "A professional kitchen designer will help see that it does."

For a list of designers in your area, visit NKBA's web site at www.nkba.org.

Kitchen/Bathroom Remodeling - Needs vs. Wants

Remodeling can be an overwhelming process, whether you're remodeling your kitchen, bathroom or any room in your home. It's easy to build an idea file that is overflowing with products and styles that you like. But, how do you turn your idea file into your dream kitchen or bath?

The National Kitchen & Bath Association (NKBA) recommends making two lists to narrow your options:

1. what you need for your new space to be functional

2. things you want, if budget permits

Some things you'll need to consider for the kitchen include:

	Need	Want
◆ cabinets	_____	_____
◆ countertops	_____	_____
◆ flooring	_____	_____
◆ oven/range/cooktop	_____	_____
◆ refrigerator/freezer	_____	_____
◆ dishwasher	_____	_____
◆ sink	_____	_____
◆ lighting	_____	_____
◆ waste disposal	_____	_____
◆ recycling bins	_____	_____
◆ desk area	_____	_____

For the bathroom, the following should be considered:

	Need	Want
◆ vanity	_____	_____
◆ separate tub/shower	_____	_____
◆ whirlpool tub	_____	_____
◆ toilet	_____	_____
◆ sink	_____	_____
◆ faucets	_____	_____
◆ storage	_____	_____
◆ flooring	_____	_____
◆ countertops	_____	_____

Keep in mind that the way you use the space(s) should also be a determining factor in the amenities that you choose for your new kitchen or bath. For example, is there one primary cook in the household, or do all family members share in the cooking process? Do you normally make heat-and-serve meals, or full-course "from scratch" meals? Is the kitchen a socializing place? Who will use the bathroom - children, guests? How many people will use the bathroom at one time? What activities will take place in the bathroom - make up application, dressing, laundry?

Since the kitchen and bath pose their own unique remodeling challenges, the NKBA recommends working with a kitchen and bathroom specialist to help you plan your new space. He/she will look at your idea file and talk with you in depth about your needs and wants. A kitchen or bathroom specialist can make recommendations for your new space based on the way you live that will save you time and money before, during and after the remodeling process. And, he/she can help you choose products and colors to fit your individual style.

To receive a list of NKBA members in your area, visit their web site at www.nkba.org.

Millions of kitchens will be built or remodeled in 1998. Some of the projects will be dreams come true. Some others could be nightmares.

When you stop and think about the effects that every alteration has on a room, you realize just how complicated remodeling or building can be. Besides the logistical questions, many decisions must be made in terms of color, hardware, appliances, lighting, plumbing fixtures, countertops, and the overall style of your new room.

"With so many decisions to make and so much to think about, the average consumer needs a professional to organize this project — someone who understands all of the complexities involved," said Doris Y. Miller, 1998 President of the *National Kitchen & Bath Association*. "Kitchen and bathroom design is a specialized trade. It requires a good deal of experience and know-how to accomplish successful projects."

The first step in creating a successful new room is a simple one — find an NKBA member to design and coordinate the construction of your room.

"Someone remodeling a kitchen or bathroom wants the project to get off to a good start, and a kitchen and bath professional is definitely the way to go," said Miller. "An NKBA member will coordinate every aspect of the design and installation. They are experienced at working with contractors, electricians, plumbers, etc., and can efficiently schedule the jobs involved. And, most important, they are experts at working with the client. They listen to client needs and translate them into the kind of rooms they want."

To help you get ready for a remodeling and work with a kitchen or bathroom designer, visit NKBA's web site at www.nkba.org.

FROM INSPIRATION TO SENSATION

Creating Your
Dream Kitchen
Or Bathroom

OFF
TO A
GOOD
START

So, you've decided to create your dream kitchen or bathroom. Great idea. You'll finally be able to apply all of those wishes you've collected on your list over the years, like that kitchen island with a cooktop (and more of that invaluable countertop and cabinet space), or maybe you've always wanted a bathtub-for-two. Whether it's the kitchen or bathroom (or both), you can look forward to an exciting transformation into the room you've always wanted.

But when you stop and think about the effects that every alteration has on a room, you realize just how complicated remodeling or building can be. Take, for instance, the kitchen island with a cooktop. Where there's a cooktop, there's smoke and steam. And where there's smoke and steam, there has to be ventilation. So an overhead hood must be added, unless you have a downventing cooktop. Also, any time you have work space like the added countertop, you need electrical outlets. So wiring will be necessary for the outlets, as well as the cooktop and vent hood. And that's just the beginning.

Besides the logistical questions, many decisions must be made in terms of color, hardware, appliances, lighting, plumbing fixtures, countertops, and the overall style of your new room.

With so many decisions to make and so much to think about, you need a professional to organize this project — someone who understands all of the complexities involved. That's where the National Kitchen and Bath Association (NKBA) comes in.

FINDING THE NKBA MEMBER FOR THE JOB

The first step in creating your new room is a simple one — find an NKBA member to design and coordinate the construction of your room. You want your project to get off to a good start, and a kitchen and bath professional is definitely the way to go.

WHY?

The National Kitchen & Bath Association is an organization of professionals who focus specifically on kitchens and bathrooms. When you deal with an NKBA member, you'll benefit from specialized expertise, years of experience, a commitment to quality, and a high degree of professionalism. They maintain showrooms with products and complete designs on display so you can get a feel for the type and quality of work they can do.

A kitchen and bath professional can offer sound advice and suggest solutions to any problems that may arise, or, better yet, prevent problems from occurring. They also understand the ways families and individuals relate to their surroundings, and therefore may be able to troubleshoot and meet needs in ways that may not occur to those who don't specialize in kitchens and bathrooms.

An NKBA member will coordinate every aspect of the design and installation. They are experienced at working with contractors — electricians, plumbers, etc. — and can efficiently schedule the jobs involved. And, most important, they are expert at working with you, the client. They listen to your needs and translate them into the kind of room you want.

Don't take chances with your investment. When you make the decision for a new kitchen or bathroom, make the decision to find an NKBA member.

HOW?

NATIONAL KITCHEN
NKBA
& BATH ASSOCIATION

I t's easy to find an NKBA member, if you know what to look for. And easy identification begins with the NKBA logo, a symbol of quality, dedication and expertise in kitchens and bathrooms.

When visiting kitchen and bath showrooms, look for the logo in windows or on the counter.

If you know anyone who has recently remodeled, talk with them. Ask them who they used and if he or she is associated with the NKBA. Referrals are an excellent source for finding an industry professional, but be sure you're dealing with someone qualified in kitchens and bathrooms specifically — an NKBA member.

You can find all of the NKBA members in your area by contacting the National Kitchen and Bath Association at 687 Willow Grove Street, Hackettstown, New Jersey 07840, or by visiting their web site at **www.nkba.org.**

HAVE YOU FINISHED YOUR HOMEWORK?

Now that you have a name in mind (or possibly more than one — you may want to talk with several NKBA professionals to find the one with whom you feel most comfortable), you can go ahead and set up an appointment to discuss your project. But before you actually sit down with the designer, there are several things you should do in preparation. (This is the fun part.)

Chances are you've been thinking about this for a while, but if not, start reading magazines geared toward the home, remodeling, architecture, and especially those that focus on kitchens and bathrooms. Clip out pictures of kitchens or bathrooms that interest you — this will help the designer get a feel for the styles you like. You may even find features that would work in your new room.

Visit kitchen and bath showrooms to see the many options for new countertops and other surfaces, and to collect brochures on fixtures, cabinets, appliances and any other items or materials that interest you.

As you visit different showrooms in your search for ideas and NKBA designers, you should make notes on each one. The best way to find the NKBA member with whom you're most comfortable is to evaluate the designers and their showrooms. Use the following checklist to help you in your decision:

Evaluating the kitchen and bath dealership

	Showrooms #1	#2	#3		Showrooms #1	#2	#3
Showroom Clean and Neat	___	___	___	Designers Ask Questions About Your Project	___	___	___
Displays Highlight Interesting Design	___	___	___	NKBA Membership Identified	___	___	___
Displays Well-Constructed and Presented	___	___	___	Firm Has Been In Business for at Least Two Years	___	___	___
Broad Range of Styles Offered	___	___	___	Firm Provides Complete Design and Installation Services	___	___	___
Staff Friendly and Helpful	___	___	___	Referrals Provided	___	___	___
Staff Knowledgeable About Products and Design	___	___	___				

As you visit showrooms and gather notes, clippings, photographs, brochures and samples, you may want to organize them into an "idea file." As your file grows, you'll see a definite style emerge from the decorating trends you've chosen — *your* style.

KITCHEN PLANNING WITH YOUR NKBA SPECIALIST

You can save a lot of time and money, and greatly reduce guesswork by first evaluating your needs. Before even your initial consultation, write down some basic lifestyle facts.

Simple facts, like how many hours a week you work, will affect how often you cook and what appliances you use. If you work a lot of hours out of the home, you may cook less often, opting instead for microwave meals, in which case you'd need your microwave in a convenient location and a lot of freezer space.

Who uses your kitchen? Is it a setting for family gatherings, or the private domain of a gourmet chef? Will it function well with two or more cooks? Do you entertain often? All of these answers will affect the size, layout and type of equipment you need for your kitchen.

When preparing your evaluation, first consider your normal cooking habits. For instance, if your family shares in the meal preparation, you may need two sinks and built-in cutting and chopping boards strategically placed throughout the kitchen to maximize food preparation areas.

Will children be active in the kitchen? If so, easy-to-clean surfaces are a must. You may also want to consider a desk or counter setup for homework and after-school snacks.

If you like to entertain, often cooking for large groups of guests, you may need two ovens and a wide-shelved refrigerator.

Do you recycle? You'll need the separating and storage space, depending on your involvement and the requirements in your area.

All of the variables mentioned here (and others your designer will pose) will affect the layout of your kitchen. Each shape — U-shaped, L-shaped, Corridor, Island, One-Wall, or Peninsula — has its own functionality and advantages. Once the NKBA kitchen specialist has laid out your kitchen, he or she will guide you in selecting components. With all of the advances in materials, appliances and designs, this selection process would be overwhelming without the help of a professional.

Your decision-making becomes much easier once you have related your needs to your lifestyle. By providing your NKBA professional with a clear picture of what works best for your family, you'll be off to a head start.

BATHROOM PLANNING WITH YOUR NKBA SPECIALIST

Do you look forward to spending time in your bathroom? Sounds like a strange question to most people. Most bathrooms are cold and claustrophobic, places where comfort is either kept to a bare minimum, or simply not an option. But with the shift in society back toward the home also come changes in the bathroom.

Bathrooms have become more than a necessity. Their role has now expanded to that of "bodyroom," incorporating such amenities as whirlpool tubs, exercise equipment, dual-head showers, heat lamps and entertainment systems.

Before you talk to an NKBA professional about your new bathroom, evaluate your needs by first looking at who will use it, and how. The best way to do that is to examine present bathroom usage. Some NKBA members suggest taking notes as you use the room on a typical weekday and weekend. By mapping out your routine, you and your bath designer will be better-equipped to create a floorplan that is efficient and incorporates the features you need.

For example, you may think the first thing you do when you step out of the shower is to reach for your towel. Keeping a diary, however, might reveal that oftentimes the first move after exiting the shower is to drip, drip, drip across the hall to the linen closet. So, by simply focusing on details and making note of them, you've discovered the need for bathroom towel storage.

If several girls or women use the bathroom, adequate circuits and outlets are necessary for hair dryers and curling irons, as well as appropriate lighting for makeup application.

Special safety and convenience features should be considered for elderly, very young and handicapped family members. High water closet seats, grab bars and locking cabinets are practical options, and your designer will likely have other suggestions.

For family bathrooms which are shared by several people, privacy zones isolating the shower, tub, lavatory and water closet will allow simultaneous use.

Your NKBA bathroom specialist will take into consideration all of these factors and more. They have the experience to anticipate potential problems and point out options that may help you with your choices.

SETTING
PRIORITIES

When your idea file is overflowing with clippings and photographs, you've thought about style and color, and evaluated your needs, there is one final step that will really help your NKBA professional: your "must-have" and "want" lists. You simply make two lists which include:

1) features you consider essential for your new room, and
2) features you'd like to have, if possible and if budget permits.

It sounds easy, right? Well, this one may force you to make some tough decisions and possibly even some sacrifices, but it is a very valuable step. Just listing and distinguishing the "must-haves" from the "wants" will help you focus on the features most important to you and your family. In fact, you may want to let each member of the family make their own lists. When you can actually see them on paper, it puts your needs into better perspective.

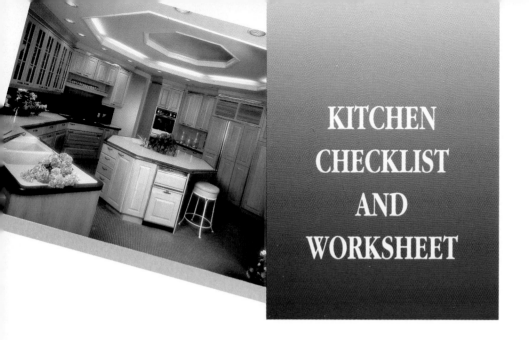

Needs and Wants

Check the items you feel your kitchen must have in the "need" column, and the items you would like, if the budget and design allow, in the "want" column. (This should be used as a preliminary guideline; they may change along the way.)

	Need	Want		Need	Want
New cabinets	____	____	Recycling bins	____	____
New countertop	____	____	More workspace	____	____
New floor	____	____	More storage	____	____
New oven(s)	____	____	Pantry	____	____
New refrigerator/freezer	____	____	Wet bar	____	____
New cooktop	____	____	New window(s)	____	____
New microwave	____	____	Desk area	____	____
New dishwasher	____	____	Eating area	____	____
New sink(s)	____	____	Media/TV center	____	____
New light fixtures	____	____	Others _____	____	____
Cutting/chopping surfaces	____	____	_____	____	____
Waste disposal	____	____	_____	____	____
Trash compactor	____	____	_____	____	____

Lifestyle/Room Use

This worksheet will give you some things to think about in your initial planning, but it's only the beginning. Your NKBA kitchen specialist will conduct an in-depth interview with you in order to create a design that suits your lifestyle and satisfies your needs and wants.

Who is the primary cook? _____

How many other household members cook? _____

Do any of these members have physical limitations? _____

What type of cooking do you normally do?
_____ Heat and serve meals
_____ Full-course, "from scratch" meals
_____ Bulk cooking for freezing/leftovers
_____ Other _____

Do you entertain frequently? _____ Formally _____ Informally

Is the kitchen a socializing place? _____

Where do you plan to sort recyclables?
___ Kitchen ___ Laundry ___ Garage ___ Other

What type of feeling would you like your new kitchen space to have?
___ Sleek/Contemporary ___ Warm & Cozy Country
___ Traditional ___ Open & Airy
___ Strictly Functional ___ Formal
___ Family Retreat ___ Personal Design Statement

BATHROOM CHECKLIST AND WORKSHEET

Needs and Wants

Check the items you feel your bathroom must have in the "need" column, and the items you would like, if the budget and design allow, in the "want" column. (This should be used as a preliminary guideline; they may change along the way.)

	Need	Want		Need	Want
New vanity	____	____	Heat lamp	____	____
Separate shower	____	____	Bidet	____	____
New lavatory (sink)	____	____	New floor/wall surfaces	____	____
Tub for two	____	____	New countertops	____	____
Whirlpool tub	____	____	Customized storage	____	____
New water closet (toilet)	____	____	Others _____	____	____
Exercise area	____	____	_____	____	____
Entertainment center	____	____	_____	____	____
Linen storage	____	____	_____	____	____
Lighting fixtures	____	____	_____	____	____

Lifestyle/Room Use

This worksheet will give you some things to think about in your initial planning, but it's only the beginning. Your NKBA bathroom specialist will conduct an in-depth interview with you in order to create a design that suits your lifestyle and satisfies your needs and wants.

Who will use this bathroom (i.e., client, spouse, child, guests)?
_____

Type of bathroom?
___ Powder   ___ Children's   ___ Mastersuite   ___ Hall

How many will use it at one time? _____

What activities will take place in the bathroom?
___ Makeup application   ___ Bathing
___ Hair care   ___ Dressing
___ Exercising   ___ Lounging
___ Laundering   ___ Other _____

Would you like his and hers facilities? _____

Do you prefer the water closet and/or bidet to be isolated from the other fixtures? _____

Would you like a closet planned as part of your new bathroom?
____ Yes   ____ No

What type of feeling would you like your new bathroom to have?
___ Sleek/Contemporary   ___ Warm/Country
___ Traditional   ___ Open & Airy
___ Personal Design Statement

THE DESIGN CONFERENCE

O.K., you've done your homework — you stand ready with your ideas, lists, samples, photographs, maybe even rough plans. And now it's time to meet with your designer.

You may first meet with the NKBA member at the showroom to look over samples and displays, but then he or she will come out to your house and really get to work. Here's where you'll begin to see what sets NKBA specialists apart from other designers. The NKBA member will take careful and thorough measurements, right down to locating the pipes in the walls (something often overlooked by those who do not specialize in kitchen and bathroom planning).

He or she will look at your idea file and talk with you in depth about your needs. This is an opportunity for both of you to discuss thoughts and opinions, ask questions and determine a direction for your room design. Think of it as an exchange of ideas, a "design conference." This is another advantage of working with an NKBA member. He or she will work *with you* to achieve the best results, instead of simply dictating a design.

One very important determinant for your new room design is your budget. You should have a figure established as you go into this — one that's realistic for your situation. And the initial design conference is the time to talk budgets. Your NKBA specialist will let you know what can be achieved — in the way of materials, construction, appliances, etc. — for what you want to spend. And together, you can set priorities for your design that will allow your new dream room to stay within your budget.

When you both agree on a general direction and a budget, you can make arrangements for payment.

With many firms, payment begins with 50% at the signing of the contract, then 40% when installation begins, and the remaining 10% upon completion of the job. Financing can be arranged through a home improvement loan, or you may be able to negotiate the price into the mortgage when purchasing a home. Remember, your new room is an investment in your home's equity. It increases with the value of your home, and may be recovered when the home is sold.

LET THE TRANS- FORMATION BEGIN

From the first meeting, you'll begin to see how working with an NKBA member will make the project easier, and the results, better. When you've got the knowledge and experience of an NKBA professional on your side, you can rest assured that your new room will be everything you dreamed it would be, and more.

First, your NKBA specialist will design the complete layout, choose the final materials, and begin coordinating the contractors — all with your approval, of course. Then, the construction begins.

Living under construction is never easy, but your NKBA professional will do everything possible to minimize the inconvenience for you. Ask him or her for tips on living under construction. For example, setting up temporary facilities for cooking and cleanup. Your NKBA designer has experience in these matters and will undoubtedly have ideas to make you more comfortable during this phase.

And now it's only a matter of time before you see your dream room become a reality. Exactly how long depends on many variables (whether or not you are having cabinets custom-designed, for example), but in somewhere between two weeks and several months, you'll see the results.

You'll soon see your room taking shape. The ideas you've envisioned, the style you've developed, the colors you've decided upon, you'll see it all materialize at the hands of the craftsmen.

ANOTHER HAPPY ENDING

I t's evening, you're dining in your new kitchen, or soaking in your new whirlpool tub. You proudly gaze around the room. For the next few weeks you'll have to open an extra drawer or two looking for the silverware. Or you may catch yourself walking across the room to where the towels *used to* be. But you'll enjoy getting to know your new room and growing with it. After all, you created it (with a little help from NKBA).

National Kitchen & Bath Association
687 Willow Grove St.
Hackettstown, New Jersey 07840
www.nkba.org

Catalogs are coded by position within the volume in numerical sequence, e.g., C345.

A

Acme Brick Co., Innovative
   Building Products, Inc.
    glass masonry units B667
    showers C565A
Aristokraft, Inc. C520

B

Basco, Inc. C585
Broan Mfg. Co., Inc.
    medicine cabinets C587
    range hoods C485; C915
    residential appliances . . . inside front cover
Bruce Floors, Bruce Hardwood
   Floors, Triangle Pacific Corp. C310
Bruce Hardwood Floors,
   Triangle Pacific Corp.
    wood flooring C246
   Triangle Pacific Corp., Bruce
   Floors
    laminate flooring C310
   Triangle Pacific Corp.,
   Premier Wood Floors
    wood floors C247

C

Century Shower Door, Inc. C593
Clarion Bathware C566B
Colorco, Ltd. C174

D

DuPont Co. C474

F

Formica Corp. C379

H

Hartford Conservatories, Inc. B575

I

Innovative Building Products,
   Inc., Acme Brick Co.
    glass masonry units B667
    showers C565A
Interceramic, Inc. C180

K

KitchenAid, Whirlpool Corp. C503
KraftMaid Cabinetry, Inc. C529

M

Melton Classics, Inc. A296
Myson, Inc. C589

P

Premier Wood Floors, Bruce
   Hardwood Floors, Triangle
   Pacific Corp. C247

R

Roberts Step-Lite Systems C949

S

Sharp Electronics Corp. C512
Sign of the Crab, Strom
   Plumbing C584
Strom Plumbing, Sign of the
   Crab .C584
Sub-Zero Freezer Co., Inc.
    refrigerators/freezers A028; C514;
                      C515; C515A

T

Triangle Pacific Corp.,
   Bruce Hardwood Floors
    wood flooring C246
   Bruce Hardwood Floors,
   Bruce Floors
    laminate flooring C310
   Bruce Hardwood Floors,
   Premier Wood Floors
    wood floors C247

W

Wellborn Cabinet, Inc. C536
Whirlpool Corp., KitchenAid C503
White River Hardwood
   Products C464
Wilsonart International, Inc. C478

Products

A

Accessible products for the disabled
see
Bathroom accessories: —disabled persons' use
Bathroom accessories: —grab bars—specific material
Cabinets: —bathroom vanity—disabled persons' use
Mirrors: —tilting
Plumbing fittings and trim
Showers: —seats for—wall-mounted
Surfacing—detectable, tactile—disabled persons' use
Washroom accessories: —disabled persons' use: —grab bars

Acoustical products
see
Specific products

Acoustic isolation and control
see
Partitions—properties

Acrylic products
see
Sinks—residential: —kitchen—acrylic, composite—specific type

Adhesives for
see also
Specific products: —adhesives for

flooring—wood
Bruce Hardwood Floors, Triangle Pacific Corp. C246

Admixtures
plasticizers
see
Sealers

Air conditioners
see
Blowers—centrifugal or axial

packaged—unitary
see
Heaters—unit

Air-conditioning equipment
see
Blowers—centrifugal or axial

Air distribution equipment
see
Blowers—centrifugal or axial
Fans
Ventilators

Air/liquid treatment equipment
see
Waste handling equipment and systems

Air pollution, quality control equipment
see
Blowers—centrifugal or axial
Vacuum cleaning systems
Ventilators: —grease containment/extractor—food service equipment

Alarms and alarm systems
horns, bells, chimes, sirens
see
Bells, buzzers, chimes (entrance and alarm)

Aluminum products
see
Doors—frames for: —aluminum—specific type
Skylights—framing: —aluminum or aluminum alloy

Appliances—residential—kitchen
see
Dishwashers—residential
Ranges and ovens—residential
Refrigerator-freezer combination: —residential—specific type
Refrigerators: —residential—specific type

Architectural artwork
cornices
see
Lath and plasterwork accessories and trim: —cove moldings
Moldings and cornices
Surfacing and paneling—interior—materials: —moldings and trim for—specific material

graphics
Colorco, Ltd. C174

ironwork—ornamental
see
Specific products

mantels
see
Mantels

Architectural artwork cont.
moldings and cornices
see
Moldings and cornices

mosaics
see
Ceramic or clay tiles: —ceramic mosaic
Glass—form
Marble: —mosaics

murals
see
Murals

niche caps, casings
White River Hardwood Products C464

Architectural woodwork
see
Woodwork

Art and decorative objects
see
Architectural artwork
Ceramic or clay tiles: —ceramic mosaic
Glass—form
Marble: —mosaics
Murals

Ash handling equipment
see
Vacuum cleaning systems

Association catalogs
see
Specific products

Athletic equipment and facilities
see
Bathtubs: —hydro-massage combination

Atriums
see also
Conservatories
Greenhouses
Solariums
Structures—modular, prefabricated
Hartford Conservatories, Inc. B575

Auditorium equipment
see
Lighting—application: —stage, cinema or theater

B

Bar furniture and equipment
elbow rests, bar tops
Wilsonart International, Inc. C478

Barrier-free design products
see
Bathroom accessories: —disabled persons' use
Bathroom accessories: —grab bars—specific material
Cabinets: —bathroom vanity—disabled persons' use
Mirrors: —tilting
Plumbing fittings and trim
Showers: —seats for—wall-mounted
Surfacing—detectable, tactile—disabled persons' use
Washroom accessories: —disabled persons' use: —grab bars

Bars
see
Bar furniture and equipment
Bathroom accessories: —grab bars—specific material
Washroom accessories: —grab bars

Bases
see
Columns
Flooring—specific material
Lath and plasterwork accessories and trim: —bases and fittings
Showers: —stall and receptor for—specific material
Wood frame construction accessories: —caps and bases—for column or post

Bathroom accessories
see also
Washroom accessories

cabinet and mirror
see also
Cabinets: —medicine
Mirrors
Aristokraft, Inc. C520
Basco, Inc. .C585
Broan Mfg. Co., Inc. C587

cabinet and mirror—with lighting fixture
see also
Lighting—application: —accent and display —cabinet and mirror
Basco, Inc. .C585
Broan Mfg. Co., Inc. C587

disabled persons' use
Basco, Inc. .C585

dispensers—facial tissue
Basco, Inc. .C585

dryers—hand or hair
see
Washroom accessories: —dryers—specific type—hand or hair

fans
see
Fans: —kitchen or bathroom

fittings
see
Plumbing fittings and trim

grab bars, safety toilet seats, safety towel bars—metal
Basco, Inc. .C585

heaters
see
Heaters—unit

Bathroom accessories *cont.*
holders—toothbrush and/or tumbler—metal
Basco, Inc. .C585

hooks—coat or robe
Basco, Inc. .C585

lighting—accent
see
Lighting—application: —accent and display

mirrors
see
Mirrors

partitions
see
Partitions—shower, toilet, urinal

shelves
see
Shelving

toilet paper holders, soap dishes—metal
Basco, Inc. .C585

towel holders
Basco, Inc. .C585
Myson, Inc. .C589
Strom Plumbing, Sign of the Crab C584

towel holders—warmers for
Myson, Inc. .C589

vanity cabinets
see
Cabinets: —bathroom vanity: —bathroom vanity—disabled persons' use

Baths
see
Bathtubs: —hydro-massage combination

Bathtubs
accessories for
Century Shower Door, Inc. C593
Clarion Bathware C566B
Strom Plumbing, Sign of the Crab C584

enclosures for
Century Shower Door, Inc. C593
Formica Corp. C379
Strom Plumbing, Sign of the Crab C584
Wilsonart International, Inc. C478

enclosures for—sliding door
Century Shower Door, Inc. C593

enclosures for—swinging door
Century Shower Door, Inc. C593

fiberglass, fiberglass-reinforced, plastic
Clarion Bathware C566B
Wilsonart International, Inc. C478

fittings for
see
Faucets—application: —bathtub
Plumbing fittings and trim

hydro-massage combination
Clarion Bathware C566B

surrounds, wall liners for
see
Bathtubs: —enclosures for

whirlpools
see
Bathtubs: —hydro-massage combination

Bathtub/shower—prefabricated units
Clarion Bathware C566B

Beads
see
Flooring—specific material

Beams, girders and rafters
anchors, hangers, accessories for—wood framing
see
Wood frame construction accessories

Bells, buzzers, chimes (entrance and alarm)
Broan Mfg. Co., Inc. . . . . inside front cover

Bicycle equipment
see
Toppings—traffic-bearing

Blocks—glass
see also
Flooring—glass block
Glass—form: —block
Panels—building—materials: —glass, glass block
Partitions—materials: —glass block
Paving: —glass block
Skylights—materials: —glass—block, corrugated, plain or wired
Windows—replacement: —glass blocks for

curved
Innovative Building Products, Inc., Acme Brick Co. B667

decorative
Innovative Building Products, Inc., Acme Brick Co. B667

framing for
Innovative Building Products, Inc., Acme Brick Co. B667

structural
Innovative Building Products, Inc., Acme Brick Co. B667

Blowers—centrifugal or axial
see also
Fans
Ventilators

variable flow control
Broan Mfg. Co., Inc. C915

ventilating or exhaust
Broan Mfg. Co., Inc. C915

Bluestone
see
Specific products—flagstone

Brackets
see
Luminaires—components: —hardware, brackets, extrusions, fasteners

Braille products
see
Surfacing—detectable, tactile—disabled persons' use

Bridges
nosings for
see
Toppings—traffic-bearing

Building panels
see
Panels—building

Buildings—modular, prefabricated
see
Structures—modular, prefabricated

Burners
range
see
Ranges and ovens—residential: —cooktops—specific type

Butt hinges
see
Hardware—door

Buzzers
see
Bells, buzzers, chimes (entrance and alarm)

C

Cabinets
bathroom vanity
see also
Bathroom accessories: —cabinet and mirror: —cabinet and mirror—with lighting fixture
Lighting—application: —cabinet and mirror
Aristokraft, Inc. C520
Basco, Inc. C585
Broan Mfg. Co., Inc. . . . inside front cover; C587
KraftMaid Cabinetry, Inc. C529
Wellborn Cabinet, Inc. C536

bathroom vanity—disabled persons' use
Basco, Inc. C585

custom-designed
Aristokraft, Inc. C520
Broan Mfg. Co., Inc. C587
KraftMaid Cabinetry, Inc. C529
Wellborn Cabinet, Inc. C536
Wilsonart International, Inc. C478

dispenser—washroom
see
Washroom accessories

doors for
see
Doors—application: —cabinet

equipment cabinets, racks, consoles—electrical, electronic
see
Storage equipment: —cabinets—specific type

hardware for
see
Hardware—cabinet

kitchen—residential
Aristokraft, Inc. C520
KraftMaid Cabinetry, Inc. C529
Wellborn Cabinet, Inc. C536

lavatory
see
Cabinets: —washroom vanity
Lavatories and accessories: —cabinets for

lighting for
see
Lighting—application: —accent and display: —cabinet and mirror

medicine
see also
Bathroom accessories: —cabinet and mirror—specific type
Basco, Inc. C585
Broan Mfg. Co., Inc. . . . inside front cover; C587

residential
Aristokraft, Inc. C520
Broan Mfg. Co., Inc. C587
KraftMaid Cabinetry, Inc. C529

Cabinets *cont.*
residential *cont.*
Wellborn Cabinet, Inc. C536

shower
see
Showers

storage
see
Storage equipment: —cabinets—specific type

tops for
DuPont Co. C474
Formica Corp. .C379
Wellborn Cabinet, Inc. C536
Wilsonart International, Inc. C478

wall storage
see
Wall storage units: —shelf/cabinet

wardrobe
see
Wardrobes: —cabinets and drawers for

washroom vanity
Broan Mfg. Co., Inc. C587
Wilsonart International, Inc. C478

wood
see
Woodwork

Cabins—log
see
Structures—modular, prefabricated

Canopies
inserts for
see
Glass
Plastic

Caps
see
Architectural artwork: —niche caps, casings
Columns
Wood frame construction accessories: —caps and bases—for column or post

Carvings—wood
see
Woodwork

Casework
see
Cabinets

Casings
see
Architectural artwork: —niche caps, casings
Lath and plasterwork accessories and trim: —casings and corner guards

Castings
see
Specific products

Ceilings
see
Ceilings—general
Ceilings—panels and tiles for

Ceilings—general
fans for
see
Fans: —wall, ceiling or pedestal

moldings for—ornamental
White River Hardwood
Products C464

Ceilings—general *cont.*
ventilators for
see
Ventilators: —ceiling, wall, window

Ceilings—panels and tiles for
glass
Innovative Building Products,
Inc., Acme Brick Co. B667

Ceramic or clay tiles
ceramic mosaic
Colorco, Ltd. .C174

custom-designed
Colorco, Ltd. .C174

glazed
Colorco, Ltd. .C174
Interceramic, Inc. C180

unglazed
Colorco, Ltd. .C174

Ceramic products
see
Ceramic or clay tiles
Flooring—clay or ceramic tile
Surfacing and paneling—interior—materials: —ceramic—specific type

Chairs
rails for
see
Lath and plasterwork accessories and trim: —rails—chair, display or map
Woodwork: —rails—chair or plate

Chimes
see
Bells, buzzers, chimes (entrance and alarm)

Church equipment
windows—inserts for
see
Glass
Plastic

Chutes
rubbish and waste
see
Waste handling equipment and systems

Clay products
see
Ceramic or clay tiles
Flooring—clay or ceramic tile
Surfacing and paneling—interior—materials: —ceramic or clay tile—specific type: —clay tile—quarry

Cleaning systems
see
Vacuum cleaning systems

Closets
see
Wardrobes

accessories for
see
Shelving

Clothes racks, hooks, hook panels
see
Washroom accessories

Clothes washers
see
Laundry equipment—specific use

Coatings
see
Coatings—wood-protective
Flooring—specific materials: —coatings for—
slip-resistant
Sealers
Surfacing and paneling—interior
Surfacing—detectable, tactile—disabled persons'
use
Toppings—traffic-bearing
Wall coverings—flexible
Wood treatments

Coatings and toppings—concrete or masonry
see
Sealers
Toppings—traffic-bearing

Coatings—wood-protective
see also
Sealers: —wood
Wood treatments
factory-applied
Formica Corp. .C379

Cold storage buildings
see
Structures—modular, prefabricated—
components for: —wall, roof panels for
thermal isolation

Column covers
wood
Melton Classics, Inc. A296

Columns
caps and bases for—fiberglass
Melton Classics, Inc. A296
caps and bases for—plastic
Melton Classics, Inc. A296
caps and bases for—simulated/
manufactured concrete, metal, stone,
wood
Melton Classics, Inc. A296
caps and bases for—stone
Melton Classics, Inc. A296
caps and bases for—wood
see
Wood frame construction accessories: —caps
and bases—for column or post
covers/enclosures for
see
Column covers
fiberglass
Melton Classics, Inc. A296
ornamental composition
Melton Classics, Inc. A296
ornamental wood
Melton Classics, Inc. A296
plastic
Melton Classics, Inc. A296
stone—simulated/manufactured
Melton Classics, Inc. A296
wood or laminated wood
Melton Classics, Inc. A296

Compactors—waste
see
Waste handling equipment and systems

Concrete
floor
see
Toppings—traffic-bearing
roof
see
Toppings—traffic-bearing

Conservatories
see also
Atriums
Greenhouses
Solariums
Structures—modular, prefabricated
Hartford Conservatories, Inc. B575

Construction systems
wood framing—manufacturers
see
Wood frame construction accessories

Controls
pest
see
Specific products
rodent
see
Specific products
vermin
see
Specific products

Cooktops
see
Ranges and ovens—residential: —cooktops:
—cooktops/grills—convertible

Cornices
see
Moldings and cornices
Surfacing and paneling—interior
Woodwork: —moldings, cornices, door and
window trim

Counters
custom-designed
Wilsonart International, Inc. C478
lighting for—accent
see
Lighting—application: —accent and display
tops for
DuPont Co. .C474
Formica Corp. C379
Interceramic, Inc. C180
Wilsonart International, Inc. C478

Covers
column
see
Column covers

Coves
see
Flooring—specific material
Lath and plasterwork accessories and trim:
—cove moldings
Luminaires—types: —cove

Curbing
roof—skylight, smokestack, ventilator
see
Skylights—general: —curb combination

Curtain walls
see
Panels—building
Storefronts

Curtain walls—window framing systems
panels for
see
Panels—building

D

Decking
see
Toppings—traffic-bearing

Decks—patio and pool
see
Toppings—traffic-bearing

Dentils
see
Moldings and cornices

Desks
tops, pads for
Formica Corp. C379

Detention equipment
see
Glass—properties: —burglar-resistant
Hardware—door
Luminaires—properties: —vandal/impact-
resistant

Diffusers—air distribution
see
Ventilators

Disabled persons' products
see
Bathroom accessories: —disabled persons' use
Bathroom accessories: —grab bars—specific
material
Cabinets: —bathroom vanity—disabled persons'
use
Mirrors: —tilting
Plumbing fittings and trim
Showers: —seats for—wall-mounted
Surfacing—detectable, tactile—disabled persons'
use
Washroom accessories: —disabled persons'
use: —grab bars

Dishes
see
Bathroom accessories: —toilet paper holders,
soap dishes—specific material

Dishwashers—residential
built-in
KitchenAid, Whirlpool Corp. C503
energy-saving
KitchenAid, Whirlpool Corp. C503
free-standing or mobile
KitchenAid, Whirlpool Corp. C503
undersink
KitchenAid, Whirlpool Corp. C503

Dispensers

facial tissue, lotion, paper cup, soap
see
Washroom accessories

Display equipment

see
Shelving

cabinets and cases
see
Cabinets

lighting for
see
Lighting—application: —accent and display

Display rails

see
*Lath and plasterwork accessories and trim:
—rails—chair, display or map*

Disposers—liquid/solid waste

see
Waste handling equipment and systems

Dividers

see
*Flooring—specific material
Partitions*

Door entrance trim

see
*Woodwork: —moldings, cornices, door and
window trim*

Door hardware

see
Hardware—door

Doors

see
*Doors—application
Doors—frames for
Doors—operation
Doors—properties
Doors—swinging—by materials/construction*

Doors—application

bathtub enclosure
see
Bathtubs

cabinet
Broan Mfg. Co., Inc. C587
KraftMaid Cabinetry, Inc. C529

entrance
see
*Doors—operation
Doors—swinging—by materials/construction
Storefronts*

inserts for
see
*Glass
Plastic*

lights for
see
*Glass
Plastic*

shower, tub
Century Shower Door, Inc. C593

tub
see
Doors—application: —shower, tub

vision lights for
see
*Glass
Plastic*

Doors—frames for

aluminum or aluminum alloy
Century Shower Door, Inc. C593

brass, bronze—custom-designed
Century Shower Door, Inc. C593

Doors—operation

sliding—frame and glass, glass
Century Shower Door, Inc. C593

swinging
see
Doors—swinging—by materials/construction

Doors—properties

watertight
Century Shower Door, Inc. C593

Doors—swinging—by materials/ construction

glass—tempered
Century Shower Door, Inc. C593

inserts for
see
*Glass
Plastic*

lights for
see
*Glass
Plastic*

Drawers

storage
see
Storage equipment: —cabinets with drawers

wardrobe
see
Wardrobes: —cabinets and drawers for

Dressing rooms, booths

see
Showers: —dressing room, compartment

Driveways

see
Toppings—traffic-bearing

Dryers

clothing
see
Laundry equipment—residential

hand or hair
see
*Washroom accessories: —dryers—specific
type—hand or hair*

residential
see
Laundry equipment—residential

Dust collectors

see
Vacuum cleaning systems

E

Edgings

see
*Flooring—clay or ceramic tile: —bases, dividers,
edgings and inserts for*

Electrical equipment

see
Heaters—unit

Electrical equipment *cont.*

see cont.
*Lighting—application
Luminaires—specific types*

Enclosures

see
*Bathtubs
Conservatories
Greenhouses
Showers
Solariums
Structures—modular, prefabricated*

Energy conservation

see
*Dishwashers—residential: —energy-saving
Specific products
Ventilators: —heat recovery, air filtering*

Entrances

see
*Doors—application
Doors—frames for
Doors—operation
Doors—properties
Doors—swinging—by materials/construction
Hardware—door
Storefronts*

Etching

see
*Glass—form: —patterned, carved, decorative,
etched, mosaic, sandblasted or textured
Plastic—form: —engraved, etched*

Exhaust systems

air
see
*Blowers—centrifugal or axial
Fans
Ventilators*

Extractors

see
*Ventilators: —grease containment/extractor—
food service equipment*

F

Facings, refacings or veneers

see
*Panels—building
Surfacing and paneling—interior
Veneers
Wall coverings—flexible*

Fans

see also
*Blowers—centrifugal or axial
Ventilators*

kitchen or bathroom
Broan Mfg. Co., Inc. C915

ventilating or exhaust
Broan Mfg. Co., Inc. C915

wall, ceiling or pedestal
Broan Mfg. Co., Inc. . . . . inside front cover

Fascias—properties

fire-resistant
Wilsonart International, Inc. C478

Fasteners

see
Adhesives for

Glass—form *cont.*

structural
see
   Panels—building—materials: —glass, glass block
   Storefronts: —structural frames, mullions for—
     glass, glass block

Glass mullion glazing
see
   Storefronts: —structural frames, mullions for—
     glass, glass block

Glass products
see
   Ceilings—panels and tiles for: —glass
   Doors—operation
   Doors—swinging—by materials/construction:
     —glass—specific type
   Mirrors: —glass
   Panels—building—materials
   Skylights—materials: —glass—block,
     corrugated, plain or wire

Glass—properties

anti-glare/shading
   Innovative Building Products,
     Inc., Acme Brick Co. B667

burglar-resistant
   Innovative Building Products,
     Inc., Acme Brick Co. B667

diffusing
see
   Glass—form: —patterned, carved, decorative,
     etched, mosaic, sandblasted or textured

heat-absorbing
   Innovative Building Products,
     Inc., Acme Brick Co. B667

insulating panel
   Innovative Building Products,
     Inc., Acme Brick Co. B667

security and detention
see
   Glass—properties

sound-resistant
   Innovative Building Products,
     Inc., Acme Brick Co. B667

Glassware washers
see
   Dishwashers—specific application

Glazed enclosures
see
   Atriums
   Conservatories
   Greenhouses
   Solariums

Glazing compounds or accessories

glass blocks
see
   Blocks—glass: —framing for

Glazing, glazing film
see
   Glass—form
   Glass—properties
   Plastic—form
   Plastic—properties

Glue
see
   Adhesives for

Golf paths
see
   Toppings—traffic-bearing

Grab bars
see
   Bathroom accessories: —grab bars—specific
     material
   Washroom accessories: —grab bars

Graphics
see
   Architectural artwork
   Murals

Grease containment/extractors
see
   Ventilators: —grease containment/extractor—
     food service equipment

Greenhouses
see also
   Conservatories
   Heaters—unit
   Solariums
   Hartford Conservatories, Inc. B575

Greenhouses—extrusions for
   Hartford Conservatories, Inc. B575

Grilles or screens
see
   Partitions

wood—fixed unit
see
   Woodwork: —decorative grillework

Grills—barbecue
see
   Ranges and ovens—residential: —cooktops/
     grills—convertible

Guards

corner—metal
see
   Lath and plasterwork accessories and trim:
     —casings and corner guards

wall
see
   Lath and plasterwork accessories and trim:
     —casings and corner guards

H

Hangers
see
   Luminaires—components: —hardware, brackets,
     extrusions, fasteners

Hangers—clothing
see
   Bathroom accessories
   Washroom accessories

Hardware—bathroom, washroom

shower
see
   Showers: —rods, hardware and tracks for

Hardware—cabinet

hinges
   KraftMaid Cabinetry, Inc. C529

Hardware—cabinet *cont.*

locks
   Wellborn Cabinet, Inc. C536

Hardware—door

hinges
   Century Shower Door, Inc. C593

knobs
   Century Shower Door, Inc. C593

Hardware—shower
see
   Showers: —rods, hardware and tracks for

Heads—shower
see
   Plumbing fittings and trim

Heaters—unit

electric
   Myson, Inc. C589

Heat reclamation equipment
see
   Ventilators: —heat recovery, air filtering

Heliports and equipment
see
   Specific products

Hinges
see
   Hardware—cabinet: —hinges
   Hardware—door

Holders

washroom, bathroom
see
   Bathroom accessories
   Washroom accessories

Hoods
see
   Ventilators

Hooks—clothing
see
   Bathroom accessories
   Washroom accessories

Hospital equipment

grab bars, safety toilet seats, safety towel bars
see
   Bathroom accessories: —grab bars—specific
     material
   Washroom accessories: —grab bars

laboratory
see
   Laboratory equipment

plumbing fittings
see
   Plumbing fittings and trim

Hotel, motel equipment

bathroom
see
   Bathroom accessories
   Washroom accessories

lighting
see
   Lighting—application

Hothouses
see
Greenhouses

HVAC terminal units
see
Heaters—unit

I

Insulation—application
panel—building
see
*Structures—modular, prefabricated—
components for: —wall, roof panels for
thermal isolation*

Ironing boards
see
*Laundry equipment—specific type: —ironing
boards—built-in*

J

Jail equipment
see
Specific products

K

Kitchen equipment—commercial or institutional
see
*Ventilators
Waste handling equipment and systems*

Kitchen equipment—residential
see
*Cabinets
Dishwashers—residential
Fans: —kitchen or bathroom
Faucets—application: —sink—kitchen
Freezers—residential
Ranges and ovens—residential
Refrigerator-freezer combination:
—residential—specific type
Refrigerators: —residential—specific type
Sinks—residential
Ventilators: —hood—residential kitchen—specific
type
Waste handling equipment and systems:
—compactors—residential or institutional*

Knobs
see
Hardware—door: —knobs

L

Laboratory equipment
plumbing fittings
see
Plumbing fittings and trim
work surfaces
Formica Corp. C379
Wilsonart International, Inc. C478

Laminates
see
*Metal laminate sheets
Plastic laminate sheets
Veneers*

Landscape accessories
lighting
see
*Lighting—application: —landscape—deck,
garden, patio/terrace, walk*

Lath and plasterwork accessories and trim
bases and fittings
White River Hardwood
Products .C464
casings and corner guards
White River Hardwood
Products .C464
cove moldings
White River Hardwood
Products .C464
rails—chair, display or map
White River Hardwood
Products .C464

Laundry equipment—residential
dryers
KitchenAid, Whirlpool Corp. C503
dryers—energy-saving
KitchenAid, Whirlpool Corp. C503
ironing boards—built-in
Broan Mfg. Co., Inc. . . . . inside front cover
washer/dryer combination
KitchenAid, Whirlpool Corp. C503
washers—front-loading
KitchenAid, Whirlpool Corp. C503
washers—front-loading—energy-saving
KitchenAid, Whirlpool Corp. C503

Lavatories and accessories
cabinets for
Wellborn Cabinet, Inc. C536
fittings and trim
see
*Faucets—application: —lavatory
Plumbing fittings and trim*
lavatories
DuPont Co. C474
Formica Corp. C379
Strom Plumbing, Sign of the
Crab C584
tops for
DuPont Co. C474
Formica Corp. C379
Wilsonart International, Inc. C478
vanity top and bowl—molded—one-piece
see also
Sinks—residential
DuPont Co. C474
Formica Corp. C379

Lighting
see
*Lighting—application
Luminaires—components
Luminaires—properties
Luminaires—types*

Lighting—application
see also
Luminaires—types
accent and display
Roberts Step-Lite Systems C949
cabinet and mirror
see also
*Bathroom accessories: —cabinet and mirror—
with light fixture*
Basco, Inc. .C585

Lighting—application *cont.*
cabinet and mirror *cont.*
Broan Mfg. Co., Inc. . . . inside front cover; C587
display
see
Lighting—application: —accent and display
entertainment
see
Lighting—application: —stage, cinema or theater
**floor proximity egress path-marking
system**
see
Lighting—application: —stair, aisle, path
hazardous location
see
*Luminaires—properties: —vandal/impact-
resistant*
**landscape—deck, garden, patio/terrace,
walk**
Roberts Step-Lite Systems C949
railing
see
Luminaires—types: —railing
showcase
see
Lighting—application: —accent and display
stage, cinema or theater
Roberts Step-Lite Systems C949
stair, aisle, path
Roberts Step-Lite Systems C949
street
see
*Lighting—application: —landscape—deck,
garden, patio/terrace, walk*
theater
see
Lighting—application: —stage, cinema or theater
walkway
see
*Lighting—application: —landscape—deck,
garden, patio/terrace, walk: —stair, aisle, path*

Lights
window
see
*Glass
Plastic*

Liquid waste disposal or treatment equipment
see
Waste handling equipment and systems

Lockers—materials
see
Cabinets

Locks
cabinet
see
Hardware—cabinet: —locks
furniture
see
Hardware—cabinet: —locks

Log cabins
see
Structures—modular, prefabricated

Louvers
see
Ventilators

P

Paint
see
Sealers
Stains

Paneling—interior
see
Surfacing and paneling—interior

Panels—building
see
Panels—building—materials
Panels—building—properties

Panels—building—materials
glass, glass block
Innovative Building Products,
Inc., Acme Brick Co. B667

Panels—building—properties
insulating
see also
Structures—modular, prefabricated—
components for: —wall, roof panels for
thermal isolation
Innovative Building Products,
Inc., Acme Brick Co. B667

Panels—ceiling
see
Ceilings—panels and tiles for

Partitions
see
Partitions—materials
Partitions—properties
Partitions—shower, toilet, urinal

Partitions—application
shower
see
Partitions—shower, toilet, urinal
toilet, urinal
see
Partitions—shower, toilet, urinal

Partitions—general
blocks for
see
Blocks—specific material
Partitions—materials: —glass block

Partitions—materials
glass block
see also
Blocks—glass
Innovative Building Products,
Inc., Acme Brick Co. B667
plastic
Wilsonart International, Inc. C478
plastic laminate-faced
Wilsonart International, Inc. C478
shoji
see
Plastic—form: —patterned or textured

Partitions—properties
fire-rated
Wilsonart International, Inc. C478
fire-resistant
Wilsonart International, Inc. C478

Partitions—properties cont.
sound-insulating or retarding—floor-to-ceiling
Innovative Building Products,
Inc., Acme Brick Co. B667

Partitions—shower, toilet, urinal
shower—plastic
Wilsonart International, Inc. C478
toilet, urinal—plastic
Wilsonart International, Inc. C478

Paste
see
Adhesives for

Patio equipment
see
Conservatories
Greenhouses
Lighting—application: —landscape—deck,
garden, patio/terrace, walk
Solariums
Structures—modular, prefabricated—specific
type

Pavers
see
Paving

Paving
see also
Surfacing—detectable, tactile—disabled persons'
use
Toppings—traffic-bearing
glass block
Innovative Building Products,
Inc., Acme Brick Co. B667
sealers for
see
Sealers

Photographic artwork
see
Architectural artwork
Murals

Physical fitness equipment
see
Bathtubs: —hydro-massage combination
Showers: —hydro-massage combination

Pigments
see
Specific products: —colors for

Pipe lighting systems
see
Luminaires—components: —pipe, tube
Luminaires—types: —tube, pipe

Piping and tubing—accessories for
see
Plumbing fittings and trim

Plaster
accessories for
see
Lath and plasterwork accessories and trim
trim for
see
Lath and plasterwork accessories and trim

Plastic
see
Plastic—form
Plastic laminate sheets
Plastic materials—custom-molded
Plastic—properties

Plastic—form
colored
DuPont Co. .C474
Formica Corp. C379
Wilsonart International, Inc. C478
corrugated or flat sheet
DuPont Co. .C474
Formica Corp. C379
Wilsonart International, Inc. C478
corrugated or flat sheet—filler strips for
Wilsonart International, Inc. C478
engraved, etched
Formica Corp. C379
patterned or textured
DuPont Co. .C474
Formica Corp. C379
sheet, coil
DuPont Co. .C474
Formica Corp. C379

Plastic laminate products
see
Partitions—materials: —plastic laminate-faced
Plastic laminate sheets
Surfacing and paneling—interior—materials:
—plastic laminate-faced

Plastic laminate sheets
DuPont Co. .C474
Formica Corp. C379

Plastic materials—custom-molded
DuPont Co. .C474

Plastic products
see
Columns: —caps and bases for—plastic:
—plastic
Flooring—wood: —plastic-impregnated
Moldings and cornices: —plastic, composite
Partitions—materials
Partitions—shower, toilet, urinal: —shower—
plastic: —toilet, urinal—plastic
Plastic materials—custom-molded
Surfacing and paneling—interior—materials:
—moldings and trim for—plastic, composite
Wall coverings—flexible

Plastic—properties
abrasion-resistant
see
Plastic—properties: —shock-resistant
chemical-resistant
DuPont Co. .C474
Formica Corp. C379
fire-resistant
DuPont Co. .C474
Formica Corp. C379
Wilsonart International, Inc. C478
moldable
Wilsonart International, Inc. C478
safety
DuPont Co. .C474
Formica Corp. C379
Wilsonart International, Inc. C478
shock-resistant
Formica Corp. C379

Plumbing fittings and trim

faucets, fixture trim
see
Faucets

shower or spray
Century Shower Door, Inc. C593
Strom Plumbing, Sign of the
Crab C584

Plumbing fixtures

see
Bathtubs
Faucets
Lavatories and accessories
Plumbing fittings and trim
Showers
Sinks—commercial or institutional
Sinks—residential

Plywood products

see
Shelving: —wood, plywood, wood fiber

Pollution control equipment and systems

see
Fans
Vacuum cleaning systems
Ventilators
Waste handling equipment and systems

Porch enclosures

see
Conservatories
Greenhouses
Solariums
Structures—modular, prefabricated—specific type

Posts

see
Columns
Wood frame construction accessories: —caps and bases—for column or post

Prefabricated structures

see
Structures—modular, prefabricated

Prison equipment

see
Specific products

Product information—associations

see
Specific products

Product information—general

see
Specific products

R

Railings—types

handrails—illuminated
see
Luminaires—types: —railing

Rails

chair
see
Lath and plasterwork accessories and trim: —rails—chair, display or map

Rails *cont.*

chair *cont.*
see *cont.*
Woodwork: —rails—chair or plate

display and map
see
Lath and plasterwork accessories and trim: —rails—chair, display or map

Ranges and ovens—residential

accessories for
KitchenAid, Whirlpool Corp. C503

cooktops
KitchenAid, Whirlpool Corp. C503

cooktops/grills—convertible
KitchenAid, Whirlpool Corp. C503

electric
KitchenAid, Whirlpool Corp. C503

gas
KitchenAid, Whirlpool Corp. C503

ovens—built-in
KitchenAid, Whirlpool Corp. C503

ovens—built-in—double
KitchenAid, Whirlpool Corp. C503

ovens—energy-saving
KitchenAid, Whirlpool Corp. C503
Sharp Electronics Corp. C512

ovens—microwave
Sharp Electronics Corp. C512

ovens—microwave/conventional combination
Sharp Electronics Corp. C512

ventilating hoods for
see
Ventilators: —hood—residential kitchen—specific type

Receptors—shower

see
Showers: —stall and receptor for—specific material

Recreational equipment

see
Bathtubs: —hydro-massage combination

Refacings or facings

see
Panels—building
Surfacing and paneling—interior
Veneers
Wall coverings—flexible

Refrigerator-freezer combination

residential
KitchenAid, Whirlpool Corp. C503
Sub-Zero Freezer Co., Inc. . A028; C514; C515; C515A

residential—built-in
Sub-Zero Freezer Co., Inc. . A028; C514; C515; C515A

residential—energy-saving
KitchenAid, Whirlpool Corp. C503
Sub-Zero Freezer Co., Inc. . A028; C514; C515; C515A

Refrigerators

see also
Refrigerator-freezer combination

residential
KitchenAid, Whirlpool Corp. C503
Sub-Zero Freezer Co., Inc. . A028; C514; C515; C515A

Refrigerators *cont.*

residential—built-in
KitchenAid, Whirlpool Corp. C503
Sub-Zero Freezer Co., Inc. . A028; C514; C515; C515A

residential—energy-saving
KitchenAid, Whirlpool Corp. C503
Sub-Zero Freezer Co., Inc. . A028; C514; C515; C515A

residential—ice, chilled water dispensers
Sub-Zero Freezer Co., Inc. . . A028; C514; C515

residential—undercounter
KitchenAid, Whirlpool Corp. C503
Sub-Zero Freezer Co., Inc. . A028; C514; C515; C515A

water cooler combination
see
Refrigerators: —residential—ice, chilled water dispensers

Registers and grilles

see
Ventilators

Rehabilitation equipment

see
Bathtubs: —hydro-massage combination

Restaurant equipment and furniture

see
Refrigerator-freezer combination
Waste handling equipment and systems

Roadway construction

see
Paving
Toppings—traffic-bearing

Rods and bars

see
Bathroom accessories: —grab bars—specific material
Showers: —rods, hardware and tracks for
Washroom accessories: —grab bars

Roof assemblies

see
Skylights

Roofing

see
Structures—modular, prefabricated—components for: —wall, roof panels—specific type

Roofing—properties

traffic-bearing—automobile, vehicular
see
Toppings—traffic-bearing

traffic-bearing—pedestrian
see
Toppings—traffic-bearing

Roofing specialties and construction products

coatings
see
Sealers
Toppings—traffic-bearing
Wood treatments

traffic-bearing
see
Toppings—traffic-bearing

Roofing specialties and construction products *cont.*

walkways, vehicular pathways
see
Toppings—traffic-bearing

Roof windows
see
Skylights

Room assemblies

dressing
see
Showers: —dressing room, compartment

partitions for
see
Partitions

shower
see
Showers: —dressing room, compartment

Room dividers
see
Partitions

Roundels
see
Moldings and cornices

S

Safety equipment

mirrors
see
Mirrors: —safety

plastic
see
Plastic—properties: —safety

Sandwich panels or walls
see
Panels—building

School equipment

display and map rails
see
Lath and plasterwork accessories and trim: —rails—chair, display or map

laboratories
see
Laboratory equipment

partitions
see
Partitions

storage
see
Storage equipment

wardrobes
see
Wardrobes

Screens

partition
see
Partitions

space divider
see
Partitions

Sealants
see
Adhesives for

Sealers

wood
Formica Corp. C379

Seats—shower, toilet
see
Bathroom accessories: —grab bars—specific material
Showers

Security and bullet-resistant equipment and products
see
Glass—properties: —burglar-resistant
Hardware—door
Luminaires—properties: —vandal/impact-resistant

Septic tanks and accessories
see
Waste handling equipment and systems

Service basins
see
Sinks—commercial or institutional

Sewage treatment equipment and systems
see
Waste handling equipment and systems

Sheet metal for fabrications
see
Metal laminate sheets

Sheets, strips, plates, coils

glass
see
Glass—form

metal laminate
see
Metal laminate sheets

plastic
see
Plastic—form

Shelving
see also
Storage equipment
Wall storage units: —shelf/cabinet

bathroom or washroom—metal
Basco, Inc. C585

wood, plywood, wood fiber
Wellborn Cabinet, Inc. C536

Showcases
see
Lighting—application: —accent and display

Shower heads
see
Plumbing fittings and trim

Showers
see also
Bathtub/shower—prefabricated units

cabinet and enclosure
Acme Brick Co., Innovative
  Building Products, Inc. C565A
Century Shower Door, Inc. C593
DuPont Co. C474
Formica Corp. C379
Innovative Building Products,
  Inc., Acme Brick Co. B667

Showers *cont.*

cabinet and enclosure *cont.*
Strom Plumbing, Sign of the
  Crab .C584

cabinet and enclosure—extrusion for
Acme Brick Co., Innovative
  Building Products, Inc. C565A

door for
see
Doors—application: —shower, tub

dressing room, compartment
Wilsonart International, Inc. C478

fitting, lever, valve for
see
Plumbing fittings and trim

hydro-massage combination
Clarion Bathware C566B

partition for
see
Partitions—shower, toilet, urinal

rods, hardware and tracks for
Basco, Inc. C585
Century Shower Door, Inc. C593
Strom Plumbing, Sign of the
  Crab .C584

seats for—wall-mounted
Century Shower Door, Inc. C593

stall and receptor for—composition
DuPont Co. C474

stall and receptor for—fiberglass
Formica Corp. C379

system
Acme Brick Co., Innovative
  Building Products, Inc. C565A
Century Shower Door, Inc. C593

Siding—materials

stone
see
Specific type

Signaling systems
see
Bells, buzzers, chimes (entrance and alarm)

Sinks—commercial or institutional

fittings and trim for
see
Plumbing fittings and trim

tops for
DuPont Co. C474
Formica Corp. C379

Sinks—residential
see also
Lavatories and accessories

bathroom—acrylic, composite—double-bowl
DuPont Co. C474

bathroom—acrylic, composite—single-bowl
DuPont Co. C474

faucets for
see
Faucets—application

fittings for
see
Plumbing fittings and trim

tops for
DuPont Co. C474
Formica Corp. C379

Skylights
see
Skylights—form
Skylights—framing
Skylights—general
Skylights—materials
Skylights—properties

Skylights—form
flat panel
Innovative Building Products,
Inc., Acme Brick Co. B667

Skylights—framing
aluminum or aluminum alloy
Innovative Building Products,
Inc., Acme Brick Co. B667

Skylights—general
curb combination
Innovative Building Products,
Inc., Acme Brick Co. B667

Skylights—materials
glass—block, corrugated, plain or wired
Innovative Building Products,
Inc., Acme Brick Co. B667

Skylights—operation
ventilators for—power-driven
see
Ventilators: —adjustable—manual or power-
operated

Skylights—properties
heat and glare-retarding
Innovative Building Products,
Inc., Acme Brick Co. B667
insulating
Innovative Building Products,
Inc., Acme Brick Co. B667

Soap, soap dispensers and holders
see
Bathroom accessories: —toilet paper holders,
soap dishes—specific material

Solar energy conversion—components for—passive
glazing—insulating
see
Glass—properties: —insulating—specific type
greenhouses
see
Greenhouses
panels—building
see
Panels—building—properties: —insulating
solariums
see
Solariums

Solariums
see also
Conservatories
Greenhouses
Hartford Conservatories, Inc. B575

Sound control products
see
Partitions—properties

Space dividers—interior
see
Partitions

Spandrel panels
see
Panels—building—materials

Sports training equipment
see
Bathtubs: —hydro-massage combination

Stage, theater and cinema equipment
lighting
see
Lighting—application: —stage, cinema or theater

Stains
wood
Bruce Hardwood Floors,
Triangle Pacific Corp. C246
Formica Corp. C379

Stair treads, risers
lighting for
see
Lighting—application: —stair, aisle, path

Stalls—shower
see
Showers

Stone
see
Specific products/types

Stone—simulated/manufactured products
see
Columns: —stone—simulated/manufactured
Moldings and cornices: —simulated/
manufactured stone
Surfacing and paneling—interior—materials:
—moldings and trim for—simulated/
manufactured stone: —stone—simulated/
manufactured

Storage and retrieval systems
see
Shelving
Specific equipment/products
Storage equipment

Storage equipment
see also
Shelving
cabinets with doors
Wellborn Cabinet, Inc. C536
cabinets with drawers
Wellborn Cabinet, Inc. C536
wall storage units
see
Wall storage units

Storefronts
structural frames, mullions for—glass, glass block
Innovative Building Products,
Inc., Acme Brick Co. B667

Stoves
see
Ranges and ovens—residential

Street, outdoor equipment
lighting
see
Lighting—application: —landscape—deck,
garden, patio/terrace, walk

Structures—modular, prefabricated—application
conservatories
see
Conservatories
greenhouses
see
Greenhouses
solariums
see
Solariums

Structures—modular, prefabricated—components for
wall, roof panels for thermal isolation
Hartford Conservatories, Inc. B575

Sun controls
see
Glass
Plastic
Skylights

Sunrooms, patio rooms, sun-windows
see
Greenhouses
Solariums
Structures—modular, prefabricated

Surfacing and paneling—exterior
see
Panels—building

Surfacing and paneling—interior
see
Surfacing and paneling—interior—general
Surfacing and paneling—interior—materials
Surfacing and paneling—interior—properties
Wall coverings—flexible

Surfacing and paneling—interior—general
custom-designed
Interceramic, Inc. C180
White River Hardwood
Products C464
Wilsonart International, Inc. C478

Surfacing and paneling—interior—materials
ceramic mosaic
Colorco, Ltd. C174
ceramic or clay tile—custom-designed
Colorco, Ltd. C174
ceramic or clay tile—glazed
Colorco, Ltd. C174
Interceramic, Inc. C180
ceramic or clay tile—patterned, sculptured or textured
Interceramic, Inc. C180
ceramic or clay tile—unglazed
Colorco, Ltd. C174

Surfacing and paneling— interior—materials *cont.*

marble tile
Interceramic, Inc. C180

metal laminate-faced
Formica Corp. C379

moldings and trim for—hardboard
White River Hardwood
Products C464

moldings and trim for—plastic, composite
see also
Moldings and cornices: —plastic, composite
DuPont Co. C474
Formica Corp. C379

moldings and trim for—simulated/ manufactured stone
see also
Moldings and cornices: —simulated/
manufactured stone
DuPont Co. C474

moldings and trim for—wood or plywood
see also
Woodwork: —moldings, cornices, door and
window trim
White River Hardwood
Products C464

moldings and trim for—wood or plywood—simulated/manufactured
DuPont Co. C474
White River Hardwood
Products C464

plastic laminate-faced
see also
Plastic laminate sheets
Formica Corp. C379
Wilsonart International, Inc. C478

plastic—sheet or tile
DuPont Co. C474
Formica Corp. C379
Wilsonart International, Inc. C478

stone—simulated/manufactured
DuPont Co. C474

wood—simulated/manufactured
DuPont Co. C474
Formica Corp. C379

Surfacing and paneling— interior—properties

fire-resistant
DuPont Co. C474
Formica Corp. C379
Wilsonart International, Inc. C478

Surfacing—detectable, tactile— disabled persons' use
Formica Corp. C379

Swimming pool equipment

flooring—safety
see
Toppings—traffic-bearing

safety decking, flooring
see
Toppings—traffic-bearing

T

Tables

tops for
DuPont Co. C474
Formica Corp. C379
Wilsonart International, Inc. C478

Tambour
see
Surfacing and paneling—interior—materials
Veneers

Terrazzo products
see
Flooring—terrazzo
Marble: —mosaics

Tessera
see
Ceramic or clay tiles
Glass
Marble

Theatrical equipment
see
Lighting—application: —stage, cinema or theater

Theft detection/protection equipment and systems
see
Glass—properties: —burglar-resistant
Hardware—door
Luminaires—properties: —vandal/impact-
resistant

Therapeutic equipment
see
Bathtubs: —hydro-massage combination
Showers: —hydro-massage combination

Timber
see
Wood frame construction accessories
Wood—treated

Tires—recycled
see
Specific products

Toilets

compartments for
see
Partitions—shower, toilet, urinal

paper, dispensers for
see
Washroom accessories: —holders—toilet paper

partitions for
see
Partitions—shower, toilet, urinal

Toppings—traffic-bearing

tile or tile form
Bruce Hardwood Floors,
Triangle Pacific Corp.,
Bruce Floors C310

Tops
see
Bar furniture and equipment: —elbow rests, bar
tops
Cabinets: —tops for
Counters: —tops for
Desks: —tops, pads for
Laboratory equipment: —work surfaces
Lavatories and accessories: —tops for
Sinks—commercial or institutional: —tops for
Sinks—residential: —tops for
Tables: —tops for

Towel bars—safety
see
Bathroom accessories: —grab bars—specific
material
Washroom accessories: —grab bars

Towels
see
Bathroom accessories: —towel holders: —towel
holders—warmers for

Tracks

shower cubicle
see
Showers: —rods, hardware and tracks for

Traffic accessories, equipment and products
see
Toppings—traffic-bearing

Treatments
see
Wood treatments

Trim
see
Lath and plasterwork accessories and trim
Moldings and cornices
Surfacing and paneling—interior—materials:
—moldings and trim for—specific material
Woodwork: —moldings, cornices, door and
window trim

Tube lighting
see
Luminaires—components: —pipe, tube
Luminaires—types: —tube, pipe

Tubs
see
Bathtubs
Bathtub/shower—prefabricated units
Doors—application: —shower, tub

U

Universal design products
see
Bathroom accessories: —disabled persons' use
Bathroom accessories: —grab bars—specific
material
Cabinets: —bathroom vanity—disabled persons'
use
Mirrors: —tilting
Plumbing fittings and trim
Showers: —seats for—wall-mounted
Surfacing—detectable, tactile—disabled persons'
use
Washroom accessories: —disabled persons'
use: —grab bars

Urinals

fittings, levers, valves for
see
Plumbing fittings and trim

partitions for
see
Partitions—shower, toilet, urinal

V

Vacuum cleaning systems
centralized, automatic operation
Broan Mfg. Co., Inc. .... inside front cover

Valves
see
Plumbing fittings and trim

Vanities
see
Cabinets: —bathroom vanity: —washroom vanity
Lavatories and accessories: —vanity top and
bowl—molded—one-piece

Varnish
stain
see
Stains

Veneers
wood or simulated/manufactured wood
Formica Corp. C379

Ventilators
see also
Blowers—centrifugal or axial
Fans
adjustable—manual or power-operated
Broan Mfg. Co., Inc. C485; C915
air quality intake
Broan Mfg. Co., Inc. ... inside front cover ; C485
ceiling, wall, window
Broan Mfg. Co., Inc. C485
grease containment/extractor—food service equipment
Broan Mfg. Co., Inc. C485
heat recovery, air filtering
Broan Mfg. Co., Inc. C485
hood—food service equipment
Broan Mfg. Co., Inc. C485
hood—residential kitchen
Broan Mfg. Co., Inc. inside front cover; C485; C915
hood—residential kitchen—fan and light combination
Broan Mfg. Co., Inc. C485; C915
hood—residential kitchen—plate warmer
Broan Mfg. Co., Inc. C485
kitchen fan
see
Fans: —kitchen or bathroom
make-up air unit—food service equipment
Broan Mfg. Co., Inc. C485
roof—curb combination
see
Skylights—general: —curb combination

W

Wainscoting
see
Surfacing and paneling—interior
Veneers
Wall coverings—flexible

Walkways
see
Toppings—traffic-bearing

Wallboard
strip channels and corner lath for
see
Lath and plasterwork accessories and trim

Wall coverings—flexible
see also
Surfacing and paneling—interior
fire-resistant
Formica Corp. C379
plastic—sheet or tile
Formica Corp. C379

Wall coverings—rigid
see
Surfacing and paneling—interior

Walls—exterior insulation and finish systems—general
see
Veneers

Wall storage units
shelf/cabinet
KraftMaid Cabinetry, Inc. C529

Wardrobes
cabinets and drawers for
Aristokraft, Inc. C520

Warehouses
see
Structures—modular, prefabricated— components for

Washers
clothes
see
Laundry equipment—residential

Washroom accessories
see also
Bathroom accessories
cabinets
see
Cabinets: — washroom vanity
disabled persons' use
Basco, Inc. C585
dispenser cabinets—toilet tissue
Basco, Inc. C585
dispensers—facial tissue
Basco, Inc. C585
dryers—electric—hand or hair
Broan Mfg. Co., Inc. .... inside front cover
grab bars
Basco, Inc. C585
holders—toilet paper
Basco, Inc. C585
holders—toothbrush and/or tumbler— metal
Basco, Inc. C585
hooks—coat or robe
Basco, Inc. C585
partitions
see
Partitions—shower, toilet, urinal
shelving
see
Shelving

Waste handling equipment and systems
compactors—residential or institutional
Broan Mfg. Co., Inc. .... inside front cover

Water conditioning equipment
see
Waste handling equipment and systems

Water conservation equipment
see
Plumbing fittings and trim

Waterproofing membranes
protection for
see
Toppings—traffic-bearing

Water supply and treatment equipment
see
Waste handling equipment and systems

Wax—floor or wall
Bruce Hardwood Floors, Triangle Pacific Corp. C246

Whirlpools
see
Bathtubs: —hydro-massage combination
Showers: —hydro-massage combination

Windows
see
Windows—replacement

Windows—general
church
see
Glass
Plastic
coatings for
see
Coatings—wood-protective
Sealers
Wood treatments
inserts for
see
Glass
Plastic
overglazing for
see
Glass
Plastic
stained or faceted glass
see
Glass
Plastic
ventilators for
see
Ventilators: —ceiling, wall, window

Windows—overglazing for
see
Glass
Plastic

Windows—properties
insulating—thermal—add-on glazing
see
Glass
Plastic

Windows—replacement

glass blocks for
Innovative Building Products,
Inc., Acme Brick Co. B667

Wood frame construction accessories

caps and bases—for column or post
Melton Classics, Inc. A296

Wood products

see
   Column covers: —wood
   Columns: —wood—specific type
   Flooring—wood
   Mantels: —wood
   Sealers: —wood
   Shelving
   Stains: —wood
   Surfacing and paneling—interior—materials
   Veneers: —wood or simulated/manufactured
     wood

Wood—simulated/manufactured products

see
   Columns: —caps and bases for—simulated/
     manufactured concrete, metal, stone, wood
   Surfacing and paneling—interior—materials:
     —wood—simulated/manufactured—specific
     type
   Veneers: —wood or simulated/manufactured
     wood

Wood—treated

see also
   Wood treatments

hardwoods
Formica Corp. C379
softwoods
Formica Corp. C379

Wood treatments

see also
   Coatings—wood-protective
   Sealers: —wood
   Stains: —wood
   Wood—treated

selection information
Formica Corp. C379

Woodwork

custom-built
KraftMaid Cabinetry, Inc. C529
Wellborn Cabinet, Inc. C536
White River Hardwood
   Products C464
decorative grillework
White River Hardwood
   Products C464
mantels
see
   Mantels: —wood
moldings, cornices, door and window trim
see also
   Surfacing and paneling—interior—materials:
     —moldings and trim for—wood or plywood
White River Hardwood
   Products C464
rails—chair or plate
White River Hardwood
   Products C464
stock
White River Hardwood
   Products C464

Woodwork—simulated/manufactured

moldings, cornices, door and window trim
see also
   Moldings and cornices: —plastic, composite
   Surfacing and paneling—interior—materials:
     —moldings and trim for—wood or plywood—
     simulated/manufactured
White River Hardwood
   Products C464

Catalogs are coded by position within the volume in numerical sequence, e.g., C345

NOTE: Sweet's has been requested by manufacturers to include the following trade names and trademarks in this index. Sweet's makes no representations or warranties as to the rights of any manufacturer to any trade name or trademark listed in this index.

O

OAKBOND (adhesives) C246
OAKMONT (oak parquet) C246
OLYMPIC (oak flooring) C247
OPTIDESIGN (heat exchangers) C585
ORNAMENTAL (walnut flooring) C247
OVER THE RANGE (convection &
microwave ovens) C512

P

PLANTATION (oak flooring) C247
PRE-FINISHED STRIP (oak strips) C246
PREMIER (wood flooring) C247

R

RANCH PLANK (oak planks) C246
REUNION (oak planks) C246
RIDGESIDE (oak strips) C246
RIDGEWOOD (oak parquet) C246
RIVERSIDE (oak planks) C246
ROBERTS STEP-LITE SYSTEMS (low-
voltage tube lighting) C949

S

SANTA FE SQUARE (custom-crafted wood
tiles) C246
SHARP (appliances & microwave ovens) C512
SHILOH (oak flooring) C247
SIERRA PLANK (oak planks) C246
SIGN OF THE CRAB (fittings, trim &
accessories) C584
SLIM LINE (surface-mounted medicine
cabinets) C585
SMART & EASY (convection & microwave
ovens) C512
SONATA (custom-crafted wood tiles) C246
SORRENTO (oak parquet) C246
SPRINGDALE (oak planks) C246
STAFFORD (oak strips) C246
STEP LIGHTS (stair, safety lighting) C949
STERLING (oak strips) C246
STERLING ENCORE PLANK (oak planks) C246
STERLING PRESTIGE PLANK (oak planks) C246
STRIP LIGHTS (step, cove, outdoor & indoor
lighting) C949
STROM (fittings, trim & accessories) C584
SUB-ZERO (refrigerators/freezers) . . A028; C514; C515;
C515A
SUMMERSIDE (oak strips) C246
SUMMIT HILL (oak planks) C246
SUTTON (oak planks) C246

T

TARA (oak flooring) C247
THE BRAND YOU CAN TRUST (laminate
floors) C310
TRAFFIC ZONE (laminate flooring) C310
TRIANGLE PACIFIC (laminate flooring) C310
TRIANGLE PACIFIC (wood flooring) C246; C247
TUBE LITES (outdoor/indoor, low-voltage
lighting) C949
TYPE 500 (standard heat exchangers) C585

U

UNFINISHED STRIP (oak strips) C246
UNIT BLOCK (oak parquet) C246

V

VALLEY VIEW (oak planks) C246
VAPOR-LOCK (moisture barriers) C246
VILLA NOVA PLANK (oak planks) C246
VILLAGE PLANK (oak planks) C246

W

WEARMASTER 3.0 (hickory, oak, maple &
basswood planks) C246
WELLBORN (kitchen & bath cabinets) C536
WESTMINSTER (oak planks) C246
WHIRLPOOL (residential appliances) C503
WHITE RIVER (architectural wood moldings,
hardwoods, ornamentals, millwork,
embossed moldings) C464
WILSONART (solid polymer fabrications) C478
WINDWARD STRIP (oak strips) C246

Melton™ Classics
Incorporated

fine architectural millwork products

Classic™
Architectural Wood Columns

Classic Design

In keeping with the Classic Orders of Architecture as recorded in the late 1500's by the renowned Renaissance architect, Vignola, Melton Classics proudly presents its complete line of architecturally correct wood columns. Available in matching round, square, or pilaster configurations, every element of the column, from the proportions and bowed taper (entasis) of the shaft to the fluting and carefully sculpted detail of the capital, is specifically crafted to carry on the timeless beauty and unmistaken authenticity of a true Architectural Column. Additionally, contemporary and custom designs are available upon special request.

For projects which call for quality designed and constructed authentic architectural wood columns, specify the Classic™ from Melton Classics.

10-Year Warranty

Melton Classics provides a 10-year limited warranty against decay and joint separation on Clear All Heart Redwood Columns when used with fiberglass caps, bases and plinths and properly installed, ventilated and painted. For complete details of this ten-year warranty contact the company direct.

Construction

Each Classic™ Column shaft is constructed of the finest clear wood available as called for in the specification. The staves are glued with Type I waterproof glue, bound under pressure and allowed to cure for at least 24 hours. The rough column shaft is then precision turned with correct entasis using state-of-the-art equipment combined with the hands-on expertise of wood-working artisans. Each shaft is treated with wood preservative, hand finished, primed and carefully inspected before shipping to assure consistent quality. Shafts designated for exterior use are coated with asphaltum on the inside for waterproofing. Classic™ Column shafts may be specified either plain or fluted and are completely load bearing.

Materials

Column shafts for exterior use are available in Clear All Heart Redwood, western red cedar, pine, and a variety of other clear western wood species. Staves for column shafts are available in both solid or finger-jointed construction. For interior application, pine, poplar, mahogany, cherry, oak or virtually any commercially available wood species may be specified.

3

A296
06400/MEL
BuyLine 9745

Classic™
Architectural
Wood Columns

Capitals, Bases and Plinths

For exterior use, Tuscan and Roman Doric capitals, bases and plinths are available in load bearing fiberglass or redwood. Cast aluminum plinths are recommended for use with redwood bases. For interior applications, wood species to match the column shafts are available.

Made in Halves and Splined for Reassembly

For installation around structural supports, columns may be manufactured in halves and splined for reassembly.

Installation/Finishing/Storage

Detailed installation instructions are provided. Special care must be taken by the installing contractor to ensure proper ventilation of the column shaft. Melton Classics accepts no responsibility for columns improperly ventilated or not installed in accordance with instructions. Two coats of high-quality oil-based paint should be applied to all exterior surfaces immediately following installation. If installation cannot be completed immediately upon delivery, columns must be stored in a dry, well-ventilated area.

When installing ornamental capitals, the following procedure should be followed. Prior to installation, all interior and exterior surfaces should be painted with at least two coats of high-quality oil-based paint. When ordered in combination with Melton Classic columns, each capital is furnished with the appropriate load bearing support to transfer the load to the column shaft. All ornamental capitals for exterior use are furnished with the necessary lead flashing to complete the proper installation procedures. To prevent moisture infiltration, premium grade caulking should be applied where the capital meets the beam and rests on the column shaft.

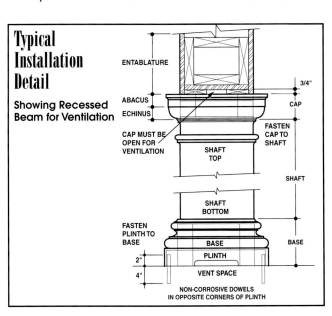

Typical Installation Detail

Showing Recessed Beam for Ventilation

ENTABLATURE

ABACUS
ECHINUS

3/4"
CAP

CAP MUST BE OPEN FOR VENTILATION

FASTEN CAP TO SHAFT

SHAFT TOP

SHAFT

SHAFT BOTTOM

SHAFT

FASTEN PLINTH TO BASE

BASE

BASE

PLINTH

2"

4"

VENT SPACE

NON-CORROSIVE DOWELS IN OPPOSITE CORNERS OF PLINTH

Classic™

Architectural Wood Columns Technical Data

Tuscan

Design # 200TN-Plain • #205TN-Fluted

TOTAL BASE	BOT. DIA.	TOP DIA.	SQUARE PLINTH		ROUND BASE		ROUND CAP	SQUARE ABACUS		TOTAL CAP
E F	A	B	C	D	E	F	G	H	I	G H
2 3/8	8	6 1/2	10 3/4	1 7/8	1 3/4	5/8	1	1 3/8	9 3/8	2 3/8
2 7/8	10	8 1/2	13 3/8	2 3/8	2 1/8	3/4	1 1/4	1 3/4	12 1/8	3
3 1/4	12	10	16 1/8	2 3/4	2 3/8	7/8	1 3/8	2	14 3/8	3 3/8
4	14	12	18 3/4	3 3/8	3	1	1 5/8	2 3/8	17 1/8	4
4 1/2	16	13 1/2	21 1/2	3 7/8	3 3/8	1 1/8	1 7/8	2 3/4	19 1/4	4 5/8
5 3/8	18	15	24 1/4	4 1/4	3 7/8	1 1/2	2 1/8	3	21 1/2	5 1/8
6	20	17	27	4 3/4	4 1/4	1 3/4	2 1/4	3 3/8	24 1/4	5 5/8
6 7/8	22	18 1/2	29 3/4	5 1/4	4 3/4	2 1/8	2 1/2	3 3/4	26 1/2	6 1/4
7 1/2	24	20	32 1/2	5 3/4	5 1/4	2 1/4	2 3/4	4 1/8	28 3/4	6 7/8
8 1/4	26	22	35	6 1/4	5 5/8	2 5/8	3	4 3/8	31 1/2	7 3/8
8 3/4	28	23 1/2	38	6 3/4	6	2 3/4	3 1/4	4 3/4	33 3/8	8
9 1/4	30	25	40 1/2	7 1/4	6 1/2	2 3/4	3 1/2	5 1/8	35 3/4	8 5/8
10	32	27	42 3/4	7 3/4	6 7/8	3 1/8	3 3/4	5 1/2	37 5/8	9 1/4
10 5/8	34	28 1/2	45 1/2	8 1/2	7 1/2	3 3/8	3 7/8	5 3/4	41	9 5/8
11 3/8	36	30	48	9	7 3/4	3 5/8	4 1/4	6 1/4	42 3/4	10 1/2

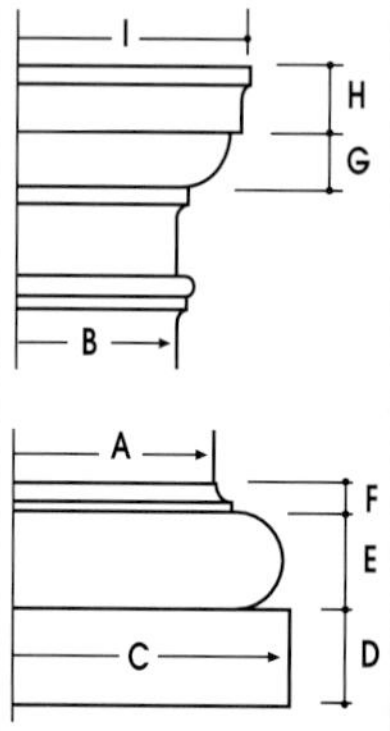

Roman Doric

Design # 210RD-Plain • #215RD-Fluted

TOTAL BASE	BOT. DIA.	TOP DIA.	SQUARE PLINTH		ROUND BASE			ROUND CAP		SQUARE ABACUS			TOTAL CAP
E F G	A	B	C	D	E	F	G	I	J	K	L	M	I J K L
2 3/8	8	6 1/2	10 3/4	1 7/8	1 7/16	7/16	1/2	5/16	13/16	7/8	5/8	9 3/4	2 5/8
3	10	8 1/2	13 3/8	2 3/8	1 3/4	5/8	5/8	3/8	1	1	3/4	12 1/2	3 1/8
3 7/16	12	10	16 1/8	2 3/4	2 1/16	11/16	11/16	7/16	1 3/16	1 1/2	7/8	14 3/4	4
4	14	12	18 3/4	3 3/8	2 3/8	7/8	3/4	9/16	1 3/8	1 5/8	1 1/8	17 1/2	4 11/16
4 7/8	16	13 1/2	21 1/2	3 7/8	2 7/8	1	1	5/8	1 5/8	1 7/8	1 1/4	19 7/8	5 3/8
5 5/8	18	15	24 1/4	4 1/4	3 1/4	1 1/8	1 1/4	3/4	1 3/4	2 1/8	1 3/8	22 1/4	6
6 1/4	20	17	27	4 3/4	3 5/8	1 1/4	1 3/8	3/4	2	2 3/8	1 5/8	25	6 3/4
6 3/4	22	18 1/2	29 3/4	5 1/4	3 7/8	1 3/8	1 1/2	7/8	2 1/8	2 5/8	1 3/4	27 3/8	7 3/8
7 1/2	24	20	32 1/2	5 3/4	4 5/16	1 7/16	1 3/4	15/16	2 3/8	2 3/4	1 13/16	29 3/4	7 7/8
8 1/8	26	22	35	6 1/4	4 5/8	1 1/2	2	1	2 9/16	3 1/8	2	32 1/2	8 11/16
8 5/8	28	23 1/2	38	6 3/4	5	1 3/4	1 7/8	1 1/8	2 3/4	3 3/8	2 1/8	34 5/8	9 3/8
9 3/8	30	25	40 1/2	7 1/4	5 3/8	1 3/4	2 1/4	1 3/16	2 7/8	3 1/2	2 3/8	37	9 15/16
17 3/4	32	27	42 3/4	7 3/4	5 3/4	1 7/8	2 3/8	1 3/16	3 1/8	3 3/4	2 1/2	39 1/4	10 9/16
19 1/4	34	28 1/2	45 1/2	8 1/2	6 1/8	2	2 5/8	1 5/16	3 3/8	4	2 5/8	42 1/8	11 5/16
20 1/4	36	30	48	9	6 3/8	2 1/8	2 3/4	1 3/8	3 5/8	4 1/4	2 3/4	44 1/8	12

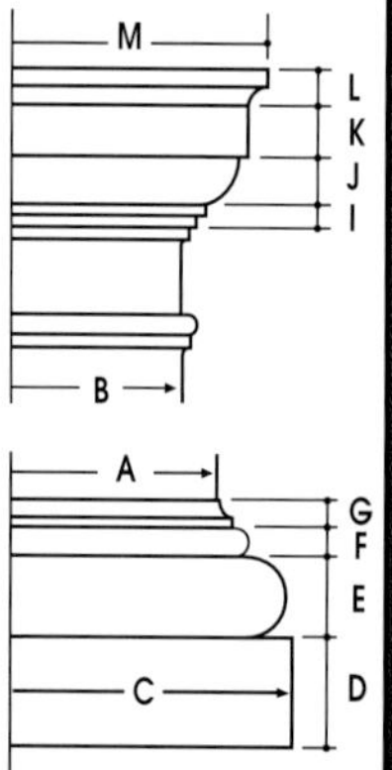

Roman Doric w/ Attic Base

Design # 220RDA-Plain • #225RDA-Fluted

TOTAL BASE	BOT. DIA.	TOP DIA.	SQUARE PLINTH		ROUND BASE				ROUND CAP		SQUARE ABACUS			TOTAL CAP
E F G H	A	B	C	D	E	F	G	H	I	J	K	L	M	I J K L
3 1/4	8	6 1/2	10 3/4	1 7/8	1 1/8	7/8	3/4	1/2	5/16	13/16	7/8	5/8	9 3/4	2 5/8
3 7/8	10	8 1/2	13 3/8	2 3/8	1 1/4	1 1/8	7/8	5/8	3/8	1	1	3/4	12 1/2	3 1/8
4 1/2	12	10	16 1/8	2 3/4	1 1/2	1 3/8	1	5/8	7/16	1 3/16	1 1/2	7/8	14 3/4	4
5 3/8	14	12	18 3/4	3 3/8	1 3/4	1 5/8	1 1/4	3/4	9/16	1 3/8	1 5/8	1 1/8	17 1/2	2 5/8
6 1/4	16	13 1/2	21 1/2	3 7/8	2 1/8	1 7/8	1 3/8	7/8	5/8	1 5/8	1 7/8	1 1/4	19 7/8	2 5/8
7 1/8	18	15	24 1/4	4 1/4	2 3/8	2 1/8	1 1/2	1 1/8	3/4	1 3/4	2 1/8	1 3/8	22 1/4	6
8 1/8	20	17	27	4 3/4	2 5/8	2 3/8	1 3/4	1 3/8	3/4	2	2 3/8	1 5/8	25	6 3/4
9	22	18 1/2	29 3/4	5 1/4	2 7/8	2 5/8	1 7/8	1 5/8	7/8	2 1/8	2 5/8	1 3/4	27 3/8	7 3/8
9 15/16	24	20	32 1/2	5 3/4	3 3/16	2 7/8	2 1/8	1 3/4	15/16	2 3/8	2 3/4	1 13/16	29 3/4	7 7/8
10 5/8	26	22	35	6 1/4	3 3/8	3 1/8	2 1/4	1 7/8	1	2 9/16	3 1/8	2	32 1/2	8 11/16
11 3/8	28	23 1/2	38	6 3/4	3 3/4	3 3/8	2 3/8	1 7/8	1 1/8	2 3/4	3 3/8	2 1/8	34 5/8	9 3/8
12	30	25	40 1/2	7 1/4	3 7/8	3 5/8	2 5/8	1 7/8	1 3/16	2 7/8	3 1/2	2 3/8	37	9 15/16

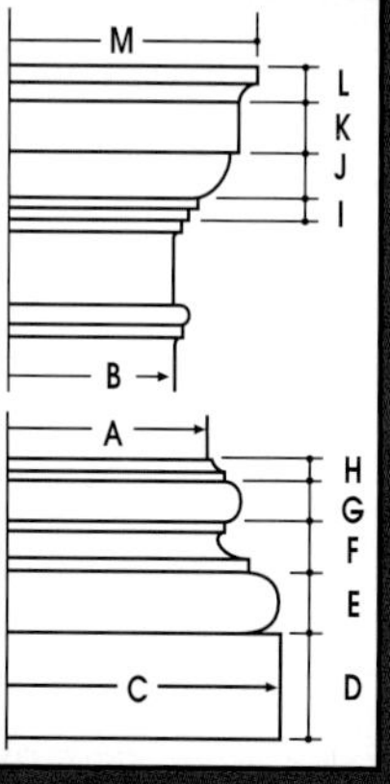

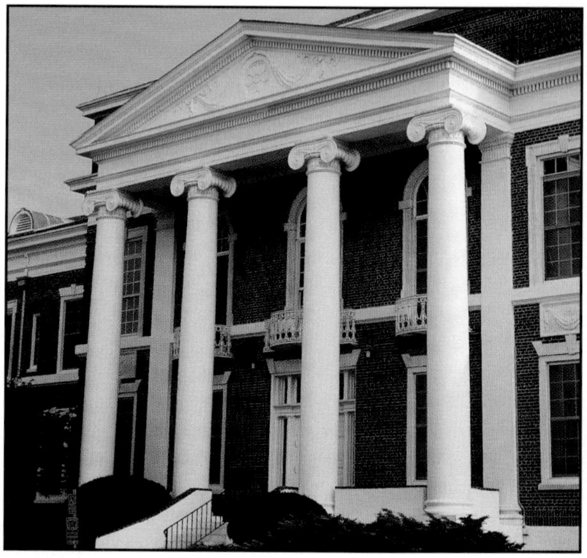

Plan Types

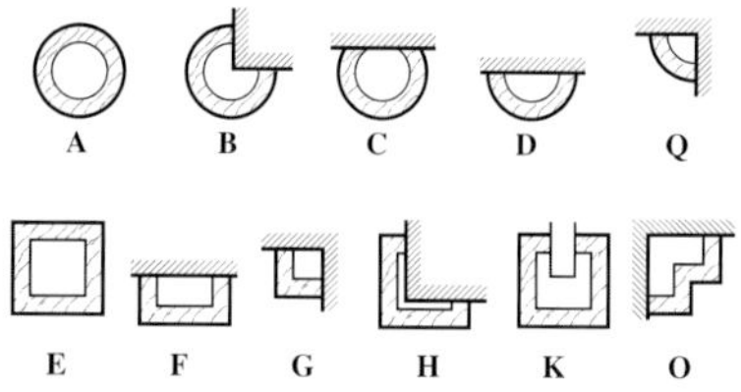

Fluting Types

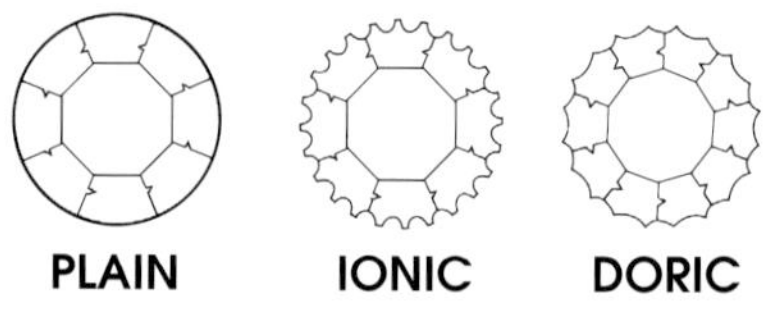

Load Bearing Capacity

Diameter	Stave Thickness		Wood Species	
	Plain	Fluted	Pine	Redwood
6″	2″	2″	2500	6,000
8″	2″	2″	4000	9,000
10″	2″	2″	5000	12,500
12″	2″	2″	6500	15,000
14″	2″	2″	11,000	17,000
16″	2″	2″	12,000	21,000
18″	2″	2″	14,000	24,500
20″	2″	2″	16,500	28,000
22″	2″	3″	18,000	32,000
24″	2″	3″	20,000	34,000
26″	3″	3″	22,000	39,500
28″	3″	3″	24,000	43,500
30″	3″	3″	25,500	47,500
32″	3″	3″	25,500	47,500
34″	3″	3″	25,500	47,500
36″	3″	3″	25,500	47,500

Load applied concentrically through axis of column. Loads valid only if uniform contact between full area of column ends and cap and base units. Loads are provided as a convenience and are not an exact value. Consult a structural engineer for accurate load estimates. Shaft thickness may vary for interior columns.

5

Classic™
Ornamental Capitals for Architectural Wood Columns

Ornamental Capitals

Hand crafted in accordance with the Orders of Architecture, every classically proportioned, crisply detailed ornamental capital is molded from durable, fiber-reinforced composition. Each capital is fired at temperatures suitable to harden the composition, and then sealed prior to being carefully packaged for shipment. Ornamental capitals from Melton Classics are available in round, square and various angular pilaster profiles.

For historical restorations, Melton Classics artisans can create a mold from as little as one-fourth of an existing capital in order to form an authentic replica of the original capital. Additionally, wooden capitals can be hand carved to complement the broad line of stain-grade hardwood columns available from Melton Classics.

Roman Ionic
Design # 230RI - Plain, 235RI - Fluted

Bottom Dia.	Cap Outside Dia.	Cap Height	Abacus Width
6"	5¼"	2¼"	6⅛"
8"	6½"	3"	8¼"
10"	9"	3⅝"	11"
12"	10½"	4½"	12½"
14"	13"	5½"	17½"
16"	13½"	6⅛"	17½"
18"	16¼"	6½"	20"
20"	18"	8¾"	25"
22"	18¾"	8¾"	25"
24"	20½"	9"	25¼"
26"	22¾"	9½"	26½"
28"	25"	12½"	32"
30"	NA	NA	NA

Scamozzi
Design # 240SC - Plain, 245SC - Fluted

Bottom Dia.	Cap Outside Dia.	Cap Height	Abacus Width
6"	5¼"	2⅝"	7¾"
8"	6¾"	3"	10¼"
10"	8½"	3⅞"	14½"
12"	11"	5"	17½"
14"	13"	6"	19½"
16"	14½"	6¼"	22¼"
18"	16"	7½"	25"
20"	18"	8½"	28½"
22"	NA	NA	NA
24"	21"	10¼"	34¼"
26"	22½"	11"	35½"
28"	25"	12¾"	39"
30"	NA	NA	NA

Roman Corinthian
Design # 250SC - Plain, 255SC - Fluted

Bottom Dia.	Cap Outside Dia.	Cap Height	Abacus Width
6"	5"	7"	9½"
8"	7¼"	10¼"	12¾"
10"	8½"	12"	15"
12"	11"	15½"	18½"
14"	12½"	17"	22"
16"	14"	20"	27"
18"	16"	23"	32½"
20"	18"	25½"	39"
22"	19½"	28½"	42"
24"	21"	28½"	42"
26"	22½"	32"	42"
28"	24"	34"	46"
30"	26"	37½"	46½"

Empire
Design # 260EM - Plain, 265EM - Fluted

Bottom Dia.	Cap Outside Dia.	Cap Height	Abacus Width
6"	5"	3⅛"	9"
8"	6½"	3¾"	10"
10"	9"	5½"	16"
12"	10¼"	6¼"	18"
14"	12½"	7¼"	20½"
16"	14"	8¾"	23"
18"	16½"	10"	32"
20"	18"	11¼"	34"
22"	NA	NA	NA
24"	20½"	12¾"	35½"
26"	22½"	13"	37"
28"	NA	NA	NA
30"	NA	NA	NA

Greek Angular Ionic
Design # 270GAI - Plain, 275GAI - Fluted

Bottom Dia.	Cap Outside Dia.	Cap Height	Abacus Width
6"	NA	NA	NA
8"	6½"	3¾"	9½"
10"	8¾"	5⅜"	14½"
12"	10½"	6"	17¼"
14"	12½"	7¼"	20¾"
16"	14½"	8⅜"	20½"
18"	16"	9¾"	24¼"
20"	18"	11"	29¾"
22"	NA	NA	NA
24"	NA	NA	NA
26"	NA	NA	NA
28"	NA	NA	NA
30"	NA	NA	NA

Empire With Necking
Design # 280EMN - Plain, 285EMN - Fluted

Bottom Dia.	Cap Outside Dia.	Cap Height	Abacus Width
6"	5"	6⅞"	9"
8"	6¼"	7¾"	10"
10"	8½"	10"	13½"
12"	10"	11"	18"
14"	12"	14½"	20½"
16"	14"	17"	23"
18"	16"	15"	32"
20"	18"	17¼"	34"
22"	NA	NA	NA
24"	20½"	19"	35½"
26"	NA	NA	NA
28"	NA	NA	NA
30"	NA	NA	NA

Greek Erechtheum Ionic
Design # 300GE - Plain, 305GE - Fluted

Bottom Dia.	Cap Outside Dia.	Cap Height	Abacus Width
6"	5"	3¼"	6¾"
8"	6¼"	3¾"	7¾"
10"	9"	5½"	12"
12"	10"	6¼"	14½"
14"	12¾"	7"	15"
16"	14½"	9"	17½"
18"	15¼"	10¼"	22"
20"	18"	11"	26"
22"	19½"	11¼"	26"
24"	20½"	13"	30½"
26"	NA	NA	NA
28"	NA	NA	NA
30"	25"	15"	45½"

Temple of Winds
Design # 330TW - Plain, 335TW - Fluted

Bottom Dia.	Cap Outside Dia.	Cap Height	Abacus Width
6"	5¼"	7"	8"
8"	7"	8"	12"
10"	9"	11⅛"	15¼"
12"	10"	11⅝"	16⅞"
14"	12"	16"	19"
16"	14"	16"	23"
18"	16"	18⅛"	26¾"
20"	17½"	21½"	28"
22"	19½"	23¼"	34½"
24"	21"	28½"	31¼"
26"	22"	24"	35"
28"	24"	28"	37"
30"	26"	30"	39"

Classic™ Wood Column Designs

A   **Roman Doric with Attic Base**
Design # 220RDA - Plain, 225RDA - Fluted

C   **Roman Corinthian**
Design # 250RC- Plain, 255RC - Fluted

E   **Greek Angular Ionic**
Design # 270GAI - Plain, 275GAI - Fluted

B   **Temple of Winds**
Design # 330TW - Plain, 335TW - Fluted

D   **Empire**
Design # 260EM - Plain, 265EM - Fluted

F   **Roman Doric**
Design # 210RD - Plain, 215RD - Fluted

G **Roman Ionic**
Design # 230RI - Plain, 235RI - Fluted

H **Scamozzi**
Design # 240SC - Plain, 245SC - Fluted

I **Roman Corinthian**
Design # 250RC- Plain, 255RC - Fluted

J **Empire with Necking**
Design # 280EMN - Plain, 285EMN - Fluted

K **Tuscan**
Design # 200TN - Plain, 205TN - Fluted

L **Greek Erechtheum Ionic**
Design # 300GE - Plain, 305GE - Fluted

DuraClassic™
Poly/Marble Composite Columns

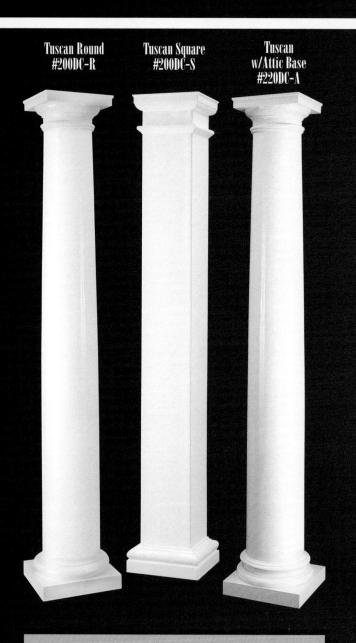

Tuscan Round
#200DC-R

Tuscan Square
#200DC-S

Tuscan
w/Attic Base
#220DC-A

Limited Lifetime Warranty

Melton Classics, Inc. warrants that its DuraClassic™ column will be free from defects in material or workmanship for the lifetime of ownership as long as the DuraClassic™ columns have been installed according to manufacturers recommended installation instructions. For complete details of this limited lifetime warranty contact the company direct.

DuraClassic™ Poly/Marble Columns

In keeping with the Melton Classic standard of quality, traditional classical designs have been combined with state-of-the-art technology to create this innovative column line. Based on the timeless Orders of Architecture, every column component from the crisply detailed Tuscan capital and base to the entasis tapered shaft are cast from fiber-reinforced polyester resin marble composite.

The DuraClassic™ Round columns are available in diameters from 8" to 18" and heights from 4' to 24'. In addition to our standard Tuscan capital and bases, we also offer Roman Doric capitals for 8", 10" and 12" shaft diameters. Square columns are available in a Tuscan design in 8", 10" and 12" shaft sizes in heights from 3' to 14'.

Tuscan Column-Round
Design # 200DC-R

BOT. DIA.	TOP DIA.	SHAFT HEIGHTS	BASE/PLINTH HEIGHT	PLINTH WIDTH	CAP HEIGHT	CAP WIDTH
8	6½	5 ft. to 10 ft.	4¼	10¾	2⅜	9¾
10	8½	5 ft. to 12 ft.	5⅛	13⅜	3⅛	12¼
12	10	5 ft. to 16 ft.	6⅛	16⅛	3¾	14⅝
14	12	5 ft. to 16 ft.	7¾	18¾	4¼	17⅛
16	13½	5 ft. to 18 ft.	9⅛	21½	4¾	19⅝
18	15	5 ft. to 24 ft.	9⅝	24¼	5⅛	21½

Tuscan Column-Square
Design # 200DC-S

BOT. DIA.	TOP DIA.	SHAFT HEIGHTS	BASE/PLINTH HEIGHT	PLINTH WIDTH	CAP HEIGHT	CAP WIDTH
8	8	3 ft. to 10 ft.	4	11¹¹⁄₁₆	2¼	10¼
10	10	3 ft. to 12 ft.	5	13⅝	3⅛	14¼
12	12	3 ft. to 14 ft.	5½	16½	3¼	15¼

Tuscan Column-with Attic Base
Design # 220DC-A

BOT. DIA.	TOP DIA.	SHAFT HEIGHTS	BASE/PLINTH HEIGHT	PLINTH WIDTH	CAP HEIGHT	CAP WIDTH
8	6½	5 ft. to 10 ft.	5⅛	10¾	2⅜	9¾
10	8½	5 ft. to 12 ft.	6¼	13⅜	3⅛	12¼
12	10	5 ft. to 16 ft.	7¼	16⅛	3¾	14⅝
14	12	5 ft. to 16 ft.	8¾	18¾	4¼	17⅛
16	13½	5 ft. to 18 ft.	10⅛	21½	4¾	19⅝
18	15	5 ft. to 24 ft.	11⅜	24¼	5⅛	21½

NOTE: 8"-12" Attic Bases are Poly/Marble
14"-18" Attic Bases are Fiberglass

A296
06400/MEL
BuyLine 9745

DuraClassic™
Ornamental Capitals and Bases

Roman Ionic
Design # 230DC

Bottom Dia.	Cap Outside Dia.	Cap Height	Abacus Width
8″	$6^1/_2$″	3″	$8^1/_4$″
10″	9″	$3^5/_8$″	11″
12″	$10^1/_2$″	$4^1/_2$″	$12^1/_2$″
14″	13″	$5^1/_2$″	$17^1/_2$″
16″	$13^1/_2$″	$6^1/_8$″	$17^1/_2$″
18″	$16^1/_4$″	$6^1/_2$″	20″

Scamozzi
Design # 240DC

Bottom Dia.	Cap Outside Dia.	Cap Height	Abacus Width
8″	$6^3/_4$″	3″	$10^1/_4$″
10″	$8^1/_2$″	$3^7/_8$″	$14^1/_2$″
12″	11″	5″	$17^1/_2$″
14″	13″	6″	$19^1/_2$″
16″	$14^1/_2$″	$6^1/_4$″	$22^1/_4$″
18″	16″	$7^1/_2$″	25″

Roman Corinthian
Design # 250DC

Bottom Dia.	Cap Outside Dia.	Cap Height	Abacus Width
8″	$7^1/_4$″	$10^1/_4$″	$12^3/_4$″
10″	$8^1/_2$″	12″	15″
12″	11″	$15^1/_2$″	$18^1/_2$″
14″	$12^1/_2$″	17″	22″
16″	14″	20″	27″
18″	16″	23″	$32^1/_2$″

Empire
Design # 260DC

Bottom Dia.	Cap Outside Dia.	Cap Height	Abacus Width
8″	$6^1/_2$″	$3^3/_4$″	10″
10″	9″	$5^1/_2$″	16″
12″	$10^1/_4$″	$6^1/_4$″	18″
14″	$12^1/_2$″	$7^1/_4$″	$20^1/_2$″
16″	14″	$8^3/_4$″	23″
18″	$16^1/_2$″	10″	32″

Greek Erechtheum Ionic
Design # 300DC

Bottom Dia.	Cap Outside Dia.	Cap Height	Abacus Width
8″	$6^1/_4$″	$3^3/_4$″	$7^3/_4$″
10″	9″	$5^1/_2$″	12″
12″	10″	$6^1/_4$″	$14^1/_2$″
14″	$12^3/_4$″	7″	15″
16″	$14^1/_2$″	9″	$17^1/_2$″
18″	$15^1/_4$″	$10^1/_4$″	22″

Temple of Winds
Design # 330DC

Bottom Dia.	Cap Outside Dia.	Cap Height	Abacus Width
8″	7″	8″	12″
10″	9″	$11^1/_8$″	$15^1/_4$″
12″	10″	$11^5/_8$″	$16^7/_8$″
14″	12″	16″	19″
16″	14″	16″	23″
18″	16″	$18^1/_8$″	$26^3/_4$″

Note: Poly/Marble capital dimensions may vary.

Roman Corinthian #250DC   Scamozzi #240DC   Temple of the Winds #330DC

Load Bearing Capacity

Diameter	Height	Load in Pounds
8″	8′	12,000
10″	8′	16,000
12″	8′	20,000

Plan Types

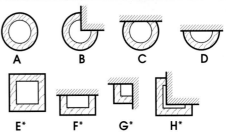

A, B, C, and D available in all sizes
*E, F, G, and H available 8″ to 12″ diameter only

FRP Classic™
Non-load Bearing Fiberglass Columns

FiberWound Classic™
Load Bearing Fiberglass Columns

FRP Classic™
Tuscan Tapered Shaft
#200FRP-T

FRP Classic™
Tuscan Straight Shaft
#200FRP-S

FiberWound Classic™
Tuscan Tapered Shaft
#200FW

FRP Classic™
Non-load Bearing Fiberglass Column Covers

Melton Classics's fiberglass column covers are designed to provide a beautiful and durable low maintenance cover for structural supports, ductwork, etc. These low maintenance columns are available in a wide range of classical or contemporary designs with entasis tapered or straight shafts from a large inventory of standard molds. Constructed from fiberglass reinforced polyester (FRP) molded with fire-rated resins and fiberglass, the FRP Classic provides a Class A fire rating and low smoke density. Custom designs are available upon request.

FiberWound Classic™
Load Bearing Fiberglass Columns

In the Melton Classics tradition of innovation, the FiberWound Classic™ load bearing fiberglass column combines aerospace technology with authentic classical column designs to create the most durable and light-weight architectural column available. Backed by a limited lifetime warranty, this low maintenance fiberglass column is created with correct entasis and classically proportioned capitals and bases to provide a lifetime of classic beauty. Aerospace filament winding technology allows high impact resistance and very high load bearing capacities to be achieved without excessive weight. The reduced weight combined with simplicity of assembly provides lower installation and handling costs making the FiberWound Classic™ one of the most durable and affordable architecturally correct columns available. FiberWound Classic™ columns can also be specified for Class A fire rating upon request.

11

MarbleTex™
Synthetic Stone Columns

MarbleTex™
Synthetic Stone Columns

Melton Classics presents the innovative MarbleTex™ line of *maintenance-free* synthetic stone columns. These classically styled columns are created in durable integral color through marble/polymer composition in a Classic White integral color through finish that requires no painting or sealants.

Our exclusive centrifugal casting process allows MarbleTex™ column shafts to be manufactured in one load bearing seamless unit which simplifies installation. Column shafts can also be manufactured in halves for reassembly around structural supports, when desired. Offered in Tuscan and Neo Doric designs, the MarbleTex™ capitals, bases and plinths are manufactured from the same durable maintenance free stone composition as the shaft. Ornamental capitals and attic styled bases are available for selected sizes.

MarbleTex™ Synthetic Stone Column Features:

• Limited Lifetime Warranty

• Prefinished integral coloration or paint grade finishes are available

• Offered in plain shaft Tuscan or Neo Doric designs with marble textured finish

• Available in diameters from 6" to 28" and in heights from 4' to 25'

These maintenance free columns are ideal companions for our **MarbleTex™ synthetic stone balustrades (see Sweet's 04720/MEL)** providing the opportunity for complete coordination of design elements. MarbleTex™ columns and balustrades are the ideal choice for any interior application, or the most demanding exterior application.

Limited Lifetime Warranty

Melton Classics, Inc. warrants that its MarbleTex™ column will be free from defects in material or workmanship for the lifetime of ownership as long as the MarbleTex™ columns have been installed according to manufacturers recommended installation instructions. For complete details of this limited lifetime warranty contact the company direct.

Load Bearing Capacity

DIAMETER	6"	8"	10"	12"	14"	16"	18"	20"	24"	28"
MAX LOAD IN POUNDS	9000	12000	16000	20000	20000	20000	20000	20000	20000	20000

Load applied concentrically through axis of column. Loads valid only if uniform between full area of column shaft ends. Loads are provided as a convenience and are not an exact value. Consult a structural engineer for accurate load estimates. Due to variations in natural stone, color of finished product may vary.

Tuscan 200MT

BOT. DIA	TOP DIA	PLINTH		BASE	CAP SQUARE		CAP RND
A*	B*	C	D	E	F	G	H
8	6½	10¾	1⅞	2⅜	10	1⅜	1
10	8½	13⅜	2⅜	2⅞	12½	1¾	1¼
12	10	16⅛	2¾	3¼	15	2	1⅜
14	12	18¾	3⅜	4	17½	2⅜	1⅝
16	13½	21½	3⅞	4½	20	2¾	1¾
18	15	24¼	4¼	5⅜	22½	3	2⅛
20	17	27	4¾	6	25	3⅜	2¼
24	20	32½	5¾	7½	30	4⅛	2¾
28	23½	38	6¾	8¾	33⅜	4¾	3¼

*Nominal

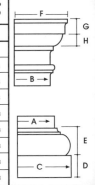

Neo Doric 210ND

BOT. DIA	TOP DIA	PLINTH		BASE	CAP SQUARE		CAP RND
A*	B*	C	D	E	F	G	H
6	5¼	9¼	1½	1¾	8¼	1¼	1⅛
8	7⅛	11¼	1¾	2¼	10¼	1¼	1¼
10	9¼	13½	1¾	2½	12½	1⅜	1½
12	10⅞	16¼	2	2¾	14½	1⅝	1¾
14	11½	18¾	2¼	3⅜	16⅛	1¾	1¾
16	13¼	21¼	2½	4	18	1¾	1¾
18	15⅜	23¾	2⅞	4	20¼	2¼	2

*Nominal

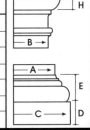

Neo Doric 210ND   **Tuscan 200MT**

Melton™ Classics
Incorporated
fine architectural millwork products

P.O. Box 465020
Lawrenceville, Georgia 30042
1-800-963-3060
(770) 963-3060
FAX: (770) 962-6988
www.meltonclassics.com

OTHER ARCHITECTURAL PRODUCTS AVAILABLE

Melton Classics offers a wide variety of other fine products as listed below. For more information, contact the factory.

• MarbleTex™ Synthetic Stone Balusters
• MarbleTex™ Synthetic Stone Newel Posts
• MarbleTex™ Synthetic Stone Hand Rails and Foot Rail All with Integral Color

For MarbleTex™ Balustrade information, refer to: SWEETS 04720/MEL

For additional information on balustrades, specifications, installation instructions or technical information refer to:

www.meltonclassics.com or call 800-963-3

Melton Classics is continually conducting product improvement and development and therefore reserves the right to change or discontinue any product without notice.

© 1998 Melton Classics, Inc. 9/98 MCI0158

See us in Sweet's
CD Online Catalog Files Directory

B575
13134/HAR
BuyLine 1336

HARTFORD CONSERVATORIES

Rooms of Distinction

HARTFORD
CONSERVATORIES, INC. ®

Call Toll Free
for information
800-963-8700

HARTFORD CONSERVATORIES

The Original Hardwood Conservatory

Originally developed in England as an elegant link between house and garden, our conservatories are a practical and beautiful way to increase your living space year round. Hartford draws on 20 years of experience in the design and manufacture of conservatories. We believe that our rooms are second to none.

Bring the outdoors into your home. The choice is yours. It's your breakfast room, your family room, your dining room, your home office or your fitness room. It can be anything, and everything you want it to be.

There's a size to match your space needs and a price to match your budget, ranging from our smallest units, which are designed as a practical entryway, or our extremely versatile and spacious family room sized units.

Spring, Summer, Winter and Fall, Hartford Conservatories are designed to be enjoyed year-round and to withstand the harshest weather conditions. Hartford Conservatories provide a versatile, affordable, and easy way to increase living space and add beauty and charm to any style home. The quality and affordability of our conservatories cannot be matched. A Hartford conservatory costs far less than a similar custom built addition and is much more desirable. Hartford Conservatories can make your dream room a reality. Our unique modular kit can be customized to meet your design requirements. Just call and ask to speak to one of our experienced installation specialists.

Victorian

Features

- Indonesian Mahogany framework, stress graded and pre-treated with a white primer or base coat preservative.
- Safety tempered, dual pane, insulated glass units for all wall panels and doors.
- Wall panels come either full height or designed to be installed on your specially built kneewall.
- Standard double French doors with elegant solid brass hardware.
- Triple walled polycarbonate roof panels.
- PVC gutters, or decorative dentil molding option.
- Modular system arrives on site with most parts pre-cut and ready to assemble.
- Heating and air conditioning can be installed for comfortable year-round living.
- Certified by US consulting engineers to meet the strictest building codes in most areas of North America.
- Do-it-yourself kits available.

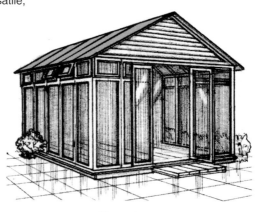

Georgian

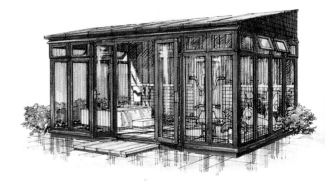

Windsor

Before

After

The graceful Victorian, the contemporary Windsor, and our newest model, the classic Georgian, add beauty and charm to any style home. Our versatile product line offers a broad range of sizes and design options easily customized to your individual specifications.

Panel Styles

Plain   **Etched**

Panel P1
Full height panel with a solid raised wood insert beneath a fixed or opening larger window.

Plain   **Etched**

Panel P2
Full height panel with a fixed larger window beneath a fixed or opening small top window.

Plain   **Etched**

Panel P3
Installed on your kneewall, panel has a fixed or opening large window

---

Conservatory Sizes & Styles

The Victorian 'D' Series, 17° Roof

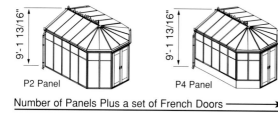

9'-1 13/16" — P2 Panel   9'-1 13/16" — P4 Panel

Number of Panels Plus a set of French Doors ⟶

10' 4" x 5' 4" D1	10' 4" x 7' 3" D2	10' 4" x 9' 4" D3	10' 4" x 11' 4" D4	10' 4" x 13' 5" D5	10' 4" x 15' 6" D6	10' 4" x 17' 6" D7
50 sq.ft.	70 sq.ft.	92 sq.ft.	112 sq.ft.	134 sq.ft.	155 sq.ft.	176 sq.ft.
6	8	10	12	14	16	18

The Victorian 'F' Series, 17° Roof

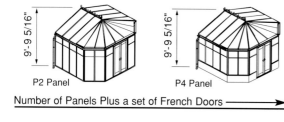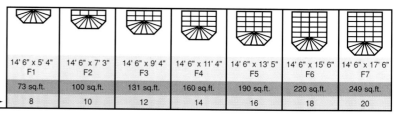

9'-9 5/16" — P2 Panel   9'-9 5/16" — P4 Panel

Number of Panels Plus a set of French Doors ⟶

14' 6" x 5' 4" F1	14' 6" x 7' 3" F2	14' 6" x 9' 4" F3	14' 6" x 11' 4" F4	14' 6" x 13' 5" F5	14' 6" x 15' 6" F6	14' 6" x 17' 6" F7
73 sq.ft.	100 sq.ft.	131 sq.ft.	160 sq.ft.	190 sq.ft.	220 sq.ft.	249 sq.ft.
8	10	12	14	16	18	20

The Victorian 'F' Series, 30° Roof

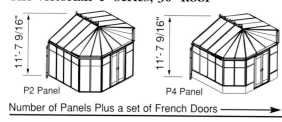

11'-7 9/16" — P2 Panel   11'-7 9/16" — P4 Panel

Number of Panels Plus a set of French Doors ⟶

14' 6" x 5' 4" F1	14' 6" x 7' 3" F2	14' 6" x 9' 4" F3	14' 6" x 11' 4" F4	14' 6" x 13' 5" F5	14' 6" x 15' 6" F6	14' 6" x 17' 6" F7
73 sq.ft.	100 sq.ft.	131 sq.ft.	160 sq.ft.	190 sq.ft.	220 sq.ft.	249 sq.ft.
8	10	12	14	16	18	20

The Victorian 'H' Series, 30° Roof

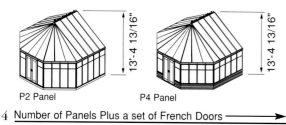

13'-4 13/16" — P2 Panel   13'-4 13/16" — P4 Panel

Number of Panels Plus a set of French Doors ⟶

20' 3" x 8' 2" H1	20' 3" x 10' 1" H2	20' 3" x 12' 2" H3	20' 3" x 14' 3" H4	20' 3" x 16' 4" H5	20' 3" x 18' 4" H6	20' 3" x 20' 5" H7
160 sq.ft.	199 sq.ft.	241 sq.ft.	283 sq.ft.	325 sq.ft.	366 sq.ft.	408 sq.ft.
12	14	16	18	20	22	24

Plain   *Etched*

Plain   *Etched*

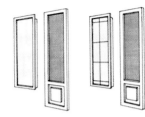

Plain   *Etched*

Panel P4
Installed on your kneewall, panel has a fixed large window beneath a fixed or opening small top window.

Clerestory
Clerestories can be added above any panel to increase the height of the room.

Screen Panel
This has a removable glazed frame turning any conservatory into the ideal screen room.

The Windsor '4-L' Series, 10° Roof

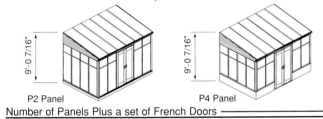

P2 Panel   P4 Panel

Number of Panels Plus a set of French Doors ⟶

8' 8" x 6' 4" 3L4	12' 9" x 8' 5" 4L6	16' 11" x 8' 5" 4L8	21' 0" x 8' 5" 4L10	25' 1" x 8' 5" 4L12
54 sq.ft.	107 sq.ft.	142 sq.ft.	176 sq.ft.	211 sq.ft.
8	12	14	16	18

The Windsor '5-L' Series, 20° Roof

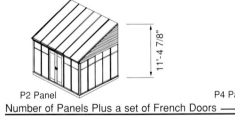 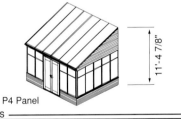

P2 Panel   P4 Panel

Number of Panels Plus a set of French Doors ⟶

12' 9" x 10' 6" 5L6	16' 11" x 10' 6" 5L8	21' 0" x 10' 6" 5L10	25' 1" x 10' 6" 5L12
133 sq.ft.	177 sq.ft.	220 sq.ft.	263 sq.ft.
14	16	18	20

The Georgian 'G' Series, 17° Polycarbonate Roof

 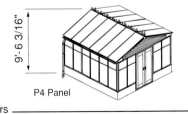

P2 Panel   P4 Panel

Number of Panels Plus a set of French Doors ⟶

12' 9" x 8' 5" G4	12' 9" x 10' 5" G5	12' 9" x 12' 6" G6
107 sq.ft.	133 sq.ft.	159 sq.ft.
12	14	16

The Georgian 'G' Series, Conventional Roof

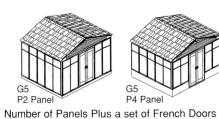  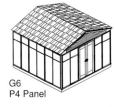 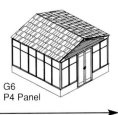

G5
P2 Panel   G5
P4 Panel   G6
P4 Panel   G6
P4 Panel

Number of Panels Plus a set of French Doors ⟶

12' 9" x 8' 5" G4	12' 9" x 10' 5" G5	12' 9" x 12' 6" G6
107 sq.ft.	133 sq.ft.	159 sq.ft.
12	14	16

Panels, French Doors and Clerestories Sizes & Styles

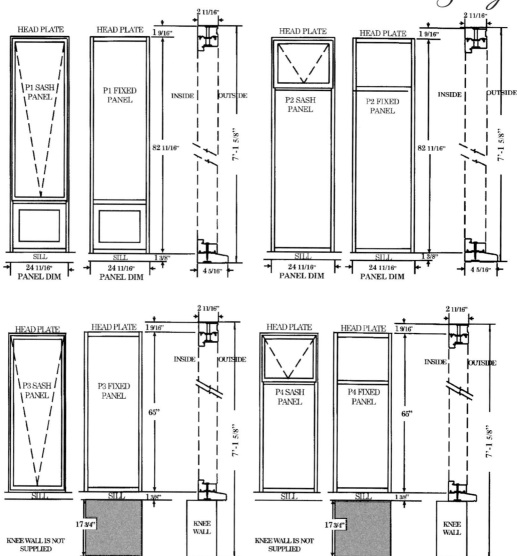

• You may purchase individual panels to enclose your existing porch.
• Decorative stain glass windows are available upon request.
• A sash panel opens and includes a screen.

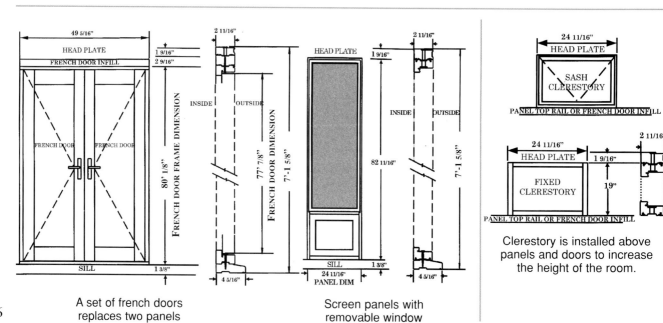

A set of french doors replaces two panels

Screen panels with removable window

Clerestory is installed above panels and doors to increase the height of the room.

Design Options

- Triple walled polycarbonate roof panels are available in clear, opal or bronze.
- Wall panels come either full height or designed to be installed on your specially built kneewall.
- Various panels configuration and clerestories can increase height.
- Tempered safety glass is available in plain or etched styles, either of which may be ordered with Low E and argon treatment for increased performance.
- Screens are supplied for all opening windows and doors.
- Panel and roof blinds are available to increase your privacy.
- A comfortable environment is created by adding our roof skylights.
- Stain or paint your conservatory any color to compliment your personal taste.

Etched glass window panels are an available option.

Standard double french doors with elegant brass hardware.

Panel blinds and roof blinds are available options.

Screen doors are also available.

7

Performance

Hartford Conservatories exceed all snow load standards set by the BOCA National Building Code, the Uniform Building Code and the American Society of Civil Engineers Standard 7-93 for almost all areas of the United States.

The polycarbonate roof used on our conservatories has been tested to withstand loads in excess of 144 pounds per square foot. Furthermore, Hartford Conservatories have been tested for wind load conditions equivalent to almost 100 mph and uplift wind pressures in excess of 43 pounds per square foot.

Hartford Conservatories have been certified by U.S. Consulting Engineers, a copy of the engineering report and certification is provided to all purchasers to assist with regulatory approvals.

Lifetime Warranty*

The superior components and craftsmanship enables Hartford Conservatories® to issue a *Lifetime Limited Warranty on the hardwood and roof plus 20 years on the insulated glass units.

For more information call our
TOLL-FREE CUSTOMER SERVICE LINE (8am to 8pm)
800-963-8700

Photographs, drawings, and plans contained in this brochure are shown for guide purposes only and the designs of the finished product may vary. Hartford Conservatories, Inc. reserves the right to alter specifications without prior notice.

HARTFORD CONSERVATORIES, INC.
96A Commerce Way, Woburn, MA 01801
tel.: 800/963-8700
fax: 781/937-9025

For further information, see us in:
Sweet's CD
Sweet's Online (http://www.sweets.com)
Hartford Conservatories Website (http://www.hartford-con.com)

IBP glass block grid system™

WINDOWS   SKYLIGHTS • FLOORS   SHOWERS   WALLS

ACME
BRICK
Since 1891

IBP Glass block Grid System™
WINDOWS • SKYLIGHTS • FLOORS • SHOWERS • WALLS

The IBP Glass Block Grid System™ combines a strong, lightweight aluminum frame with glass block and weatherproof sealant, to provide cost-effective glass block installation without mortar. Applications of the IBP Grid System are limited only by the imagination. Over sixty thousand successful installations worldwide include store fronts, windows, curtain walls, mosaics, shower enclosures, floors, retail displays, signage, furniture, and sun spaces.

Installation
IBP grid assemblies are available in many standard sizes, and can be custom-manufactured to meet your specifications. Installers simply nail or screw the grid assembly into place. Glass block are then wrapped with insulating foam tape, inserted into the grid, and sealed. A frame can be assembled and installed either by professionals or by do-it-yourselfers.

Durability
The IBP Glass Block Grid System, unlike mortar installations, allows both for building movement and for expansion/contraction of glass block and surrounding materials. The result is a glass block installation that retains its beauty and integrity over time.

Appearance
Gray mortar joints tend to limit the aesthetic appeal of traditional glass block installations. IBP assemblies replace the mortar look with a variety of grid colors which harmonize well with any building design. A wide array of Trimline glass block patterns and colors add further design choices.

Versatility
With the IBP grid system, it's easy to achieve a new effect simply by replacing existing glass block with a new pattern or color. Again, this replacement process takes only minutes and requires no special tools or labor.

Design Assistance
IBP offers free professional design services for all customers. Details are also available on all IBP products in AutoCAD® Release 12 format. To inquire about this service, or to ask for any additional information on the IBP Glass Block Grid System, please call Acme Brick Company at **1-800-932-2263**. Outside the US dial 010-817-820-2532.

Security
The IBP Glass Block Grid System offers the same advantage as security bars, making it one of the most secure components of any building structure. Even if block are broken and removed, the grid system performs like burglar bars and impedes entry.

Sound Transmission
Traditional windows and skylights transmit more than light. They also transmit or possibly amplify sounds from raindrops, hailstones, traffic, and aircraft. When the IBP Glass Block Grid System is utilized, sounds are subdued and muted by the mass of the block. Light passes freely, but sound doesn't.

Cost
Because skilled labor is generally not required, an IBP grid system can cost less to install than traditional mortared glass block or glass pavers.

Insulation
The acceptable U-value standard, according to the American Architectural Manufacturers Association (AAMA), for a double-pane window is .69. The IBP Glass Block Grid System has a U-value of .49, more than 25 percent better than the accepted standard. Additionally, this system has an air and water infiltration rate of 0.00.

Repair
To replace a damaged block, a maintenance person simply cuts away the sealant, removes the block from the grid, inserts the new block, and reseals. Skilled labor and special tools aren't required, and the repair process takes only a few minutes. To replace a damaged block in a mortar installation, a skilled mason must carefully chip out the mortar and replace the block. When the new mortar dries, it may or may not match the existing mortar.

WINDOWS AND WALLS

IBP window and wall grids enhance the appearance of glass block installations. The IBP system assures a proper, uniformly spaced glass block installation without using the time-consuming method of mortar and spacers. IBP window performance factors such as thermal efficiency, air infiltration, water penetration, and security surpass most competing window installations.

The versatility of the IBP Glass Block Grid System™ extends far beyond the standard grid sizes depicted on the project to the right. Stair-stepped windows and the service island counter pictured below are just two examples of the infinite number of design possibilities. Other applications include work space enclosures, interior partitions, curtain walls, and room dividers

New York, NY; New York City Transit Authority

Designed by Boyer Glass & Mirror

Krebs, OK; Terry D. Miller, Designer

WINDOW HEAD
WOOD STUD / BRICK VENEER

WINDOW HEAD
(Jamb Similar)
Mounting Flange Installation

WINDOW HEAD
(Jamb Similar)
Flushmount Installation

WINDOW SILL
WOOD STUD / BRICK VENEER

Standard grid colors are shown below. Silver and Gold are anodized. Custom colors are available.

White	Bronze	Taupe	Black	Red	Silver	Gold
Interior/Exterior	*Interior/Exterior*	*Interior/Exterior*	*Interior Grid*	*Interior Grid*	*Interior Grid*	*Interior Grid*

SKYLIGHTS

IBP *glass block* skylights provide features unavailable in conventional *plastic* skylights. By selecting various block patterns and colors, designers can customize an IBP skylight to meet the aesthetic, energy efficiency, and lighting requirements of a project. Because security is always important, the grid system serves as security bars even if block are broken and removed. IBP skylights provide greater sound insulation qualities than conventional skylights. Additionally, the durability and beauty of aluminum and of glass block make this a superior skylight.

IBP skylights accommodate typical curb and flashing construction as detailed. Standard skylight models span areas up to 49" x 80" (six block wide by ten block long) without additional support. Custom skylights can be designed to span larger areas.

Louisville, KY; Designed by Rodney Wells

Bonita Springs, FL; Bonita Springs Medical Center

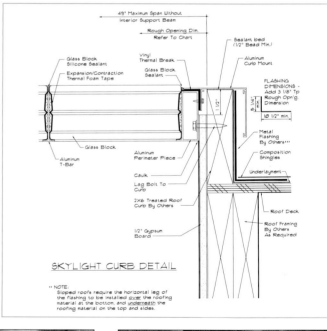

SKYLIGHT CURB DETAIL

Bonita Springs, FL; Bonita Springs Medical Center

Skylight grid with curb mount.

Installation of glass block

Application of the sealant

SHOWER ENCLOSURES

Today's most beautiful shower enclosures are fashioned from glass block, and IBP's new shower enclosure system renders glass block showers practical for the first time. Aluminum extrusions link together in 22.5° increments to turn corners as shown below. A flush aluminum finishing piece easily attaches the grid panels to adjoining walls and to the shower base. To prevent leaks, the interior side of the shower is sealed with a mildew-resistant silicone. IBP offers a self-supporting glass block door header frame to further enhance the shower's aesthetic appeal.

IBP shower enclosures can be designed to fit your specific requirements. Examples shown at right are just a few of the many design configurations available. Many shower designs are installed within two hours, and usually at less cost than traditional glass block shower installations.

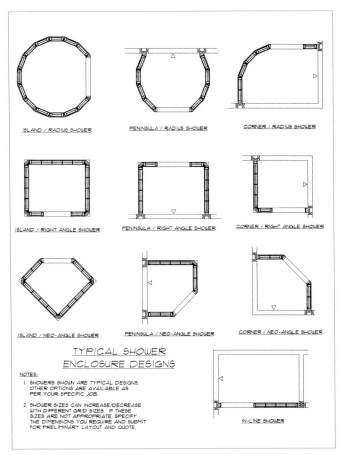

ISLAND / RADIUS SHOWER   PENINSULA / RADIUS SHOWER   CORNER / RADIUS SHOWER

ISLAND / RIGHT ANGLE SHOWER   PENINSULA / RIGHT ANGLE SHOWER   CORNER / RIGHT ANGLE SHOWER

ISLAND / NEO-ANGLE SHOWER   PENINSULA / NEO-ANGLE SHOWER   CORNER / NEO-ANGLE SHOWER

TYPICAL SHOWER ENCLOSURE DESIGNS

NOTES:

1. SHOWERS SHOWN ARE TYPICAL DESIGNS. OTHER OPTIONS ARE AVAILABLE AS PER YOUR SPECIFIC JOB.

2. SHOWER SIZES CAN INCREASE/DECREASE WITH DIFFERENT GRID SIZES. IF THESE SIZES ARE NOT APPROPRIATE, SPECIFY THE DIMENSIONS YOU REQUIRE AND SUBMIT FOR PRELIMINARY LAYOUT AND QUOTE.

IN-LINE SHOWER

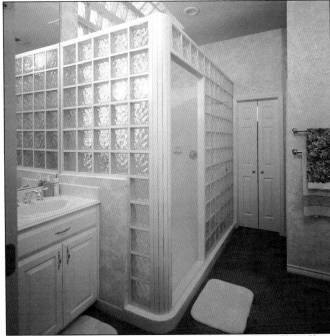

Fort Worth, TX; Custom Unique Homes

Austin, TX; Newmark Homes

FLOORS AND CEILINGS

IBP's engineered grid system assures easy installation of glass paver floors and ceilings. The lightweight structural aluminum grid, which is assembled on site, can span up to 7'6" without additional reinforcement. In the pedestrian bridge application pictured below, the floor also serves as a large skylight. Durability and beauty make IBP grids and glass pavers a logical choice for floors and ceilings.

The IBP grid system for floors was developed to provide an alternative method for installing glass paver units. This system eliminates the problems associated with conventional glass paver installations. Before the IBP system was available, glass paver units were set in grout within heavy and cumbersome prefabricated floor panels. The inflexibility of the typical concrete paver system can result in cracked or broken pavers. To prevent this problem, the IBP aluminum grid system utilizes a neoprene boot which encases the sides and bottom edges of each glass paver unit. The boot creates a cushion between the glass and the aluminum. A silicone sealant is applied to a narrow channel around each paver unit. The completed IBP floor system is beautiful and cost effective. Additionally, the IBP system circumvents the limitations of prefabricated concrete floor panels.

J. Wise Smith Associates, Inc.

Wm. Graves, Inc. Architects

Wm. Graves, Inc. Architects

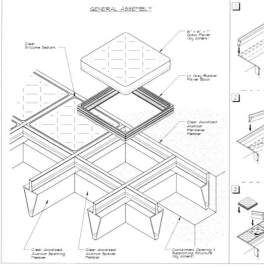

GENERAL ASSEMBLY

- Clear Silicone Sealant
- 6" x 6" x 1" Glass Paver (by others)
- Lt. Gray Rubber Paver Boot
- Clear Anodized Aluminum Perimeter Member
- Clear Anodized Aluminum Spanning Member
- Clear Anodized Aluminum Spacer Member
- Containment Opening & Supporting Structure (by others)

1. INSTALL PERIMETER MEMBERS INTO CONTAINMENT OPENING.

2. INSTALL ONE SPANNING MEMBER AT EACH END.

3. INSERT GLASS BLOCK PAVER UNITS INTO RUBBER BOOTS. ALTERNATELY INSTALL ONE GLASS BLOCK PAVER UNIT, THEN ONE SPACER MEMBER, SIMULTANEOUSLY WORKING IN FROM EACH CORNER TOWARD MID-SPAN, LEAVING OUT THE CENTERMOST PAVER UNIT.

4. REPEAT STEPS 2 AND 3, SIMULTANEOUSLY WORKING IN FROM EACH END TOWARDS THE CENTER LEAVING OUT THE CENTERMOST SPANNING MEMBER, CORRESPONDING SPACER MEMBERS AND GLASS BLOCK PAVER UNITS.

5. INSTALL LAST SPANNING MEMBER AND CORRESPONDING SPACER MEMBERS.

6. INSTALL REMAINING GLASS BLOCK PAVER UNITS AND SEAL.

PHOTO GALLERY

Spokane, Washington; Law/Kingdon, Inc., Architects

Seattle, Washington; Seattle Glass Block

Baton Rouge, LA; Roy Hendrick, Architect

Dallas, TX

Richmond American Homes

San Antonio, TX; Rita Heck, Designer

GUIDE SPECIFICATION: IBP WINDOWS AND WALLS

PART 1 - GENERAL

1.1. SCOPE

1.1.1. Furnish and install all window perimeter frame pieces, T-Bar grid members, glazing materials, expansion-contraction thermal foam tape, sealants, framing, flashings, and other items necessary for complete window installation as indicated on the Drawings and specified herein.

1.1.2. Related work specified elsewhere: 1.1.2.1. Glass and Glazing 1.1.2.2. Sealants 1.1.2.3. Flashings

1.2. Guarantee

1.2.1. Window manufacturer shall guarantee for a period of one year from the date of purchase that the windows will be free of defects in materials and factory workmanship, and that defective materials will be repaired or replaced immediately, after proper notification.

1.2.2. The installing contractor shall guarantee for a period of one year against faulty installation workmanship or water leakage due to on-site errors.

1.3. Submittals

1.3.1. Submit assembly instructions and installation drawings as required to indicate methods on construction, location and spacing of anchorage, joinery, finishes, sizes, shape, thickness and alloy materials, glazing materials, and relationship to the adjoining work.

1.4. Material Storage and Handling

1.4.1. Store material in dry place, off the ground, where temperature will not exceed 90 degrees Fahrenheit.

1.4.2. Handle material to prevent damage to finished surfaces. Do not install scratched or damaged components.

1.4.3. After installation, protect finished surfaces from damage caused by ensuing work.

PART 2 - PRODUCTS

2.1. Materials

2.1.1. IBP Glass Block Grid System: Extruded aluminum Glass Block Grid System for Windows as manufactured by Innovative Building Products, Inc., 2917 W. 7th Street, Fort Worth, TX 76107.

2.1.2. Expansion-Contraction Thermal Foam tape: Adhesive backed, closed cell foam, 1/16" or 3/32" thick, furnished.

2.1.3. Sealant: TradeMate Glass Block Sealant, furnished.

2.1.4. Finish: Selected from manufacturer's standard finishes and colors.

2.1.5. Glass block units: 7 3/4" x 7 3/4" x 3 1/8" thick, partially evacuated hollow units, made of clear or colored glass as manufactured by Pittsburgh Corning, Solaris, or Weck.

PART 3 - EXECUTION

3.1. Field Conditions

3.1.1. Verify all applicable field dimensions and adjust as necessary to accommodate window frame.

3.1.2. Examine supporting frame to which window will be attached. Correct any conditions which are not constructed according to installation instructions furnished by window manufacturer.

3.2. Installation

3.2.1. Assemble and seal glass block grid system for window according to instructions furnished by manufacturer.

3.2.2. Apply continuous sealant bead to back of window Z-bar. Place assembled glass block grid system frame into properly prepared and sized rough opening and adjust until plumb and level. Screw or nail grid system in place utilizing all predrilled holes in nailing flange.

3.2.3. Adhere foam tape gasket to each glass block according to instructions furnished by glass block grid system manufacturer. Carefully insert glass blocks into grid system from exterior side of window so that each block is pressed against T-Bar and foam tape does not roll back.

3.2.4. Apply sealant to completely fill channel around each glass block and wipe flush with surface. Apply sealant to exterior frame corners according to instructions furnished by grid system manufacturer.

3.3. Cleanup

3.3.1. Clean all exposed surfaces of aluminum glass block grid system with clean, soft cloth and mild hand soap using gentle rubbing action. Do not use abrasive or solvent-type cleaners, detergents or paint removers.

3.3.2. Remove all labels from glass block and clean with soft cloth and water.

GUIDE SPECIFICATION: IBP GRID SYSTEM FOR SKYLIGHTS

PART 1 - GENERAL

1.1. SCOPE

1.1.1. Furnish and install all skylight perimeter frame pieces, T-Bar grid members, glazing materials, expansion-contraction thermal foam tape, sealants, curbs, flashings, and other items necessary for complete skylight installation as indicated on the Drawings and specified herein.

1.1.2. Related work specified elsewhere: 1.1.2.1. Glass and Glazing 1.1.2.2. Sealants 1.1.2.3. Flashings

1.2. Guarantee

1.2.1. Skylight manufacturer shall guarantee for a period of one year from the date of purchase that the skylights will be free of defects in materials and factory workmanship, and that defective materials will be repaired or replaced immediately, after proper notification.

1.2.2. The installing contractor shall guarantee for a period of three years against faulty installation workmanship or water leakage due to on-site errors.

1.3. Submittals

1.3.1. Submit assembly instructions and installation drawings as required to indicate methods on construction, location and spacing of anchorage, joinery, finishes, sizes, shape, thickness and alloy materials, glazing materials, and relationship to the adjoining work.

1.4. Material Storage and Handling

1.4.1. Store material in dry place, off the ground, where temperature will not exceed 90 degrees Fahrenheit.

1.4.2. Handle material to prevent damage to finished surfaces. Do not install scratched or damaged components.

1.4.3. After installation, protect finished surfaces from damage caused by ensuing work.

PART 2 - PRODUCTS

2.1. Materials

2.1.1. IBP Glass Block Grid System: Extruded aluminum Glass Block Grid System for Skylights as manufactured by Innovative Building Products, Inc., 2917 W. 7th Street, Fort Worth, TX 76107.

2.1.2. Expansion-contraction thermal foam tape: Adhesive backed, closed cell foam, 1/16" or 3/32" thick, furnished.

2.1.3. Sealant: TradeMate Glass Block Sealant, furnished.

2.1.4. Fasteners: Tamper-proof cadmium plated steel for attaching skylight perimeter frame to curb.

2.1.5. Finish: Selected from manufacturer's standard finishes and colors.

2.1.6. Glass block units: 7 3/4" x 7 3/4" x 3 1/8" thick, partially evacuated hollow units, made of clear or colored glass as manufactured by Pittsburgh Corning, Solaris, or Weck.

PART 3 - EXECUTION

3.1. Field Conditions

3.1.1. Verify all applicable field dimensions and adjust as necessary to accommodate skylight frame.

3.1.2. Examine supporting curb and structural support to which skylight frame will be attached. Correct any conditions which are not constructed according to installation instructions furnished by skylight manufacturer.

3.2. Installation

3.2.1. Assemble and seal glass block grid system for skylight according to instructions furnished by manufacturer.

3.2.2. Apply continuous sealant bead around top of skylight supporting curb. Place assembled glass block grid system frame on curb and press down to seat properly and overlap flashings. Attach frame to curb with specified fasteners and tighten.

3.2.3. Adhere foam tape gasket to each glass block according to instructions furnished by glass block grid system manufacturer. Carefully insert glass blocks into grid system from exterior side of skylight so that each block is pressed against T-Bar and foam tape does not roll back.

3.2.4. Apply sealant to completely fill channel around each glass block and wipe flush with surface. Apply sealant to frame caps according to instructions furnished by grid system manufacturer.

3.3. Cleanup

3.3.1. Clean all exposed surfaces of aluminum glass block grid system with clean, soft cloth and mild hand soap using gentle rubbing action. Do not use abrasive or solvent-type cleaners, detergents, or paint removers.

3.3.2. Remove all labels from glass block and clean with soft cloth and water.

GUIDE SPECIFICATION: IBP GRID SYSTEM FOR FLOORS

PART 1 - GENERAL

1.1. SCOPE

1.1.1. Furnish all floor system perimeter pieces, spanning members, spacer members, paver boots, paver units, sealants, all other materials and labor necessary for complete floor system installation as indicated on the Drawings and specified herein.

1.1.2. Related work specified elsewhere: 1.1.2.1. Glass and Glazing 1.1.2.2. Sealants 1.1.2.3. Containment Opening

1.2. Guarantee

1.2.1. Floor system manufacturer shall guarantee for a period of five years from the date of purchase that the floor system will be free of defects in materials and factory workmanship, and that defective materials will be repaired or replaced immediately, after proper notification.

1.2.2. The installing contractor shall guarantee for a period of five years against faulty installation workmanship due to on-site errors.

1.3. Submittals

1.3.1. Submit assembly instructions and shop drawings as required to indicate methods of construction, location and spacing of anchorage, joinery, finishes, sizes, shape, thickness and alloy materials, paver units, and relationship to the adjoining work.

1.4. Material Storage and Handling

1.4.1. Store material in dry place, off the ground, where temperature will not exceed 90 degrees Fahrenheit.

1.4.2. Handle material to prevent damage to finished surfaces. Do not install scratched or damaged components.

1.4.3. After installation, protect finished surfaces from damage caused by ensuing work.

PART 2 - PRODUCTS

2.1. Materials

2.1.1. IBP Glass Block Grid System for Floors: Extruded aluminum Glass Block Grid System for Floors as manufactured by Innovative Building Products, Inc., 2917 W. 7th Street, Fort Worth, TX 76107.

2.1.2. Paver Unit Boots: EPDM Ethylene Propylene Diene Terpolymer, a man-made, UV and oil resistant compound furnished with IBP Glass Block Grid System.

2.1.3. Sealant: TradeMate Glass Block Sealant, furnished with IBP Glass Block Grid System.

2.1.4. Finish: Clear anodized matte finish.

2.1.5. Glass block paver units: Nominal 6" x 6" x 1" thick, solid glass paver units, in color and pattern as selected.

PART 3 - EXECUTION

3.1. Field Conditions

3.1.1. Verify all applicable field dimensions and adjust as necessary to accommodate floor system.

3.1.2. Examine supporting structure and containment opening to which floor system will be installed. Correct any conditions which are not constructed according to installation instructions and approved shop drawings furnished by floor system manufacturer.

3.2. Installation

3.2.1. Insert each paver unit into paver boot.

3.2.2. Assemble glass block grid floor system according to instructions furnished by manufacturer into prepared containment opening. Top surface of glass block pavers shall finish flush with adjoining surface and exposed aluminum surface joints unless shown otherwise on the drawings.

3.2.3. Apply sealant to completely fill channel around each glass block paver unit and joints between aluminum grid members and wipe flush with top surface. Perform all sealant work in accord with the requirements of the Sealant Section of the specifications.

3.3. Cleanup

3.3.1. Clean all exposed surfaces of aluminum glass block grid system with clean, soft cloth and mild hand soap using gentle rubbing action. Do not use abrasive or solvent-type cleaners, detergents, or paint removers.

3.3.2. Remove all labels from glass block and clean with soft cloth and water.

www.ibpglassblock.com

IBP-SWT-A1-11/97

Fabrications of
Ceramic, Glass and Stone

Classic Glass & Stone Mosaics
Hand Painted Mosaics
Water Jet Cutting
Shattered Mosaics
Historical/Restorations
Photomurals

Colorco

For centuries ceramic, glass and stone pieces have been used to enhance the appearance of art. Their use as decorative dressing to the outside of buildings dates as far back as recorded history. In fact the pharaohs of Egypt used it extensively. Interestingly enough, the methods used in the design and manufacture of such large scale tiling projects has not changed much from those ancient beginnings. That is until now...

Colorco is a complete turn-key tile image design/manufacturing service. We will convert any image you supply into a beautiful tile rendering. Colorco can also supply this same service in glass, ceramics, stone, metal and some wood products. There is a complete range of images that can be transformed.

Applications

It's hard to imagine a building project that can't be enhanced with the addition of a tile image. With your choice of glass, ceramic or stone tiles, your imagination is our only limit. From corporate logos, to swimming pools, Colorco has demonstrated its abilities. Go ahead, let us help brighten up that bath or dramatize the entrance hallways. A beautiful color mosaic design can draw attention to your entire building with an eye catching glass tiled wall that illuminates from within. Outdoor company logos in "real color" will outlast any painted sign. The Colorco advantage makes it easier than it ever has been

Shattered and Classic Mosaics

Water Jet Cut Leaf Design

Classic European Stone Mosaic

Procedure

Even if you've never worked with these materials before, designing with Colorco is easy.

It all starts with a copy of the architectural plans for the space into which the image must be placed. This gives us the overall dimensions and mechanical specifications of the work.

Next, you provide a painting or complete picture of the image you wish transformed into tile. This artwork will act as the master from which our system will produce your product. Therefore it is important that the image we receive be correct.

From here the tile image may be created using existing tile colors or your choice of substitute ones. You'll receive a shop drawing(s) of your artwork as the computer has received it, and a tiled rendering of the image output on a high resolution pen plotter which is precisely scaled. Each tile on the drawing is shown in its exact color assuring accuracy. Even the effect of grout is simulated. Your approval of the artwork puts you in business.

Completing the assignment, Colorco offers the service of delivering completely assembled tile sheets ready for placement. You'll receive a quotation which lists both the cost of the tile as delivered and the cost of Colorco installing the finished project. The overall ceramic tile image is divided up into smaller sections measuring one by two feet. Each sheet is marked according to its placement in the image. Along with the supplied assembly instructions, your workers will find completing the tile work for your job one of their easiest tasks. Glass tile sections are pre-assembled and ready for placement.

Whole Tile Imaging is Porcelain and Glass

Painted Ceramic Wall with Water Jet Cut Floor Medallion

Porcelain Mosaic with Shattered Fish

Colorco – List of Accomplishments

- *Invented imaging with tile.*
- *Pioneered the use of the shattered mosaic style for large applications.*
- *Early pioneer using abrasive water to cut stone and tile.*
- *Invented custom cut & glazed mosaics.*
- *Invented film technology used in manufacturing process.*
- *Invented production systems used in manufacturing process.*
- *Invented design tools used in producing advanced mosaics.*
- *Invented readable imagery whereby the image is composed of discretely colored letters which make up the image.*
- *Invented the use of poly carbonate file to surface level mosaic tile.*
- *Colorco has perhaps received more CTDA Spectrum awards for excellence than any other company, eight awards in four years. Including four highest honors.*

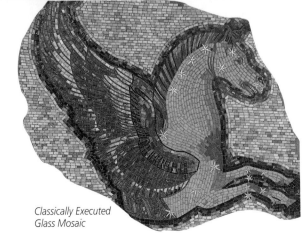

Classically Executed Glass Mosaic

Hand Painted Classic Mosaic Detail

Hand Painted Mosaics & Classic Glass Mosaics

Colorco Glass and Hand Painted Mosaics represent the ultimate in artistic expression. Your artwork or design can be fabricated by the master of crafts men and women at Colorco.

Colorco offers contemporary styles as well as the classic styles.

Installation Using Hand Painted Mosaic Tile

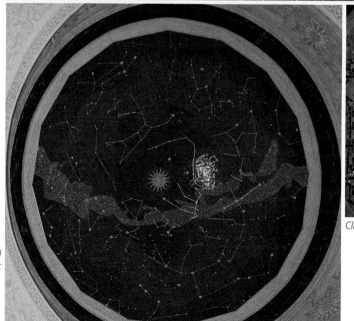
Classic Glass and Gold Mosaic

Classic Glass Mosaic

Colorco Classic Stone Mosaics

Colorco Classic Mosaics represent the ultimate in stone mosaics. These hand crafted works of art are hand crafted by some of the finest artisans in this country. In the Colorco Classic Stone Mosaic series, each mosaic is hand cut and placed.

The execution style is done in the classic European tradition.

Classic Byzantine Mosaic

Classic Stone, Floor, Wall and Molding

Classic Mosaic Using Antiqued Stone

Classic Mosaic Tile Portraiture Reproductions

are available from your artwork or photograph. Colorco's classically trained artists will translate into any size mosaic. The finished piece will be constructed of glazed ceramics mosaics. These mosaics are durable to last for many centuries, potentially lasting till the end of civilization itself. Available only from Colorco.

Hand Painted Classic Mosaic

Water-Jet Cutting

When your budget doesn't allow for classic mosaic work then jet-cutting is a way to achieve dramatic results without the expense of intricate fabrication. With jet-cutting, any material may be used. Again, BE CREATIVE and have fun. The results transcend the material itself.

The following pages contain photographs of projects which use Water-Jet cutting in the fabrication process.

JET-CUT MATERIALS: All Ceramic, Glass, Stone, Metal, Tile, Paver etc.

Water Jet
Floor Medallion

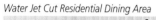

Water Jet Cut Residential Dining Area

Water Jet Cut Map Using Grid Overlay

Water Jet Cut Mosaics

Porcelain Mosaic Inlaid into 1 inch Porcelain Field

Shattered Mosaics

Never before have such incredible mosaic floors been available at such a reasonable cost. The design complexities possible are limited only by humankinds ability to imagine, dream and create. All one has to do to design and incredible mosaic floor is the following:

- *Sketch the overall design concept onto the outline drawing of the floor or wall requiring the mosaic.*

- *The design motifs may be developed individually or all at the same time.*

- *Black ink on white paper (8.5"x11") define the graphic elements.*

- *Colors are selected from the American Olean and Dal-Tile mosaic tile pallets. Colorco then takes your graphic information and does the rest.*

From design translation through installation, Colorco does it all. Or, if you choose, a competent local tile contractor can install the work.

Through the use of solid pigmented tile, your art work can possibly last for centuries.

Remember size is <u>no problem</u>. Go wild.

MATERIALS: Ceramic, Glass, Stone, & Paver products

...tered Mall Medallion

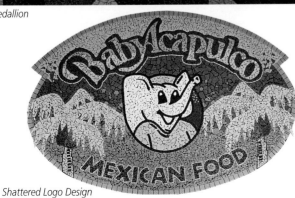

Shattered Logo Design

Custom Shattered Porcelain Mosaic

Historical Restorations

Colorco's extensive knowledge of materials from around the world and knowledge of older and traditional methods of tile and stone work has resulted is designers and architects calling upon Colorco to execute classical restorations.

Colorco, from New York Subways to old style ceramic and stone installations... Colorco does it all.

Photomurals/
Square Tile Designs

Colorco's most economical way to achieve incredible mosaic designs is to use whole tile imagery. From simple designs using only a few colors through complex designs using hundreds of colors.

No More Coloring Grids.
Just submit your refined sketches, artwork or photography, along with the outline drawing and Colorco will do the rest.

Portraits and graphics can be translated into large tile murals. The tile can range in size from 1/4" through 2". Large surfaces are a specialty of Colorco.

The following is a partial list of Colorco projects in New York City where you can visit to see the level of quality and expertise that Colorco works to.

- Iridium Restaurant, in Empire Hotel, diagonal from Lincoln Center (Porcelain)
- St. Paul the Apostle, 59th Street, behind Columbus Circle on the upper west side (Glass and Stone Mosaics)
- Godiva Chocolatier, 70I 5th Avenue (Stone Mosaics)
- 570 Lexington Avenue (Stone Mosaic, Slab and Brass)
- Ramada Renaissance, Public bathrooms, near Times Square (Custom Glass)
- Broad Street subway station, intersection of Broad Street and Wall Street (Custom Porcelain)
- Christopher and Houston Street on the 1/9 Train (Custom Porcelain)

COLORCO
MASTERS OF MOSAICS

Mail: P.O. Box 456 • Merrimack, NH 03054-0456
Factory: 33 Elm Street • Merrimack, NH 03054-6431
Tel: 603/424-9602 Fax: 603/429-1935

 See us in Sweet's
CD
Online
Directory

Commercial Wall & Floor Tile Products.

Interceramic, USA

THE BEST THE WORLD HAS TO OFFER.

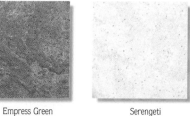

Empress Green

Serengeti

Blue Ridge

Corinthian

Angel Fire

Rajah

FLAGSTONE

Random

- Natural slate-like surface
- Skid inhibiting
- Coordinating 6x6 & 3x12 bullnose trim
- Impact & acid resistant
- Frost resistant
- Group IV

SIZES: 6 x 6, 6 x 12, 12 x 12

BULLNOSE

6" x 6"

3" x 12"

CASTLE GATE

Random

- Aged stone-like surface
- Skid inhibiting
- Coordinating 6x6 & 3x12 bullnose trim
- Impact & acid resistant
- Frost resistant
- Group IV

SIZES: 6 x 6, 6 x 12, 12 x 12
12 x 18, 18 x 18

BULLNOSE

6" x 6"

3" x 12"

VIGNÉ

Random

- Weathered stone surface
- Skid inhibiting
- Coordinating 6x6 & 3x12 bullnose trim
- Impact & acid resistant
- Frost resistant
- Group IV

SIZES: 6 x 6, 6 x 12, 12 x 12, 18 x 18

BULLNOSE

6" x 6"

3" x 12"

CASTLE GATE

Avila

Carcassonne

Montford

VIGNÉ

Bordeaux

Chablis

Champagne

Chardonnay

Vigné Decorative Tiles:

6 x 12 Fascia Listel

6 x 6 Corner

6 x 6 Corner Grouping

Deco A

Deco B

Deco C

Deco D

6 x 12 Mosaic

3 x 12 Listel

INTERCERAMIC TILE MEETS ALL RECOMMENDED AMERICAN NATIONAL STANDARD SPECIFICATIONS FOR CERAMIC TILE FOR ANSI A 137.1.

Wall Tile

SIZE AVAILABLE	4 1/4 x 4 1/4	6 x 6	8 x 8
IC BRITES	●	●	
IC MATTES	●	●	
IC CRYSTALS	●		
BOLD TONES	●	●	
EGYPTIAN SLATE		●	
PEARL BRITES	●	●	
PEARL MATTES	●	●	
ASTRATTO			●
CLASS			●

Technical Data
4 1/4 x 4 1/4 and 6 x 6 Wall Tile

	Interceramic Tile	ANSI Test
Warpage	.23%	ASTM C 485
Thickness	.018 in	ASTM C 499
Thermal Shock	resistant	ASTM C 484
Scratch Hardness	5	MOHS Scale
Breaking Strength	141 lbs	ASTM C 648
Wedging	.40%	ASTM C 502
Water Absorption	17%	ASTM C 373
Bond Strength	110 psi	ASTM C 482
Facial Dimension	.98%	ASTM C 499

SHADE & TEXTURE SPECTRUM

low   moderate   high   random

Low STS - Least amount of shade and texture variation attainable in naturally fired clay products.

Moderate STS - Moderate shade and texture variation within each carton.

High STS - High shade and texture variation within each carton.

Random STS - Very high shade and texture variation within each carton.

FLOOR TILE TECHNICAL DATA

APPLICATION SPECIFICATIONS

RECOMMENDED APPLICATION: GROUP III PRODUCTS
Medium traffic: All residential and light commercial applications. Not recommended for commercial entryways.

RECOMMENDED APPLICATION: GROUP IV PRODUCTS
Heavy traffic: All residential and most commercial applications. Shopping malls & most public areas.

RECOMMENDED APPLICATION: GROUP V PRODUCTS
Heavy plus traffic: All residential and all commercial applications where extra heavy wearability is required.

COEFFICIENT OF FRICTION (Avg. Results)[+]

	Skid-inhibiting (1)
Dry Leather	0.82
Dry Rubber	0.80
Dry Neolite	0.78
Wet Leather	0.63
Wet Rubber	0.67
Wet Neolite	0.72

Smooth surface tiles are not recommended for areas exposed to direct outside traffic. Skid-inhibiting surfaces are inherently more difficult to clean. Attention to this characteristic should be noted when product is specified.

ADA

Meets Recommended Guidelines for American's With Disabilities Act for Horizontal Surfaces.

TECHNICAL DATA[+]	Interceramic Tile	ANSI/ASTM Tests
Water Absorption	3% or less	ASTM C-373
Abrasive Hardness index number	170 Avg.	ASTM C-501
Breaking Strength	390 lbs. Avg.	ASTM C-648
Thermal Shock	Resistant	ASTM C-484
Scratch Hardness of Glaze	5.0-9.0	MOHS Scale
Frost Resistance	Resistant	Hobert-Goodrich
Bonding Strength	Over 147 p.s.i.	ASTM C-482

[+]These test results vary by item. Detailed information may be obtained from Interceramic. 800-365-6733

MAINTENANCE
Interceramic tile is vitreous with a hard-glaze surface. Normal precautions should be observed during setting and grouting, and the grout manufacturer's instructions should be carefully followed. The characteristics of skid-inhibiting tile, while providing greater safety, will require more extensive cleaning procedures than the smooth finish tiles.

VARIATIONS IN SHADE OR COLOR
Variations in shade or color are inherent in all fired clay products and are one of the natural qualities which help create the beautiful effect characteristic of tile. Blending of tiles from at least six different boxes during installation is recommended to achieve best results. This is especially important when installing skid-inhibiting tiles, as shine can differ under certain lighting conditions.

SIZES
All sizes are sold on a nominal (approximate) basis. Size tolerance: plus or minus 1.5%. Exact measurements are available from Interceramic.

COLOR ILLUSTRATIONS AND SAMPLES
Color charts, color illustrations, and reproduction in catalogs and other publications of Interceramic are not represented to match the exact color or shade of the tile represented. Color illustrations of tile are offered at approximations only.
All samples are submitted as representative of a type of tile, a color, a shade, or a kind of finish; and the tile furnished in a shipment may vary from such samples.

LIMITS OF LIABILITY
Tests are performed on random samples of Interceramic tile by an independent testing laboratory and are believed to be representative of the general quality of the tile. There is no guarantee by Interceramic that these exact results will be guaranteed on every tile. Interceramic extends no guarantees, expressed or implied, as to glaze slipperiness, wear-time periods, gloss or maintenance procedures. Test procedures and individual results are available from Interceramic.

ANSI A-137.1
Interceramic tile achieves the necessary values for the ANSI A 137.1-P188 (American National Standards Institute) requirement. This is the most complete testing done on ceramic tile and includes tests on thickness, facial dimension, warpage, wedging, water absorption, crazing, thermal shock, bonding strength and breaking strength.

MONTANA

- Light grain texture
- Skid inhibiting surface
- Eight solid colors
- Coordinating trim
- Impact & acid resistant
- Frost resistant
- Group IV

SIZES: 8 x 8, 12 x 12

Moderate

BULLNOSE	COVE BASE
4" x 8"	6" x 8"
4" x 4" Crn	1" x 6" Corner

METALLIC

- Cut granite-like finish, in 10 solid colors
- Skid inhibiting surface
- Coordinating trim
- Impact & acid resistant
- Frost resistant
- Group IV

SIZES: 8 x 8, 12 x 12

Moderate

BULLNOSE	COVE BASE
4" x 8"	6" x 8"
4" x 4" Crn	1" x 6" Corner

MAXIMA / ACCENTS

- Skid inhibiting surface
- Coordinating trim
- Maxima 20 year wear warranty
- Impact & acid resistant
- Frost resistant
- Group V, IV Accents

SIZES: 8 x 8, 12 x 12

Moderate

BULLNOSE	COVE BASE
4" x 8"	6" x 8"
4" x 4" Crn	1" x 6" Corner

MONTANA

Arena	Alpine	Grafito	Granito
Platinum	Canyon	Vail	Tahoe

METALLIC

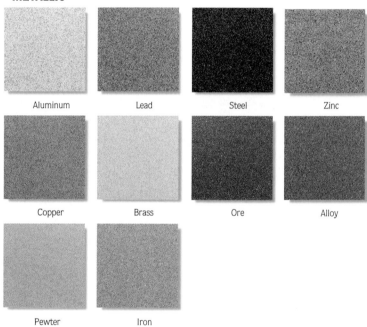

Aluminum	Lead	Steel	Zinc
Copper	Brass	Ore	Alloy
Pewter	Iron		

Exclusive 20-Year Wear Warranty

20 YEAR LIMITED WARRANTY

MAXIMA

Cobalt	Plata	Niquel	Topaz

MAXIMA ACCENTS

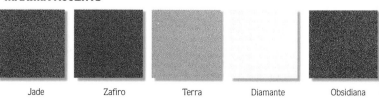

Jade	Zafiro	Terra	Diamante	Obsidiana

IC CRYSTALS

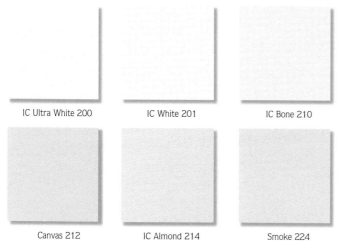

| IC Ultra White 200 | IC White 201 | IC Bone 210 |

| Canvas 212 | IC Almond 214 | Smoke 224 |

EGYPTIAN SLATE

| Cairo 805 | Pyramid 815 | Sphinx 825 |

| Oasis 875 | Pharaoh 885 |

ASTRATTO

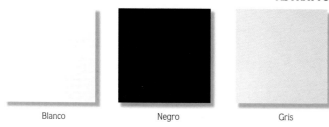

| Blanco | Negro | Gris |

CLASS

| Blanco | Azul | Amarillo |

IC CRYSTALS

- Finely textured crystalline surface
- Coordinates with most name brand fixture colors
- Coordinating trim
- Spacer lugs
- Beveled edge

SIZES: 4 1/4 x 4 1/4
Thickness: 7.5 mm

RECOMMENDED APPLICATION:

	COMMERCIAL	RESIDENTIAL
FLOORS		• (bathrooms)
WALLS	•	•
COUNTERS		•

Meets All Recommended Specifications for ANSI - A 137.1

EGYPTIAN SLATE

- Sculptured stone surface, matte finish
- Coordinates with Interceramic floor tile
- Coordinating trim
- Spacer lugs
- Beveled edge

SIZES: 6 x 6
Thickness: 7.5 mm

RECOMMENDED APPLICATION:

	COMMERCIAL	RESIDENTIAL
FLOORS		• (bathrooms)
WALLS	•	•
COUNTERS		•

Meets All Recommended Specifications for ANSI - A 137.1

ASTRATTO / CLASS

- Deep, rich, high-gloss smooth finish on Astratto
- High-gloss, undulated surface on Class
- Coordinating decorative listels
- Coordinating trim
- Easy to clean

SIZES: 8 x 8

RECOMMENDED APPLICATION:

	COMMERCIAL	RESIDENTIAL
FLOORS		
WALLS	•	•
COUNTERS		

IC BRITES & IC MATTES

- Deep, rich, high-gloss finish on brites
- Non-reflective, pearl-like finish on mattes
- Coordinates with most name brand fixture
- Coordinating trim
- Spacer lugs
- Beveled edge

SIZES: 4 1/4 x 4 1/4 & 6 x 6
Thickness: 7.5 mm

RECOMMENDED APPLICATION:

	COMMERCIAL	RESIDENTIAL
FLOORS		• bathroom (IC Mattes)
WALLS	•	•
COUNTERS		•

Meets All Recommended Specifications for ANSI - A 137.1

PEARL BRITES / PEARL MATTES

- Undulated, slate-like surface
- Rich, high-gloss finish on brites
- Non-reflective, pearl-like finish on mattes
- Coordinating trim
- Spacer lugs
- Beveled edge

SIZES: 4 1/4 x 4 1/4 & 6 x 6
Thickness: 7.5 mm

RECOMMENDED APPLICATION:

	COMMERCIAL	RESIDENTIAL
FLOORS		• bathroom (P Mattes)
WALLS	•	•
COUNTERS		•

Meets All Recommended Specifications for ANSI - A 137.1

BOLD TONES

- Deep, rich, high-gloss, smooth finish
- Coordinating trim
- Spacer lugs
- Beveled edge

SIZES: 4 1/4 x 4 1/4 & 6 x 6
Thickness: 7.5 mm

RECOMMENDED APPLICATION:

	COMMERCIAL	RESIDENTIAL
FLOORS	•	•
WALLS		
COUNTERS		

Meets All Recommended Specifications for ANSI - A 137.1

IC BRITES / MATTES

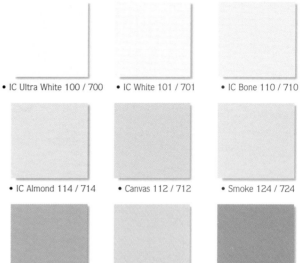

- Available in IC Brites & IC Mattes. All others are IC Brites.

(High-gloss finishes may show scratches)

- IC Ultra White 100 / 700   • IC White 101 / 701   • IC Bone 110 / 710

- IC Almond 114 / 714   • Canvas 112 / 712   • Smoke 124 / 724

Mocha 117   Mint 171   Moss 175

Sunrise 151   Blossom 163   Harbor 182

PEARLS BRITES / MATTES

IC Ultra White 3100 / 3700   IC White 3101 / 3701   IC Bone 3110 / 3710

BOLD TONES

Yellow Jacket 545   Classic Navy 589   Bluebonnet 585

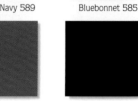

Pure Cobalt 587   Colonial Blue 583   Absolute Black 529

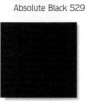

Teal 575   Evergreen 579   Plum 568

Wineberry 567   Dusty Rose 566   Antique Red 557

DAKOTA

Bismarck

Prairie

Bison

Tioga

Custer

ALASKA

Timberline

Kodiak

Tundra

Yukon

Gold Rush

CONQUEST

Trojan Gray

Titan Green

Samurai Beige

Spartan White

Viking Blue

MEDITERRANEAN

Marsala

Valencia

Crete

Palermo

DAKOTA

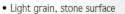
Moderate

- Rustic stone surface
- Skid inhibiting
- Coordinating bullnose trim
- Impact & acid resistant
- Frost resistant
- Group IV

SIZES: 6 x 6, 12 x 12, 18 x 18

BULLNOSE

6" x 6"

3" x 12"

ALASKA

High

- Light grain, stone surface
- Skid inhibiting
- Coordinating bullnose trim
- Impact & acid resistant
- Frost resistant
- Group IV

SIZES: 6 x 6, 6 x 12, 12 x 12

BULLNOSE

6" x 6"

6" x 6" Crn

CONQUEST

Moderate

- Natural weathered slate surface
- Skid inhibiting
- Coordinating bullnose trim
- Impact & acid resistant
- Frost resistant
- Group IV

SIZES: 6 x 6, 6 x 12, 12 x 12

BULLNOSE

6" x 6"

3" x 12"

MEDITERRANEAN

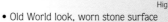
High

- Old World look, worn stone surface
- Skid inhibiting
- Coordinating bullnose trim
- Impact & acid resistant
- Frost resistant
- Group IV

SIZES: 6 x 6, 6 x 12, 12 x 12, 12 x 18, 18 x 18

BULLNOSE

6" x 6"

3" x 12"

ARCHITECTURAL SPECIFICATION - SECTION 09300

PART I-GENERAL

A. **Related Work Specified Elsewhere**
1. Lathing and cement scratch coat   Section_____
2. Waterproof membranes or wallboard   Section_____
3. Handrails in bathroom areas   Section_____
4. This section should include all work required before the installation of the tile.

B. **Description of Work**
1. This is to include all work and materials required to furnish and install ceramic tile as indicated on the drawings.

C. **Quality Assurance**
1. Provide Interceramic samples as well as samples of the grout and thinset as approved by the architect.
2. Use quality and skilled tile installers who are thoroughly trained and experienced in the installation methods being specified.
3. Work shall be executed and tested in accordance with current editions of the following standards:
     (a) ANSI A108.1 - Installation of Ceramic Tile with Portland Cement
     (b) ANSI A108.4 - Installation of Ceramic Tile with Water Resistant Organic Adhesives
     (c) ANSI A108.5 - Installation of Ceramic Tile with Dry Set Portland Cement Mortar
     (d) ANSI A108.6 - Installation of Ceramic Tile with Chemical Resistant
     (e) Consult the Tile Council of America's Handbook for Ceramic Tile Installation for other types of specifications.

D. **Submittals**
1. The manufacturer shall assure that all the tile being used is in compliance with ANSI A 137.1-1988.
2. If applicable, a Master Grade certificate may be required with both the signature of the manufacturer and the tile contractor.
3. Submit a 12" square sample of each color, pattern and type of tile being specified.

E. **Product Handling**
1. The cartons should be delivered to the job site unopened and undamaged with all labels intact.
2. Keep tile cartons dry.
3. An additional 2% of each tile used should be ordered for the owner's emergency use.

F. **Environmental Project Conditions**
1. Maintain environmental conditions during and after the installation in accordance with reference standards and accordance with manufacturer's printed recommendations.

PART II - PRODUCTS

A. **Tile**
1. The tile shall be manufactured by Interceramic, Inc. in accordance with the published specification of ANSI A 137.1-1988.
2. The tile shall be:
     (a) Wall tile Series _____   (b) Floor tile   Series _____
                 Color _____   Color _____
                 Size _____   Size _____
3. Provide the pattern to be used for the installation
4. Provide the trims of the same or coordinating colors, size and finish of the adjacent flat tile. Check the Interceramic product catalogs for a description of the trims available.

B. **Setting Materials**
1. Consult the Tile Council of America's Handbook for Ceramic Tile Installation or the Ceramic Tile Institute for the specifications to properly install ceramic tile. Consult the manufacturer of premixed setting materials for correct installation procedures.
     (a) Portland cement mortar   (d) Dry set mortar
     (b) Metal lathe   (e) Latex mortar
     (c) Membrane   (f) Epoxy mortar

C. **Grouting Materials**
1. The grout chosen should conform to the Group Specification Guide published on Page 9 of the Tile Council of America's Handbook for Ceramic Tile Installation. Refer to the grout manufacturer for more specific information regarding the grout and method chosen for the installation.
     (a) Commercial cement grout   (d) Latex Portland cement grout
     (b) Dry set grout   (e) Epoxy grout
     (c) Sand-Portland cement grout

D. **Sealants**
1. Use sealants in control joints, tub and showers, etc... that meet FSTT-S-001543 Class A or B (COM-NBS).

E. **Thresholds and Edge Strips**
1. Provide thresholds or edge strips to provide for a proper transition between the tile and other adjacent surfaces.

PART III - INSTALLATION

A. Acceptability of Surface
1. Before installation of ceramic tile, the substrate surface cannot show variations in excess of:

	Floor	Wall
Dry set mortar	1/8" in 10'	1/8" in 8'
Latex Portland cement mortar	1/8" in 10'	1/8" in 8'
Epoxy	1/8" in 10'	1/8" in 8'
Organic Adhesives	1/16" in 3'	1/8" in 8'

2. The substrate surface must be free of all loose dirt, oil, grease, wax, dust, or curing compounds. If the substrate contains these materials, sand blast, grind or sand to remove the materials and scarify the surface.

B. **Layout**
1. Locate all movement or expansion joints prior to determining the layout of the tile.
2. Layout all tile work so as to minimize cuts less than one-half tile in size.
3. Layout all tile work so that cuts in both walls and floors are to be least conspicuous.
4. Align all floor and wall joints to give straight and uniform grout lines.

C. **Setting Materials**
     (Methods shown are only examples. Specify method that is required).
1. On Dimensionally Stable Concrete Subfloor: ANSI A108.1 (Reference TCA Method F112, Cement Mortar, Bonded)
2. On Non-Dimensionally Stable Concrete Subfloor: ANSI A108.1 (Reference TCA Method F111, Cement Mortar, Cleavage Membrane)
3. On Wood Subfloor: ANSI A108.1 (Reference TCA Method F141, Cement Mortar)
4. See TCA Handbook for Ceramic Tile Installation for other methods for installing ceramic tile.

D. **Grouting**
1. Follow grout manufacturer's recommendations as to grouting procedures and precautions.
2. Remove all grout haze, observing grout manufacturer's recommendations as to the use of various cleaners.
3. Thoroughly rinse all tile work before and after the use of cleaners and chemicals, if required.

E. **Protection of Tile Surface**
1. Finished installation should be free of all chipped, cracked, defective or unbonded tile.
2. Cover all tile floors with heavy duty construction or kraft paper masked in place to avoid stains or damage from construction traffic.
3. No foot and wheel traffic can use the floor for a minimum of 3 days, preferable 7 days.
4. Place large, flat sheets of wood in high traffic areas to protect newly tiled floor.

This specification is designed for your use as a helpful guide. You should modify it if job requirements deem it necessary.
If you require Interceramic samples for architectural color boards or client submittals, please contact your local Interceramic distributor or call 800-365-6733.

Printed in USA   SKU: INSMSWTBRO

The Natural Choice ®

Bruce®

Factory Finished and Contract Unfinished Hardwood Floors

Universal Studios retail store — Orlando International Airport
WearMaster® Oak EWM-3100 Golden Wheat

Introduction:

Bruce Hardwood Floors, a division of Triangle Pacific Corp., is the world's largest manufacturer of hardwood floors. Since 1884, architects, builders and consumers have trusted Bruce to provide the best quality and value in hardwood floors.

With manufacturing facilities in Center, Texas; Nashville and Jackson, Tennessee; West Plains, Missouri; Port Gibson, Mississippi; and Beverly, West Virginia, Bruce provides our national and international, independent distributor network with a complete line of hardwood flooring products.

Contents:

From the cover: :Photo by Michael Lowry, Southern Living Magazine
WearMaster Maple EWM-3200 Maize color floor with EWM-3101 Mocha Glaze border

Acrylic Impregnated Hardwood Floors

WearMaster
Maple Hardwoods

EWM-3200 Maize

EWM-3202 Classic Cocoa

EWM-3209 Berry

EWM-3210 Galaxy

EWM-3213 Canyon

WearMaster
Basswood

EWM-3411 Midnight

EWM-3412 Empire

Technical Information:

WearMaster floors are factory-finished, 3-ply engineered plank floors. The planks are 3/8" thick (9.53 mm), 3" wide (76.20 mm) and are random in length ranging from 12" to 60" (304.80 - 1,524.00 mm). WearMaster has tongue and groove construction, square end and side surface edges, and a smooth, low gloss, commercial finish. WearMaster also carries a Class B Flame Spread Rating, and meets the advisory recommendations of the American's With Disabilities Act Regulations for Slip Resistance for Accessible Routes. The acrylic impregnated wood and color layer is available in four hardwood species (oak, maple, hickory, and basswood).

Testing Standards:

ASTM D 2394-83, Sections 18-22 - Test Method for Indentation Resistance Using a Falling Ball. Indent depth (inches) Oak: 0.010 Maple: 0.006 Hickory: 0.008 Basswood: 0.015.

ASTM D 2394-83, Sections 33-37 - Test Method for Static Slip Resistance. Oak: 0.63 Maple: 0.70 Hickory: 0.63 Basswood: 0.60 Meets the advisory recommendations of the American's With Disabilities Act Regulations for Slip Resistance for Accessible Routes.

ASTM D 4060-95 - Test Method for Abrasion Resistance of Organic Coatings by the Taber Abraser. All species average: 1800 using the S-33 wheel with 500 grams of weight per wheel.

ASTM E 648-94a - Test Method for Critical Radiant Flux of Floor Covering Systems Using a Radiant Heat Energy Source. Oak: 0.68 Maple: 0.61 Hickory: 0.68 Basswood: 1.08.

ASTM E 84-95 - Test Method for Surface Burning Characteristics of Building Materials. Oak: Class B Maple: Class B Hickory: Class B Basswood: Class B.

Description:

WearMaster floors are designed, engineered and manufactured specifically to handle the rigorous demands of commercial applications. Therefore every aspect of Wearmaster floors feature the most advanced technology available to ensure superior performance. The end result is a hardwood floor that is in a class of its own.

Wearmaster floors are manufactured using our patented* acrylic impregnation process that completely fills and seals the open cells in the wood. This yields a hardwood floor of maximum muscle and extreme durability, a hardwood floor over 50% harder than standard, unimpregnated hardwood floors.

WearMaster, recognized for years as the ultimate in hardwood flooring, is ten times tougher than its predecessor. WearMaster features our extremely durable PERMION™ finish which suspends aluminum oxide crystals in ultra-violet cured urethane. Since aluminum oxide is a very hard, high-melting crystalline solid, it gives the floor an iron-like shield to protect the fortified wood below. And it assures incredible ease of care and unsurpassed stain resistance.

Wearmaster floors also feature a unique, pressurized Colorjet Infusion™ process that results in stain penetration through the entire wear layer.

And on top of it all, WearMaster floors are backed by the most comprehensive warranty in the hardwood flooring industry...your assurance of lasting beauty and durability in any commercial or residential application.

Product Usage:

WearMaster acrylic impregnated hardwood floors are designed for use in heavy and light commercial applications as well as residential use.

Note: Hardwood floors (including WearMaster) are not recommended for use in areas with high humidity, excessive moisture, or on concrete with compressive strength of less than 2000 psi.

*U.S. Patent Nos. 5,605,767; 5,609,915 and 5,683,820

3

"Store of the Future," featuring WearMaster, designed by Chute Gerdeman, Columbus, OH

WearMaster Oak Hardwood

Installation:

WearMaster floors can be installed on, above or below grade level, and over most existing SOUND, DRY AND LEVEL SUBFLOORS including existing solid wood floors (installed at right angle only), APA approved exterior grade 5/8" (15.88mm) or greater plywood, 3/4" (19.05mm) PS2-92 OSB, concrete (minimum 90 lb. density reinforced), ceramic tile, or resilient tiles and sheet vinyl if over an above-mentioned subfloor (staple down).

WearMaster can be installed over all radiantly heated concrete floors providing the concrete meets the requirements listed above.

- Bruce does not recommend installation over lightweight or acoustical concrete subfloors.

- All subfloors should be sound, clean, thoroughly dry, smooth, and level/flat within 3/16" (4.76mm) in a 10' (3m) span or 1/8" (3.18mm) in a 6' (1.83m) span.

- For a copy of WearMaster installation instructions, call toll free 1-800-722-4647. It is imperative that all jobsite and flooring preparations as stated in the instructions are followed prior to installing the floor.

- Always follow the adhesive manufacturer's recommendations for installation regarding trowel notch size, rolling requirements and flash time.

- If staple-down installation is preferred, use 1" or longer, glue-coated staples with the Senco® SLS20HF stapler.

EWM-3100
Golden Wheat

EWM-3101
Mocha Glaze

Acrylic Impregnated Hardwood Floors

WearMaster
Hickory Hardwoods

EWM-3301
Sierra Brown

EWM-3302
Cordovan Brown

EWM-3304
Rustic Wood

EWM-3305
Violet Mist

EWM-3308
Cayenne

WearMaster Oak EWM-3101 Mocha Glaze

Maintenance: WearMaster Acrylic Impregnated Products

WearMaster floors provide unprecedented ease of maintenance. The acrylic impregnated wear layer features a tough, low gloss, commercial urethane finish that practically takes care of itself. It resists damage from most spills and stains. With prompt attention, most spills and stains wipe perfectly clean.

WearMaster floors require no special cleaning equipment or procedures. Routine maintenance is simply vacuuming to remove dirt and grit and occasional light cleaning with Dura-Luster® Commercial Cleaner Concentrate.

Please call toll free 1-800-722-4647 for a Floor Care Guide which details care and maintenance information.

Availability:

Bruce Hardwood Floors are sold through an international distribution network including the United States, Canada, Mexico, Europe and Japan.

Warranty:

Bruce WearMaster products carry a Full Lifetime Warranty on Structural Integrity, Adhesive Bond and Subfloor Moisture Protection. Bruce includes a 25-Year Warranty on the acrylic impregnated wood layer in that it will not wear through or separate from its multi-ply, engineered construction.

WearMaster's Permion finish is warranted for 3 years in commercial settings and 10 years in residential settings.

For complete details of Bruce product warranties, call toll-free 1-800-722-4647.

How to Specify WearMaster Acrylic Impregnated Floors:

A. Flooring shall be Bruce 3/8" X 3" (9.53 mm X 76.20mm) WearMaster flooring (specify product item number) in the (specify wood species) grade of wood as manufactured by Bruce Hardwood Floors, a division of Triangle Pacific Corp.

B. Flooring shall be manufactured in a 3-ply, engineered construction that utilizes the Bruce ColorJet Infusion™ process to create a minimum 1/12" thick, pressurized wood color layer in the color (specify color name and number).

C. Flooring shall feature a minimum 1/12" thick acrylic impregnated wear surface utilizing the patented Bruce WearMaster impregnation process. U.S. Patent Nos. 5,609,915 and 5,605,767 and 5,683,820.

D. Factory finished, engineered WearMaster flooring shall be provided with Permion urethane finish; a stain resistant, ultra-violet cured, low gloss, commercial urethane finish.

E. Factory finished, acrylic impregnated wood flooring will have no less than a Class B Flame Spread Rating (ASTM Test E-84-95).

F. Installed product will meet the Fuel Contribution and Smoke Density standards established for a product with a Class B Flame Spread Rating by the American Society for Testing and Materials (ASTM Test E-84-95).

G. Product to be installed will pass the Critical Radiant Flux Test with a minimum Class I Rating (ASTM Test E-648-94a).

H. Installed flooring material will have a finish that meets the advisory recommendations of the American's With Disabilities Act Regulations for Slip Resistance for Accessible Routes of a minimum .60 coefficient of friction rating (ASTM Test D-2394-83).

I. Installation of WearMaster floors shall be made in accordance with instructions provided in each carton.

Meridian Stone® Custom Crafted Wood Tile — H-4020 Sedona with H-316 Creme Diamond Accents

Description:

The Bruce Benchmark™ Collection features the widest assortment of colors, styles, and patterns in the hardwood flooring industry. Benchmark floors are manufactured from the finest, premium-grade hardwoods to assure an outstanding consistency of grain pattern and texture. Benchmark products are available in the Bruce Dura-Luster® urethane finish and the Dura-Satin® wax finish.

Dura-Luster urethane finish products are recommended for all residential areas, including kitchens.

Dura-Satin wax finish products are recommended for light commercial and residential use, including high traffic areas.

Maintenance: Dura-Luster Urethane Finish Products

For the Dura-Luster urethane finish, Bruce recommends good general maintenance practices that include sweeping or vacuuming to remove dirt and grit. For a more thorough cleaning, simply clean with Bruce No-Wax Cleaner. The Bruce Dura-Luster finish is a no-wax finish and does not require buffing. However, if buffing is desired after cleaning, use only a soft polishing attachment such as a lamb's wool pad.

Dura-Luster Urethane Finish

3/4" Solid Oak Strip and Planks

Sterling® Strip
Random lengths and a standard 2 1/4" width.
Square edges and ends. Tongue and groove.
Size: 3/4" X 2 1/4"

C-720 Natural	C-7220 Auburn
C-721 Gunstock	C-7222 Vintage Brown
C-722 Spice	C-7223 Glacial White
C-723 Winter White	

Sterling Encore Plank®
Random lengths and alternate widths. Square
edges and ends. Tongue and groove.
Size: 3/4" X 2 1/4" - 3 1/4"

B-740 Natural   B-741 Gunstock

Devon® Plank
Random lengths and alternate widths. Eased
edges and square ends. Tongue and groove.
Size: 3/4" X 2 1/4" - 3 1/4"

B-640 Natural	B-642 Spice
B-641 Gunstock	B-643 Winter White

Windward® Strip
Random lengths and a standard 2 1/4" width.
Eased edges and square ends. Tongue and
groove. Size: 3/4" X 2 1/4"

C-620 Natural	C-623 Winter White
C-621 Gunstock	C-6220 Auburn
C-622 Spice	C-6224 Driftwood

Sterling Prestige Plank®
Random lengths and a standard 3 1/4" width.
Square edges and ends. Tongue and groove.
Size: 3/4" X 3 1/4"

C-730 Natural	C-732 Spice
C-731 Gunstock	C-733 Winter White

American 🍁 Maple
COLLECTION

Kennedale™ Strip
Random lengths and a standard 2 1/4" width.
Slightly eased edges and ends. Tongue and
groove. Size: 3/4" X 2 1/4"

CM-700 Natural	CM-728 Cherry
CM-710 Country Natural	CM-733 Cinnamon

5/16" Solid Oak Strip

Natural Reflections®
Random lengths and a standard 2 1/4" width.
Square edges and ends. Tongue and groove.
Size: 5/16" X 2 1/4"

C-5010 Natural	C-5021 Quartz
C-5011 Gunstock	C-5028 Cherry
C-5012 Spice	C-5029 Mink Grey
C-5013 Ivory White	C-5030 Prairie
C-5014 Mellow	C-5031 Walnut
C-5016 Butterscotch	

3/8" Engineered Strip and Planks

Reunion Plank®
Random lengths and a standard 3" width. 5-ply
engineered oak. Square edges and ends. Tongue
and groove. Size: 3/8" X 3"

E-710 Toast	E-7120 Auburn
E-711 Gunstock	E-7122 Vintage Brown
E-712 Mellow	E-7123 Glacial White
E-713 Ivory White	

LeClaire® Plank
Random lengths and a standard 3" width. 3-ply
engineered oak with eased edges and ends.
Tongue and groove.

E-820 Toast	E-823 Ivory White
E-821 Gunstock	E-824 Spice

Charlemont® Plank
Random lengths and widths. 3-ply engineered
oak with eased edges and ends. Tongue and
groove. Size: 3/8" X 3" - 5" - 7"

E-840 Toast   E-841 Gunstock

Harborlight™ Plank
Random lengths and a standard 5" width. 5-ply
engineered maple with square edges and ends.
Tongue and groove. Size: 3/8" x 5"

E-1610 Natural	E-1620 Sedona
E-1611 Cinnamon	

Northshore™ Plank
Random lengths and a standard 5" width. 5-ply
engineered oak with square edges and ends.
Tongue and groove. Size: 3/8" x 5"

E-8510 Natural	E-8517 Saddle
E-8511 Gunstock	E-8522 Vintage Brown
E-8516 Butterscotch	

Caruth® Plank
Random lengths and a standard 3" width. 5-ply
engineered maple with square edges and ends.
Tongue and groove. Size: 3/8" X 3"

E-910 Toast	E-913 Creme
E-911 Caramel	E-920 Sedona

Antell® Plank
Random lengths and alternate widths. 3-ply
engineered oak with eased edges and ends.
Tongue and groove. Size: 3/8" X 3" - 5"

E-830 Toast   E-831 Gunstock

Hancock™ Plank
Factory installed pegs. Random lengths and
widths. 3-ply engineered oak with eased edges
and ends. Tongue and groove.
Size: 3/8" X 3" - 5" - 7"

E-851 Gunstock   E-854 Spice

Stafford™ Strip
Random lengths and a standard 2 1/4" width. 3-
ply engineered oak with square edges and ends.
Tongue and groove. Size: 3/8" X 2 1/4"

E-410 Toast	E-416 Butterscotch
E-410U Unfinished	E-417 Saddle
E-411 Gunstock	E-420 Auburn
E-413 Ivory White	E-421 Quartz

Installation:

Bruce Dura-Luster urethane products are recommended for all
residential areas, including the kitchen.

Solid oak products can be installed on or above grade. Engineered
products can be installed on, above or below grade level, including
basements. Detailed installation instruction sheets are provided in every
product carton.

Benchmark™ Collection:

3/8" Engineered Custom Wood Tile and Parquet

Debut®
3-ply engineered oak, single unit. Eased edges, tongue and groove. Size: 3/8" X 9" X 9"
K-2010 Toast   K-2011 Gunstock

Jeffersonian™ II
3-ply engineered oak, three-piece construction. Eased, butt edges. Size: 3/8" X 8" X 8"
H-1710 Toast   H-1711 Gunstock

Sonata®
3-ply engineered maple center/oak pickets, five-piece construction. Eased, butt edges.
Size: 3/8" X 12" X 12"
H-4621 Creme Center/Quartz Pickets
H-4625 Creme Center/Peachtree Pickets

Santa Fe Square™
3-ply engineered oak, one unit with one diagonally cut corner to accept diamond insert. Eased edges, tongue and groove. Diamond inserts ordered separately. Size: 3/8" X 9" X 9"
K-2110 Toast   K-2111 Gunstock

Meridian Stone®
3-ply engineered maple, one unit with eased, butt edges. Four corners diagonally cut to accept diamond inserts. Diamond inserts ordered separately. Size: 3/8" X 12" X 12"
H-4010 Toast   H-4020 Sedona
H-4016 Creme

Diamond Accents
3-ply engineered maple, one unit with eased, butt edges. For use with Santa Fe Square and Meridian Stone only. Size: 2 7/8" X 2 7/8"

H-310U Unfinished	H-325 Parchment
H-316 Creme	H-326 Sherwood
H-320 Sedona	H-327 Wood Violet
H-322 Espresso	H-328 Sahara
H-324 Charcoal	

Herringstrip®
3-ply engineered oak, one unit with eased edges. Variety of pattern/design options. Tongue and groove. Size: 3/8" X 3" X 15"
H-1010 Toast   H-1022 Vintage Brown
H-1011 Gunstock

5/16" Solid Oak Custom Wood Tile and Parquet

Oakmont®
Single unit contains oak fillets joined with a soft metal spline. Square edges. Tongue and groove. Size: 5/16" X 12" X 12"

L-70 Desert	L-77 Tudor
L-71 Chestnut	L-720 Auburn
L-72 Mellow	L-721 Quartz
L-76 Ivory White	L-724 Driftwood

Dura-Luster Testing Standards:

ASTM D 968 - The Falling Sand Test. Results represent the amount, in milliliters, of sand that falls on a controlled area before the finish is worn away. The higher the number, the better the finish.

Bruce Dura-Luster urethane finish - 88,000 milliliters per mil of finish.

Competitive urethane finish - 48,000 milliliters per mil of finish.

ASTM D 2394-83, Sections 33-37 - Test Method for Static Slip Resistance. Oak and Maple: Exceeds 0.60

Meets the advisory recommendations of the American's With Disabilities Act Regulations for Slip Resistance for Accessible Routes.

ASTM E 648-94a - Test Method for Critical Radiant Flux of Floor Covering Systems Using a Radiant Heat Energy Source. Oak: 0.68, Maple: 0.68

Color Fastness: Results represent in numerical value the amount of shift from the original color toward a yellow coloration. The lower the number the better the color/finish.

Raw Oak Test Score: 8.055

Bruce Ivory White Test Score: 4.919

Bruce Desert/Natural Test Score: 3.003

Note: Bruce parquet products with a self-stick foam backing are available on a special order basis. Contact your distributor for details.

Warranty:

All Bruce Hardwood Flooring products carry a Full Lifetime Warranty on Structural Integrity, Adhesive Bond and Subfloor Moisture Protection. Benchmark Collection Dura-Luster urethane products carry a Full Five-Year Finish Wear Layer Warranty for residential applications. For complete details of Bruce product warranties, call toll-free 1-800-722-4647.

Dura-Luster Urethane Finish

Coastal Woodlands™

1/2" Engineered Plank

ECW-124 Oak Nutmeg

ECW-126 Oak Butterscotch

ECW-121 Oak Natural

ECW-200 Plantation Beech

ECW-161 Beech

ECW-171 Maple Natural

ECW-170 Country Maple

ECW-131 Asian Pine

ECW-141 Iroko

ECW-151 Kempas

ECW-181 Cherry Natural

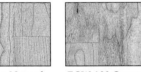
ECW-188 Country Cherry

ECW-191 Nyatoh

ECW-211 Merbau Natural

Coastal Woodlands™ — Kempas Color–ECW151

Description:

Designed for floating floor installations, Coastal Woodlands products consist of three strips of hardwoods pre-assembled on 1/2" thick, 7 11/16" wide and 86 5/8" (1.4cm x19.5cm x 220.0cm) long planks. Precision tongue and groove construction and true square edges combine for a flat, smooth surface.

Installation:

Coastal Woodlands products are installed over Bruce ComfortGuard™ underlayment as a floating floor. The rolled foam underlayment provides a cushioning effect, sound absorption and moisture protection.

How to Specify Benchmark Products:

A. Flooring shall be Bruce (state name, size and/or width) strip, plank, custom wood tile or parquet in the grade of (specify wood species) with a surface color/finish of (state color item number) as manufactured by Bruce Hardwood Floors, a division of Triangle Pacific Corp.

B. Factory-finished engineered strip, plank, or parquet and solid strip, plank or parquet shall be sanded for a smooth finish and have a (specify desired finish) Dura-Luster ultra-violet cured urethane finish or Dura-Satin baked-in wax finish that includes a soya and linseed penetrating stain and carnauba wax.

C. Installation must be made in accordance with the installation instruction sheets provided in each carton.

D. Installation of all 3/8", 3-ply products can be either nailed, stapled, or glued using properly recommended tools.

E. Use Bruce Tribond Wood Flooring adhesive for glue-down installation. Bruce Tribond Wood Flooring adhesive shall be used for all 3/8" strip, plank, and parquet (5/16" and 3/4"). Adhesive for end fastening 3/4" random planks shall be Bruce Oakbond or PL-400 as recommended by Bruce Hardwood Floors.

F. Trowel for spreading Bruce Tribond Adhesive shall be notched as required by Bruce Hardwood Floors.

G. Nailing Machines: 2" barbed fasteners or approved staples should be used for installing Bruce 3/4" strip or plank flooring, and nailing machines with 1 1/4" cleats should be used for nail-down installation of 3/8" strip or plank as required by Bruce Hardwood Floors.
For 3/8", 3-ply products that are 3" wide or less, use one inch or longer glue-coated staples with the Stanley Bostitch® #S3297-LHF stapler or the Senco® SLS20HF stapler.

9

Dillard's Department Store — Little Rock, Arkansas — Monterey Plank E-20 Gunstock

Description:

Bruce Dura-Satin wax finish floors are specifically designed for light commercial and residential use, including high traffic areas. The Dura-Satin finish epitomizes the old-world richness and patina of soft, baked-in stain and wax. The exclusive Bruce 13-step penetrating stain and wax finish creates a protective barrier that provides lasting durability against traffic, wear, soil and stains. The Bruce Dura-Satin wax finish is an outstanding choice for beauty and durability in light commercial applications.

Maintenance:

Bruce recommends good general maintenance practices for Dura-Satin wax finish products.

Commercial Maintenance
• Sweep or vacuum daily to remove grit.
• Using a commercial floor buffer, buff daily with a fiber bristle polishing brush.
• Using a lamb's wool applicator or equivalent, apply Bruce floor care products once every two weeks or as required in extreme traffic areas. Follow with buffing.

Residential Maintenance
• Use quality solvent-based cleaners and waxes.
• Buffing between waxing will restore the floor's sheen.
• High traffic areas can be waxed without waxing the entire floor.
• Waxing too often may cause a wax build-up and dull the finish.
• Do not use water base waxes. Water may dull the finish and cause additional maintenance problems.

Dura-Satin Testing Standards:

ASTM D 4060-95 - Test Method for Abrasion Resistance of Organic Coatings by the Taber Abraser. Oak: 0.011 Maple: 0.010

ASTM E 84-95 - Test Method for Surface Burning Characteristics of Building Materials. Oak: Class C Maple: Class C

Warranty:

All Bruce hardwood flooring products carry a Full Lifetime Warranty on Structural Integrity, Adhesive Bond, and Subfloor Moisture Protection.

Benchmark Collection Dura-Satin wax products carry a Full Five-Year Finish Wear Layer Warranty for residential applications and Full One-Year Finish Wear Layer Warranty in approved commercial applications. For complete details of Bruce product warranties, call toll-free 1-800-722-4647.

Dura-Satin Wax Finish

3/4" Solid Oak Strip and Planks

Westminster® Plank
Wrought iron nails for end fastening. Random lengths and widths. Beveled edges and ends. Tongue and groove. Size: 3/4" X 3" - 5" - 7"
A-3 Mellow Textured

Cathedral® Plank
Factory installed pegs. Random lengths and widths. Beveled edges and ends. Tongue and groove. Size: 3/4" X 3" - 5" - 7"
A-5 Toast   A-7 Gunstock

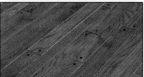

Ranch Plank®
Factory installed pegs. Random lengths and alternate widths. Beveled edges and ends. Tongue and groove. Size: 3/4" X 2 1/4" - 3 1/4"
B-3 Gunstock

Cambridge® Plank
Random lengths and widths. Beveled edges and ends. Tongue and groove. Size: 3/4" X 3" - 4" - 6"
A-20 Toast   A-21 Gunstock

Fireside® Plank
Random lengths and alternate widths. Beveled edges and ends. Tongue and groove.
Size: 3/4" X 2 1/4" - 3 1/4"
B-4 Gunstock   B-8 Toast

Country Oak® Plank
Factory installed pegs. Random lengths and widths. Beveled edges and ends. Tongue and groove. Size: 3/4" X 3" - 4" - 6"
A-25 Rustic

Homestead Plank®
Textured finish. Random lengths and alternate widths. Beveled edges and ends. Tongue and groove. Size: 3/4" X 2 1/4" - 3 1/4"
B-5 Mellow Textured

Prefinished Strip
Random lengths, standard 2 1/4" width. Beveled edges and ends. Tongue and groove.
Size: 3/4" X 2 1/4"
C-1 Natural   C-4 Gunstock
C-3 Bronzetone

3/4" Solid Oak Parquet

Unit Block
Single unit with 6 tongue and groove fillets joined with a soft metal spline. Beveled edges.
Size: 3/4" X 9" X 9"
G-7 Natural   G-8 Gunstock

3/8" Engineered Plank

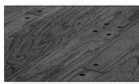

Village Plank®
Factory installed pegs. 3-ply engineered plank. Random lengths and widths. Beveled edges and ends. Tongue and groove. Size: 3/8" X 3" - 5" - 7"
E-1 Mellow   E-11 Gunstock

Villa Nova Plank®
3-ply engineered plank. Random lengths and widths. Beveled edges and ends. Tongue and groove. Size: 3/8" X 3" - 5" - 7"
E-12 Gunstock

Sierra Plank®
3-ply engineered plank. Random lengths and alternating widths. Beveled edges and ends. Tongue and groove. Size: 3/8" X 3" - 5"
E-30 Gunstock

Monterey™ Plank
3-ply engineered plank. Random lengths and standard 3" width. Beveled edges and ends. Tongue and groove. Size: 3/8" X 3"
E-20 Gunstock

Classic™ Plank
5-ply engineered plank. Square edges, random lengths and standard 3" width. Square edges and ends. Tongue and groove. Size: 3/8" X 3"
E-510 Toast   E-511 Gunstock

3/8" Engineered Parquet

Heritage Square®
3-ply engineered oak. One unit, with beveled edges. Tongue and groove. Size: 3/8" X 9" X 9"
K-25-TG Gunstock   K-27-TG Mellow
K-26-TG Toast   Textured

Dover Strip — CB-128 Merlot

Description:

Kensington™ Collection products are manufactured from specially selected hardwoods chosen with natural characteristics for a more rustic, casual style. Kensington products are available in the Bruce Dura-Luster urethane finish and the Dura-Satin wax finish.

Dura-Luster urethane finish floors receive multiple coats of urethane cured with ultraviolet light between each coat. This produces a tough, durable finish that repels most household spills, never requires waxing, and is very easy to maintain.

Dura-Satin wax finish products are the result of a 13-step penetrating stain and wax process that creates a protective barrier which provides lasting durability against traffic, wear, soil and stains. Dura-Satin wax finish products are specifically designed for light commercial and residential use, including high traffic areas.

Installation:

Bruce Dura-Luster urethane products are recommended for all residential areas, including the kitchen.

Solid oak products can be installed on or above grade. Engineered products can be installed on, above or below grade level, including basements.

Detailed installation instruction sheets are provided in every product carton.

Dura-Luster Testing Standards:

Refer to the Dura-Luster testing standards on page 8.

Dura-Luster Urethane Finish

3/4" Solid Oak Strip and Plank

Laurel™ Strip
Random lengths and a standard 2 1/4" width. Eased edges with square ends. Tongue and groove. Size: 3/4" X 2 1/4"
CB-910 White Oak Natural   CB-924 Gunstock
CB-921 Natural   CB-926 Butterscotch
CB-922 Spice   CB-927 Saddle
CB-923 Winter White

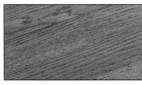

Bayport™ Strip
Random lengths and a standard 2 1/4" width. Square edges with square ends. Tongue and groove. Size: 3/4" X 2 1/4"
CB-820 Auburn   CB-824 Gunstock
CB-821 Natural   CB-826 Butterscotch
CB-822 Spice   CB-827 Saddle

Valley View™ Plank
Random lengths and a standard 3 1/4" width. Eased edges with square ends. Tongue and groove. Size: 3/4" X 3 1/4"
CB-931 Natural   CB-934 Gunstock

Dover™ Strip
Random lengths and a standard 2 1/4" width. Eased edges with square ends. Tongue and groove. Size: 3/4" X 2 1/4"
CB-110 Dune   CB-128 Merlot
CB-112 Sundance   CB-130 Seashell
CB-111 Faun

5/16" Solid Oak Parquet

Sorrento® Parquet
Single unit contains oak fillets joined with a soft metal spline. Square edges.
Size: 5/16" X 12" X 12"
L-92 Mellow   L-94 Chestnut
L-93 Desert   L-95 Quartz

3/8" Engineered Oak Strip and Planks

Riverside™ Plank
Random lengths with a standard 3" width. 5-ply engineered oak with square edges and ends. Tongue and groove. Size: 3/8" X 3"
EB-720 Toast   EB-724 Spice
EB-721 Gunstock   EB-726 Butterscotch
EB-723 Ivory White   EB-727 Saddle

Springdale™ Plank
Random lengths with a standard 3" width. 3-ply engineered oak with square edges and ends. Tongue and groove. Size: 3/8" X 3"
EB-520 Toast   EB-526 Butterscotch
EB-521 Gunstock   EB-527 Saddle
EB-525 Mellow

Glen Cove™ Plank
Random lengths and a standard 3" width. 3-ply engineered oak with eased edges and ends. Tongue and groove. Size: 3/8" X 3"
EB-880 Toast   EB-884 Spice
EB-881 Gunstock   EB-886 Butterscotch
EB-883 Ivory White   EB-887 Saddle

Summerside™ Strip
Random lengths and a standard 2 1/4" width. 3-ply engineered oak with square edges and ends. Tongue and groove. Size: 3/8" X 2 1/4"
EB-620 Toast   EB-626 Butterscotch
EB-621 Gunstock   EB-627 Saddle
EB-625 Mellow

Warranty:

All Bruce products carry a Full Lifetime Warranty on Structural Integrity, Adhesive Bond, and Subfloor Moisture Protection.

Kensington Collection Dura-Luster urethane products carry a Full Three-Year Finish Wear Layer Warranty for residential applications. For complete details of Bruce product warranties, call toll-free 1-800-722-4647.

How to Specify Kensington Collection Products:

A. Flooring shall be Bruce (state name, size and/or width) strip, plank, custom wood tile or parquet in the grade of (specify wood species) with a surface color/finish of (state color item number) as manufactured by Bruce Hardwood Floors, a division of Triangle Pacific Corporation.

B. Factory-finished engineered strip, plank, or parquet and solid strip, plank or parquet shall be sanded for a smooth finish and have a (specify desired finish) Dura-Luster ultra-violet cured urethane finish or Dura-Satin baked-in wax finish that includes a soya and linseed penetrating stain and carnauba wax.

C. Installation must be made in accordance with the installation instruction sheets provided in each carton.

D. Installation of all 3/8", 3-ply products can be either nailed, stapled, or glued using properly recommended tools.

E. Use Bruce Tribond Adhesive for glue-down installation. Bruce Tribond Adhesive shall be used for all 3/8" strip, plank, and parquet (5/16" and 3/4"). Adhesive for end fastening 3/4" random planks shall be Bruce Oakbond or PL-400 as recommended by Bruce Hardwood Floors.

F. Trowel for spreading Bruce Tribond Adhesive shall be notched as required by Bruce Hardwood Floors.

G. Nailing Machines: 2" barbed fasteners or approved staples should be used for installing Bruce 3/4" strip or plank flooring, and nailing machines with 1 1/4" cleats should be used for nail-down installation of 3/8" strip or plank as required by Bruce Hardwood Floors.
For 3/8", 3-ply products that are 3" wide or less, use one inch or longer glue-coated staples with the Stanley Bostitch® #S3297-LHF stapler or the Senco® SLS20HF stapler.

13

Kensington™ Collection:
Dura-Satin Wax Finish

3/4" Solid Oak Strip and Planks

Madison Plank®
Random lengths and widths. Beveled edges and ends. Tongue and groove. Size: 3/4" X 3" - 4" - 6"
A-51 Gunstock   A-52 Toast

Manchester® Plank
Random lengths and alternating widths. Beveled edges and ends. Tongue and groove.
Size: 3/4" X 2 1/4" - 3 1/4"
B-11 Toast   B-14 Gunstock

Prefinished Strip
Random lengths and standard 2 1/4" width. Beveled edges and ends. Tongue and groove.
Size: 3/4" X 2 1/4"
CB-21 Toast   CB-24 Gunstock

Brookhollow™ Strip
Random lengths and standard 2 1/4" width. Eased edges and square ends. Tongue and groove.
Size: 3/4" X 2 1/4"
CB-91 Natural   CB-94 Gunstock

3/8" Engineered Oak Planks

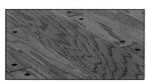

Brookside™ Plank
Factory installed pegs. Random lengths and widths. Beveled edges and ends. Tongue and groove. Size: 3/8" X 3" - 5" - 7"
E-50 Gunstock Textured

Brandon™ Plank
Random lengths and widths. Beveled edges and ends. Tongue and groove. Size: 3/8" X 3" - 5" - 7"
E-52 Gunstock Textured

Sutton™ Plank
Random lengths and standard 3" width. Beveled edges and ends. Tongue and groove.
Size: 3/8" X 3"
E-51 Gunstock   E-55 Toast
     Textured

3/8" Engineered Oak Parquet

Ridgewood® Parquet
3-ply engineered oak. Center unit surrounded with 2 pickets. Beveled, butt edges.
Size: 3/8" X 8" X 8"
H-84 Gunstock Textured

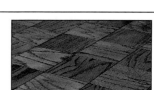

Heritage Square®
3-ply engineered oak. One unit with beveled edges. Tongue and groove. Size: 3/8" X 9" X 9"
K-28-TG Gunstock Textured

Installation:

Bruce Dura-Satin wax finish products are recommended for both residential and light commercial applications, including high traffic areas.

Solid oak products can be installed on or above grade. Engineered oak products can be installed on, above or below grade level, including basements.

Detailed installation instruction sheets are provided in every product carton.

Dura-Satin Testing Standards:

Refer to the Dura-Satin testing standards on page 10.

Warranty:

All Bruce products carry a Full Lifetime Warranty on Structural Integrity, Adhesive Bond, and Subfloor Moisture Protection.

Kensington Collection Dura-Satin wax products carry a Full Three-Year Finish Wear Layer Warranty in residential applications and a One-Year Finish Wear Layer Warranty in approved commercial applications. For complete details of Bruce product warranties, call toll-free 1-800-722-4647.

Maintenance: Dura-Satin Wax Finish Products

Bruce recommends good general maintenance practices for Dura-Satin wax finish products.

Commercial Maintenance
• Sweep or vacuum daily to remove grit.
• Using a commercial floor buffer, buff daily with a fiber bristle polishing brush.
• Using a lamb's wool applicator or equivalent, apply Bruce floor care products once every two weeks or as required in extreme traffic areas. Follow with buffing.

Residential Maintenance
• Use quality solvent-based cleaners and waxes.
• Buffing between waxings will restore the floor's sheen.
• High traffic areas can be waxed without waxing the entire floor.
• Waxing too often may cause a wax build-up and dull the finish. Twice yearly should be sufficient for normal residential traffic areas.
• Do not use water base waxes. Water may dull the finish and cause additional maintenance problems.

Contract
Unfinished Products

Contract Unfinished CU-740. Custom finished in a Gunstock color.

Description:

Bruce manufactures a complete line of contract unfinished products for job site finishing. These products are kiln dried prior to milling and go through the identical manufacturing process as all other Bruce products with the exception of finishing. Contract Unfinished Floors are available in both solid and engineered oak.

Warranty:

Bruce Contract Unfinished products carry a Full Lifetime Warranty on Structural Integrity, Adhesive Bond, and Subfloor Moisture Protection. For complete details of Bruce product warranties, call toll-free 1-800-722-4647.

3/4" Signature Series
Solid Oak Plank

Available with square ends. Side edges may be square or beveled. The 3/4" solid oak series is available in red or white oak, and in 3", 4", 5", 6" or 7" widths in random lengths. Sizes can be mixed to achieve alternate or random patterns.

Installation: Nail down, on or above grade level.

3" Plank	4" Plank	5" Plank	6" Plank	7" Plank
Item#				
CU-3RB	CU-4RB	CU-5RB	CU-6RB	CU-7RB
CU-3RS	CU-4RS	CU-5RS	CU-6RS	CU-7RS
CU-3WB	CU-4WB	CU-5WB	CU-6WB	CU-7WB
CU-3WS	CU-4WS	CU-5WS	CU-6WS	CU-7WS

R = Red Oak W = White Oak B = Beveled Edges S = Square Edges

Engineered Flooring

Engineered oak construction with square ends and edges and tongue and groove milling. Traditional red and white oak boards available in 2 1/4" and 3" widths and random lengths.

Installation: Glue down, on above or below grade level.

1/2" Strip and Plank

size	Select & Better Red Oak	Select & Better White Oak	#1 Common Red Oak	#1 Common White Oak
1/2" X 2 1/4"	CU-600	CU-610	CU-615	CU-625
1/2" X 3"	CU-640	CU-650	CU-635	CU-645

3/8" Strip and Plank

size	Select & Better Red Oak	Select & Better White Oak	#1 Common Red Oak	#1 Common White Oak
3/8" X 2 1/4"	CU-700	CU-710	CU-715	CU-725
3/8" X 3"	CU-740	CU-750	CU-735	CU-745

How to Specify Contract Unfinished Floors:

A. Flooring shall be Bruce (state name, size and/or width) strip or plank in the species of oak or maple (state item number) as manufactured by Bruce Hardwood Floors, a division of Triangle Pacific Corporation.

B. Bruce unfinished strip or CU plank shall be installed, sanded and finished at the job site according to the job specification. Engineered strip and plank shall be presanded at the factory for minimum job site sanding.

C. Installation must be completed in accordance with the installation instruction sheets provided in each carton.

D. Installation of all Contract Unfinished 3/8", 3-ply products can be either nailed, stapled, or glued using properly recommended tools.

E. Use Bruce Tribond Wood Flooring adhesive for glue-down installation. Adhesive shall be used for all 1/2" and 3/8" thick strip and plank products. Adhesive for end fastening of 3/4" random strip or planks shall be Bruce Oakbond or PL-400 as recommended by Bruce Hardwood Floors.

F. Trowel for spreading Bruce Tribond Wood Flooring adhesive shall be notched as required by Bruce Hardwood Floors.

G. Nailing Machines: 2" barbed fasteners or approved staples should be used for installing Bruce 3/4" strip or plank flooring, and nailing machines with 1 1/4" cleats should be used for nail-down installation of 3/8" strip or planks as required by Bruce Hardwood Floors.
For 3/8", 3-ply products that are 3" wide or less, use one inch or longer glue-coated staples with the Stanley Bostitch® #S3297-LHF stapler or the Senco® SLS20HF stapler.

al Dente Restaurant featuring WearMaster — Bally's Las Vegas

Installation Products:

- **Adhesives.** Bruce Tribond Wood Flooring adhesive is used for installation of all 3/8" strip, plank and custom wood tile or parquet (5/16" and 3/4") except when the parquet is self-stick, dry foam back or a vapor barrier is involved. Check adhesive label for trowel specifications.

- Bruce Oakbond Adhesive is required for end fastening some of the solid oak, random width, nail-down strip or plank floors.

- **Trim and Molding.** Bruce's complete line of trim and molding products are available either factory-finished or unfinished.

- **Installation Accessories.** Bruce offers specially notched trowels for spreading adhesives to the proper specifications, cork expansion products, nails and other installation products to complete the job.

- **Nailing machines.** Recommended nailers and staplers, along with proper fasteners are available through your Bruce distributor. Follow required nailing schedules and subfloor recommendations.

Maintenance/Repair Products

Bruce offers a complete line of routine maintenance products formulated specifically for each type of Bruce finish. In addition, a full line of repair products such as stains, fillers and finishes are available.

Sales and Specifier Support

Bruce has a complete library of sales and specifier support materials available, and a nationwide network of distributor representatives ready to assist you at the local level.

Additional Information

For the name of your local Bruce distributor or dealer, please call toll free: **1-800-722-4647**. Visit our website at **www.brucehardwoodfloors.com**.

The Natural Choice®

Maple Treasures™, shown in Natural.

Chaparral™ Strip, shown in Brandywine.

PREMIER
W O O D   F L O O R S

A division of Triangle Pacific Corp.

For All The Favorite Rooms In Your Life™

Plantation™ Strip shown in Natural

Founder's™ Collection

The Founder's Collection is a superior line of flooring exclusively milled from premium-grade American hardwoods. The Founder's Collection features Premier's durable Everguard™ no-wax finish.

Plantation™ Strip & Plank Engineered Oak

- 3/8" thick, 2 1/4" wide (strip) or 3/8" thick, 3" wide (plank) cross-ply engineered oak, three ply
- Random lengths of 10" to 48"
- Patented Flexform™ milling system
- Available in square edges and ends (plank & strip)
- and eased edges and square ends (plank only)
- Tongue and groove side construction with Level-Lock end system
- Available in all Founder's Collection stain choices
- Install on, above or below grade

New Orleans™ Strip Solid Oak

- 3/4" thick, 2 1/4" wide solid oak
- Random lengths of 9" to 84"
- Square edges and ends
- Tongue and groove construction
- Available in Natural, Autumn, Brandywine and Golden Oak
- Install on or above grade only

Founder's Collection Colors

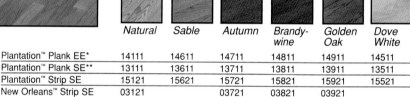

	Natural	Sable	Autumn	Brandy-wine	Golden Oak	Dove White
Plantation™ Plank EE*	14111	14611	14711	14811	14911	14511
Plantation™ Plank SE**	13111	13611	13711	13811	13911	13511
Plantation™ Strip SE	15121	15621	15721	15821	15921	15521
New Orleans™ Strip SE	03121		03721	03821	03921	

* Eased Edges ** Square Edges

Jewels of Nature™

In this rare collection you'll find Cherry, Maple, Pecan and Walnut hardwoods. And as part of the Founder's Collection, the same five year warranty applies. Cherry Royale™, 3/8" x 3"; Maple Treasures™, 3/8" x 2 1/4"; Noble™ Pecan, 3/8" x 3"; and an Ornamental™ Walnut Feature Strip, 3/8" x 1 1/2".

- 3/8" thick, cross-ply engineered hardwoods, 3-ply
- Random lengths of 10" to 48"
- Square edges and ends
- Tongue and groove side construction with Level-Lock end system
- Patented Flexform™ milling system
- Install on, above or below grade

Noble™ Pecan shown in Amber.

Jewels of Nature™ Collection Colors:

Maple

Pecan

Walnut

Cherry

Natural	Cinnabar	Garnet	Natural	Amber	Smokey Topaz	Walnut	Cherry Royale
27121	27721	27421	23111	23211	23911	23391	23411

For additional product and warranty information, please call 1-800-588-1707 or visit our website at www.premierwoodfloors.com.

Landmark™ Collection

Landmark Collection floors are manufactured from American oak hardwoods that are specially chosen for their distinctive natural characteristics. Landmark Collection floors feature the Premier Everguard™ no-wax finish.

Olympic™ Plank shown in Sable

Olympic™ Strip & Plank Engineered Oak

- 3/8" thick, 2 1/4" wide (strip) or 3/8" thick, 3" wide (plank) cross-ply engineered oak, three ply
- Random lengths of 10" to 48"
- Patented Flexform™ milling system
- Available in square edges and
- ends (plank & strip) and eased edges and square ends (plank only)
- Tongue and groove side construction with Level-Lock end system
- Available in all Landmark Collection stain choices
- Install on, above or below grade

Tara™ Oak Parquet Solid Oak

- 5/16" thick, 12" x 12" solid oak
- Square edges
- Tongue and groove construction
- Available in Natural, Autumn, Brandywine and Golden Oak
- Install on or above grade only

Chaparral™ Strip & Shiloh® Strip Solid Oak

- 3/4" thick, 2 1/4" wide solid oak
- Random lengths of 9" to 84"
- Square edges and ends (Chaparral Strip), or eased edges and square ends (Shiloh Strip)
- Tongue and groove construction
- Available in Natural, Autumn, Brandywine and Golden Oak
- Install on or above grade only

Landmark™ Collection Colors

	Natural	Sable	Autumn	Brandy-wine	Golden Oak
Olympic™ Plank EE	14112	14612	14712	14812	14912
Olympic™ Plank SE	13112	13612	13712	13812	13912
Olympic™ Strip SE	15122	15622	15722	15822	15922
Shiloh™ Strip EE	02122		02722	02822	02922
Chaparral™ Strip SE	03122		03722	03822	03922
Tara™ Oak Parquet	01102		01702	01802	01902

For additional product and warranty information, please call 1-800-588-1707 or visit our website at www.premierwoodfloors.com.

Founder's Collection

Warranty: All Premier wood floors first quality products have a full lifetime construction warranty and all Premier engineered products have a full lifetime adhesive and subfloor moisture protection warranty. Founder's Collection products with the Everguard urethane wear surface are guaranteed not to wear through or separate from the wood for a full five years from the date of purchase when used in normal residential traffic conditions.

Landmark Collection

Warranty: All first quality Landmark Collection floors have a full lifetime construction warranty and all Premier engineered products have a full lifetime adhesive and subfloor moisture protection warranty. Landmark Collection products with the Everguard urethane wear surface are guaranteed not to wear through or separate from the wood for a full three years from the date of purchase when used in normal residential traffic conditions.

Premier's Patented Flexform™ Milling System

The Flexform milling system is a standard feature on all Premier engineered products, and insures that the floor will lay flat, even when installed over subfloors with slight irregularities.

The Flexform construction process starts with 3 layers of solid hardwoods glued together in a cross-ply process.

Premier then applies a tongue and groove interlocking system and the Flexform milling process of tension relief grooves with computer aided manufacturing techniques. This results in the Level Lock end system, whereby ends are locked in position by the precision tongue and groove side construction. This combination dramatically improves

the floors ability to remain stable under normal seasonal humidity changes and to conform to irregular subfloors.

Premier floors with the patented Flexform milling system help eliminate the popping sound often encountered when hardwood floors bridge depressions in the subfloor.

Easy Care Everguard™ Finish

The Premier Everguard finish consists of multiple layers of tough, durable urethane resins cured by ultra-violet light between each layer. The result is a hard,

durable shell that forms a traffic-resistant shield and protects the wood from wear and spills. The Everguard finish resists most household spills and stains.

Maintenance is as simple as vacuuming and cleaning occasionally with Premier Spray-N-Wipe™.

How to Specify Premier Wood Floors:

A. Premier products are designed for residential and light commercial use.

B. Flooring shall be Premier (specify name, size and/or width) strip, plank or parquet in the grade of (specify wood species) with a surface color/finish of (state color item number) as manufactured by Premier Wood Floors, a division of Triangle Pacific Corporation.

C. Factory finished engineered strip or plank and solid strip or parquet shall be sanded for a smooth finish and have an ultra-violet cured urethane finish.

D. Installation must be made in accordance with the installation instruction sheets provided in each carton.

E. Installation of 3/8", 3-ply products can be glued using properly recommended tools or stapled using the Senco® SLS20HF Stapler over wood and wood substrates.

F. Use Premier Adhesive for glue-down installation. Premier Adhesive can be used for all 3/8" strip, plank and 5/16" parquet.

G. Trowel for spreading Premier Adhesive shall be notched as required by Premier Wood Floors.

H. Nailing machines: 2" barbed fasteners or approved staples should be used for installing Premier 3/4" strip flooring as required by Premier Wood Floors.

I. For additional product information, please call **1-800-588-1707** or visit our website at www.premierwoodfloors.com.

PREMIER
W O O D F L O O R S

A division of Triangle Pacific Corp.

16803 Dallas Parkway, Dallas, TX 75248

Sweet's brochure # PRMSWT ©1998,1997 Premier™ Wood Floors
a division of Triangle Pacific Corp. Printed in U.S.A. 8/98

Bruce® Laminate Floors

A division of Triangle Pacific Corp.

TRAFFIC ZONE®

High-Performance FLOORS

Superior Performance

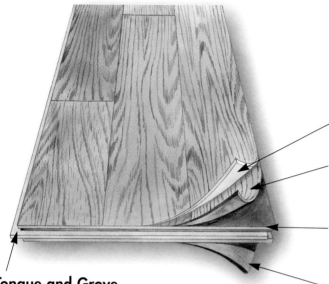

Description

Traffic Zone® high-performance laminate floors are precision engineered in a 4-ply construction that is fused together under tremendous heat and pressure to form a single plank of unprecedented strength and durability.

Crystal-Guard™ Finish
A durable wear and stain resistant finish with superior resilience.

Image Design Paper Layer
Product patterns are printed on this layer in various styles including wood, stone and contemporary designs.

Magnum HDF™ Core
A moisture resistant, high-density fiberboard core that maintains the structural integrity of each precision engineered plank.

Moisture Guard Backer
Seals the bottom of each plank for additional stability and moisture protection.

Tongue and Grove
Precision-milled to be solid and secure...generating a tightness of fit that helps keep the floor flat, dimensionally stable, and prevents peaking.

Installation

Installation Type: Floating Floor Suspension System. Traffic Zone products are glued to each other, not directly to the floor.

Subfloor: Must be smooth, clean, level, dry and structurally sound.

Level: Subfloor surface should be level within 3/16" per ten foot span.

Grade: Install on, above and/or below ground level.

Surfaces: Old floor coverings (except carpet), concrete, metal, wood and radiant heated surfaces (operating below 85° F).

Underlayment: ComfortGuard™ open cell foam with poly moisture barrier.

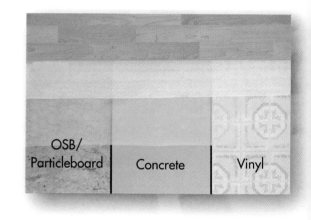

OSB/Particleboard | Concrete | Vinyl

Traffic/Wear Resistant

Pet Resistant

Fade Resistant

Allergy Aid

Stain Resistant

Burn Resistant

Scrub Resistant

Ecologically Friendly

Creative Combinations

▲ Pearl, Forest, Indigo and Cranberry Planks

Mountain Oak/Chestnut Plank with Adobe/Spanish Clay Tile Accents

Create your very own custom-designed, color-coordinated, floor fashion with Traffic Zone Tiles, Planks, Blocks, and Designer Feature Squares. By combining the wood, marble, stone, and abstract patterns, you can create a look and style that's custom-matched to your decor. Here are a few imaginative examples.

How to Specify Traffic Zone High-Performance Laminate Floors

A. Flooring shall be Bruce (state name, pattern and/or size) plank, block, tile or designer feature square as manufactured for Bruce Laminate Floors, a division of Triangle Pacific Corp.

B. Factory-finished laminate planks, blocks, tiles or designer feature squares shall have a Crystal-Guard™ finish constructed of aluminum oxide crystals set into a cellulosic web and fused with a melamine thermosetting resin.

C. Installation must be made in accordance with the installation instruction sheets provided in each carton.

D. Adhesive for joining planks, blocks, tiles or designer feature squares shall be Bruce Ever-Seal™ adhesive utilizing the top-of-tongue adhesive system as required by Bruce Laminate Floors.

E. Underlayment shall be Bruce ComfortGuard™ which includes a poly moisture barrier lining one side as required by Bruce Laminate Floors.

3

Care and Maintenance

Traffic Zone floors feature a no-wax Crystal-Guard™ finish that delivers exceptional stain resistance and easy care. Routine vacuuming will easily remove surface dust and dirt. Over time, grit and grime build-up will require an occasional cleaning. Using specially formulated Bruce® No-Wax Floor Cleaner, it is easy to wipe the floor clean to restore a "like-new" look. For really tough spots like tar, shoe polish, and most burn marks, nail polish remover will quickly and easily remove any marks.

The most stubborn stains wipe harmlessly off the Crystal-Guard™ finish.

Easy care starts with simple vacuuming to remove loose dirt and debris.

Easy care ends with an occasional wipe-over with Bruce No-Wax Floor Cleaner.

▲ Merbau Plank

▼ Hartford Maple/Natural Plar

Planks

Only Bruce could capture the true wood-grain beauty and richness
of natural hardwoods in a laminate floor. With a variety of
twenty-seven designer colors, Bruce's wood-patterned,
laminate Planks can complement the creativity of
any interior design.

Product Dimensions: 5/16" x 7 5/8" x 50 5/8"
(8 mm x 19.4 cm x 128.6 cm)

Red Oak/Natural #Z00331	Red Oak/Honey #Z00332	Red Oak/Chestnut #Z00333
Maple #Z00325	Summer Maple #Z00335	Hartford Maple/Natural #Z00360
Mountain Oak/Chestnut #Z00162	Mountain Oak/Natural #Z00161	Merbau #Z00363
Beech #Z00324	Alder #Z00126	Antique Birch #Z00130
Indigo #Z00344	Pearl #Z00346	Forest #Z00343
Birch #Z00128	Apple #Z00238	Autumn Maple #Z00334
Natural Cherry #Z00336	Royal Cherry #Z00337	Cherry #Z00327
Autumn #Z00347	Pine #Z00222	Marble #Z02102
Cranberry #Z00342	Gray #Z00345	White Oak #Z00339

5

▲ Toledo Fontana Color with Toledo Rossa as an Accent

Tiles

Add a new dimension to your favorite room with this imaginative collection of striking colors and distinctive patterns presented in Tiles. Elegantly etched stone, marble, and granite reproductions display a texture and richness inspired by nature.

Product Dimensions: 5/16" x 15 3/16" x 15 3/16" (8 mm x 38.6 cm x 38.6 cm)

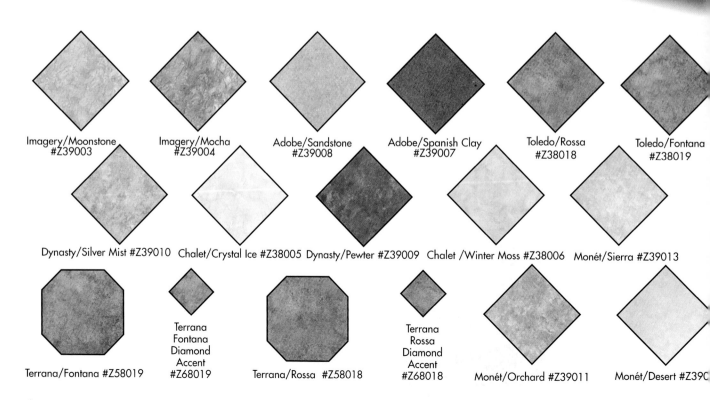

Imagery/Moonstone #Z39003

Imagery/Mocha #Z39004

Adobe/Sandstone #Z39008

Adobe/Spanish Clay #Z39007

Toledo/Rossa #Z38018

Toledo/Fontana #Z38019

Dynasty/Silver Mist #Z39010

Chalet/Crystal Ice #Z38005

Dynasty/Pewter #Z39009

Chalet /Winter Moss #Z38006

Monét/Sierra #Z39013

Terrana/Fontana #Z58019

Terrana Fontana Diamond Accent #Z68019

Terrana/Rossa #Z58018

Terrana Rossa Diamond Accent #Z68018

Monét/Orchard #Z39011

Monét/Desert #Z390

Blocks

Traffic Zone Blocks create bold patterns of slate, ceramic and marble, and can be combined with other Traffic Zone products for custom patterns.

Product Dimensions:
5/16" x 15 3/16" x 25 1/4"
(8 mm x 38.6 cm x 64.1 cm)

ress/Sunset #Z48016

Empress/Nordic #Z48015

ara/Fossil White #Z48014

Imperial Slate/Brushed Beige #Z48017

▲ Empress/Sunset Block

Designer Feature
Squares

Add a splash of color and design creativity to your Traffic Zone floors with these stylish Designer Feature Squares. These versatile Squares can be used together with Blocks, Tiles, and Planks to create eyecatching color accents!

Product Dimensions:
5/16" x 7 5/8" x 7 5/8"
(8 mm x 19.4 cm x 19.4 cm)

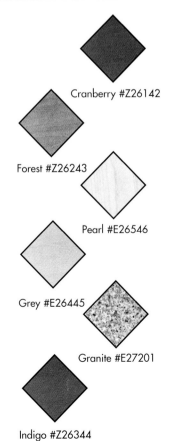

Cranberry #Z26142

Forest #Z26243

Pearl #E26546

Grey #E26445

Granite #E27201

Indigo #Z26344

◀ Indigo/Pearl
Designer Feature Squares

CARNIVAL™ Value Priced Laminate Flooring

Carnival floors are crafted with all the features and benefits that make laminate floors so popular with today's homeowners.

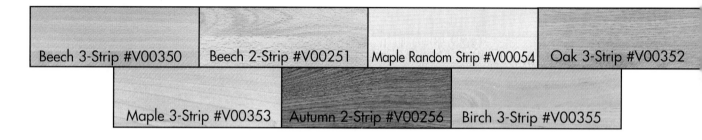

Beech 3-Strip #V00350 | Beech 2-Strip #V00251 | Maple Random Strip #V00054 | Oak 3-Strip #V00352

Maple 3-Strip #V00353 | Autumn 2-Strip #V00256 | Birch 3-Strip #V00355

- Easy Care, No-Wax Finish
- 7000 Cycles
- Fiberboard Core
- 9/32" thick (7 mm)
- Moisture Guard Bottom Layer

- 10-Year Finish Warranty
- 10-Year Fade Resistance Warranty
- 10-Year Stain Resistance Warranty
- Lifetime Structural Warranty

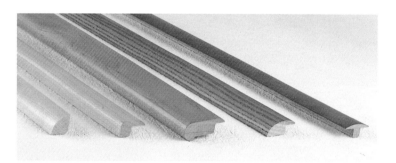

Finishing Touches

The Traffic Zone flooring system includes color-coordinated wood trim and molding products to add the perfect finishing touch to any installation

 # A Warranty You Can Trust

- *FULL Lifetime Structural Warranty **
- *FULL 15-Year Commercial Fade & Stain Warranty*
- *FULL 5-Year Commercial Wear Warranty*

- *FULL 15-Year Residential Wear Warranty*
- *FULL 15-Year Residential Fade-Resistance Warranty*
- *FULL 15-Year Residential Stain-Resistance Warranty*

*For comprehensive warranty information, ask your retailer for a copy of the Traffic Zone Buyer Protection Brochure.

For additional information or the name of your local Bruce distributor or dealer, please call toll free: **1-800-722-4647**. Visit our website at **www.brucelaminatefloors.com**

 **Bruce**® Laminate Floors

A division of Triangle Pacific Co.

Formica Ligna® wood surfacing

Formica® brand laminate

Formica®

Brand Products

Formica DecoMetal® collection

**From the introduction
of the first high pressure laminate
to today's dazzling array
of surfacing material collections,
Formica Corporation has led the way
for more than eight decades
with surfacing materials for
the places where we live and work.**

Formica Surell® solid surfacing material

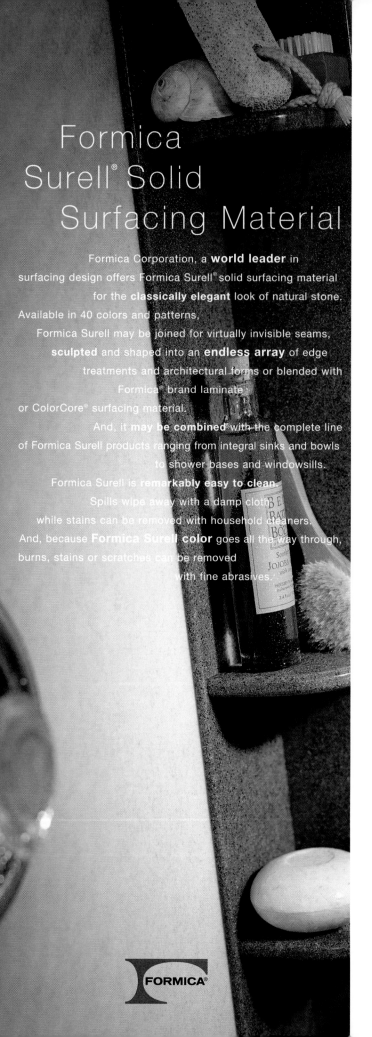

Formica Surell® Solid Surfacing Material

Formica Corporation, a **world leader** in surfacing design offers Formica Surell® solid surfacing material for the **classically elegant** look of natural stone. Available in 40 colors and patterns, Formica Surell may be joined for virtually invisible seams, **sculpted** and shaped into an **endless array** of edge treatments and architectural forms or blended with Formica® brand laminate or ColorCore® surfacing material. And, it **may be combined** with the complete line of Formica Surell products ranging from integral sinks and bowls to shower bases and windowsills. Formica Surell is **remarkably easy to clean.** Spills wipe away with a damp cloth while stains can be removed with household cleaners. And, because **Formica Surell color** goes all the way through, burns, stains or scratches can be removed with fine abrasives.

TECHNICAL DATA

Formica Surell® solid surfacing material is a solid homogeneous material suitable for many functional and decorative applications. It is a fully densified composite of modified resin and mineral filler. The product is available in the following forms:

- Sheet stock in ¼" (6.4mm), ½" (12.7mm), ¾" (19.1mm) and 1" (25.4mm) (factory order only)
- Kitchen sinks, single and double bowl designs
- Lavatory bowls, universal designs (ADA specification and water conservation)
- Vanity tops with integral bowl and backsplash
- Shower bases and shower walls with optional recessed soap dish
- Bathtubs and bath walls with optional recessed soap dish
- Edge strips and windowsills
- Laboratory sink
- Utility/bath sink

Formica Surell solid surfacing material is ideally suited for domestic use in the kitchen and bathroom. It is also widely specified for a full range of uses in offices, banks, restaurants, hospitals and other commercial applications. It has:

- Excellent heat resistance
- Full renewability
- Can be finished to a matte, satin or polished surface
- Inconspicuous seams
- Standard class 1(A) Flame/smoke rating
- Listed by the National Sanitation Foundation (NSF) for use in commercial and residential food service areas
- New York State for fire gas toxicity (value = 74g)
- HUD Bulletin UM-73a
- New York City MEA 190-90M
- Sinks and bowls certified by CSA

HOW TO SPECIFY

Solid surfacing material shall be Formica Surell® solid surfacing material provided by Formica Corporation, Cincinnati, OH. To order, please specify the following information:

Sheet Stock

Thickness	Width
Color	Length

Edge Strip/Windowsill

Color	Width
Thickness	Length

Lavatory Bowl

Model No.	Color
Size	

Kitchen Sink/Utility Sink

Model No.	Color
Size	

Vanity Top

Size	Bowl Position
End Splash	No. of Bowls
Color	

Shower Base

Model No.	Color
Size	

Shower Wall Surrounds

Model No.	Color

Bathtub

Model No.	Color
Size	

Bath Wall Surrounds

Size	Color

PRODUCT AVAILABILITY CHART

Consult this chart for available colors, patterns and forms.

	Almondine	Arctic	Frost	Greystone	Peach	Sail White	Sand	Silk	Berrydust	Cobalt	Firestone	Graphite	Moonlight	Mossdust	Peachdust	Pepperdust	Pinedust	Rockyrose	Sandstorm	Silverado	Teal	Tidal Sand	Winterhaze	Cayenne	Dawn Mist	Ginger Root	Night Mist	Periwinkle Mist	Pesto	Sandy Mist	Spanish Paprika	Spruce Mist	Carnival	Confetti White	Glacier Ore	Starry Night	Tornado	Constellation	Basilica	Black Lava
SHEETS																																								
1/4" Sheets	■	■	■				■	■		■		■	■		■		■	■	■	■	■	■	■		■					■		■								
1/2" Sheets	■	■	■	■	■	■	■	■	■	■	■	■	■	■	■	■	■	■	■	■	■	■	■	■	■	■	■	■	■	■	■	■	■	■	■	■	■	*	*	*
Edge Strips	■	■	■	■	■	■	■	■	■	■	■	■	■	■	■	■	■	■	■	■	■	■	■	■	■	■	■	■	■	■	■	■	■	■	■	■	■	■	■	■
KITCHEN SINKS																																								
K104, KS21, KS25	■	■	■			■	■	■																																
All Other Kitchen Sinks		■	■																																					
LAVATORY BOWLS																																								
VTUM	■	■	■	■	■	■	■	■			■	■	■		■			■		■		■	■											■						
VTA 2, 3, 4		■	■																																					
VANITIES																																								
Vanities		■	■																																					
End Splashes		■	■																																					
SHOWERS/BATHTUBS**																																								
Shower Bases		■	■																																					
Shower Surrounds		■	■										■		■		■			■					■					■										
Bathtub Surrounds		■	■										■		■		■			■					■					■										
5' & 6' Bathtubs		■	■																																					
Soap Dishes		■	■																																					
Small Coves		■	■										■		■		■			■					■					■										
Large Coves																																								
Overlay Panels		■	■										■		■		■			■					■					■										

Solid Collection — Almondine … Silk
Granite Collection — Berrydust … Winterhaze
Mist Collection — Cayenne … Spruce Mist
Revolution® Collection — Carnival … Tornado
Innovation™ Collection — Constellation … Black Lava

*30" x 144"(76cm x 366cm) only   **individual components and kits

For detailed specification and product information, refer to SweetSource, the CD-ROM version of the *Sweets Catalog*.

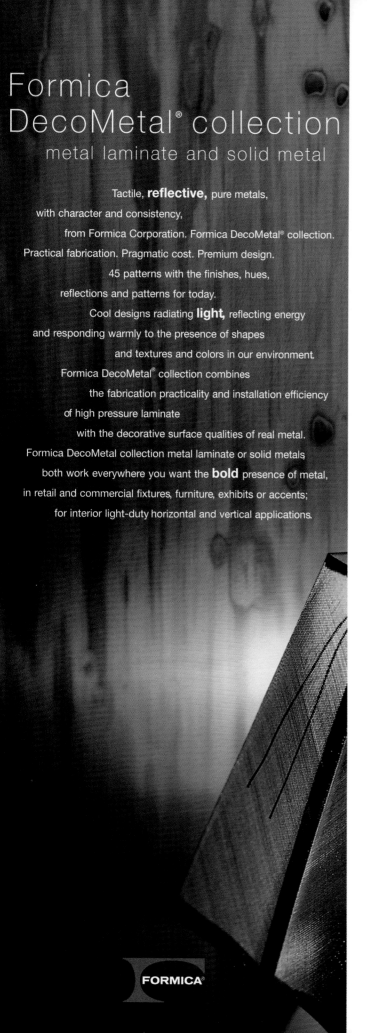

Formica
DecoMetal® collection
metal laminate and solid metal

Tactile, **reflective,** pure metals,

with character and consistency,

from Formica Corporation. Formica DecoMetal® collection.

Practical fabrication. Pragmatic cost. Premium design.

45 patterns with the finishes, hues,

reflections and patterns for today.

Cool designs radiating **light,** reflecting energy

and responding warmly to the presence of shapes

and textures and colors in our environment.

Formica DecoMetal® collection combines

the fabrication practicality and installation efficiency

of high pressure laminate

with the decorative surface qualities of real metal.

Formica DecoMetal collection metal laminate or solid metals

both work everywhere you want the **bold** presence of metal,

in retail and commercial fixtures, furniture, exhibits or accents;

for interior light-duty horizontal and vertical applications.

FORMICA®

TECHNICAL DATA

Recommended Application Formica DecoMetal® collection includes real metal foil laminated to a phenolic core or solid metal with no backer. Metal laminate is suitable for interior light-duty horizontal or vertical applications such as furniture, exhibits, accents, etc., where the bold look and design of metal are required.

Surface Finishes Aluminum surface laminate (brushed, cross-brushed, finematte, satin and embossed) has an epoxy coated aluminum surface and, depending on the design, is available in natural, goldtone, coppertone, bronzetone, and steeltone.

Polished aluminum surface laminate has an anodized aluminum surface available in natural, goldtone, coppertone, and smoky gray, in plain or embossed design.

Copper surface laminate has a polyurethane resin-coated copper surface and, depending on the design, is available in plain, embossed, natural, patina, and antique appearance.

Stainless steel surface laminate has a real stainless steel surface available in a brushed design.

HOW TO SPECIFY

Surface shall be DecoMetal® collection metal laminate or DecoMetal® collection solid metal from Formica Corporation, Cincinnati, Ohio.

Color Number
Color Name
Grade
Size

For detailed specification and product information, refer to SweetSource, the CD-ROM version of the *Sweets Catalog.*

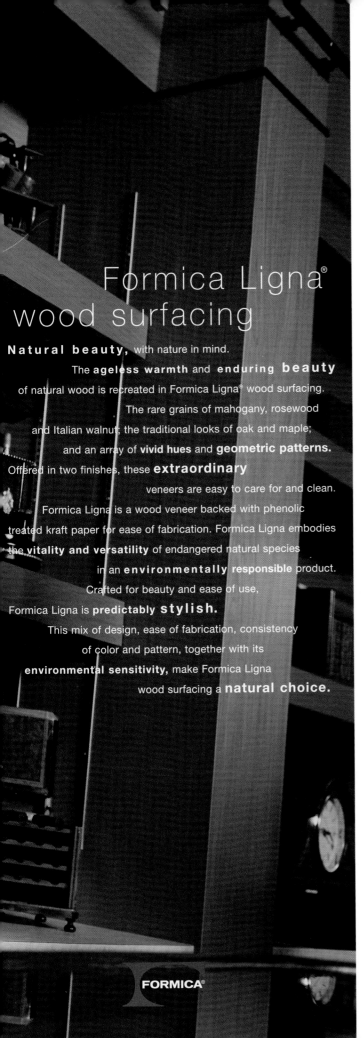

Formica Ligna® wood surfacing

Natural beauty, with nature in mind.

The **ageless warmth** and **enduring beauty** of natural wood is recreated in Formica Ligna® wood surfacing.

The rare grains of mahogany, rosewood and Italian walnut; the traditional looks of oak and maple; and an array of **vivid hues** and **geometric patterns.** Offered in two finishes, these **extraordinary** veneers are easy to care for and clean.

Formica Ligna is a wood veneer backed with phenolic treated kraft paper for ease of fabrication. Formica Ligna embodies the **vitality and versatility** of endangered natural species in an **environmentally responsible** product.

Crafted for beauty and ease of use, Formica Ligna is **predictably stylish.**

This mix of design, ease of fabrication, consistency of color and pattern, together with its **environmental sensitivity,** make Formica Ligna wood surfacing a **natural choice.**

FORMICA®

TECHNICAL DATA

Recommended Application Formica Ligna® wood surfacing is real wood laminated to a phenolic core. Formica Ligna combines the beauty of natural wood with exotic designs and more consistent quality and ease of use than wood veneers, while demonstrating sensitivity to the environment. Formica Ligna is made from real wood veneer; consequently slight color and pattern variation may occur and does not indicate a product defect. As with natural wood, exposure to direct sunlight can produce color change. Any slight change in color over time does not indicate a product defect.

Formica Ligna Surfaces:

• Unfinished surface is intended for application to dry interior, light-duty horizontal or vertical surfaces where design, appearance and quality are required. Surface properties are dependent on the finish applied by the fabricator. Do not leave the surface unfinished.

• Polyurethane surface is intended for application to dry interior, light-duty horizontal or vertical surfaces where design, appearance, quality and resistance to stain and heat from ordinary sources are required. Formica Ligna is not recommended for kitchen countertop use.

Grades:

• Postformable (ALP) grade is heat formable to a 180 wrap on ¾" core of MDF or particle board. Thickness of ALP grade is .027"

• Non-forming (ALN) grade is thicker (.050") and more appropriate for wall applications, reception areas, and light-duty horizontal applications (conference tables, accent furniture).

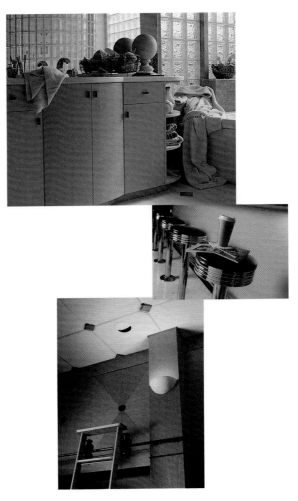

For detailed product information, refer to SweetSource, the CD-ROM version of the *Sweets Catalog.*

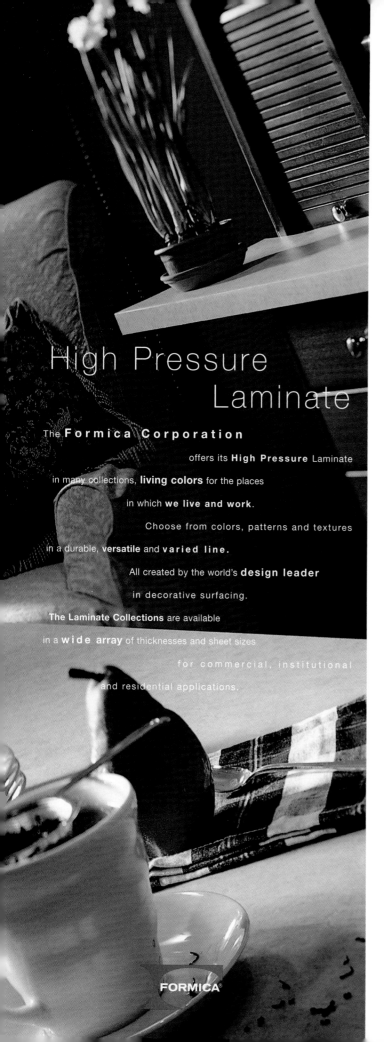

High Pressure
Laminate

The **Formica Corporation**

offers its **High Pressure** Laminate

in many collections, **living colors** for the places

in which **we live and work**.

Choose from colors, patterns and textures

in a durable, **versatile** and **varied line**.

All created by the world's **design leader**

in decorative surfacing.

The Laminate Collections are available

in a **wide array** of thicknesses and sheet sizes

for commercial, institutional

and residential applications.

FORMICA

FORMICA® BRAND LAMINATE

For more than 80 years, Formica® brand laminate has served the places where we live and work. As sparkling countertops and cabinet facings. As durable furniture and work surfaces in offices, hospitals and laboratories. And as inviting displays, counters and tabletops in shops and restaurants. Created with melamine-impregnated decorative paper bonded to a phenolic treated kraft paper backing, Formica brand laminate offers a distinctive combination of economy, versatility and trend-leading design.

- Unparalleled choice of solids, patterns, woodgrains and pearlescents.
- Matte, polished and textured finishes.
- Postforming grades ranging from ⅜" to ½" minimum radius.
- Fire-rated, lab, flooring grades and NSF approved.

FORMICA CHEMTOP™

Formica Chemtop™ laminate is resistant to chemicals, stains, impact and heat. It also meets the ISO and NEMA standards. Available in 20 colors. All are post-formable and easy to fabricate, install and maintain.

LAB GRADE LAMINATE

Both chemical- and stain-resistant, Formica® brand Lab Grade is designed for laboratories, hospitals and other environments where potentially destructive elements and solutions are common. Lab Grade is postformable and meets the International Standards Organization and National Electrical Manufacturers Association performance standards. Lab Grade is available in matte black only.

FIRE RATED LAMINATE

Formica® brand Fire Rated Laminate meets Class 1(A) flame spread ratings and is available in a selection of solid colors, patterns and woodgrains. It is listed by Underwriters Laboratory Inc., and meets the following standards:

FAA Part 25.853 (A&B) Noncommercial aircraft
U.S. Coast Guard, Subpart 164.012
MIL-P-17171 E (SH), Type IV
MIL-STD-1623 D (SH)
Canadian Reference: ULC Classification as per
ASTM #84 (ULC 723) and NFPA 255.

With two grades suitable for general purpose, non-postforming applications, this laminate is ideal for most military and marine applications.

THICK STOCK LAMINATE

Formica® brand Thick Stock laminate is available in thicknesses up to 1". Its exceptional strength allows the product to be used as a structural material. Uses include toilet partitions, lockers, furniture, countertops, transportation panels, doors, play equipment and other assemblies requiring high strength and resistance to impact, water and humidity. Available with decorative surface on one side, both sides, or no sides, Thick Stock can be drilled, sanded, shaped and cut with standard carbide-tipped tools.

BACKING SHEETS AND CABINET LINERS

Formica® brand Backing Sheets and Cabinet Liner sheets provide balancing and moisture control for utilitarian surfaces. Available in two grades and a wide variety of sizes, the undecorated phenolic backing sheets have a flat, dark brown finish. Cabinet liners are available in four colors and two sizes, all with a flat, non-decorative finish suitable for cabinet interiors.

COLORCORE® SURFACING MATERIAL

Featuring the high-performance characteristics of standard laminate, ColorCore® surfacing material brings you the added dimension of solid-through color. Available in 18 solid colors in matte finish and black and white in polished finish, ColorCore eliminates the familiar dark edge of standard laminate, creating a sense of mass versus surface.

- Matte and polished finishes with matte appropriate for general purpose applications and polished for vertical and light-duty horizontal applications.
- Concealed seams.

GRADE SELECTION GUIDE

Consult this chart to determine the recommended grades for typical applications.

	Horizontal										Vertical					
	General Purpose				General Purpose Postform		Fire Rated	Backing Sheet		Lab Grade	General Purpose	General Purpose Postform	Fire Rated	Cabinet Liner	Backing Sheet	
NEMA	HGS	HCS	HCS	HGS	HGP	HGP	HGF	BGF	BGS	LGP	VGP	VGP	VGP	CLS	BLF	BLS
Formica Brand Product/Grade	Grade 10	Grade 41	Grade 43	Grade 51	Grade 12	Grade 52	Grade 50	Grade 89	Grade 92	Grade 12	Grade 20	Grade 30	Grade 32	Grade 72	Grade 87	Grade 91
	●	●	○	○	○	○		○	○	●	○	●	○	○	○	
Nominal Thickness	.048" (1.2mm)	.051" (1.3mm)	.062" (1.6mm)	.050" (1.2mm)	.038" (1.0mm)	.039" (1.0mm)	.048" (1.2mm)	.048" (1.2mm)	.048" (1.2mm)	.038" (1.0mm)	.028" (0.7mm)	.039" (1.0mm)	.032" (0.8mm)	.020" (0.5mm)	.028" (0.7mm)	.020" (0.5mm)
Commercial Work Surfaces Teller Stations — Conference Tables — Restaurant Tables Nurses Stations — Desks — Bar Tops	●	●		○	○	○			○							○
Commercial Cabinetry and Furniture Store Fixtures — Dormitory Furniture — Bookcases Library Equipment — Study Carrels — Column Covers	●	●	○	○	○	○		○	○		○	○	○	○	○	
Commercial Doors and Partitions Interior Passage Doors — Toilet Compartments Elevator Cabs — Moveable Partitions	●	●	○	○	○	○	○									
Residential Work Surfaces Kitchen Countertops — Bar Tops Vanity Tops — Windowsills	●	●		○	○	○	○									
Residential Cabinetry and Furniture Kitchen Cabinets — Occasional Furniture — Case Goods Tables — Bookcases	●	●	○	○	○	○			○		○	●		○		○
Laboratory Work Surfaces										●						

How to specify Formica® Brand Laminate

PART I – GENERAL

Contractor shall supply and install high pressure laminate as shown on drawings and specified herein.

1.1 Product Delivery and Storage High pressure laminate to be stored with top face-down and a caul board on top to protect material from damage and from warping. Laminate to be protected from moisture and from contact with floors or outside walls.

1.2 Preconditioning Laminate and substrate to acclimate for at least 48 hours at same ambient condition. Optimum conditions being approximately 75°F and relative humidity of 45 to 55%. Air circulation to be provided around product.

PART II – PRODUCTS

2.2 High Pressure Laminate High pressure laminate should be Formica brand laminate from Formica Corporation, Cincinnati, Ohio.

PL-1 Color Number	PL-2 Color Number
Color Name	Color Name
Grade (Name/Number)	Grade (Name/Number)
Finish (Name/Number)	Finish (Name/Number)

2.2 Adhesives (for standard and postforming grade laminates) Contact, semi-rigid (PVAc) or rigid (Urea, Resorcinol) adhesives are recommended. Fabricator to follow adhesive manufacturer's recommendations.

2.3 Adhesives (ColorCore® surfacing material) Semi-rigid (PVAc) or non-pigmented contact adhesives are recommended. Fabricator to follow adhesive manufacturer's recommendations.

2.4 Substrates Laminate to be bonded to a suitable substrate such as medium-density fiber board (MDF) or a 45# density particle board (CS 236-66; Type 1,

Grade B, Class 2). The following materials are not recommended for use: plywood, plaster, gypsum board, concrete. Maximum panel widths to be 24" for Grade 20.

2.5 Backing Sheets Backing sheets to be provided as necessary to balance assembly and prevent warping.

PL-1 Color Number	Grade (Name/Number)
Color Name	

PART III – EXECUTION

3.1 Inspection All surfaces to be laminated are to be inspected to determine if they are sound, clean and free of surface defects. All defects found are to be corrected.

3.2 Preparation Surfaces to be sanded and prepared as required to provide a surface that is smooth, clean, free of oil or grease and uniform in thickness.

3.3 Installation

A. Material equipment and workmanship should conform to industry-standard practices, conditions, procedures and recommendations as specified by ANSI/NEMA LD3-1995 Section 4, Architectural Woodwork Quality Standards.

B. Panel assemblies should be laminated with suitable backer sheets to minimize warping.

C. Maximum panel widths to be 24" for Grade 20.

D. All inside corners of cutouts to be radiused as large as possible (⅛" minimum). All edges and corners to be filed smooth, free of chips and nicks. Surface shall be Formica brand laminate, manufactured by Formica Corporation.

PL-1 Color Number	Grade (Name/Number)
Color Name	Finish (Name/Number)

Choose from the Complete Line of Formica® Brand Decorative Surfacing

For information about Formica® brand high pressure laminate, DecoMetal® collection metal laminate and solid metal, Formica Ligna® wood surfacing, and Surell® solid surfacing material, refer to Sweets Catalog Code Number C477 06650/FOS Buyline 6819. For detailed information on all of our products, refer to **Formica Corporation** in SweetSource CD-ROM.

For Complete Information

Complete information on all Formica® brand decorative surfaces, including Surface Level, sample sets, fabrication guides, care and maintenance guides, warranty information and technical data available through our Zip Chip™ hotline. In the United States call, toll free, **1-800-FORMICA.™** In Canada, call 1-800-363-1405. In Mexico, call 525-530-3135. Or, contact your nearest Formica Corporation regional sales office.

Surell, Revolution, Formica Ligna, DecoMetal, Formica and the Formica Logo are registered trademarks of Formica Corporation or its subsidiaries. Innovation, Zip Chip and 1-800-FORMICA are trademarks of Formica Corporation or its subsidiaries.

REGIONAL OFFICES

CENTRAL

Formica Corporation
10155 Reading Road
Cincinnati OH 45241
513-786-3525 phone
513-786-3566 fax

EASTERN

Formica Corporation
476 Lincoln Blvd.
Middlesex NJ 08846
732-469-1559 phone
732-469-5917 fax

FLORIDA

Formica Corporation
5300 N. Powerline Rd.
Suite 1B
Fort Lauderdale FL 33309
954-489-9250 phone
954-489-9252 fax

MIDWEST

Formica Corporation
1400 East Touhy Avenue
Suite 430
Des Plaines IL 60018
847-390-9500 phone
847-390-9507 fax

NORTHEAST

Formica Corporation
131 Stedman St. #1
Chelmsford MA 01824
508-458-4666 phone
508-458-2999 fax

NORTHWEST

Formica Corporation
3500 Cincinnati Avenue
Sunset Whitney Ranch CA 95765
916-645-0390 phone
916-645-1577 fax

SOUTHERN

Formica Corporation
5525 Westfield Dr. SW
Atlanta GA 30336
404-349-9909 phone
404-349-2995 fax

SOUTHWEST

Formica Corporation
902 W. North Carrier Parkway
Grand Prairie TX 75050
972-623-4150 phone
972-623-4158 fax

WESTERN

Formica Corporation
2601 Saturn, Suite 103
Brea CA 92821
714-993-0393 phone
714-993-0182 fax

PUERTO RICO

Formica Corporation
Calle B, Lote 6
Amelia Industrial Park
Guaynabo PR 00968
787-793-1230 phone
787-793-6555 fax

EASTERN CANADA

Formica Canada, Inc.
25 rue Mercier
St. Jean sur Richelieu
Quebec, Canada J3B 6E9
514-347-7541 phone
514-347-5065 fax

CENTRAL CANADA

Formica Canada, Inc.
33 International Blvd.
Etobicoke, ON, Canada M9W 6H3
416-675-3747 phone
416-675-3803 fax

WESTERN CANADA

Formica Canada, Inc.
D-105, 19720-94A Avenue
Langley, B.C., Canada V3A 4P8
604-882-9494 phone
604-882-9495 fax

MEXICO

Formica de Mexico S.A. de C.V.
Viaducto Miguel Aleman No. 55
06780 **Mexico D.F.**
525-530-3135 phone
525-530-4248 fax

White River™

HARDWOODS·WOODWORKS, INC.

YOUR ONESOURCE FOR DECORATIVE HARDWOOD MOULDING

MON REALE™ - AN EXCLUSIVE SELECTION OF SCULPTURED HARDWOOD MOULDING

ORNAMENTALLY EMBOSSED • TRADITIONAL SMOOTH • EMBOSSED MDF

Curved Work Our Specialty

PAINT OR STAIN • LONG LENGTHS UP TO 16′ • EASY TO INSTALL

Manufactured in Fayetteville, Arkansas USA

Phone 501-442-6986 • www.mouldings.com • Fax 501-442-0257

AVAILABLE THROUGH DISTRIBUTION NATIONWIDE:

ALABAMA Georgia Flush (770) 819-2870 Millwork Sales (615) 256-3539 **ARKANSAS** Paxton (501) 565-5661
SO. CALIFORNIA Orepac (909) 627-4043 El & El (909) 591-0339 **NO. CALIFORNIA** Coastal Lumber-Straight Line Div. (916) 387-5193
Higgins 1-800-241-1883 **EA. CONNECTICUT** Rugby (508) 823-0404 **WE. CONNECTICUT** Rugby (860) 282-0818
DIST OF COLUMBIA Rawles Aden 1-800-446-1818 **GEORGIA** Georgia Flush (770) 819-2870 **HAWAII** Higgins 1-800-241-1883
SO. ILLINOIS Koetter (812) 923-8875 **NO. ILLINOIS** River City (815) 965-9439 Markwood Products (847) 428-8383
INDIANA Koetter (812) 923-8875 **NO. INDIANA** Hass (219) 287-1501 **KANSAS** Paxton (816) 483-5009
KENTUCKY Koetter (812) 923-8875 **LOUISIANA** River Side (504) 242-6624 Allen (318) 868-6541 **MAINE** Rugby (207) 283-0138
EA. MASSACHUSETTS Rugby (508) 823-0404 Lynn Lumber (617) 590-0400 **WE. MASSACHUSETTS** Rugby (860) 282-0818
MICHIGAN Jim Mackie Sales (313) 427-3810 **SO. WE. MICHIGAN** Hass (219) 287-1501 **MISSISSIPPI** Millwork Sales (601) 981-3667
MISSOURI Paxton (816) 483-5009 **NEVADA** Rugby 1-800-488-2322 Austin (702) 362-1633 Higgins 1-800-241-1883
NEW HAMPSHIRE Rugby (802) 763-8331 **NEW JERSEY** Black Millwork (201) 934-0100 A-1 Millwork (609) 767-5233 Bossen Arch. Millwork
(609) 786-1100 **SO. NEW JERSEY** A-1 Millwork (609) 767-5233 **NEW YORK** Black Millwork (201) 934-0100
Millwork Specialties (518) 463-1141 **NEW YORK CITY** Royal Doors (718) 243-2000 Black Millwork (201) 934-0100
NO. CAROLINA Jenkins 1-800-262-5972 **OHIO** B & B (216) 292-6555 Paxton (513) 984-8200
NO. EA. OKLAHOMA Mill Creek (918) 747-2000 **CENTRAL OKLAHOMA** General Builder's Supply (405) 947-7227
OREGON Woodcrafters (503) 231-0226 **PENNSYLVANIA** Adelman (412) 231-0770 A-1 Millwork (609) 767-5233
Bossen Arch. Millwork (609) 786-1100 **RHODE ISLAND** Rugby (508) 823-0404 **SO. CAROLINA** Jenkins 1-800-262-5972
TENNESSEE Millwork Sales (615) 256-3539 Koetter (812) 923-8875 **TEXAS** Texas Wholesale (972) 245-2907
Fisher Millwork (210) 698-3280 **UTAH** Moulding Specialties (801)887-7050 **VERMONT** Rugby (802) 763-8331
VIRGINIA Rawles Aden 1-800-446-1818 **WASHINGTON** Galco (253) 272-3366 **WE. VIRGINIA** Rawles Aden 1-800-446-1818
Koetter (812) 923-8875 **WISCONSIN** Builder's World (414) 542-8883 See Northern Illinois

ALL OTHER AREAS CALL 1-800-558-0119

CORNICE, CROWN & COVE MOULDINGS

Poplar in-stock • Red Oak denoted • UltraFlex for curved applications • Scale 1/4" = 1"

CR841 13/16" x 6 1/4"

CR850 3/4" x 2 3/4" OAK

CR860 13/16" x 7"

CR862 13/16" x 7" OAK

CO705 13/16" x 5 1/4"

CO707 3/4" x 3 1/2"

CO720 3/4" x 3/4" OAK

CO723 1/2" x 1 1/2"
(Fits cope on MB192)

CO730 7/8" x 1 1/2"

CR800 13/16" x 7" OAK

CM81 1 1/16" x 4 3/4"

CM82 1 1/16" x 5 7/8"

CM83 13/16" x 5 1/2" OAK

CM84 13/16" x 6 1/4"

CM69 3/4" x 2 3/4"

CM70 13/16" x 4 3/8"

CM71 13/16" x 4 1/2"

CM72 13/16" x 3 3/4" OAK

CM73 13/16" x 5 1/2" OAK

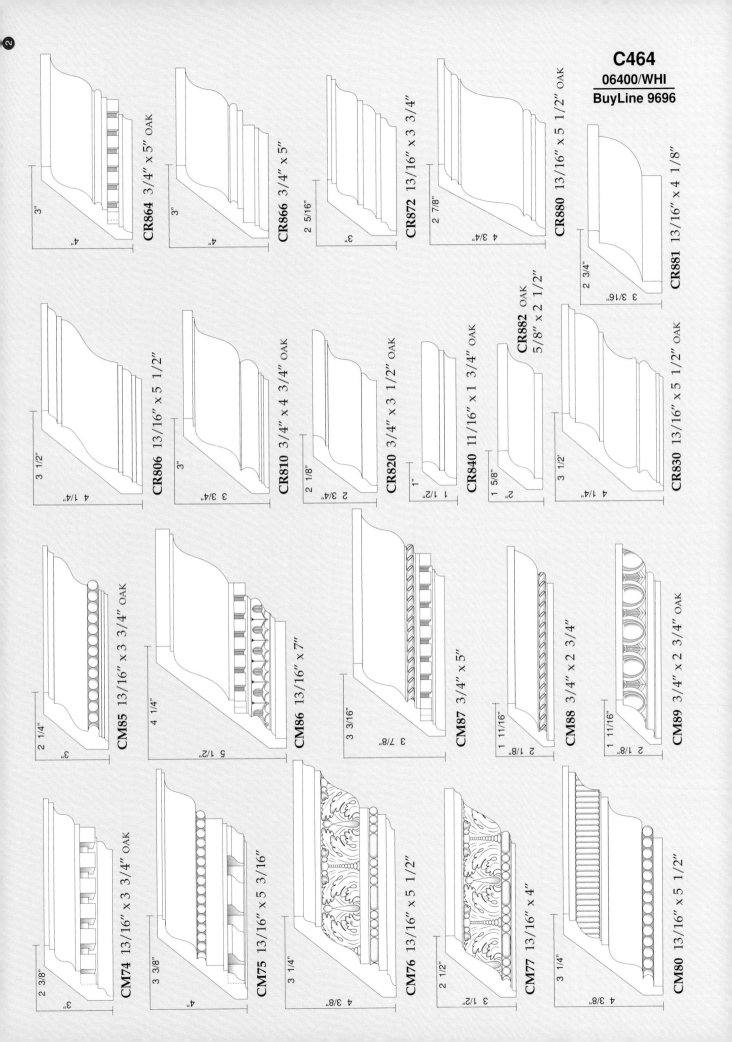

CR864 3/4" x 5" OAK

CR866 3/4" x 5"

CR872 13/16" x 3 3/4"

CR880 13/16" x 5 1/2" OAK

CR881 13/16" x 4 1/8"

CR806 13/16" x 5 1/2"

CR810 3/4" x 4 3/4" OAK

CR820 3/4" x 3 1/2" OAK

CR840 11/16" x 1 3/4" OAK

CR882 OAK
5/8" x 2 1/2"

CR830 13/16" x 5 1/2" OAK

CM85 13/16" x 3 3/4" OAK

CM86 13/16" x 7"

CM87 3/4" x 5"

CM88 3/4" x 2 3/4"

CM89 3/4" x 2 3/4" OAK

CM74 13/16" x 3 3/4" OAK

CM75 13/16" x 5 3/16"

CM76 13/16" x 5 1/2"

CM77 13/16" x 4"

CM80 13/16" x 5 1/2"

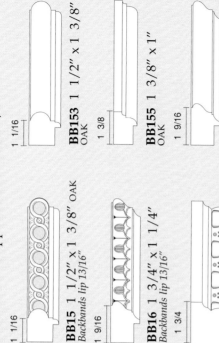

CASINGS & BACKBANDS

Poplar in-stock • Red Oak denoted • UltraFlex for curved applications • Scale 1/4" = 1"

BB153 1 1/2" x 1 3/8" OAK

BB155 1 3/8" x 1" OAK

BB156 1 3/4" x 1 1/4"

BB158 2 1/8" x 1 11/16" (lips 1 1/16")

CH689 1 3/4" x 2 1/2"

MM195 1 3/4" X 5 7/8"

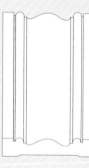

BB15 1 1/2" x 1 3/8" OAK *Backbands lip 13/16"*

BB16 1 3/4" x 1 1/4" *Backbands lip 13/16"*

BB17 1 3/4" x 2 1/2" *Backbands lip 13/16"*

BB18 1 5/8" x 1 1/4" *Backbands lip 13/16"*

CR68 1 3/4" x 2 1/2" *Backbands lip 13/16"*

MANTLE MOULDS

MM187 1 1/4" x 4 3/8"

CA356 11/16" x 2 1/4" OAK

CA360 13/16" x 3 1/2"

CA362 1 1/16" x 4 1/2"

CA363 13/16" x 3 1/4" OAK

CA364 13/16" x 3 1/2" OAK

CA323 3/4" x 4" OAK

CA324 3/4" x 4" OAK

CA325 3/4" x 6 1/2" OAK
CA325 can adapt to 5 1/2", 4 1/2", 3 1/2" width by jobsite modifications.

CA326 3/4" x 3 1/4" OAK

CA30 13/16" x 3 3/4"

CA31 13/16" x 4"

CA33 13/16" x 3 1/4" OAK

CA36 13/16" x 3 1/4" OAK

CA37 1 1/16" x 4"

DOOR HEADERS & TOP CAPS

TC140 1" x 2 1/8"
OAK

1 1/16"

TC150

DH190

TC150 1 3/4" x 2 1/4"
OAK
DH190 1 1/16" x 5 1/4"
OAK

TC120 1" x 2 1/8"
OAK

1 5/8"

TC150

DH99

TC150 1 3/4" x 2 1/4"
OAK
DH99 1 1/16" x 5 1/4"
OAK

MODILLION BLOCKS FOR CROWN APPLICATIONS

2 3/4"

2"

1 3/4"

MB191 1 3/4" x 2 3/4" x 2"
(Blocks are pre-cut to 2")

MB192
(front view)

3"

2"

3 1/4"

3"

MB189 1 3/4" x 2 3/4"
(Sold as lineal footage)

2 1/4"

MB192
(Sold as block with attached coved top.)

CO723 1/2" x 1 1/2"
*(Fits cope on MB192)
Order CO723 as
separate lineal footage.*

*Generally, Modillion Blocks
are placed 6" on center,
therefore ordered two blocks
per running foot.*

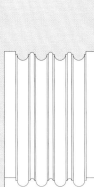

CA368 13/16" x 2 3/4" OAK

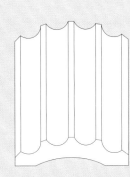

CA380 1 1/4" x 4"

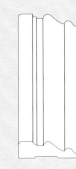

CA382 1 1/16" x 3 1/4"

CA388 1 1/16" x 4"

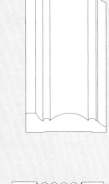

CA389 1 1/16" x 4 1/2"

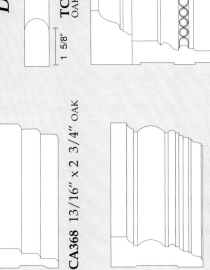

CA327 3/4" x 4" OAK

CA328 1 5/16" x 5 1/8"

CA335 13/16" x 2 1/2" OAK

CA342 13/16" x 3 1/2"

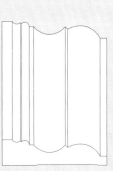

CA344 13/16" x 3 1/2" OAK

CA38 1 1/4" x 4"

CA39 13/16" x 3 1/2" OAK

CA300 13/16" x 3" OAK

CA302 13/16" x 4" OAK

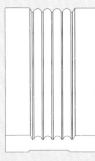

CA322 3/4" x 4"

BASE & CHAIRRAIL MOULDINGS
Poplar in-stock • Red Oak denoted • UltraFlex for curved applications • Scale 1/4" = 1"

DENTIL MOULDINGS

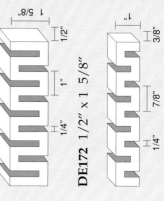
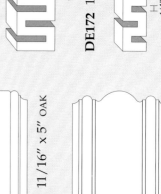

DE168 1/2" x 1/2" OAK

DE169 3/4" x 1" OAK

DE170 5/8" x 1 1/2" OAK

DE171 3/4" x 2" OAK

DE172 1/2" x 1 5/8"

DE173 3/8" x 1"

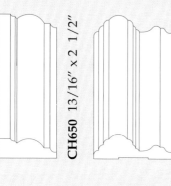

CH650 13/16" x 2 1/2"

CH659 1" x 3 1/2"

CH690 11/16" x 3" OAK

CH693 11/16" x 5" OAK

CA324 3/4" X 4" OAK

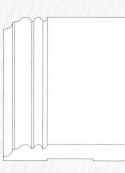

B469 11/16" x 5 1/2"

CHAIRRAIL MOULDINGS

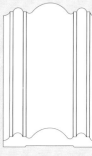

CR61 13/16" x 2 1/2"

CR63-A 1 1/16" x 3 1/4"

CR64 1 1/16" x 3"

CR65 13/16" x 2 1/2" OAK

B416 5/8" x 5"

B435 5/8" x 3 3/4" OAK

B444 9/16" x 3 1/4" OAK

B460 3/4" x 5" OAK

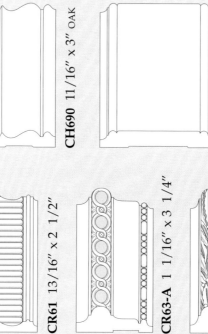

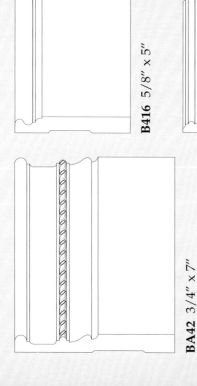

BA42 3/4" x 7"

BA43-C 3/4" x 5 1/2" OAK

BA44 with PM22-pl 3/4" x 7 3/4"
BA44 3/4" x 6
PM22-pl (lips 1/4") 11/16" x 1 3/4"

DOOR STOPS, BASE SHOES & CORNERS

 **DS100** 1/2" x 1 1/2" OAK

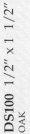 **DS110** 1/2" x 1 1/2" OAK

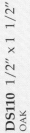 **DS111** 3/8" x 2"

 BS126 3/4" x 1/2" OAK

 QR105 3/4" x 3/4" OAK

LINEAL MOULDINGS

LM90 1 1/16" x 3 1/2" OAK
Pattern repeats every 6 3/8"

LM91 1 1/16" x 3 1/2"

LM92 1 1/16" x 3 1/2"

LM93 1 1/16" x 3 1/2"

*Our solid hardwood mouldings are all in-stock in Poplar in all patterns to paint or stain.
In-stock Red Oak mouldings are denoted.
All hardwood mouldings shipped unfinished.*

CR66 1" x 3 1/2"
Ribbon pattern repeats on center every 7 1/2"

CR67 13/16" x 2 1/8" OAK

CR68 1 3/4" x 2 1/2"

CR69 1 1/8" x 2 1/4"

CH610 3/4" x 3" OAK
(lips 1/2" - 3/4")

CH640 1 1/16" x 3"

B462 3/4" x 6"

B463 11/16" x 5 1/2" OAK

B464 3/4" x 6" OAK

B468 11/16" x 4 1/2" OAK

BA46 11/16" x 5 1/2" OAK

B400 5/8" x 4 1/2" OAK

B401 3/4" x 6" OAK

B403 3/4" x 5"

PANEL MOULDINGS • Poplar in-stock • Red Oak denoted • UltraFlex for curved applications • Scale 1/4" = 1"

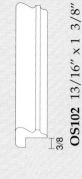 

RE104 9/16" x 1 5/8"

RE107 3/8" x 3/4"

OS101 13/16" x 13/16" OAK

OS102 13/16" x 1 3/8"

5/8

3/8

DIMENSIONAL HARDWOODS
In-Stock Poplar and Red Oak

DS1x2 3/4 x 2
DS1x4 3/4 x 3 1/2
DS1x6 3/4 x 5 1/2
DS1x8 3/4 x 7 1/4
DS1x10 3/4 x 9 1/4
DS1x12 3/4 x 11 1/4

CDS1x4 3/4 x 4
CDS1x6 3/4 x 6

JA458 3/4 x 4 5/8
JA658 3/4 x 6 5/8

 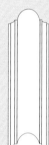      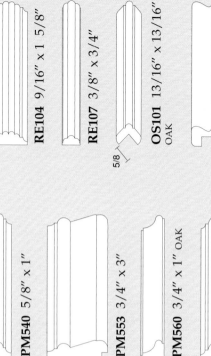    

PM540 5/8" x 1"

PM553 3/4" x 3"

PM560 3/4" x 1" OAK

PM561 3/4" x 3/4" OAK

PM569 3/4" x 1" OAK

PM570 3/4" x 2" OAK

PM577 3/4" x 2 3/8" OAK (lips 1/2" - 3/4")

PM580 3/4" x 1 3/4" OAK (lips 3/4")

PM582 3/4" x 1 3/8" (lips 3/4")

PM505 3/4" x 2" OAK (lips 1/2" - 3/4")

PM511 13/16" x 1 3/4" OAK

PM520 11/16" x 1 3/4" OAK (lips 1/4")

PM521 1" x 1 3/4" OAK

PM525 11/16" x 1 3/4" OAK

PM526 1 1/16" x 2 1/8" OAK

PM527 1 x 2 1/2"

       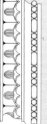 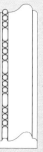

PM26 1 1/16" x 2 1/8"

PM27 3/4" x 2"

PM28 3/4" x 1 1/2"

PM29 1" x 1 1/2"

PM50 3/4" x 1 1/4" OAK

PM52 13/16" x 1 3/4" OAK

PM54 11/16" x 1 1/2"

PM55 13/16" x 1 1/4"

PM56-B 1/2" x 7/8"

PM07 5/8" x 1 1/8"

PM08 5/8" x 1 1/4"

PM09 5/8" x 1 1/4"

PM10 5/8" x 1 1/4" OAK

PM11 7/16" x 5/8"

PM12 5/8" x 1 1/8"

PM14 1/2" x 1" OAK

PM20 13/16" x 2"

PM22 11/16" x 1 3/4"

PM8536 1' x 2 3/4"
Repeats 2 5/8"

PM8540 5/8" x 1
Repeats 3/4"

PM8541 7/8" x 1 1/2"
Repeats 1 1/4"

PM8545 9/16" x 1"
Repeats 3/4"

PM8546 7/8" x 1 3/4"
Repeats 1 1/4"

PM8552 13/16" x 2"
Repeats 4 3/4"

PM8553 Repeats 8"
1 1/8" x 2 3/4"

PM595 5/8" x 3/4"
(See Friezes)

PM585 1/2" x 1"

PM586 3/4" x 1 1/2"

PM590 1 1/2" x 2 1/2"
OAK

PM593 1" x 1 1/4"

PM595 5/8" x 3/4"

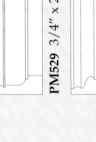

PM8532 Repeats 8"
1 1/8" x 2 3/4"

PM8535 Repeats 1 3/4"
3/4" x 1 1/2"

PM529 3/4" x 2" OAK

PM530 3/4" x 1 1/8"

PM535 5/8" x 1 1/4" OAK

PM537 1/2" x 1/2" OAK

PM538 1/4" x 1 1/2"

PM539 1/2" x 5/8" OAK

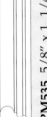

PM8528 5/8" x 1"
Repeats 2 3/8"

PM8529 7/8" x 1 1/2"
Repeats 5"

PM8531 13/16" x 2"
Repeats 3 1/2"

Mon Reale ™

Mon Reale is a fine-grained overlay, contoured to traditional hardwood mouldings. These sculptured designs will allow you to create a look of unsurpassed elegance. Poplar in-stock only. Ultra Flex for curved applications. Scale 1/4" = 1"

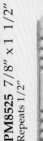

PM8525 7/8" x 1 1/2"
Repeats 1/2"

PM8526 9/16" x 1"
Repeats 2 3/8"

PM8527 7/8" x 1 3/4"
Repeats 5"

PM57 5/8" x 1 1/4"
(lips 1/4")

PM58 5/8" x 1"

PM59 5/8" x 3/4" OAK

PM70 3/4" x 2 3/8"
(lips 1/2" - 3/4")

PM500 5/8" x 2 1/4"
(lips 3/4")

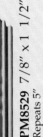

PM8522 9/16" x 1"
Repeats 1/4"

PM8523 7/8" x 1 3/4"
Repeats 1/2"

PM8524 Repeats 1/4"
5/8" x 1"

PM22-pl 11/16" x 1 3/4"
(lips 1/4")

PM23-B 3/4" x 2"

PM24 3/4" x 2"

PM25 1" x 2 1/2"

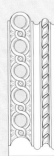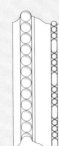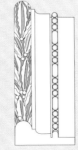

Panel Mouldings

PM8511 13/16" x 2"
Repeats 2 1/4"

PM8520 7/8" x 2"
Repeats 1"

Concerning our Friezes

MT indicates "Maximum Thickness" of moulding where overlay may be thicker than 13/16".

Backbands fit our Friezes and add width, depth and detail.

PM595 can be added to all Friezes to give them a symmetrical look.

CA8326 1 1/4" x 4 1/2"
Repeats 4 3/4"

CA8330 1 7/8' x 5" Repeats 8"

CA8336 1 7/8" x 5" Repeats 8"

FR8950 13/16" x 5 1/2" MT= 1 1/16"
Repeats 26"

FR8953 13/16" x 5 1/2" MT=1 1/8"
Repeats 7 1/2"

FR8956 13/16" x 5 1/2" MT=1"
Repeats 24"

*Frieze shown
with Backband*

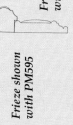

*Frieze shown
with PM595*

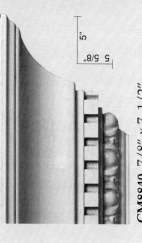

5 5/8" | 5"

CM8840 7/8" x 7 1/2"

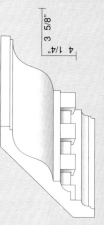

4 1/4" | 3 5/8"

CM8850 13/16" x 5 1/2"
Dentil is overlay

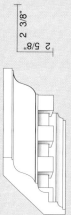

2 5/8" | 2 3/8"

CM8852 13/16" x 3 1/2"
Dentil is overlay

FRIEZES

FR8920 13/16" x 3 3/4" MT=3/4"
Repeats 7/8"

*Friezes are used with Crowns,
as Chairrails, Basecaps,
Casings and more.*

CORNICE MOULDINGS

4 3/4" | 3 3/4"

CM8801 7/8" x 6" Repeats 7"

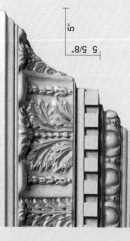

5 5/8" | 5"

CM8808 7/8" x 7 1/2" Repeats 7 1/2"

3 3/4" | 3"

CM8810 15/16" x 4 3/4"
Repeats 4 3/4"

4 7/8" | 3 3/4"

CM8812 1" x 6"

BACKBANDS

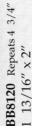

BB8110 Repeats 1"
1 13/16" x 1 1/2"

BB8111 Repeats 2 7/8"
1 3/4" x 2 1/2"

BB8120 Repeats 4 3/4"
1 13/16" x 2"

BB8121 Repeats 3 1/2"
1 13/16" x 2"

BB8122 Repeats 2 1/4"
1 13/16" x 2"

FR8960 13/16" x 5 1/2" MT=1"
Repeats 16"

FR8965 13/16" x 5 1/2" MT=7/8"
Repeats 11 1/2"

CASINGS

CA8320 1 1/4" x 4 1/2"
Repeats 2 1/4"

CA8322 1 1/16" x 4 1/2"
Repeats 1 1/4"

FR8921 13/16" x 3 3/4" MT=1"
Repeats 6 1/8"

FR8922 13/16" x 3 3/4" MT=1"
Repeats 2"

FR8923 13/16" x 3 3/4" MT=7/8"
Repeats 19"

FR8940 13/16" x 3 3/4" MT=7/8"
Repeats 12 1/2"

CM8820 13/16" x 2 3/4"
Pattern repeats 2 7/8"
1 3/4"
2 1/4"

CM8823 1" x 3 3/4"
Pattern repeats 3"
2 1/2"
3"

CM8825 1" x 7 1/2"
4 3/4"
5 7/8"

CM8830 7/8" x 6" Repeats 13 1/2"
3 3/4"
4 3/4"

CM8837 7/8" x 7"
5 1/4"
4 3/4"

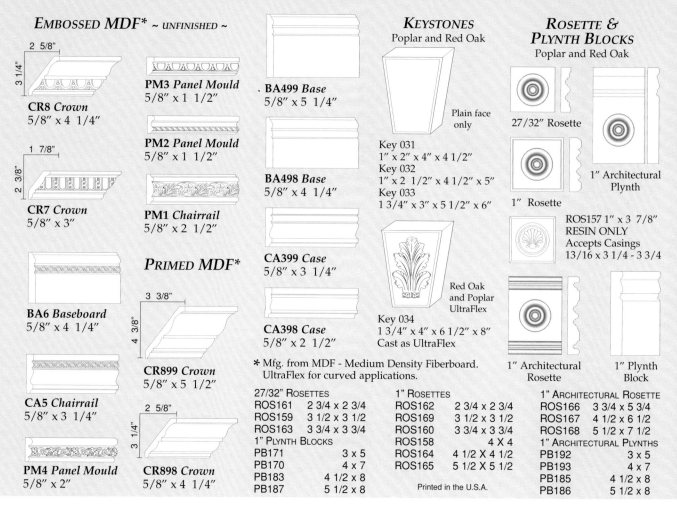

EMBOSSED MDF* ~ UNFINISHED ~

2 5/8"
3 1/4"
CR8 *Crown*
5/8" x 4 1/4"

PM3 *Panel Mould*
5/8" x 1 1/2"

PM2 *Panel Mould*
5/8" x 1 1/2"

1 7/8"
2 3/8"
CR7 *Crown*
5/8" x 3"

PM1 *Chairrail*
5/8" x 2 1/2"

BA6 *Baseboard*
5/8" x 4 1/4"

PRIMED MDF*

3 3/8"
4 3/8"
CR899 *Crown*
5/8" x 5 1/2"

CA5 *Chairrail*
5/8" x 3 1/4"

2 5/8"
3 1/4"
CR898 *Crown*
5/8" x 4 1/4"

PM4 *Panel Mould*
5/8" x 2"

BA499 *Base*
5/8" x 5 1/4"

BA498 *Base*
5/8" x 4 1/4"

CA399 *Case*
5/8" x 3 1/4"

CA398 *Case*
5/8" x 2 1/2"

KEYSTONES
Poplar and Red Oak

Plain face only

Key 031
1" x 2" x 4" x 4 1/2"
Key 032
1" x 2 1/2" x 4 1/2" x 5"
Key 033
1 3/4" x 3" x 5 1/2" x 6"

Red Oak and Poplar UltraFlex

Key 034
1 3/4" x 4" x 6 1/2" x 8"
Cast as UltraFlex

* Mfg. from MDF - Medium Density Fiberboard. UltraFlex for curved applications.

ROSETTE & PLYNTH BLOCKS
Poplar and Red Oak

27/32" Rosette

1" Architectural Plynth

1" Rosette

ROS157 1" x 3 7/8"
RESIN ONLY
Accepts Casings
13/16 x 3 1/4 - 3 3/4

1" Architectural Rosette

1" Plynth Block

27/32" ROSETTES		1" ROSETTES		1" ARCHITECTURAL ROSETTE	
ROS161	2 3/4 x 2 3/4	ROS162	2 3/4 x 2 3/4	ROS166	3 3/4 x 5 3/4
ROS159	3 1/2 x 3 1/2	ROS169	3 1/2 x 3 1/2	ROS167	4 1/2 x 6 1/2
ROS163	3 3/4 x 3 3/4	ROS160	3 3/4 x 3 3/4	ROS168	5 1/2 x 7 1/2
1" PLYNTH BLOCKS		ROS158	4 X 4	1" ARCHITECTURAL PLYNTHS	
PB171	3 x 5	ROS164	4 1/2 X 4 1/2	PB192	3 x 5
PB170	4 x 7	ROS165	5 1/2 X 5 1/2	PB193	4 x 7
PB183	4 1/2 x 8			PB185	4 1/2 x 8
PB187	5 1/2 x 8			PB186	5 1/2 x 8

Printed in the U.S.A.

White River™
HARDWOODS•WOODWORKS, INC.

1197 Happy Hollow Road
Fayetteville, Arkansas 72701 U.S.A.

S P E C I F Y I N G   C O R I A N ®

CORIAN®
DUPONT®

Corian®.
A world apart from other materials.

CORIAN® is an advanced composite of natural minerals and pure acrylic polymer,* developed for one purpose: to create an ideal surface for the rigors of life.

CORIAN® is a uniquely durable solid surface material. With installations in high-traffic areas for more than 30 years that still looks like new, CORIAN® has shown outstanding resistance to wear and tear. CORIAN® has the versatility to be used in multiple residential and commercial applications.

Color and pattern run all the way through and cannot wear away. CORIAN® cannot delaminate. Joints are unobtrusive, impermeable, hygienic and seamless in appearance.

CORIAN® has a rich, natural translucence and is inviting to the touch.

CORIAN® offers design versatility, function and durability far beyond the scope of conventional materials. Yet CORIAN® surfaces can be fabricated with conventional tools.

CORIAN®. CREATED FOR LIFE.™

CORIAN® gives architects and designers the freedom to create beautiful interior and exterior designs that stand up to the most demanding conditions.

CORIAN® is created to stand up to the hard knocks life can dish out. As a result, CORIAN® makes any environment easy to live with.

Easy to clean
Everyday stains clean up with just soapy water and cleanser.**

Resists stains
CORIAN® resists stains because liquids can't penetrate. CORIAN® has no pores or voids like ceramic tile, granite or marble. It is unaffected by food stains and common disinfectants. Stubborn stains from cigarette burns, marking pens and hair dyes can be removed easily with abrasive cleanser and a scouring pad.**

Resists impacts
CORIAN® resists fracture, chipping and cracking better than most marble, stone or polyester products. Minor cuts and scratches can be removed with fine sandpaper.**

Resists heat
CORIAN® resists heat better than many other surface materials. However, the use of a hot pad under hot cookware or electrical appliances is recommended.**

Class I and Class A flammability rating
All Colors of CORIAN® have Class I and Class A flammability ratings, making them suitable for any private, public, commercial or military application.

NSF compliance
All Colors of CORIAN® are certified by the *National Sanitation Foundation ANSI/NSF Standard 51: Plastic Materials and Components Used In Food Equipment*. This means CORIAN® can be used anywhere food is prepared or served, including areas where food will routinely come into contact with the surface of CORIAN®. This makes CORIAN® ideal for use in food service areas such as restaurants, healthcare and educational facilities, office buildings, and public buildings.

Hygienic
Independent laboratory tests clearly show that nonporous CORIAN® will not promote the growth of fungi, mildew and bacteria such as staph or other germs.

Additional information on radioactive compounds, HIV (AIDS) cleanup and use in the chemical laboratory is available through a series of bulletins issued by DuPont: *Removing Radioactive Compounds from CORIAN® (H-03843); Removing HIV (AIDS) from CORIAN® (H-14362); Chemical Resistance of CORIAN® Solid Surface Products (H-47329)*.

Renewable
CORIAN® surfaces are renewable, usually with ordinary abrasive cleansers and a scouring pad.** Renewability and durability make CORIAN® inherently environmentally friendly: In effect, CORIAN® recycles itself as time goes by. Or, when needed, CORIAN® can be reworked to create new surfaces.

Inert, nontoxic, chemically nonreactive, hypoallergenic
There is virtually no off-gassing from CORIAN® at normal room temperatures. Even when exposed to direct flame, CORIAN® is one of the least toxic materials available. No wonder CORIAN® is the material of choice for such sensitive applications as museum archival storage

and display cases, and for walls and work surfaces in hospital operating rooms and intensive care facilities.

Barrier-free design
The versatility of CORIAN® lends itself to barrier-free design. Whether in ADA-compliant vanity tops, unobtrusive thresholds or accessible shower pans, CORIAN® allows design for any lifestyle need.

APPLICATIONS

The versatility of CORIAN® is almost limitless in scope. So it is impossible to list every conceivable use for CORIAN®. Some typical applications for Healthcare, Hospitality, Institutions, Public Spaces, Corporate Environments, Retail Spaces, and Residential, Public and Military Housing are listed below:

- Countertops ▪ Vanity tops
▪ Lavatories ▪ Sinks ▪ Shower and bath surrounds ▪ Wall cladding ▪ Work surfaces ▪ Windowsills ▪ Wainscotting ▪ Signage ▪ Indoor and outdoor shop fronts ▪ Furniture ▪ Display cases ▪ Elevators ▪ Shelves ▪ Trash receptacles ▪ Bar tops ▪ Service areas

FABRICATION

CORIAN® products can be fabricated in the shop or on-site, because CORIAN® has working characteristics similar to those of fine hardwood. Unlike marble or granite, CORIAN® can be thermo-formed to many shapes and easily cut or joined to create smooth surfaces of any size that appear seamless. CORIAN® may be combined with wood, brass, tile, acrylics and other CORIAN® colors to create a wide variety of unique designs and edge treatments. Surface effects, logos and graphics can be routed, sandblasted or laser-etched. And the translucent quality of CORIAN® means it can be backlit for visual impact.

---

* Methyl methacrylate.
** For more information, refer to *DuPont CORIAN® Care & Maintenance Tips Card* (H-56461).

C474
06650/DUP
Buy Line 0665

WARRANTY

DuPont warrants all CORIAN® products to be free from material defects for a period of 10 years. If failure occurs due to any material defects, DuPont will pay both labor and material costs to repair or replace the defective material. Refer to the DuPont CORIAN® 10-Year Product Warranty for details.

COLORS

Colors of CORIAN® are born in nature, made with natural color pigments from the earth itself. Unlike dyes, these natural pigments resist fading, even when exposed to long periods of harsh sunlight. Colors of CORIAN® have a subtle, compelling translucency. These colors are easy to design with. Easy to live with.

Genesis Series
Bisque, Bone, Cameo White, Champagne, Dusty Rose, Glacier White, Peach, Pearl Gray, Seagrass, Tea Rose, Vanilla

Venaro Series
Dawn Beige, Venaro Champagne, Venaro Gray, Venaro Peach, Venaro Rose, Venaro White

Sierra Series
Aqua, Aurora, Beach, Burnt Amber, Dusk, Eclipse, Evergreen, Lavender, Malachite, Midnight, Mojave, Oceanic, Pink Coral, Primrose, Sandstone, Sunset, Tarragon

Jewel Series
Azure, Black Pearl, Black Quartz, Cobalt, Emerald, Garnet, Jade, Ruby, Sapphire

Summit Series
Blue Ridge, Everest, Kilimanjaro, Matterhorn, Mont Blanc, Pepper Ivory, Pyrenees, Sequoia, Spruce, Vesuvius

Magna Series
Antarctica, Mediterranean, Platinum, Rain Forest, Rosetta, Sahara, Terra

Design Portfolio
Festival, Hot, Kiwi, Lilac, Mandarin, Mardi Gras, Nocturne, Sun

SHEETS & SHAPES

All colors of CORIAN® are available in ½″ × 30″ × 145″ sheet stock. Many are also available in ¼″* and ¾″ thicknesses and variable widths.**

A wide variety of shaped products are available, including sinks, lavatories and One-Piece Vanity Tops & Bowls. CORIAN® is readily available through a national network of Authorized Distributors.

ACCESSORIES

DuPont Joint Adhesive for CORIAN®—
for bonding CORIAN® to CORIAN®. Available in a wide variety of colors, it can be used to create decorative inlay designs.

Silicone Sealant for CORIAN®—for
installing backsplashes and reveal edges; for sealing tub and shower seams.

ENGINEERED PRODUCTS

Custom Tub & Shower Wall Systems
Engineered to give you creative freedom, combined with the superior value of

prefabricated components. With so many choices of components and colors, it's easy to design a coordinated bathroom suite that fits your client's needs, budget and physical requirements. Size options are unlimited. Installation is easy, even over existing tile.

Ready-To-Install Tub & Shower Wall Kits
Precut, prepackaged components install in five easy steps. Even over existing tile. Designed with thoughtful features that both installers and end users will appreciate. Colors coordinate with CORIAN® One-Piece Vanity Tops & Bowls.

One-Piece Vanity Tops & Bowls
Vanity, bowl and coved backsplash are fabricated as one smooth, sleek unit. Simple. Elegant. With no sink lips, grout or visible seams to spoil the clean lines by trapping water and dirt.

Lavatories
The ideal counterpart to a CORIAN® vanity top. Available in a variety of sizes and styles, including undermount, seamed-undermount or bevel-mount models.

Sinks
Single- or double-bowl units offer extraordinary flexibility in color and placement options. Undermount, seamed-undermount or bevel-mount models are available. Integrated drainboards are available in left- and right-hand units.

* ¼″ sheets are recommended for vertical applications only.
** Contact your Authorized Distributor or DuPont CORIAN® for more information.

How to Specify Corian®

The following suggested write-ups are included to assist you when specifying CORIAN®.

One-Piece Vanity Tops & Bowls
Vanity bowls and tops shall be of a one-piece, monolithic design, made of CORIAN® (methyl methacrylate binder) manufactured by DuPont. Color and pattern shall be selected by the architect, and physical properties shall conform to the manufacturer's standard specifications. The material shall be homogenous, not coated or laminated. Installation shall be in a workmanlike manner, in accordance with the manufacturer's instructions.

Surfaces
Surfaces shall be CORIAN®: manufactured by DuPont; color and pattern shall be selected by the architect. CORIAN® sheets shall be ½″ (13mm) or ¾″ (19mm) for horizontal applications. Backsplashes, where specified, shall be ¼″ (6mm), ½″ (13mm) or ¾″ (19mm). Vertical applications shall be ¼″ (6mm) unless otherwise specified. Physical properties shall conform to the manufacturer's standard specifications. The material shall be homogenous, not coated or laminated. Installation shall be in a workmanlike manner, in accordance with the manufacturer's instructions.

When specifying CORIAN® for applications that are wider than 30″ (760mm) or require a seam, specify "DuPont Joint Adhesive for CORIAN®." It can be used to form a smooth, inconspicuous seam. "DuPont Silicone Sealant for CORIAN®" should be used for caulking tub and shower wall seams and edges.

Generic specifications that can be customized for your applications of CORIAN® are available from your local Authorized Distributor of CORIAN®. Both electronic and hard copy versions are available in several of the most popular specification formats.

For More Information on Corian®…

For the latest information regarding sizes, shapes, colors and engineered products, contact your local Authorized Distributor of CORIAN®. A variety of literature and samples, including the *CORIAN® Product Catalog* and the *CORIAN® On Call CD-ROM Interactive Multimedia Library*, are available worldwide.

For additional information or to share an innovative application for CORIAN®, please contact DuPont at:

www.corian.com

DuPont CORIAN®
Wilmington, DE 19805
1-800-4-CORIAN®
(1-800-426-7426)

Technical Data—Corian® Surfaces

Property	Typical Result	Test
Tensile Strength	6000 psi	ASTM-D-638
Tensile Modulus	1.5×10^6 psi	ASTM-D-638
Flexural Strength	8000 psi	ASTM-D-790
Flexural Modulus	1.2×10^6 psi	ASTM-D-790
Elongation	0.4% min.	ASTM-D-638
Hardness	>85 ASTM-D-785	Rockwell "M" Scale
	56 ASTM-D-2583	Barcol Impressor
Thermal Expansion	3.02×10^{-5} in./in./°C (1.80×10^{-5} in./in./°F)	ASTM-D-696
Gloss (60° Gardner)	5–75 (matte—highly polished)	ANSI-Z124
Color Stability	No change	NEMA-LD-3-3.10
Wear and Cleanability	Passes	ANSI-Z124.3 & Z124.6
Stain Resistance: Sheets	Passes	ANSI-Z124.3 & Z124.6
Fungus and Bacteria Resistance	No attack	ASTM-G-21 & G-22
Boiling Water Surface Resistance	No visible change	NEMA-LD-3-3.5
High Temperature Resistance	No change	NEMA-LD-3-3.6
Izod Impact (Notched Specimen)	0.28 ft.-lbs./in. of notch	ASTM-D-256 (Method A)
Impact Resistance: Sheets	No fracture—½ lb. ball: ¼″ slab—36″ drop ½″ slab—144″ drop ¾″ slab—204″ drop	NEMA-LD-3-3.3
Point Impact: Bowls	No cracks or chips	ANSI-Z124.3 & Z124.6
Weatherability	No change	ASTM-D-1499
Specific Gravity*	1.7	
Water Absorption	Long-term 0.4% (¾″) 0.6% (½″) 0.8% (¼″)	ASTM-D-570
Toxicity	99 (solid colors) 66 (patterned colors)	Pittsburgh Protocol Test ("LC50" Test)
Flammability (Class I and Class A)	All Colors**	ASTM-E-84 & NFPA255
Flame Spread	<25	
Smoke Developed	<30	

* Approximate weight per square foot
¼″ (6mm) 2.2 lbs. • ½″ (13mm) 4.4 lbs. • ¾″ (19mm) 6.6 lbs.

** ¼″ (6mm) results reflect material adhered to both masonry surfaces and
standard grade ½″ (13mm) thick gypsum board, using DuPont Panel Adhesive
for CORIAN® and tested as a composite.

CORIAN®

DuPont®

Wilsonart® Laminate

You want a broad range of choices. You want a surface that lasts. Yet, you have a budget

you must maintain. Relax. Wilsonart Laminate combines the best of design, durability,

and value in a surfacing material that looks great in any setting.

Choose from our unique palette of over 250 colors and patterns, ranging from solid

tones to woodgrains and marbles or patterns. A designer finish, such as Crystal, may be added. And, as always, a matching edge

treatment lends dimension and flair to any decor. No matter what your budget, Wilsonart Laminate has the right combination for you.

Wilsonart® Custom Edges

Nothing sets off the look of your countertop like a well-chosen edge treatment. Available in a wide variety of durable, affordable

surfacing materials, Wilsonart Custom Edges add expression to your interior decor. All colors and patterns have been thoughtfully

designed to coordinate with our complete line of laminate and SSV materials. And when matched with any of our various profiles

and styles, there's no limit to the effects a Custom Edge can achieve.

On the lower end of the cost spectrum, choose a beveled edge in any of our 250

laminate designs. Or move up to our more traditional Red Oak or Hard Maple wood

moldings, available in three styles and numerous profiles. For a more modern look,

consider one of our Acrylic, SSV, or Gibraltar moldings, with over 32 complementary

colors and patterns available for your choosing. Single-color moldings are standard.

Mixed designs are slightly more.

For a surface that adds style to any decor, nothing completes a Wilsonart countertop

better than Wilsonart Custom Edges. Our edges carry a 10-year warranty against

delamination.

For information on product,
samples or literature,
call toll free (800) 433-3222.

Wilsonart® SSV™ Solid Surfacing

Until now, the price of solid surfacing has been as upscale as the look. Wilsonart SSV Solid Surfacing provides the style so many homeowners admire, at a cost approximately one-third less than traditional solid surfacing. And SSV is still backed by a 10-year installed, transferable, limited warranty when installed by a certified fabricator.

Wilsonart SSV Solid Surfacing is a one-eighth-inch-thick solid surfacing material that is entirely renewable. Slight scratches and burns can be buffed away with a Scotch-Brite® pad. And the look is simply sophisticated.

Choose from 32 solid colors and stone-like patterns in all, each designed to complement our full line of integrated sinks and bowls. Wilsonart SSV Solid Surfacing also coordinates with a broad range of standard and upgrade edges to create the perfect countertop look or style. For elegant durability at a reasonable price, consider SSV from Wilsonart.

Wilsonart® Gibraltar® Solid Surfacing

Few materials of any sort command the attention or create the mystique of stone-like, premium-grade Wilsonart Gibraltar Solid Surfacing. Its beautiful, sculpted appearance affirms its underlying strength and durability, plus it's backed by a 10-year installed, transferable, limited warranty when installed by a certified fabricator. Its half-inch-thick substance lends a wood-like workability to its form. Scratch it or burn it, and it buffs back to "like new" condition under the stroke of a Scotch-Brite® pad. Match any of 32 solid colors and stone-like patterns with a coordinating sink, bowl, or edge and you'll create a showcase countertop.

Starting with solid colors, and moving up to the slightly higher-priced stone-like patterns, Wilsonart Gibraltar Solid Surfacing looks spectacular when matched with a standard one-color or premium two-color edge profile.

Wilsonart® SSV™ Solid Surfacing &
Wilsonart® Gibraltar® Solid Surfacing

Solid Colors (standard)

● SSV only
▲ Gibraltar only

Designer White	Frosty White	Ivory	Antique White	Natural Almond	Bone	Orchid Glow
D354-SL*	1573-SL*	9076-SL*	1572-SL*	D30-SL*	9035-SL●	9011-SL*●

Patterns — Mirage and Tempest Groups (upgrade)

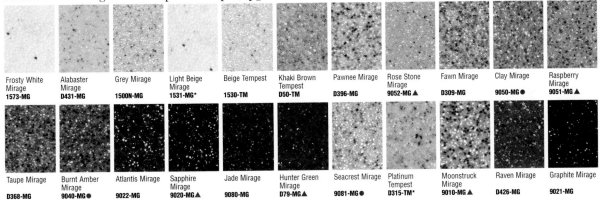

Frosty White Mirage 1573-MG | Alabaster Mirage D431-MG | Grey Mirage 1500N-MG | Light Beige Mirage 1531-MG* | Beige Tempest 1530-TM | Khaki Brown Tempest D50-TM | Pawnee Mirage D396-MG | Rose Stone Mirage 9052-MG▲ | Fawn Mirage D309-MG | Clay Mirage 9050-MG● | Raspberry Mirage 9051-MG▲

Taupe Mirage D368-MG | Burnt Amber Mirage 9040-MG● | Atlantis Mirage 9022-MG | Sapphire Mirage 9020-MG▲ | Jade Mirage 9080-MG | Hunter Green Mirage D79-MG▲ | Seacrest Mirage 9081-MG● | Platinum Tempest D315-TM* | Moonstruck Mirage 9010-MG▲ | Raven Mirage D426-MG | Graphite Mirage 9021-MG

Patterns — Melange Group (premium)

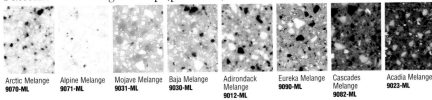

Arctic Melange 9070-ML | Alpine Melange 9071-ML | Mojave Melange 9031-ML | Baja Melange 9030-ML | Adirondack Melange 9012-ML | Eureka Melange 9090-ML | Cascades Melange 9082-ML | Acadia Melange 9023-ML

Wilsonart® SSV™ Solid Surfacing

Standard Edge   Upgrade Edges

Self Edge | *Gibraltar Edge* | *SE Molding* | *XP Molding* | *Wood Edge*

Wilsonart® Gibraltar®

Standard Edges   Upgrade Edges

Roundover | *Bevel/Chamfer* | *Ogee* | *Bullnose* | *Inlay* | *Insert*

Wilsonart® Laminate

Standard Edges   Upgrade Edges

Waterfall | *No Drip* | *Accent Color* | *Self Edge* | *Bullnose* | *Rounded Edge*

*Kitchen sinks and vanity bowls available to match. Platinum Tempest and Light Beige Mirage available in coordinating solid colors only.

Wilsonart® Laminate

Manufacturer

Wilsonart International
2400 Wilson Place
P.O. Box 6110
Temple, Texas 76503-6110
Phone: (254) 207-7000
FAX: (254) 207-2384

For more information and delivery of samples,
just call: (800) 433-3222.

Short Specification Form

Type:	(specify 107, 335 or 350)	
Surface:	Color Number:	
	Color Name:	
Finish:	Number:	Name:
Edge Trim:	Color Number:	
	Color Name:	
Adhesive:	Name:	
	Grade/Type:	
	Brand: Lokweld®	

Care and Maintenance

1. To clean the surface, use a damp cloth or sponge and a mild soap or detergent.
2. Difficult stains such as coffee or tea can be removed using a mild household cleaner/detergent and a soft bristle brush, repeating as necessary.
3. If a stain persists, use a paste of baking soda and water and apply with a soft bristled brush. Light scrubbing for 10 to 20 strokes should remove most stains. Although baking soda is a low abrasive, excessive scrubbing or exerting too much force could damage the decorative surface, especially if it has a gloss finish.
4. Stubborn stains that resist any of the above cleaning methods may require the use of undiluted household bleach or nail polish remover. Apply the bleach or nail polish remover to the stain and let stand no longer than two minutes. Rinse thoroughly with warm water and wipe dry. This step may be repeated if the stain appears to be going away and the color of the laminate has not been affected. WARNING: Prolonged exposure of the laminate surface to bleach will cause discoloration.

Your area sales representative will provide free copies of the "Care and Maintenance Guide," which covers care and maintenance of most Wilsonart products, for your own information, for project manuals and for provision to clients and contractors involved with interior construction and finishing.

Limited Warranty

Wilsonart International warrants that, under normal use and service, the material and workmanship of its products shall conform to the standards set forth on the applicable technical data sheets for a period of twelve (12) months from the date of sale to the first consumer purchaser. Dealers and distributors are provided with the technical data sheets which contain specific standards of performance for the products. In the event that a Wilsonart International product does not perform as warranted, the first purchaser's sole remedy shall be limited to repair or replacement of all or any part of the product which is defective, at the manufacturer's sole discretion.

This warranty applies only to product:

1. In its original installation; and
2. Purchased by the first consumer purchaser.

This warranty is not transferable, and expires upon resale or transfer by the first consumer purchaser.

This warranty shall not apply to defects or damage arising from any of the following:

1. Accidents, abuse or misuse;
2. Exposure to extreme temperature;
3. Improper fabrication or installation; or
4. Improper maintenance.

No other warranties, expressed or implied, are made. Under no circumstances shall the manufacturer be liable for any loss or damage arising from the purchase, use or inability to use this product, or for any special, indirect, incidental or consequential damages. No fabricator, installer, dealer, agent or employee of Wilsonart International has the authority to modify the obligations or limitation of this warranty. This warranty gives you specific legal rights, and you may also have other rights which vary from state to state; therefore, some of the limitations stated above may not apply to you. It is to your benefit to save your documentation upon purchase of a product.

Availability Summary

Sheet Widths:	30", 36", 48", 60"
	(762mm, 914mm, 1219mm, 1524mm)
Sheet Lengths:	96", 120", 144"
	(2438mm, 3048mm, 3658mm)
Sheet Thicknesses:	
General Purpose Type 107:	
	0.048" ± 0.005"
	(1.219mm ± 0.127mm)
Vertical Surface Type 335:	
	0.028" ± 0.004"
	(0.711mm ± 0.101mm)
Postforming Type 350:	
	0.039" ± 0.005"
	(.990mm ± 0.127mm)

For information on product,
samples or literature,
call toll free (800) 433-3222.

Sinks and Bowls (limited colors)

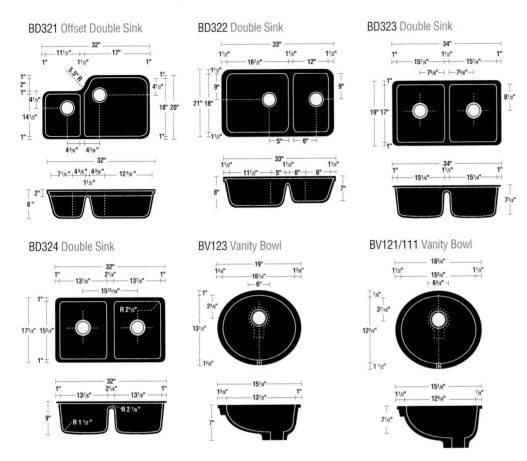

BD321 Offset Double Sink

BD322 Double Sink

BD323 Double Sink

BD324 Double Sink

BV123 Vanity Bowl

BV121/111 Vanity Bowl

Edge Diagrams

Bevel Edge Style - FE, SE

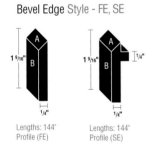

Lengths: 144"
Profile (FE)

Lengths: 144"
Profile (SE)

Available Patterns/Finishes: All Wilsonart Laminate, Chemsurf, Colorthrough Laminate, and SSV

Bevel Edge Style - XP, L

Lengths: 144"
Profile (XP)

Lengths: 144"
Profile (L)

Available Patterns/Finishes: All Wilsonart Laminate, Chemsurf, Colorthrough Laminate, and SSV

Acrylic Style - AT -1, AT-2

Lengths: 144"
Profile (AT-1)
1 5/8" Bullnose

Lengths: 144"
Profile (AT-2)
1 5/8" Roundover

Gibraltar Style - GB -11, GB-12

Lengths: 144"
Profile (GB-11: 1/2")

Lengths: 144"
Profile (GB-12: 3/8")

Wood Style - HT-1, HT-11, KT-1

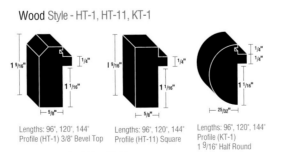

Lengths: 96", 120", 144"
Profile (HT-1) 3/8" Bevel Top

Lengths: 96", 120", 144"
Profile (HT-11) Square

Lengths: 96", 120", 144"
Profile (KT-1)
1 9/16" Half Round

Available Species: Red Oak, Hard Maple*

Backsplash Style - SS, BS

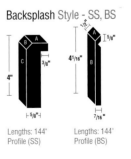

Lengths: 144"
Profile (SS)

Lengths: 144"
Profile (BS)

Available Patterns/Finishes: All Wilsonart Laminate, Chemsurf, Colorthrough Laminates, and SSV

Recommended Uses

Wilsonart® Laminate is suitable for use on fine quality residential and contract furniture and casework; and for architectural application on columns, wainscoting, valances, cornices, interior doors and divider systems.

General Purpose Type 107 is most frequently used for work surfaces on counters, islands, vanities, desks and tables. Typical vertical uses include surfacing for wall panels, teller cages and the front panels of work stations, such as those in hospitals, airports and restaurants.

Vertical Surface Type 335 is the usual choice to surface cabinet walls, doors and drawer panels. It often appears on the vertical surfaces of desks, restaurant booths and maitre d' stations, and as architectural cladding.

Postforming Type 350 adds the decorative capability of the soft edge to any typical laminate use. Formed edges for counters and desk tops and for cabinet doors and drawer panels are familiar applications of postforming laminates.

Basic Limitations

Wilsonart Laminate is for interior use only, and is not recommended for direct application to plaster or concrete walls or gypsum wallboard. This laminate is not a structural material, and must be bonded to a suitable substrate.

Do not subject these laminates to extremes in humidity, or to temperatures of over 275°F (135°C) for sustained periods of time, or to intense, continuous, direct sunlight.

Fabrication and Assembly

Wilsonart Laminate must be bonded to a substrate of reliable quality, such as particleboard, medium-density fiberboard, or plywood with one A face. Recommended substrate material is 45-lb. industrial-grade particleboard. High pressure laminate, plaster, concrete and gypsum board should not be considered suitable substrates. Basic Types laminate may not be used as structural members.

Bond with adhesives and follow the techniques recommended by the adhesive manufacturer.

Recommended adhesives are permanent types, such as urea and polyvinyl acetate (PVA); and contact types. Lokweld® Adhesives are recommended for most bonding conditions.

Take care to ensure an appropriate moisture balance between the laminate and the substrate prior to fabrication. The face and backing laminates and the substrate should be conditioned in the same environment for 48 hours before fabrication.

Recommended conditioning temperature is about 75°F (24°C). Laminates should be conditioned at about 45% relative humidity.

With postforming machinery, a sheet will form, throughout its thickness, at a nominal temperature of 325°F (163°C) in 20 ± 5 seconds.

Tools: Carbide-tipped saw and router blades should be used for cutting. High tool speed and low feed speed are advisable. Cutting blades should be kept very sharp, and use a hold-down to prevent any vibration.

Methods: Fabrication should follow approved methods. Assembled pieces should meet the specifications of DLPA (Decorative Laminate Products Association), ANSI A-161.2-1995, and "Architectural Woodwork Quality Standards, Guide Specifications and Quality Certification Program" guidelines of the Architectural Woodwork Institute where applicable.

To avoid stress cracking, do not use square-cut inside corners. All inside corners should have a minimum of 1/8" (3.175mm) radius and all edges should be routed smooth.

Drill holes for bolts or screws oversized. Screws or bolts should be slightly countersunk into the face side of a laminate-clad substrate.

Optional Finishes

Wilsonart Laminate may be specified in other optional designer finishes. Contact your local representative for availability.

#1 High Gloss. A mirror sheen finish which gives a smooth, brilliant appearance.

Glossometer reading: MD and CD 90 minimum.

#7 Textured Gloss. A textured finish which reproduces the high sheen of waxed wood furniture.

Glossometer reading: MD and CD 36 ± 3.

#41 Gloss Diagonal. Semigloss diagonal finish.

Glossometer reading: MD and CD 75 ± 5.

#50 Touchstone. A pebbled texture with the look and feel of coarse-grained sand.

Glossometer reading: MD and CD 10 ± 2.

#60 Matte. A textured finish with a moderate reflective quality.

Glossometer reading: MD and CD 10 ± 1.

#81 Cathedral Grain. An embossed finish that offers the look and feel of true flatcut wood.

Glossometer reading: MD and CD 25 ± 6.

#90 Crystal. A very finely beaded texture which minimizes smudges and finger marks and improves scratch resistance.

Glossometer reading: MD and CD 13 ± 3.

NOTE: Glossometer readings made at 60° angle of incidence. MD means the machine direction of a laminate sheet, and CD refers to the cross direction.

Wilsonart® SSV™ Solid Surfacing & Wilsonart® Gibraltar® Solid Surfacing

Care And Maintenance

1. Wilsonart Gibraltar Solid Surfacing and SSV Solid Surfacing offer exceptional beauty and durability. Routine care is as simple as wiping the surface with a damp cloth.

2. Most stains will wash away with soap and water. For tougher stains (on a matte finish*), apply an abrasive cleanser and buff with a Scotch-Brite® pad using a circular motion.

3. Minor burns (on a matte finish*) may also be removed using an abrasive cleanser and buffing the surface with a Scotch-Brite pad.

4. Hot pans and heat-producing appliances should be placed on heat shields or hot pads.

* If you have a high-gloss finish, contact your dealer or fabricator before attempting repairs.

Recommended Uses

Wilsonart SSV and Gibraltar Solid Surfacing panels are recommended for interior and exterior decorative and functional applications where a prestigious appearance, high stain resistance, ease of maintenance and extensive customizing capabilities are beneficial.

Wilsonart SSV is also fire-rated to a code compliance Class II per ASTM-E-84.

Gibraltar Solid Surfacing panels are Class 1 (A) fire-rated, which further enhances their usefulness in high-end contract, commercial and institutional applications.

Appropriate horizontal applications include tops for counters, tables, vanities, bars and laboratory work surfaces.

These materials may also be used to create windowsills and store fixtures, as well as fine custom furniture.

Typical vertical applications include paneling for walls, elevators, counter facades; partitions for toilets and dressing rooms; and interior signage.

Because of their chemical makeup, panels are appropriate for many hospital surfaces. Gibraltar Solid Surfacing panels may be bonded to each other with watertight seals.

Watertight seals can be created with Wilsonart SSV by using Lokweld® 8215 Adhesive (see corresponding tech data).

Basic Limitations

Gibraltar Solid Surfacing sheet goods are designed for interior and exterior use. When specifying Gibraltar Solid Surfacing for exterior applications, the design, fabrication and installation procedures must consider extreme concurrent temperature contrasts which could result in seam failure. Gibraltar Solid Surfacing is not recommended for building facade and facia applications.

Wilsonart SSV is designed for interior use. It should be bonded to particleboard, medium-density fiberboard or plywood (please refer to Fabrication Manual for details regarding substrate selection).

Gibraltar Solid Surfacing panels do not require bonding to substrates, and should not be bonded to solid wood, plaster, concrete, gypsum wallboard or other brands of solid surfacing. They do, however, require a supporting material or framework.

Wilsonart® SSV™ Solid Surfacing

Availability Summary

Panel Widths:	30", 36", 48"*, 60"*	(762mm, 914mm, 1219.2mm*, 1524mm*)
Panel Lengths:	60"*, 72"*, 96", 144"	(1524mm*, 1829mm*, 2438mm, 3658mm)
Thickness:	Product Type 013	0.115" ± 0.010"

*Available in limited colors

Wilsonart® Gibraltar® Solid Surfacing

Short Specification Form

Type:	See specific types under Product Description/Product Definition
Surface:	Color/Design Number: Color/Design Name:
Finish:	(specify desired texture of completed application)
Sink Type:	Color/Design Name/Model Number:
Decorative Functional Treatments:	
Adhesive:	Gibraltar Seam Kit Adhesive, color-matched to panels to be seamed. Color/Design Number: Color/Design Name:
Caulk/Sealant:	Gibraltar Color-Matched Silicone Sealant Color/Design Number: Color/Design Name: Fastening System:
Certification:	Surface shall be UL rated, Class 1 (A)

Availability Summary

Panel Widths:	30", 36"*	(762mm, 914mm*)
Panel Lengths:	96", 144"	(2438mm, 3658mm)
Thickness:	Product Type 051	1/2" (13mm) Nominal
Strips:	Width - 1 3/4", 5 3/4"	(44mm, 146mm)
	Length - 144"	(3658mm)

*Available in limited colors

Shaped Goods: (inside dimensions only)	
BK128-Round Sink	16 3/4" x 16 3/4" x 7 1/2"
BK222-Square Sink	16 3/4" x 16 3/4" x 8"
BK323-Rectangle Sink	10 1/4" x 16 3/4" x 8"
BK324-Rectangle Sink	21" x 15 3/4" x 7 1/2"
BK325-Bar Sink	9" x 12" x 5 1/2"
BK327-Disposal Sink	8" x 15 3/4" x 5 1/2"
BK426-D Bowl	21" x 16 3/4" x 7 1/2"
BV111, BV121-Vanity Bowl (BV111 is a drop-in)	12 3/4" x 15 3/4" x 7 1/2"
BV122-Vanity Bowl (ADA)	12 3/4" x 15 3/4" x 5 1/4"
BV123-Vanity Bowl	13 1/2" x 16 1/4" x 7"
BD321-Offset Double Sink	30" x 16" x 8"
BD322-Double Sink	30" x 18" x 8"
BD323-Double Sink	32" x 17" x 7 3/4"

Wilsonart® Gibraltar® Solid Surfacing

Warranty Information

Wilsonart International warrants to the consumer in the U.S. and Canada that Gibraltar Solid Surfacing, when installed by a recognized Gibraltar Solid Surfacing fabricator in the Gibraltar Fabricators Guild program, shall be free from defects in material, workmanship, fabrication and installation under normal use and service, for a period of ten years from date of sale to the consumer.

This warranty shall not apply to damage arising from any of the following:

1. Accidents, abuse or misuse;
2. Exposure to extreme heat;
3. Improper maintenance; or
4. Alteration or repair by anyone other than a recognized Gibraltar Solid Surfacing fabricator.

This warranty applies only to installations in which the Gibraltar Solid Surfacing product is affixed to the location (e.g. kitchen and bath countertops, vanity tops). This warranty extends to the original purchaser and may be transferred to the new purchaser of the location, provided the new purchaser submits a warranty registration card and provides proof of purchase. A warranty registration card can be obtained by notifying the manufacturer at the address listed below. The transferred warranty shall apply only for the remainder of the original ten year period.

No other warranties, expressed or implied, are made, including merchantability or fitness for a particular purpose. Under no circumstances shall Wilsonart International be liable for any loss or damage arising from the purchase, use or inability to use this product, or for any special, indirect or consequential damages.

To make a claim under this warranty, the consumer must contact Wilsonart International at the following address: 2400 Wilson Place, P.O. Box 6110, Temple, Texas 76503-6110.

This warranty gives you specific legal rights, and you may also have other rights which may vary from state to state. Some states do not allow the exclusion of implied warranties or of incidental or consequential damages, so the above limitation or exclusion may not apply to you. Return of owner registration card is not a condition precedent to warranty coverage. No fabricator, installer, dealer, agent or employee of Wilsonart International has the authority to increase or alter the obligation or limitation of this warranty.

Wilsonart® SSV™ Solid Surfacing

Warranty Information

Wilsonart International, Inc., warrants that, under normal use and service, installed Wilsonart® SSV™ Solid Surfacing products shall be free from defects in material and workmanship for a period of ten (10) years from the date of sale to the consumer purchaser. In the event that the product does not perform as warranted, the consumer purchaser's sole remedy shall be limited to repair or replacement, at manufacturer's discretion, of all or any part of the product which is defective. This warranty applies only to product that is attached to the building (such as kitchen or bathroom countertops) and was purchased by the original consumer purchaser.

This warranty shall not apply to any defects or damages arising from any of the following:

1. Accidents, abuse or misuse
2. Exposure to extreme temperatures
3. Improper installation or fabrication
4. Improper maintenance
5. Improper adhesive, grout, or caulk
6. Alteration or repair by anyone other than an authorized Smart Source Fabricator

This warranty applies only to product which has been fabricated and installed by an authorized Smart Source Fabricator and is in its original installation location. This warranty extends to the original purchaser and may be transferred to the new purchaser of the location, provided the new purchaser submits a warranty registration card and provides proof of purchase.

No other warranties, express or implied, are made, including merchantability or fitness for a particular purpose. Under no circumstances shall the manufacturer be liable for any loss or damage arising from the purchase, use or inability to use this product, or for any special, indirect, incidental, or consequential damages. No fabricator, installer, dealer, agent or employee of Wilsonart International has the authority to modify the obligations or limitations of this warranty.

This warranty gives you specific legal rights, and you may also have other rights which may vary from state to state. Some states do not allow the exclusion of implied warranties or of incidental or consequential damages, so the above limitation or exclusion may not apply to you. Return of owner registration card is not a condition precedent to warranty coverage.

To receive a warranty registration form, call toll free (800) 433-3222.

Corporate Headquarters
2400 Wilson Place
P.O. Box 6110
Temple, TX 76503-6110
Toll Free: (800) 433-3222
Mon.-Fri. 7:00 am-7:00 pm CST
Phone: (254) 207-7000
Fax: (254) 207-2384
Internet: www.wilsonart.com

THE SMART SOURCE

WILSONART
INTERNATIONAL

BROAN®

Range Hoods

Introducing Finesse.™
Performance dramatically styled for today's kitchens.

See page 15 for all performance specifications and installation requirements.

Finesse By **BROAN**

Finesse is an innovative vision of what range hoods are meant to be. Graceful, contoured lines beautifully complement today's popular new range and cooktop designs. Yet its form follows function.

- Powerful, quiet dual centrifugal blower — 250 CFM (81000 Series) and 400 CFM (83000 Series) models available.

- Select horizontal or vertical exhausting.

- Convertible to vent-free operation with exclusive Microtek® System filters that are 25 times more effective than vent-free filters of other manufacturers (available separately).

- Smoked, tempered-glass visor elegantly accentuates the clean, sweeping lines of this range hood, while improving overall performance.

- Infinite-speed touch controls are color-matched to the hood and form-fitted for a clean, stylish appearance.

- Indicator light lets you know the blower is on.

- Dual 75-watt lights provide 150-watts of illumination (bulbs not included); dual prismatic lenses help eliminate harsh glare.

- Fully enclosed underside is easy to keep clean.

- Dishwasher-safe filters run the full width of the range hood; filters lift out easily with no tools necessary.

- Duct connector with built-in damper included (vented models only).

- Available in 30" and 36" widths.

- Choose white, almond, black or stainless steel finish.

3

When your customers step beyond simple "remodeling" to dream kitchens with facilities for serious cooking... Rangemaster® by Broan.

High-performance, restaurant ranges are one of the hottest trends in kitchen remodeling today. When your customers select one of these commercial-look, high B.T.U. units, show them the range hood designed for these ranges: Rangemaster.

Top line features in all Rangemaster hoods include:

■ Heavy-gauge, double-wall steel construction for years of service.

■ Easy-to-clean stainless steel interior with no sharp edges.

■ Two, 15" fluorescent tubes for two-level, cooktop lighting (bulbs not included).

■ Two, 250-watt infrared food warming lamps "hold" one dish while you finish preparing others (bulbs not included).

■ Extra large, easily removable, dishwasher-safe grease filters.

■ Exclusive Heat Sentry™ automatically turns blower to high speed when excess heat is detected.

■ Infinite, solid-state speed control with blower memory "remembers" last setting selected.

Custom options fit Rangemaster to any range; any kitchen.

■ Select eight sizes (widths) from space-saving 30" to spacious 72".

■ Select HVI-certified 600 CFM or 1200 CFM interior blowers, or 600 CFM or 900 CFM exterior blowers for maximum ventilation performance. See page 14 for blower choice.

■ Restaurant quality stainless steel backsplash with fold-down food warming shelves provide the ultimate in "commercial" looks and ease of cleaning.

■ Matching soffit chimneys for kitchens with higher "cathedral" ceilings; vertical ducting only, two soffit maximum.
■ Select horizontal or vertical exhausting.

■ Select stainless steel, white, almond or black

Optional backsplash with condiment shelves that fold down for food warming.

4

When customers demand a hood with a disappearing act ... show them our Eclipse® or Silhouette® Series.

Eclipse downdraft ventilator.

Silhouette slide-out range hood.

page 14 for all performance specifications and installation requirements.

Eclipse downdraft system for island and peninsula cooking where updraft venting is impractical.

Features of all Eclipse ventilators:

■ Sleek, trim line styling complements any cooktop style or color.

■ Compatible with virtually all cooktops.

■ Discreet, integral, easy-to-reach blower control.

■ Blower discharges to right, left or down and side-to-side to avoid floor joists.

■ Space-saving design saves valuable under-counter cabinet space.

■ Access panel allows easy cleaning.

Eclipse options to suit any kitchen layout:

■ Select 30" or 36" wide models (fits all standard kitchen cabinets).

■ Powerful, quiet 500 CFM internal or 900 CFM external blower.

■ Stainless steel cover standard. White or black optional.

Silhouette hoods fit under kitchen cabinets, and slide out of sight when not in use.

Features found in all Silhouette Series range hoods:

■ Powerful performance – HVI- certified 300 CFM. For vented installations only.

■ Ultra-quiet performance – HVI-certified 4.5 Sones.

■ Compact, trim line styling maximizes kitchen cabinet space.

■ Dramatic glass visor slides out to turn on blower; slides in to turn off.

■ 24" fluorescent light with prismatic glass lens provides bright cooktop lighting (bulb not included).

■ Easy to reach, "up-front" infinite blower control.

■ Exclusive Heat Sentry automatically turns blower to high speed when excess heat is detected.

■ Dual connector with built-in damper.

Options available in Silhouette Series:

■ 30" or 36" width hoods (fits all standard kitchen cabinets).

■ Available in white or black. Fits any contemporary kitchen decor.

Industry-leading, exclusive features make Broan Deluxe Range Hoods the obvious choice for your preferred customers.

Heat Sentry™, Auto Temp, Blower Memory, Microtek® System filters...they're the features that define deluxe range hoods today and only Broan has them.

Broan 90000 Series. Take control of every cooking task with the most technologically advanced conventional range hood in North America.

Deluxe features in all 90000 Series range hoods:

- Powerful, quiet 360 CFM / 5.5 Sone (vertical discharge) or 350 CFM / 6.0 Sone (horizontal discharge) performance (HVI certified).

- Also available vent-free with exclusive Microtek System filter that's 65 times more effective than vent-free filters of other manufacturers (available separately).

- Popular 30", 36" and 42" widths.

- Advanced function electronic touchpad controls, flush-mounted for easy cleaning.

- LED indicators signal all operating functions whenever hood is operating.

- Exclusive Heat Sentry automatically turns blower to high speed when excess heat is detected.

- Auto Temp continuously monitors cooking conditions; automatically adjusting blower to appropriate ventilation levels.

- High Heat Signal sounds alarm whenever overheating occurs on cook-top (Heat Sentry and High Heat Signal activate at all times; even when blower is off).

- Two 75-watt bulbs offer three light settings, including "night light" (bulbs not included).
- Test function enables monitoring of all features.

- Broan's dual blower system is the quietest, high-performance system available in a conventional range hood.

- Choose white-on-white, white, almond, black or stainless steel finish.

8000 Series deluxe hood.

Broan 88000 Series. A top-performing, great-looking hood that would be the top of anyone else's line.

These features are found in all Broan 88000 Series range hoods:

- Powerful, quiet 360 CFM/5.5 Sone (vertical discharge) or 350 CFM/6.0 Sone (horizontal discharge) performance (HVI certified).

- Convertible to vent-free operation with exclusive Microtek® System filter that's 65 times more effective than vent-free filters of other manufacturers (available separately).

- Popular 30", 36" and 42" widths.

- Convenient, contemporary slide controls.

- Exclusive Blower Memory automatically returns to last setting selected.

- Exclusive Heat Sentry automatically turns blower to high speed when excess heat is detected.

- Two 75-watt bulbs offer bright cooktop lighting and night-light settings (bulbs not included).
- Infinite blower controls.

- Choose white-on-white, white, almond, black or stainless steel finish.

Broan 89000 Series. Perfect for high-performance cooktops or indoor gas or electric grilles.

Same great feature complement as Broan 88000 Series, plus:

- Super-performing 460 CFM/6.0 Sone (vertical discharge) or 440 CFM/7.0 Sone (horizontal discharge) dual centrifugal blowers (HVI certified).

- Available in 30", 36", 42" and 48" widths (and additional special order sizes).

- Choose white, almond, black, or stainless steel finish (additional special order colors available).

89000 Series deluxe hood.

See page 14 for all performance specifications and installation requirements.

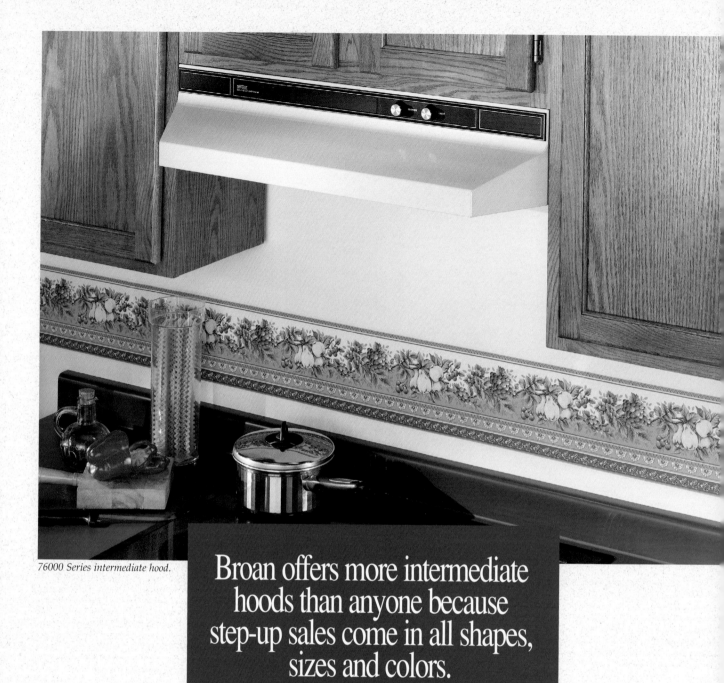

76000 Series intermediate hood.

Broan offers more intermediate hoods than anyone because step-up sales come in all shapes, sizes and colors.

Broan 76000 Series. More performance, quality and value than any hood in its class.

All these great features are found in every 76000 Series hood:

- Powerful, quiet 200 CFM/5.5 Sone (vertical discharge) or 200 CFM/6.0 Sone (horizontal discharge) performance (HVI certified).

- Convertible to vent-free operation with exclusive Microtek® System filter that's 25 times more effective than vent-free filters of other manufacturers.

- 11-5/8" by 6-5/8" dishwasher safe aluminum grease filters (vented models).

- Popular 24", 30", 36" and 42" widths.

- Infinite rotary blower speed control.

- 75-watt cooktop lighting with polymeric lens.

- Duct connector with built-in damper.

- Choose white-on-white, white, almond, black or stainless steel finish.

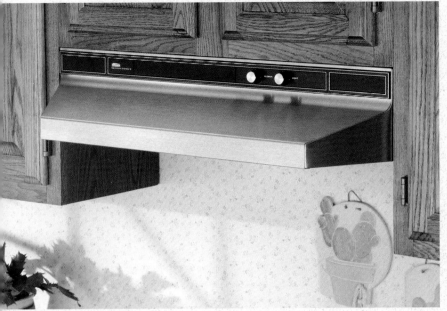

5000 Series intermediate hood.

Broan 75000 Series. Same great features as 76000 Series with more powerful blowers.

■ Powerful, quiet 250 CFM/6.5 Sone (vertical discharge) or 250 CFM/6.0 Sone (horizontal discharge) performance (HVI certified).

■ Popular 30", 36" and 42" widths.

■ Choose white-on-white, white, almond, black or stainless steel finish.

Broan 68000 and 67000 Series. Simple, understated elegance in range hood design.

Features common to 68000 (7" round vented) and 67000 (vent-free) Series range hoods:

■ 230 CFM/7.0 Sone (vertical discharge) performance (68000 only) (HVI certified).

■ Simple, elegant, easy-to-clean black or white "glass look" styling.

■ Popular 30", 36" and 42" widths.

■ Two-speed control inside hood presents clean, uncluttered front.

■ 75-watt cooktop lighting with lens (bulb not included).

■ Dishwasher safe aluminum grease filter and damper (68000 only).

■ Combination vent-free filter (67000 only).

■ Choose monochromatic white or black finish.

8000 Series intermediate hood.

Broan 48000 and 47000 Series. Straight side styling offers that subtle difference preferred by many consumers.

Features common to 48000 (7" round vented) and 47000 (vent-free) Series range hoods:

■ 230 CFM/7.0 Sone (vertical discharge) performance (HVI certified).

■ Popular 30", 36" and 42" widths.

■ 75-watt cooktop lighting with lens (bulb not included).

■ Dishwasher safe aluminum grease filter and damper (48000 only).

■ Combination vent-free filter (47000 only).

■ Choose white, almond or stainless steel finish.

48000 Series intermediate hood.

See pages 14 and 15 for all performance specifications and installation requirements.

46000 Series with optional, matching backsplash.

Simple. Dependable. Affordable. No wonder Broan economy range hoods lead the category.

Broan 46000 Series. When performance, profits and value are critical, you can rely on this great, step-up economy model.

Standard features of 46000 Series include:

- 180 CFM/7.0 Sone (vertical discharge) and 180 CFM/6.5 (horizontal discharge) performance (HVI certified).

- Convertible to vent-free operation with exclusive Microtek® System filter that's 10 times more effective than vent-free filters of other manufacturers.

- Microtek System filter included.

- Popular 30", 36" and 42" widths.

- Infinite rotary fan speed control.

- 75-watt cooktop lighting with polymeric lens (bulb not included).

- Duct connector with built-in damper included (vented models).

- Choose white, almond or stainless steel finish.

1000 Series economy hood with optional, matching backsplash.

0000/42000 Series economy hood with optional, matching backsplash.

Broan 42000, 41000 and 40000 Series. The industry's best-featured economy hoods.

Standard features of 42000, (7" round vented) 41000 (vent-free) and 40000 (vented) Series range hoods:

■ 190 CFM/5.5 Sone (vertical discharge) performance (42000 Series) (HVI certified).

■ 160 CFM/5.5 Sone (vertical discharge) or 160 CFM/6.5 Sone (horizontal discharge) performance (40000 Series) (HVI certified).

■ 10-1/2" diameter dishwasher safe aluminum grease filter (42000 Series).

■ Requires Broan #87 damper (available separately) (42000 Series).

■ Microtek® System filter included that's 9 times more effective than vent-free filters of other manufacturers (41000 Series).

■ 75-watt cooktop lighting with polymeric lens (bulb not included).

■ Duct connector with built-in damper included (40000 Series).

■ 10-1/2" by 8-3/4" dishwasher safe aluminum grease filter (40000 Series).

■ Popular 24", 30" and 36" widths (41000 and 40000 Series); 30" and 36" widths (42000 Series).

■ Choose white, almond or stainless steel finish.

See page 15 for all performance specifications and installation requirements.

For customers who want a custom look in kitchen ventilation, look to Broan.

Hideaway Hood (inside cabinets)-Model 113023.

Wood Hood Kit-Model 103023.

Hideaway...great ventilation performance. Great flush look.

■ Expandable 24"-30" height accommodates 30" face frame with cabinet doors.

■ Powerful, quiet 360 CFM/4.5 Sone (vertical or horizontal discharge) performance (HVI certified).

■ Blower and light automatically turn on when hood is pulled out.

■ Exclusive Heat Sentry™ automatically turns blower to high speed when excess heat is detected.

■ Bright cooktop lighting (bulb not included).

■ For vented installations only; not available vent-free.

■ Requires rough-in kit Model 113123.

Wood Hood...high-performance ventilation in a rich, traditional look.

■ Fits into wood hoods from 28-1/4" to 28-7/8" wide (and adapts to hoods up to 42" in width).

■ Powerful, quiet 360 CFM/5.0 Sone (vertical discharge) or 360 CFM/4.5 Sone (horizontal discharge) performance (HVI certified).

■ Exclusive Heat Sentry automatically turns blower to high speed when excess heat is detected.

■ 24" fluorescent tube lighting (bulb not included).

■ Duct connector with built-in damper for 3-1/4" by 10" vents.

■ For vented installations only; not available vent-free.

■ Requires rough-in kit Model 103123.

See page 15 for all performance specifications and installation requirements.

Micromate™. A powerful range hood. A place for your microwave. In one unit.

- Accommodates virtually any brand microwave oven.

- Installs vented or vent-free (Microtek® filter sold separately).

- Powerful, quiet 300 CFM/4.5 Sone (vertical discharge) performance (HVI certified).

- Bright cooktop lighting (bulb not included).

Micromate-120000 Series.

Canopy Hood. A warm, traditional, "heart-of-the-home" look.

- 190 CFM/6.0 (vertical discharge) or 200 CFM/6.5 Sone (horizontal discharge) performance (HVI certified).

- Convertible to vent-free operation with exclusive Microtek System filter that's 10 times more effective than vent-free filters of other manufacturers (available separately).

- Cooktop lighting with your choice of 100-watt bulb or 150-watt flood lamp (lamps sold separately).

- Textured, hammered finish in white, almond, harvest, avocado and coffee.

1000 Series Wall Canopy Hood.

page 15 for all performance specifications and installation requirements.

Range Hood Accessories and Blower Systems

Accessories	
Model #	Description
634	Roof cap with backdraft damper and safety screen, 3-1/4" x 10" or up to 8" round duct
644	Aluminum roof cap with backdraft damper and safety screen, 3-1/4" x 10" or up to 8" round duct
639	Wall cap 3-1/4" x 10" duct with backdraft damper with safety screen
641	Aluminum wall cap with backdraft damper with safety screen fits 6" round duct
643	Aluminum wall cap fits 8" round duct
647	Aluminum wall cap fits 7" round duct
649	Aluminum wall cap fits 3-1/4" x 10" duct with backdraft damper with safety screen
87	7" vertical discharge damper
97	7" spring-loaded, in-line damper
99	9" spring-loaded, in-line damper
401	3-1/4" x 10" duct, 2' section
406	6" round duct, 2' section
407	7" round duct, 2' section
410	10" round duct, 2' section
411	3-1/4" x 10" to 6" round transition
412	3-1/4" x 10" to 7" round transition
413	3-1/4" x 10" to 8" round transition
414	8" to 10" expander
415	7" adjustable elbow (carton of four)
418	10" adjustable elbow (individual)
419	6" adjustable elbow (individual)
421	10" round section with in-line damper
423	Vertical transition, 4-1/2" x 18-1/2" to 10" round
424	Rear transition, 4-1/2" x 18-1/2" to 10" round
425	Horz. left transition, 4-1/2" x 18-1/2" to 10" round
426	Horz. right transition, 4-1/2" x 18-1/2" to 10" round
453	Right end boot
454	Left end boot
428	3-1/4" x 10" vertical elbow
429	3-1/4" x 10" horizontal elbow
430	Short eave elbow for 3-1/4" x 10" duct with backdraft damper and grille
431	Long eave elbow for 3-1/4" x 10" duct with backdraft damper and grille
437	High capacity roof cap – up to 1200 CFM exhaust
441	Wall cap with gravity damper, 13-1/8" sq. fits 10" round duct
35	Wall hanging kit (for mounting hoods to wall when not hung from overhead cabinets)

Broan 331 (600 CFM) and 332 (900 CFM) exterior blowers.

Broan's new 600 CFM and 900 CFM exterior blowers offer your customers powerful ventilation performance with all the benefits of exterior mounting (roof or wall), and one benefit they won't find anywhere else… Broan quality.

- Reduce kitchen noise by locating range hood blowers on roof or outside walls.

- Select either Model 331 or the 332 exterior blower with 332K rough-in kit for Rangemaster® depending on cooking style and ventilation needs; the 332 is recommended for the Eclipse® downdraft.

- New, low-profile design fits unobtrusively with all home exterior styles.

- Durable, weather-resistant all aluminum construction.

- Safety screen keeps small animals and debris away from blower and motor.

Broan splash plates.

Stock and display splash plates for add-on sales:

- Durable 19-gauge enamel finish (appliance colors) or 24-gauge stainless steel.

- Select white, almond, black, stainless steel, avocado, coffee or harvest wheat.

- Available in 24", 30", 36" or 42" widths; all 24" high.

- Simplifies kitchen clean-up.

- Easily installed with four screws.

- See Broan price list for colors, models and prepacked display/dispenser.

RANGEMASTER®...see page 4

Width	Stainless Steel	White	Black	Almond
30"	603004	603001	603023	603008
36"	603604	603601	603623	603608
42"	604204	604201	604223	604208
48"	604804	604801	604823	604808
54"	605404	+	+	+
60"	606004	+	+	+
66"	606604	+	+	+
72"	607204	+	+	+

Options Selection Table

	Backsplash	Soffit Chimney			
Width	Stainless Steel	Stainless Steel	White	Black	Almond
30"	RP3004	RN3004	RN3001	RN3023	RN3008
36"	RP3604	RN3604	RN3601	RN3623	RN3608
42"	RP4204	RN4204	RN4201	RN4223	RN4208
48"	RP4804	RN4804	RN4801	RN4823	RN4808
54"	RP5404	RN5404	+	+	+
60"	RP6004	RN6004	+	+	+
66"	RP6604	RN6604	+	+	+
72"	RP7204	RN7204	+	+	+

+ Available as special order

Blower Selection Table and Specifications

Model	Mounting	CFM	Volts	Hz	Amps*	Vent Size
325	Interior	600	120	60	7.6	7" Round
326	Interior	1200	120	60	8.1	4-1/2" x 18-1/2" **
331	Exterior	600	120	60	2.3	10" Round
332**	Exterior	900	120	60	5.8	10" Round

++ Model 332K rough-in kit required for mounting.
Model no. 421 10" in-line damper recommended.
* Includes 4.5 Amps representing all lights.
** Transitions to 10" round available. (see accessory section on page 13)

Replacement bulbs:
Fluorescent: F14T12/SW (Soft White) Any F14T8 or F14T12 15" long preheat fluorescent lamp will fit.
Heat Lamps: 250-Watt, R40 Infrared (Bulbs and lamps not included).

ECLIPSE®...see page 5

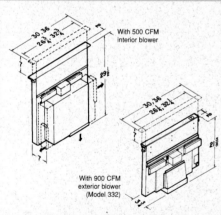

With 500 CFM interior blower

With 900 CFM exterior blower (Model 332)

To Fit Nominal Cooktop Size	Model	Description	Cover Color
30"	273003	Interior Blower Unit	Stainless Steel
36"	273603	Interior Blower Unit	Stainless Steel
30"	283003	Exterior Blower Unit*	Stainless Steel
36"	283603	Exterior Blower Unit*	Stainless Steel
30"	273001C	Optional Cover	White
36"	273601C	Optional Cover	White
30"	273023C	Optional Cover	Black
36"	273623C	Optional Cover	Black

* Exterior unit utilizes Model 332 Exterior-Mounted Blower, available separately.

Specifications**

Model	Volts	Amps	CFM	Vent
27000	120	4.0	500	3-1/4" x 10"
28000	120	4.0	900	3-1/4" x 10"

** Cooktops, countertops and cabinets vary in dimension and support systems depending upon manufacturer. These factors may impact the Eclipse's ability to fit with every worktop/cabinet combination. Specifications subject to change without notice.

SILHOUETTE®...see page 5

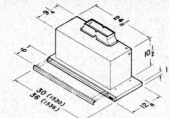

Allow 18 inches minimum from cooking surface to bottom of hood.

Width	White	Black
30"	153001	153023
36"	153601	153623

Specifications

Volts	Amps	Sones	CFM	Vent
120	3.7	4.5	300	3-1/4" x 10" (vertical)

Fluorescent Tube - 24", F20T12 (not included).

EXTERIOR BLOWERS...see page 13

For use with Rangemaster and Eclipse models.

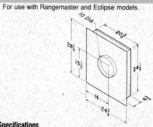

Specifications

Model	Volts	Amps	CFM	Vent
331	120	2.3	600	10" round
332	120	5.8	900	10" round

90000 SERIES...see page 6

Width	White	Almond	White on White	Black	Stainless
30"	903001	903008	903011	903023	903004
36"	903601	903608	903611	903623	903604
42"	904201	904208	904211	904223	904204

Order Microtek® System IV filter 97007662 for vent-free operation.

Specifications

Volts	Amps	Sones Ver.	Sones Hor.	CFM Ver.	CFM Hor.	Vent-Free RHP Index	Vent
120	4.5	5.5	6.0	360	350	59.09	3-1/4" x 10"

89000 SERIES...see page 7

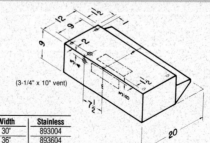

(3-1/4" x 10" vent)

Width	Stainless
30"	893004
36"	893604
42"	894204
48"	894804

Specifications

Volts	Amps	Sones Ver.	Sones Hor.	CFM Ver.	CFM Hor.	Vent
120	6.0	6.0	7.0	460	440	3-1/4" x 10"

88000 SERIES...see page 7

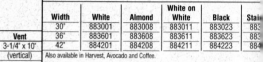

(3-1/4" x 10" vent)

Width	White	Almond	White on White	Black	Stai
30"	883001	883008	883011	883023	883
36"	883601	883608	883611	883623	883
42"	884201	884208	884211	884223	884

Also available in Harvest, Avocado and Coffee.

Specifications

Volts	Amps	Sones Ver.	Sones Hor.	CFM Ver.	CFM Hor.	Vent-Free RHP Index	Ve
120	4.5	5.5	6.0	360	350	59.09	3-1/4"

76000 SERIES...see page 8

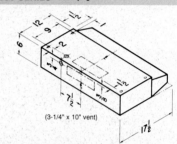

(3-1/4" x 10" vent)

Width	White	Almond	White on White	Black	Stain
24"	762401	762408	762411	762423	762
30"	763001	763008	763011	763023	763
36"	763601	763608	763611	763623	763
42"	764201	764208	764211	764223	764

Also available in Harvest, Avocado and Coffee.

Specifications

Volts	AMPS	Sones Ver.	Sones Hor.	CFM	Vent-Free RHP Index	Ve
120	3.0	5.5	6.0	200	22.73	3-1/4"

75000 SERIES...see page 9

Width	White	Almond	Stainless
30"	753001	753008	753004
36"	753601	753608	753604
42"	754201	754208	754204

Specifications

Volts	AMPS	Sones Ver.	Sones Hor.	CFM	Vent-Free RHP Index	Ve
120	3.6	6.5	6.0	250	25.0	3-1/4"

68000 SERIES...see page 9

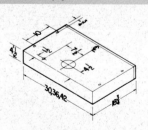

7" Round Vent

Width	White	Black
30"	683001	683023
36"	683601	683623
42"	684201	684223

Specifications

Volts	AMPS	CFM	Sones
120	2.5	230	7.0

00 SERIES...see page 9

Vent-Free

Width	White	Black
30"	673001	673023
36"	673601	673623
42"	674201	674223

...ifications

Volts	AMPS	CFM	Sones
120	2.0	Vent-Free	Vent-Free

000 SERIES...see page 9

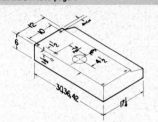

...und Vent

Width	White	Almond	Stainless
30"	483001	483008	483004
36"	483601	483608	483604
42"	484201	484208	484204

...ifications

Volts	AMPS	CFM	Sones
120	2.5	230	7.0

000 SERIES...see page 9

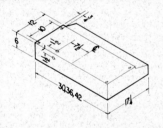

...Free

Width	White	Almond	Stainless
30"	473001	473008	473004
36"	473601	473608	473604
42"	474201	474208	474204

...ifications

Volts	AMPS	CFM	Sones
120	2.0	Vent-Free	Vent-Free

...NESSE...see page 3

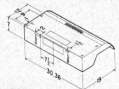

...0 Series (250 CFM)

...idth	White	Almond	Black	Stainless
...0"	813011	813018	813025	813004
...6"	813611	813618	813625	813604

...0 Series (400 CFM)

...idth	White	Almond	Black	Stainless
...0"	833011	833018	833025	833004
...6"	833611	833618	833625	833604

46000 SERIES...see page 10

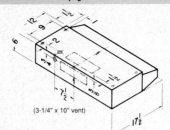

(3-1/4" x 10" vent)

Width	White	Almond	Stainless
30"	463001	463008	463004
36"	463601	463608	463604
42"	464201	464208	464204

Also available in Harvest, Avocado and Coffee.

Specifications

Volts	AMPS	Sones Ver.	Sones Hor.	CFM	Vent-Free RHP Index	Vent
120	2.5	7.0	6.5	230	7.0	3-1/4" x 10"

42000 SERIES...see page 11

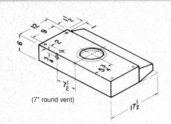

(7" round vent)

7" Round Vent

Width	White	Almond	Stainless
30"	423001	423008	423004
36"	423601	423608	423604

Also available in Harvest, Avocado and Coffee.

Specifications

Volts	AMPS	Sones Ver.	Sones Hor.	CFM	Duct-Free RHP Index	Vent
120	2.5	5.5	–	190	–	7" Round

Economy hoods are not convertible.

41000/40000 SERIES...see page 11

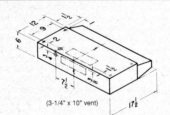

(3-1/4" x 10" vent)

41000 Vent-Free

Width	White	Almond	Stainless
24"	412401	412408	412404
30"	413001	413008	413004
36"	413601	413608	413604

Also available in Harvest, Avocado and Coffee.

41000 Specifications

Volts	AMPS	Sones Ver.	Sones Hor.	CFM	Vent-Free RHP Index
120	2.0	Vent-Free	Vent-Free	Vent-Free	8.70

40000 Vented

Width	White	Almond	Stainless
24"	402401	402408	402404
30"	403001	403008	403004
36"	403601	403608	403604

Also available in Harvest, Avocado and Coffee.

40000 Specifications

Volts	AMPS	Sones Ver.	Sones Hor.	CFM	Vent-Free RHP Index	Vent
120	2.0	5.5	6.5	160	–	3-1/4" x 10"

Economy hoods are not convertible.

HIDEAWAY-Model 113023...see page 12

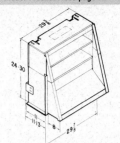

Specifications

Volts	Amps	Sones	CFM	Vent
120	3.7	4.5	360	3-1/4" x 10"

WOOD HOOD-Model 103023...see page 12

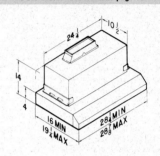

Specifications

Volts	Amps	Sones Ver.	Sones Hor.	CFM	Vent
120	3.7	5.0	4.5	360	3-1/4" x 10"

MICROMATE™-120000 Series...see page 13

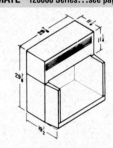

Specifications

Volts	Amps	Sones	CFM	Vent-Free RHP Index	Vent
120	2.7	4.5	300	9.8	3-1/4" x 10"

11000 SERIES...see page 13

Traditional Wall Canopy Hood

(3-1/4" x 10" vent)

11000 Series

Width	Hammered White	Hammered Almond	Hammered Harvest	Hammered Avocado	Hammered Coffee
30"	113036	113042	113047	113048	113049

Specifications

Volts	AMPS	Sones Ver.	Sones Hor.	CFM Ver.	CFM Hor.	Vent-Free RHP Index	Vent
120	3.0	6.0	6.5	190	200	9.80	3-1/4" x 10"

15

Broan delivers what customers want in kitchen ventilation.

Product: Broan offers the largest selection of range hoods in North America. Choose from Premium, Deluxe, Intermediate, Economy or Specialty models in more styles, sizes and colors than any other manufacturer.

Quality: All painted parts and weldments are inspected to assure a quality finish. All dimensional specifications are verified electronically to assure a quality fit and feel. And all shipments are inspected to be certain you receive the quality product you ordered, the way you ordered it. No shortcuts. No exceptions.

Value: State-of-the-art manufacturing and a continuing commitment to innovation ensure customers always receive the quality, reliability and performance they want, in every price category.

Performance: Exclusive features, available on a wide variety of products, allow you to turn prospects into customers:

- Heat Sentry™ – Automatically turns blower to high speed when excess heat is detected.

- AutoTemp – Monitors cooking conditions and automatically adjusts blower to appropriate ventilation levels.

- Blower Memory – Returns fan speed to the last setting used, so your customers don't have to reset the control.

Marketing support that works for you.

National Consumer Advertising: Broan is the leading residential range hood advertiser, with more than 415 million impressions each year in leading shelter magazines.

Public Relations: Broan maintains direct contact with more than 230 consumer and trade publications, ensuring that information on our range hood innovations gets to consumers.

In-Store Displays: Broan designs and builds custom range hood displays in our own

fully-equipped display department, so you can demonstrate our products for maximum exposure and sales.

Merchandising Support: Broan range hood ad slicks and logo sheets help you compose ads and fliers, and our instruction sheets are written to make installation especially easy.

Microtek® Filters: Broan Microtek replacement filters are a built-in sales and profit opportunity. Order in convenient, prepacked shipper displays.

Service: Broan sales and merchandising experts help you plan orders and promotions to maximize sales and profits. Our customer service representatives are available to help you between 7:30AM and 6:00PM Central Time. Call 1-800-558-1711.

BROAN®
A NORTEK COMPANY

P.O. Box 140, Hartford, WI 53027 **1-800-548-0790**
In Canada: Broan Limited **905-670-2500**

ALL THE COMFORTS OF HOME™

Printed in the U.S.A.

9985014
B

FOR THE WAY YOU LIVE...
FOR THE WAY YOU WORK...
FOR THE WAY IT'S MADE...

KitchenAid®

INTRODUCING

the New Architect™ Series from KitchenAid®

For generations, KitchenAid® appliances have enriched the kitchen experience for homeowners, whether cooking, entertaining, or just spending time with family.

Now, our stunning new Architect Series™ promises to make kitchen experiences even more rewarding. The Architect Series™ is the stainless steel line you have been waiting for - a sleek, streamlined design that blends in easily with any decor, contemporary or traditional. It's an ideal professional-caliber alternative to industrial-looking products. And, of course, it comes with KitchenAid® brand's enduring quality and thoughtful design, for the perfect combination of timeless beauty and performance.

KitchenAid®
FOR THE WAY IT'S MADE®

FOR A NEW LOOK IN
KITCHEN DESIGNS

KitchenAid®

FOR THE WAY IT'S MADE*

We call our new color Biscuit.

Take a fresh look at KitchenAid®. Our new Biscuit line of appliances is further evidence of our commitment to design appliances that feature quality engineering and timeless styling.

With the established trend towards natural, subtle colors in kitchen and bath areas, KOHLER Co. and DuPont CORIAN® have already introduced colors like "Biscuit" in their product lines. These colors are among their leading sellers.

The Biscuit line of appliances is a natural response to this growing trend. When no other color will do - look for the brand you trust.

CodeC503
11452/KIT
BuyLine 1405

"Biscuit" sink and faucet by KOHLER.®
"Biscuit" countertop surfaces by DuPont CORIAN.®
KitchenAid thanks both manufacturers for their contribution.

FOR THE
DESIGNER'S CHOICE

KitchenAid® will accent your great design with a choice of styles and colors. Fresh, contemporary styling with the Sculptura™ family look. Traditional styling with our Classic look. Either way, it's a KitchenAid® appliance leading the industry.

KitchenAid® is an industry leader in:
Design - Function - Features - Durability
Quietness - Style - Innovation

KitchenAid® Dishwashers
Longest Lasting Dishwasher in America

For styling choice

KitchenAid® offers two unique styles for design flexibility. The KitchenAid® KD25 has models featuring Sculptura™ "family look" styling as well as a traditional "classic" flush front styling.

For quiet

Using a state-of-the-art sound laboratory, KitchenAid® engineers created a dishwasher with features that provide some of the most efficient sound insulation possible. The new KitchenAid® Dishwasher line is quieter and you can hear the difference.

For performance

Models with SensorSure™ Soil Sensor offer better cleaning performance by removing soiled water earlier in the cycle. Super Scrub™ wash option gets crusted baking dishes clean and Sure Dry™ convection dries completely to a clear finish.

Traditional Classic

Contemporary Sculptura™

KitchenAid® Laundry Products

Clothes Look Better and Last Longer!

C503
11452/KIT
BuyLine 1405

For gentle fabric care

KitchenAid® Washers and Dryers provide gentle protection for all your fabrics. At the heart of every KitchenAid® washer is the Sure Care® Wash System with 3-speed operation and the oversized, Dual-Action Sure Care® Agitator. This agitator is so powerful, it can clean effectively at speeds as low as 90 strokes per minute.

When you pair your KitchenAid® washer with a Kitchenaid® dryer, you have even more fabric care options. The CUSHIONED HEAT™ System gently cools your clothing to prevent them from overdrying and protect them from wrinkling.

With all these quality features, you'll see why, when your choice is KitchenAid®, your clothes will look better and last longer.

For quiet operation

KitchenAid® Washers and Dryers offer a 30-Day Money-Back Guarantee if your new SUPERBA® Washer and Dryer is not quieter than your previous washer and dryer. KitchenAid® SUPERBA® Washers are the quietest top-loading washers in the industry.

KITCHENAID® BUILT-IN COOKING
A SYMBOL OF LASTING QUALITY

For integrated elegance

KitchenAid® Built-In Cooking Products are known for their looks, or rather, how they accentuate your kitchen design. Whether your kitchen is contemporary or traditional, you'll appreciate the smooth lines and rounded corners - both signatures of the KitchenAid® brand - that invite you to take a closer look at the entire kitchen. Plus, new Biscuit and Stainless color options (available on select models) give you more design flexibility than ever before.

For convection

For more than a decade, KitchenAid® convection ovens have been helping experienced chefs and novices alike create culinary masterpieces. Today, to meet the increased demand for this feature, KitchenAid® Built-In Ovens offer the Industry's Most Complete Convection Cooking Line!

KitchenAid® SUPERBA® built-in ovens offer a unique third hidden element design with the T.H.E. Convection Cooking System. In addition to "true" convection cooking, the T.H.E. System provides features like the EasyConvect Conversion System and a CONVECT FULL MEAL Option that make it easy for you to reap the benefits of convection cooking.

For customer satisfaction

KitchenAid® Built-In Cooking Products deliver sought-after, premium features. In premium kitchens, appliances - especially cooking products - are more than after-thoughts. You research, shop, and look for the best - and the best is precisely what you'll get with the KitchenAid® brand.

From halogen oven lights and frameless cooktops to easy-to-use convection controls and 14,000 BTU gas burners, we deliver all the top-shelf features you look for - and much more.

KitchenAid® Refrigeration
The Best Temperature Management System in the Industry!

For freshness

We know that fresh food is important to you. KitchenAid® Refrigerators Lock in Freshness with high-efficiency features including the ExtendFresh™ Temperature Management System - "The Best Temperature Management System in the Industry!"

But KitchenAid® refrigerators do more than keep food fresh. The AquaSense™ Water Filtration System† uses activated carbon to provide better-tasting, cleaner ice and water - 500 gallons between filter changes. That's why we call it the Twice-the-Life™ Water Filter.* You can see why KitchenAid® SUPERBA® large side-by-side refrigerators are rated #1 by a leading consumer magazine.

†on select side-by-side refrigerators

*KitchenAid Twice-the-Life Water Filters remove lead, chlorine, particulates, and turbidity. Competitive filters remove lead, chlorine, particulates, turbidity, and cysts.

For convenience

The thoughtful design of KitchenAid® refrigerators makes it easy to get at foods. With RollerTrac™Plus Roll-Out Adjustable SpillClean™ Glass Shelves* and slide-out freezer baskets KitchenAid® Refrigerators provide easy access to all the foods you store.

*on bottom-mount and select side-by-side refrigerators

For your home

Whatever you need to store, a KitchenAid® refrigerator can make room for it. With ClearVue™ Crispers, removable can racks, and even a RollerTrac™ Plus Roll-Out Freezer Floor,* KitchenAid® Refrigerators need to be seen to be believed.

*on select top-mount refrigerators

KITCHENAID® SPECIALTY PRODUCTS
WINE CELLARS, AUTOMATIC CLEAR ICE MAKERS,
TRASH COMPACTORS, HOT WATER DISPENSERS,
AND FOOD WASTE DISPOSERS

*For a home that is
more than a sum
of it's parts.*

For your home.

It's your choice.

KitchenAid®
FOR THE WAY IT'S MADE®

SHARP.

setting new standards for performance

MICROWAVE OVENS

Carousel®

MICROWAVE *ovens*

Leadership in design is often an indicator of excellence beyond the surface issues. With its popular Over the Range Carousel® microwave ovens, Sharp continues to lead the industry in both styling and feature innovations. Setting standards in every category, Sharp's revolutionary "firsts" have become the measure by which all others are judged. Like the world's first Carousel® turntable system in an Over the Range microwave, Smart & Easy™ Sensor Technology, Interactive Displays, and more. All developed to make it easy for any user to achieve mistake-proof results. The products of intuitive engineering, enlightened design, and enduring quality, Sharp microwave ovens represent an outstanding value to consumers. No doubt it's why they've been the #1 brand of microwave ovens for so many years.

Removable rack increases capacity.

ENHANCED CAPABILITIES...
Power...Capacity...Information

Sharp's newest Over the Range models offer 1000 watts of cooking power and a large 1.6 cu. ft. capacity. A new rack makes it possible to heat several dishes simultaneously without crowding, while the ON/OFF turntable easily accommodates an oversized dish. There even a new 2-line, 16-digit Interactive Display which provides more easy-to-read information, faster.

GREATER CONVENIENCE...
"More from your Microwave"

31 "More from your Microwave" menu options allow users to cook a variety of breakfast, lunch, and one-dish dinners, defrost popular foods and prepare beverages, as well.....all automatically. Combined with Sharp's Smart & Easy Sensor settings, there are 44 automatic choices in all! There's even Sharp's all new Super Defrost that makes certain defrosting jobs up to 50% faster.

TOTAL FLEXIBILITY...
Convection Microwave

Sharp's Convection Microwave ovens offer everything consumers love about conventional cooking and more. They get convection baking, broiling and combination roasting and baking, plus microwave convenience — all in one space-saving oven.

DRAMATIC STYLING...*Stainless Steel*

Sleek lines and cool textures. Only stainless steel can create the high-tech professional culinary look consumers want today. That's why Sharp offers it in two countertop models with convenient built-in options. Beautifully in sync with all the latest kitchen designs, stainless steel is as luxurious as it is enduring.

These elegantly-styled, large capacity stainless steel microwave ovens convey the sophisticated look of a product with smart, innovative engineering. A look that definitely says, there's some serious cooking going on here. Designed to meet the growing demand for professional-type equipment in the home, durable stainless steel is as practical as it is beautiful. However, sleek styling isn't all that sets these ovens apart. Packed with advanced performance to meet every cooking and entertaining need, they offer a wide array of timesaving features that eliminate cooking and programming guesswork. Available with a 16" turntable, 1.8 cu. ft. capacity (R-530BS) or 14 1/8" turntable, 1.4 cu. ft. capacity (R-430CS), both models have 1100 watts of high-speed cooking power. Perfect on the countertop or built-in (using optional RK-51S27 or RK-51S30 stainless-look Built-in Kits for R-530BS only), stainless steel makes everything look more professional, even the person using it.

R-530BS
R-430CS[+]

Sleek, Sophisticated,
STAINLESS STEEL STYLING.

R-530BS

R-530BS

features:

SMART & EASY SENSOR SETTINGS
automatically determine and set cooking times and power levels for such popular foods as popcorn, baked potatoes, rice, seafood, frozen main dishes, and more.

NEW! 2-LINE, 2 COLOR INTERACTIVE DISPLAY
provides clear word prompts to help the user get optimum cooking results. With 2 lines (12-digit R530BS / 16-digit R-430CS), communication is faster to read and easier to follow.

INTERACTIVE COOKING SYSTEM
offers step-by-step instructions to guide user through programming steps, special options, and cooking tips.

CUSTOM HELP™
makes it easy to program special options such as Child Lock, audible signal elimination, Auto Start, language / weight options — in English, Spanish, or French.

NEW "MORE FROM YOUR MICROWAVE"
provides 31 additional cooking / reheating / defrosting selections. Enables users to defrost, cook, and heat a variety of breakfast and lunch items as well as popular one-dish dinners, all automatically. Recipes provided, of course! (R-430CS only)

[*] R-430CS: complete specifications available on request or visit www.sharp-usa.com

1

R-1610 R-1611
R-1612

MORE AUTOMATIC *Convenience* THAN EVER BEFORE.

Sharp's new 1000 watt, 1.6 cu. ft. capacity Over the Range Carousel microwaves represent the latest in advanced technology and user convenience. The new 2-line, 16-digit display makes communication faster and easier to read. A new removable rack increases capacity and 44 automatic menu selections greatly expand cooking/ reheating convenience. Also new is Memory Cook, which quickly recalls one set of cooking instructions previously stored in memory. Plus Super Defrost, that's up to 50% faster. Available in black, white or almond, these ovens feature a new pearlescent handle to complement any decor or cabinetry hardware. The powerful ventilation system has a 2-speed fan to remove smoke and steam from range-top cooking. Installation, whether vented to the outside or recirculating, is easier than ever. Includes a convenient work light and night light.

R-1611

R-1610

features:

NEW 2-LINE, 16-DIGIT INTERACTIVE DISPLAY
makes programming communication faster and easier to read. Guides user through the cooking process and offers a variety of helpful hints in English, Spanish, and French.

NEW "MORE FROM YOUR MICROWAVE"
provides 31 additional cooking / reheating / defrost selections. Enables users to defrost, cook, and heat a variety of breakfast and lunch items as well as popular one-dish dinners, all automatically. Recipes provided, of course!

TURNTABLE ON/OFF
setting enables users to put the extra-large 13" turntable in "OFF" position in order to use oblong dishes (up to 4-quart, 10"x15"). Makes it much easier to cook for a crowd.

REMOVABLE COOKING RA
increases capacity, accommodating mul dishes without crowding.

13 SMART & EASY SENSOR SETTINGS
automatically select optimum cooking and power levels for popular food grou including Popcorn and Reheat.

NEW SUPER DEFROST
automatically defrosts 1-lb. portions of ground beef and boneless chicken breast to 50% faster. COMPU DEFROST™ au matically defrosts virtually any food cate

POWERFUL 300 CFM VENTILATION SYSTEM
offers three convenient venting options. Comes READY-TO-RECIRCULATE the charcoal filter provided making it ea than ever to install. May also be ducted outside, either vertically or horizontally.

R-1600 R-1601
R-1602

Beauty IS AS *Beauty* DOES.

One look at these stunning Over the Range Carousel microwave ovens and it's easy to see their appeal. Three sophisticated matte finishes (black R-1600, white R-1601, almond R-1602) and a new pearlescent handle beautifully complement any environment. Innovative styling aside, it's the performance that really attracts attention. A new 2-line, 16-digit display makes programming faster and easier, while a removable rack for two-level cooking increases capacity. Also new: Memory Cook which lets users quickly recall one set of cooking instructions previously stored in memory. An impressive line-up of timesaving automatic features ensures mistake-proof microwaving. With high-speed cooking power of 1000 watts and a 1.6 cu. ft. capacity, these ovens can easily handle a wide range of microwaving needs. Also included: a handy work light and night light.

R-1600

features:

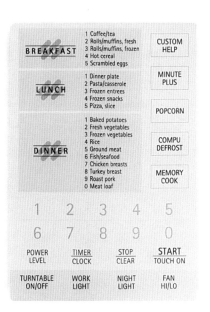

R-1601

NEW INTERACTIVE COOKING SYSTEM WITH 2-LINE, 16-DIGIT DISPLAY makes programming communication faster and easier to read. Simple instructions guide user through the cooking process in English, Spanish, or French.

NEW MEMORY COOK speeds up the cooking process by letting user recall one set of cooking instructions previously placed in memory.

TURNTABLE ON/OFF SETTING enables users to put the extra-large 13" turntable in "OFF" position in order to use oblong dishes (up to 4-quart, 10"x15"). Makes it much easier to cook for a crowd.

REMOVABLE COOKING RACK increases capacity, accommodating multiple dishes without crowding.

POWERFUL 300 CFM VENTILATION SYSTEM offers three convenient venting options. Comes READY-TO-RECIRCULATE with the charcoal filter provided making it easier than ever to install. May also be ducted to the outside, either vertically or horizontally.

BREAKFAST, LUNCH, AND DINNER settings automatically prepare 20 popular food items.

R-1850 R-1851
R-1852

CONVECTION MICROWAVE: THE *Ultimate* IN
COOKING *Versatility.*

R-1850

With these Over the Range convection microwave ovens, Sharp brings new meaning to multifunctional convenience. Now consumers can brown, bake, broil, crisp, and roast with microwave, convection, combination, and broil options. One oven does it all, without taking up a lot of space. They even come in a choice of designer colors: R-1850 (black-on-black), R-1851 (white-on-white), and R-1852 (almond-on-almond)– to suit any decor. A generous 1.1 cu. ft. stainless steel interior easily handles a variety of cooking needs and 850 watts offer cooking power to spare.

R-1851

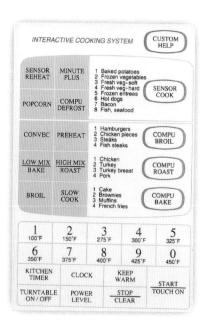

R-1851

features:

LARGE 13-INCH DIAMETER CERAMIC TURNTABLE with **ON/OFF** flexibility to handle oversized or oblong-shaped dishes or containers.

BUILT-IN EXHAUST SYSTEM offers horizontal or vertical discharge or ductless recirculation. Comes with hood light and powerful fan.

7-DIGIT, TWO-COLOR INTERACTIVE DISPLAY spells out programming steps on a lighted easy-to-read display. **CUSTOM HELP** key offers helpful cooking hints and step-by-step instructions for special features such as Child Lock and Auto Start.

SMART & EASY SENSOR settings automatically determine and cooking or reheating times and pow levels for a variety of popular foods including baked potatoes, frozen ent vegetables, hot dogs, bacon, fish/seaf

COMPU BROIL™, COMPU ROAST™, COMPU BAKE™ settings provide a new level of autom ease. Broil a steak, roast a chicken, b a cake to perfection at the touch of a

HIGH RACK included for two-level baking.

LOW RACK may be used for baking, roasting, or broiling.

It's everything anyone could want in a convection microwave oven...and more. Available with metallic charcoal cabinet (R-930AK) or white-on-white (R-930AW), with a stainless steel interior, this oven may be used as a countertop unit or installed as a wall oven with optional Built-in Kit. Both incorporate Sharp's advanced Interactive Cooking System with a 2-Color Display that provides easy-to-follow cooking steps and programming instructions. The large 1.5 cu. ft. capacity with 15 3/8-inch diameter porcelain enamel turntable can easily handle a wide range of conventional and microwave cooking needs. It's the most convenient way to create everything from cakes and casseroles to steaks and roasts to potatoes and popcorn. Output power: 900 watts.

R-930AK
R-930AW

THE BROWNING, BAKING, BROILING, CRISPING, MICROWAVING
All-In-One INTERACTIVE SYSTEM.

R-930AK

R-930AK

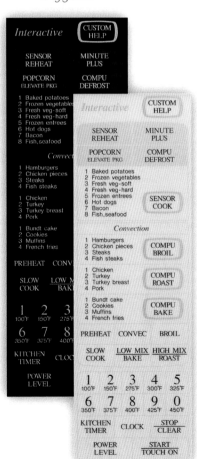

R-930AW

features:

4-WAY SYSTEM browns, bakes, broils, crisps. Two combination settings for roasting and baking are included. Broil key automatically preheats oven, signals when ready.

SMART & EASY SENSOR eliminates guesswork by automatically determining microwave cooking/reheating times and setting power levels for 8 different food categories.

COMPU BROIL, COMPU ROAST, COMPU BAKE automatically compute broiling, roasting, and baking times/temperature settings. High and low racks satisfy multiple cooking needs.

7-DIGIT TWO-COLOR INTERACTIVE DISPLAY WITH CUSTOM HELP KEY provides easy-to-read programming steps, cooking hints, and special options.

Many time and worksaving extras include:
SLOW COOK, LOW MIX/BAKE, HIGH MIX/ROAST, COMPU DEFROST, 10 VARIABLE POWER LEVELS, REHEAT & POPCORN SENSORS, MINUTE PLUS, TIMER.

R-930AW

specifications:

MODEL	R-1612, R-1611, R-1610	R-1602, R-1601, R-1600	R-1852, R-1851, R-1850	R-930AK, R-930AW	R-530BS
OVEN CAPACITY	1.6 cu. ft.	1.6 cu. ft.	1.1 cu. ft.	1.5 cu. ft.	1.8 cu. ft.
COOKING UNIFORMITY	Turntable or stirrer system; 13" diameter glass turntable	Turntable or stirrer system; 13" diameter glass turntable	Turntable or stirrer system; 13" diameter ceramic turntable	Carousel Turntable system; 15^3/$_8$" diameter porcelain enamel turntable	Carousel Turntable system; 16" diameter glass turntable
DISPLAY	2-line, 16-digit interactive	2-line, 16-digit interactive	7-digit Interactive 2-color	7-digit Interactive 2-color	2-line, 12-digit Interactive
CONVECTION OVEN TEMPERATURE CONTROL			100°, 150°, 275°-450° F in 25° increments	100°, 150°, 275°-450° F in 25° increments	
DESIGN	R-1612: Almond R-1611: White R-1610: Black	R-1602: Almond R-1601: White R-1600: Black	R-1852: Almond R-1851: White R-1850: Black	R-930AK: Metallic charcoal cabinet; black front R-930AW: White-on-white	Stainless steel front; Silver painted cabinet
OUTPUT POWER	1000W	1000W	850W	900W	1100W
OUTSIDE DIMENSIONS (W x H x D)	29^{15}/$_{16}$" x 16^3/$_8$" x 17^1/$_{16}$"*	29^{15}/$_{16}$" x 16^3/$_8$" x 17^1/$_{16}$"*	29^{15}/$_{16}$" x 16^{11}/$_{32}$" x 15^9/$_{32}$"	24^5/$_8$" x 14^7/$_8$" x 18^3/$_4$"	23^{15}/$_{16}$" x 13^7/$_{16}$" x 19^1/$_4$"
OVEN DIMENSIONS (W x H x D)	21" x 8^7/$_8$" x 14^7/$_{16}$"	21" x 8^7/$_8$" x 14^7/$_{16}$"	17^1/$_8$" x 8^1/$_{16}$" x 13^{13}/$_{16}$"	16^1/$_8$" x 9^5/$_8$" x 16^1/$_8$"	16^{13}/$_{16}$" x 10^1/$_{16}$" x 18^5/$_8$"
OVEN INTERIOR	Acrylic with light	Acrylic with light	Stainless steel with light	Stainless steel with light	Acrylic with light
APPROX. WEIGHT	Net: 55 lbs. Shipping: 63 lbs.	Net: 55 lbs. Shipping: 63 lbs.	Net: 71 lbs. Shipping: 81 lbs.	Net: 60 lbs. Shipping: 68 lbs.	Net: 41 lbs. Shipping: 46 lbs.
AC LINE VOLTAGE	All models: 120V, single phase, 60Hz, AC only			1.55kW, 13.0A	1.65kW, 14.0A
AC POWER REQUIRED	1.64kW, 14A	1.64kW, 14A	1.6kW, 13.2A		
SAFETY COMPLIANCE	All models: FCC, DHHS, UL listed				
SUPPLIED ACCESSORIES	Rack, RK-230 Charcoal Filter for non-ducted installations+	Rack, RK-230 Charcoal Filter for non-ducted installations+	High and low racks	High and low racks	
UPC CODES	R-1612: 07400063759 R-1611: 07400063758 R-1610: 07400063757	R-1602: 07400063756 R-1601: 07400063755 R-1600: 07400063754	R-1852: 074000635739 R-1851: 074000635524 R-1850: 074000635517	R-930AK: 074000606036 R-930AW: 074000606043	R-530BS: 074000636996
OPTIONAL ACCESSORIES (AVAILABLE AT EXTRA COST)			RK-220 Charcoal Filter for non-ducted installations+	R-930AK: Built-in Kit RK-66A (black) R-930AW: Built-in Kit RK-66WB (white) for in-the-wall installation+	30" Built-in Kit RK-51S30 (Stainless look) 27" Built-in Kit RK-51S27(Stainless look) for in-the-wall installation+

Specifications subject to change without notice. +Refer to Operation Manual for installation recommendations. Output wattage based on IEC-705 1988 Test Procedure. Models R-930AK/AW have UL approval to build-in over General Electric brand 27" electric wall oven models JKP18BW/WW/AW. Model R-530BS has UL approval to build-in over General Electric brand 30" electric wall oven model ZET837SYSS, Thermador 30" electric wall oven model CT130S, or Thermador 27" electric wall oven model CT127NS.

* Depth Dimension excludes handle.

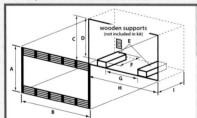

wooden supports (not included in kit)

Your Sharp Microwave Oven can be built into your kitchen wall or cabinet using the appropriate Sharp Built-in Kit. Complete hardware and easy-to-follow instructions are included. Prepare cabinet or wall opening according to the illustration at left, providing access to a separate 3-pronged, 120V AC outlet, 15 amps. or larger.

	A	B	C	D	E	F	G	H	I
RK-66A, RK-66WB	19^7/$_8$"	26^7/$_8$"	17^1/$_8$" (+ ht. of wood)	17^1/$_8$"	nominal 2" x 2"; actual 1^9/$_{16}$" x 1^9/$_{16}$" x 15"	18^3/$_8$"±^{1}/$_8$"	15	25^1/$_4$"±^{1}/$_8$"	min. 19^1/$_2$"
RK-51S27	18^1/$_8$"	26^{11}/$_{16}$"	16^7/$_8$"±^{1}/$_8$"	—	not used	—	—	24^1/$_2$"±^{3}/$_{16}$"	min. 20"
RK-51S30	18^1/$_8$"	29^{11}/$_{16}$"	16^7/$_8$"±^{1}/$_8$"	—	not used	—	—	24^1/$_2$"±^{3}/$_{16}$"	min. 20"

To receive the most current specifications, call Dimension Express at (702) 833-3600 from a fax machine. Enter code 9026 for instructions and a directory of Sharp microwave oven products.

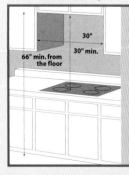

Each Sharp Over The Range microwave oven can be easily adapted for either outside ventilation (vertical or horizontal) or nonvented, ductless recirculation. Make sure top of oven will be at least 66" from the floor and at least 30" from the cooking surface. A separate 15 amp. or greater electrical receptacle must be located in the cabinet directly above the microwave oven.

LIMITED WARRANTY (R-930AK, R-930AW, R-530BS): 5 years on magnetron tube, 1 year on all other parts, 1 year on related labor and carry in service.*
See Operation Manual or your dealer for complete details.

*1 year in-home service will be provided when built-in using applicable Sharp Built-in Kit.

LIMITED WARRANTY (R-1612, R-1611, R-1610, R-1602, R-1601, R-1600)
7 years on magnetron tube, 1 year on all other parts, 1 year on related labor and in-home service.
See Operation Manual or your dealer for complete details.

LIMITED WARRANTY (R-1852, R-1851, R-1850)
7 years on magnetron tube, 2 years on all other parts, 2 years on related labor and in-home service.
See Operation Manual or your dealer for complete details.

SHARP®

FROM SHARP MINDS COME SHARP PRODUCTS™

MW-06-059

Sharp Electronics Corporation
Sharp Plaza, Mahwah, NJ 07430-2135
For more information call: 1-800-BE-SHARP
www.sharp-usa.com
©1999 Sharp Electronics Corporation

Built~in Home Refrigeration
Designed for Beauty and Performance

The first choice in kitchens of distinction

In remodeling and new construction, the look of distinction in kitchens begins with the beauty of built-in appliances and built-in refrigeration by Sub-Zero. That's why leading custom kitchen designers choose Sub-Zero first. Classic in styling and unequaled for storage, convenience and quality, Sub-Zero true built-ins are the ultimate in elegant home refrigeration.

Enjoy the elegance of built-in refrigeration

Sub-Zero home refrigeration is designed to enhance the beauty of any decor by blending compatibly with other kitchen furnishings. This is possible because of its simple design...removable decorative panels and the fact it is the same 24″ depth as most base kitchen cabinets. A Sub-Zero is designed with a minimum of external hardware, making it hardly noticeable when built into a kitchen. It also has an exclusive toe-base feature, important in kitchen appliances, which lines up with kitchen cabinets.

All units are constructed with the 24″ depth which enables the face to fit flush with most standard base cabinets. A typical free-standing refrigerator protrudes into the room 4 to 6 inches beyond cabinets, creating an unsightly appearance and takes up valuable space in the room.

Sub-Zero built-ins are designed to accept removable exterior panels of any material on the front and sides. In doing so, the unit practically disappears into the overall kitchen, blending completely into the decor instead of dominating the kitchen appearance, as a free-standing unit does. And, because the panels are removable, they can be changed, should the room decor change.

These true built-in features mean your home refrigeration need not be an unattractive standout but can now complement the over-all style of the kitchen and function as an integral part of the total kitchen design. They allow individual styling and expression of your personal taste.

Built-in work savers

Truly an accent to the kitchen of distinction, Sub-Zero built-in refrigeration offers all of the time and work saving features that today's lifestyles require...like convenient usable storage, easy up-keep, simplified cleaning, automatic defrosting and automatic ice maker.

The shallow depth makes it easier to find what you are looking for, eliminating the need to search for items that have found their way to the back shelf area (as in other refrigerators). This, along with the fact that all shelves are fully adjustable, gives even greater flexibility for storage arrangements.

Easy up-keep is achieved because of the quality materials and craftsmanship used in the construction of a Sub-Zero, ...interior, exterior and mechanical.

Cleaning is simplified because of two reasons: First the unit's built-in feature eliminates cracks and crevices that would normally collect dust and also eliminates the chore of pulling the refrigerator out to clean behind it.

Secondly, all shelves in Sub-Zero full-size units are removable to allow for ease of cleaning.

The automatic defrost feature is standard on all full-size models as well as the undercounter models (except

Model 550

249R). This eliminates the need to shut down the refrigerator to defrost and clean the unit.

Another standard feature of the full-size units is the automatic ice maker which produces an adequate supply of ice automatically without the need to handle awkward ice trays.

Many models to choose from

Whatever your space or usage requirements, Sub-Zero offers a selection of over 12 models to fit your needs and specifications. Choose from the popular side-by-side, the over-n-under (freezer on the bottom), the all-freezer and all-refrigerator units, compact undercounter refrigerators and an ice maker. Ranging in width from 18″ to 48″, Sub-Zero units offer capacities to 30.0 cubic feet. The combination all-refrigerator and all-freezer together provide as much as 40.0 cubic feet of food storage.

Sub-Zero 12-Year Protection Plan

Sub-Zero has always backed what it has manufactured, and offers a warranty package no one can match — the Sub-Zero 12-Year Protection Plan. From the day your Sub-Zero is installed, you have a full five-year (parts and labor) warranty and limited sixth through twelfth-year (parts) warranty on the sealed system, consisting of the compressor, condenser, evaporator, drier and all connecting tubing. You also have a full two-year (parts and labor) warranty on the entire product. (See warranty for non-residential use and other exceptions). Sub-Zero stands behind every refrigerator and freezer they manufacture, ensuring you of the finest in service and trouble-free maintenance.

Outstanding performance and craftsmanship

Sub-Zero is a leader in the industry in engineering functional refrigeration. Because Sub-Zero full-size units use a refrigerant in both the refrigerator and freezer compartments, proper and even temperatures are maintained more consistently throughout. This is the same type system used in some commercial refrigerators and is a standard feature in Sub-Zero home units, to insure top performance and operation. Complete factory testing of every Sub-Zero unit is your assurance of quality workmanship.

More than just refrigeration, Sub-Zero quality craftsmanship is a tradition, custom designed to enhance the value and elegance of your home for years to come.

Maximum storage with the 500 SERIES Models 501R and 501F

For large families or those people who need maximum storage, Sub-Zero offers the convenience of its new Eurostyled all-refrigerator (Model 501R) and all-freezer (Model 501F) with a total storage capacity of 40 cubic feet. The "all-refrigerator's" 20 cubic foot capacity makes this exclusive unit the largest built-in all-refrigerator on the market. One of the advantages of these units is the flexibility of planning your kitchen. The units can be installed side-by-side or with a convenient counter between them or at opposite ends of the room, depending on your kitchen layout. Adjustable shelving in both the refrigerator and freezer gives even more storage versatility. The 501F has an automatic ice maker. The "all-refrigerator" Model 501R is also ideal for people who have existing freezer storage. **Separate detailed specification sheets on models 501R and 501F available upon request.**

501F 501R

ALL FREEZER
Model 501F—Automatic defrost. Freezer is equipped with automatic ice maker.
ALL REFRIGERATOR
Model 501R—Automatic defrost refrigerator.

Model	501F	501R
Capacity	20.0 cu. ft.	20.0 cu. ft.
Dimensions	Height 73" Width 36" Depth 24"	Height 73" Width 36" Depth 24"
Finished Roughing-In Dimensions	35½"x72¾"	35½"x72¾"
Weight (lbs.)	363 crated	376 crated

* Additional shelves available at extra cost.

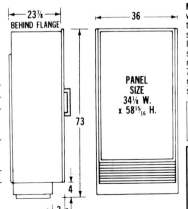

← 23⅞ → BEHIND FLANGE

← 36 →

PANEL SIZE 34⅛" W. x 58¹⁵/₁₆" H.

73

4

← 3

Minimum height required (when levelers in) is 72⁷/₁₆"

NOTE: Roughing-in width is 71½" when these models are installed side by side. If mullion is used to separate cabinets, add mullion width to 71½" dimension. Filler must be used when installed hinge to hinge.

One 115 volt, 60 cycle single phase, 15 amp. wall outlet must be provided.

Refer to 500 series "Installation Instruction" booklet for detailed installation and panel requirements.

Model 561

Model 561 Interior

®

Side by Side Combination
Models 561 and 532

The new 500 series incorporates exciting engineering innovations, with built-in beauty and elegant Eurostyled interiors. This series also features the new satin-brushed aluminum exterior trim and simplicity of design. The elegant combination of white and clear interiors, together with the built-in appearance, offers breathtaking beauty.

Sub-Zero's model 561 features an 8.9 cu. ft. freezer and 12.5 cu. ft. refrigeration in convenient top-to-bottom, side-by-side storage. Its two compressors provide independent temperature control of the freezer and refrigerator compartments. The freezer compartment has four pull-out storage baskets, automatic ice maker with removable ice storage drawer and adjustable door storage.

Model 561

COMBINATION REFRIGERATOR-FREEZER
Model 561 — Automatic defrost model. Freezer compartment equipped with automatic ice maker.

Capacity:	12.5 cu. ft. Refrigerator 8.9 cu. ft. Freezer
Dimensions:	Height 84″ Width 36″ Depth 24″
Finished Rough-In Dimensions	35¹/₂″x83³/₄″
Weight (lbs.):	480 lbs. crated

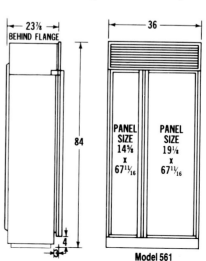

← 23⅛ →
BEHIND FLANGE

← 36 →

84

PANEL SIZE 14⅝ x 67¹¹/₁₆

PANEL SIZE 19¼ x 67¹¹/₁₆

4

3

Model 561

One 115 volt, 60 cycle single phase, 15 amp. wall outlet must be provided.

Minimum height required (when levelers in) is 82⁷/₈″ (smaller grille recommended).

Refer to 500 series "Installation Instruction" booklet for detailed installation and panel requirements.

Model 532   Model 532 Interior

Sub-Zero's huge 30 cu. ft. combination refrigerator/freezer model 532 is one of the largest home built-in units made. It incorporates new engineering innovations and Eurostyled interior. It has an 11.2 cu. ft. freezer and 18.8 cu. ft. refrigerator with convenient top-to-bottom storage.

The freezer compartment has four pull-out storage baskets, an automatic ice maker with roll-out removable ice storage drawer and adjustable door storage. The refrigerator has four self-sealing crispers, each with independent humidity control. It also features an adjustable roll-out utility drawer, adjustable door storage shelves and adjustable glass shelves. This model also has two compressors to provide independent temperature control in both the freezer and refrigerator compartments.

This unit is available in the 48 inch format with water and ice dispensed through the refrigerator door. This is not an option but another addition to our full line called the Model 590.

Detailed specification sheets on model 532, 561 and 590 are available on request.

Optional solid panel grilles that accept matching panels are available for 532 and 561. The panel grille is standard on the 590. Detailed specification sheets on the three units and grilles available upon request.

Model 532

COMBINATION REFRIGERATOR-FREEZER
Model 532—Automatic defrost model Equipped with automatic ice maker.

Capacity:	18.8 cu. ft. Refrigerator 11.2 cu. ft. Freezer
Dimensions:	Height 84″ Width 48″ Depth 24″
Finished Rough-In Dimensions:	47½″ x 83¾″
Weight (lbs.):	563 crated

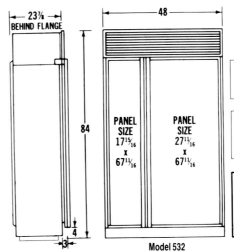

← 23⅞ →
BEHIND FLANGE

← 48 →

84

4

3

One 115 volt, 60 cycle single phase, 15 amp. wall outlet must be provided.

Minimum height required (when levelers in) is 82⅞″ (smaller grille recommended).

PANEL SIZE
17¹⁵⁄₁₆
x
67¹¹⁄₁₆

PANEL SIZE
27¹¹⁄₁₆
x
67¹¹⁄₁₆

Refer to 500 series "Installation Instruction" booklet for detailed installation and panel requirements.

Model 532

Model 550

Model 550 Interior

Over-N-Under (freezer on bottom) Models 550 and 511

For those who prefer, Sub-Zero offers a convenient arrangement with freezer on the bottom. This design was prompted by the fact that the refrigerator section is used more often than the freezer, thereby providing the greatest convenience and best accessibility. The refrigerated top half offers full width storage on adjustable shelves while frozen foods below are easily accessible with a pull-out drawer.

The over-n-under units in the 500 series also incorporate exciting engineering innovations with built-in beauty and elegant Eurostyled interiors. These units also feature the new satin-brushed aluminum exterior trim and simplicity of design.

Sub-Zero's 22.1 cu. ft. model 550 over-n-under combination unit has a 6.4 cu. ft. slide-out, double-tier freezer drawer in the

Model 550

COMBINATION REFRIGERATOR-FREEZER
Model 550 — Automatic defrost model. Freezer compartment equipped with automatic ice maker.

Capacity:	15.7 cu. ft. Refrigerator 6.4 cu. ft. Freezer
Dimensions:	Height 84″ Width 36″ Depth 24″
Finished Rough-In Dimensions	35½″x83¾″
Weight (lbs.):	468 crated

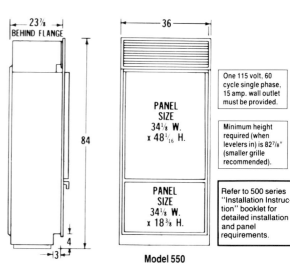

23⅛″ BEHIND FLANGE

36

84

PANEL SIZE 34⅛″ W. x 48¹/₁₆″ H.

PANEL SIZE 34⅛″ W. x 18⅜″ H.

4

3

One 115 volt, 60 cycle single phase, 15 amp. wall outlet must be provided.

Minimum height required (when levelers in) is 82⅞″ (smaller grille recommended).

Refer to 500 series "Installation Instruction" booklet for detailed installation and panel requirements.

Model 550

6

(Optional panel grille shown)　　　Model 511

Model 511 Interior

bottom. The freezer has an automatic ice maker with removable ice storage container. The top pull freezer handle and double-tier design provide easy access. The refrigerator has two self-sealing crispers, each with independent humidity control. It has a roll-out utility drawer, adjustable glass shelves and fully adjustable door storage.

The model 511 features a 5.2 cu. ft. slide-out double-tier freezer drawer and a 12.7 cu. ft. refrigerator compartment. Again the freezer has an automatic ice maker with removable ice storage container. Like the model 550, easy freezer access is provided by top pull handle and roll-out double-tier design.

These over-n-under models are extremely versatile for kitchen designs used alone or in various combinations, such as the kitchen shown on the cover of this brochure.

Both units have two compressors which provides independent temperature control in both the refrigerator and freezer compartments. These units are backed by Sub-Zero's exclusive Twelve-Year Protection Plan.

Optional solid panel grilles that accept matching panels also available. Specification sheet available upon request. Detailed specification sheets on models 550 and 511 are available upon request.

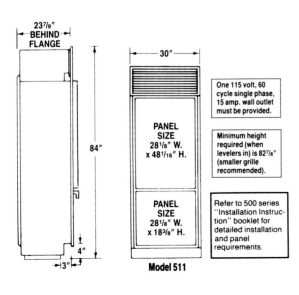

23⅞"
BEHIND
FLANGE

30"

84"

4"

3"

PANEL
SIZE
28⅛" W.
x 48¹/₁₆" H.

PANEL
SIZE
28⅛" W.
x 18⅜" H.

One 115 volt, 60 cycle single phase, 15 amp. wall outlet must be provided.

Minimum height required (when levelers in) is 82⅞" (smaller grille recommended).

Refer to 500 series "Installation Instruction" booklet for detailed installation and panel requirements.

Model 511

COMBINATION REFRIGERATOR-FREEZER
Model 511 — Automatic defrost model. Freezer compartment equipped with automatic ice maker.

Capacity:	12.7 cu. ft. Refrigerator 5.2 cu. ft. Freezer
Dimensions:	Height 84" Width 30" Depth 24"
Finished Rough-In Dimensions	29½" x 83¾"
Weight (lbs.):	375 crated

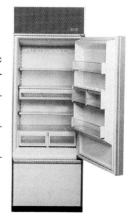

Model 511

7

Features of full-size, built-in units

1. Convenient Storage

All Sub-Zero units are 24″ in depth to conform to most kitchen base cabinet units. This not only improves appearance of finished installation but provides more accessible storage on interior shelves.

2. Sub-Zero 12-Year Protection Plan

Full five-year (parts and labor) warranty and limited sixth through twelfth-year (parts) warranty on the sealed system, consisting of the compressor, condenser, evaporator, drier and all connecting tubing; and a full two-year (parts and labor) warranty on the entire product from the date of installation. (Does not include installation.) (See warranty for non-residential use and other exceptions.)

3. Automatic Ice Maker

Makes and stores crescent-shaped ice pieces. Although several conditions affect the amount of ice that is produced in a given period of time, an adequate supply is provided. (Model 532 and 561 icemaker shown)

4. Automatic Defrosting

Automatically eliminates frost accumulation in both refrigerator and freezer sections.

5. Accepts Removable Decorative Door Panels

Front panels of virtually any material, not exceeding 1/4″ in thickness are easily installed. Raised panels may also be used when perimeter edge does not exceed 1/4″. **(We recommend routing, recessing or optional extended handles for finger clearance when using raised panels.) Refer to Installation Instruction Guide for detailed information. Only colored and stainless steel panels are available from the factory. (50# per door panel weight limit.)**

6. Side Panels

Unit is made to accept side panels if sides are exposed. Only colored and stainless steel panels are available from the factory.

7. Front-Vented

Allows for true built-in installation and eliminates over heating.

8. Removable and Adjustable Shelves

Cantilever type glass shelves in the refrigerator and wire shelves in the freezer for easy cleaning and flexible storage.

9. Deluxe Crispers

Spacious, self-sealing crispers have easy-glide roller design and adjustable, independent humidity control to assure food freshness.

10. Interiors

Award-winning Eurostyled white and clear interior.

11. Magnetic Door Gasket

Surrounds entire door with a pull that assures a positive seal.
NOTE — Because of a perfect seal, allow a slight delay before reopening door.

12. Right or Left Door Swing

Available, when specified, on all over-n-under and single door units (all side-by-side units are hinged on outside). Doors are not reversible.

13. Portable Egg Trays

Convenient and versatile, they may be carried to the table or preparation area.

14. Adjustable Dairy Compartment

Versatile, positive sealing compartment for dairy items.

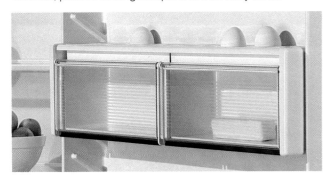

15. Adjustable Utility Basket

Adjustable roll-out refrigeration basket offers handy storage for small items.

16. Clean Trim

No visible screws.

17. Colored Panels

Decorator front and side steel panels are available from Sub-Zero in the following colors: Harvest Gold, Almond, Avocado, Coffee, Stainless Steel and White.

18. Grilles

Standard grille height is 11″. Other available grille heights range from 10″ to 15″ in 1″ increments. Optional decorative, solid panel grilles that accept matching panels also available in these sizes.

Panel grille

19. Toe Space Base

Integral part of cabinet. Inset is 4″ high by 3″ deep — meeting specifications of American Institute of Architects and conforming with most bases of kitchen cabinets.

20. Door Handles

Standard as shown in photographs throughout this literature.

21. Door Closers

All models equipped with door closers.

22. Door Stops

Although most installations do not require a door stop (door opens to 130°), an optional kit is available if needed. The Door Stop Kit allows the door to open to 90°.

23. Rollers

Unit has rollers and convenient leveling system for ease of installation.

24. Additional Shelves

Available at additional cost.

> **IMPORTANT:** For proper operation and use, the door must open at least a full 90°. A minimum 2″ filler should be used in corner installations to assure a 90° door opening. Remember to allow enough clearance in front of unit for full door swing.

Undercounter models

Sub-Zero undercounter refrigerators, freezers, combinations and ice makers are ideal for the bar, den, family room, yacht or office. They are designed to be installed under a counter. However, some may also be used as free-standing units.

All under-counter models are self-venting, have foamed-in-place insulation, have durable ABS easy to clean interiors and accept front door panels of practically any material to harmonize with cabinets or other equipment. They also have right to left door swings which are interchangeable in the field (kit required except model 245). All of these features and more are backed by Sub-Zero's 12-Year Protection Plan – providing a full five-year (parts and labor) warranty and limited sixth through twelfth year (parts) warranty on the sealed system, consisting of the compressor, condenser, evaporator, drier and all connecting tubing; and a full two year (parts and labor) warranty on the entire product from the date of installation. (Does not include installation.) (See warranty for non-residential use and other exceptions.)

The Sub-Zero combination model 245 provides automatic defrost, refrigerator storage, freezer storage and automatic ice making.

Sub-Zero also offers "all-refrigerator" and "all-freezer" undercounter units. The model 249RP "all-refrigerator" features automatic defrost, door storage and adjustable compartment shelving. Our model 249FF "all-freezer" features automatic defrost, adjustable compartment shelving and can be equipped with an automatic ice maker, but it must be installed at the factory.

A unit for those who desire primarily refrigerator storage with some freezer storage is the model 249R. This unit is a manual defrost, with a small full-width freezer, door storage and adjustable compartment shelving.

Model 249R

We also offer a built-in ice maker for those who entertain in style. Requirements for clear ice can be satisfied with the model 506, which provides an abundance of crystal-clear cubes in a unit that requires only an 18″ width. Featuring a drop-down hopper-type door, this unit stores up to 35 pounds of 3/4″ cubes. This unit requires a drain or pump.

Separate specification sheet on each undercounter model is available upon request.

Undercounter Model	249R	249RP	249FF	245	506
Capacity	4.4 cu. ft. Refrigerator .7 cu. ft. Freezer	4.9 cu. ft. Refrigerator	4.6 cu. ft. Freezer	3.0 cu. ft. Refrigerator 1.9 cu. ft Freezer	Stores 35 lbs. of ice
Unit Dimensions [Levelers in] (H x W x D in inches)	$33^{13}/_{16}$ x $23^{7}/_{8}$ x 24	$33^{13}/_{16}$ x $23^{7}/_{8}$ x 24	$33^{13}/_{16}$ x $23^{7}/_{8}$ x 24	34 x $23^{7}/_{8}$ x 24	$34^{13}/_{32}$ x $17^{7}/_{8}$ x $23^{7}/_{8}$
Weight (lbs.)	120 crated	117 crated	135 crated	139 crated	110 crated

Note: Refer to "Installation Instruction" booklet for detailed water, electrical and other installation requirements.

Model 249R

Model 249RP

**Model 249FF
(ICEMAKER OPTIONAL)**

Model 245

Model 506

Installation specifications

Following are the installation specifications for all Sub-Zero full-size and undercounter models. The dimensions shown in the chart correlate with the schematic drawings. For further details refer to the **Installation Instruction Booklet.**

Schematic drawing

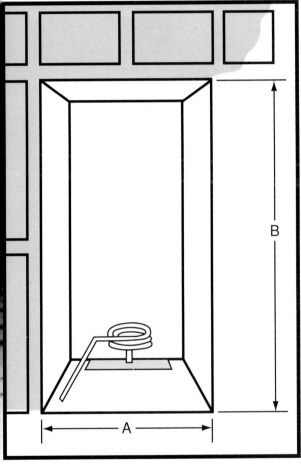

Door Clearance Schematic Drawing Top View

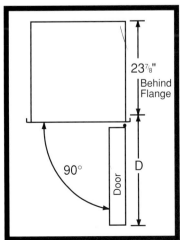

Wood grille not available from Sub Zero.

Model No.	Finished Rough Opening Dimensions		Door Panel Dimensions (width x height)	Minimum Door Clearance Requirement at 90°
	A	B	C	D
550	35¹/₂″	83³/₄″	34¹/₈″ x 48¹/₁₆″ & 34¹/₈″ x 18³/₈″	36¹/₁₆″
511	29¹/₂″	83³/₄″	28¹/₈″ x 48¹/₁₆″ & 28¹/₈″ x 18³/₈″	30¹/₈″
561	35¹/₂″	83³/₄″	14⁵/₈″ x 67¹¹/₁₆″ & 19¹/₈″ x 67¹¹/₁₆″	20³/₄″
532	47¹/₂″	83³/₄″	17¹⁵/₁₆″ x 67¹¹/₁₆″ & 27¹¹/₁₆″ x 67¹¹/₁₆″	29¹/₄″
501R	35¹/₂″	72³/₄″	34¹/₈″ x 58¹⁵/₁₆″	36¹/₁₆″
501F	35¹/₂″	72³/₄″	34¹/₈″ x 58¹⁵/₁₆″	36¹/₁₆″
590	47¹/₂″	83³/₄″	15¹/₈″ x 67¹¹/₁₆″ & 20⁹/₁₆″ x 67¹¹/₁₆″	29¹/₄″
245	24″	34¹/₂″	23¹/₂″ x 28¹/₈″	25¹³/₁₆″
249R	24″	34¹/₂″	23⁵/₈″ x 30″	25³/₈″
249RP	24″	34¹/₂″	23⁵/₈″ x 30″	25³/₈″
249FF	24″	34¹/₂″	23⁵/₈″ x 30″	25³/₈″
506	18″	34¹/₂″	17″ x 13³/₁₆″ & 17″ x 11¹⁵/₁₆″	11³/₄″

(Optional panel grille shown)

How to buy

Sub-Zero home refrigeration can be seen and purchased at top custom kitchen dealers and appliance stores in all major cities across the United States and many Canadian cities. If not available in your area, feel free to contact Sub-Zero direct for the distributor nearest you. Call 800-222-7820.

Service

There are hundreds of authorized service centers throughout the country to provide warranty service and perform other service functions. These centers maintain a stock of Sub-Zero approved parts and a staff of qualified repair technicians. The service center nearest you may be found in the yellow pages or by contacting the dealer you purchased the unit from. If service cannot be found, contact Sub-Zero direct: 800-356-5826.

SUB-ZERO FREEZER CO., INC.

Post Office Box 44130
Madison, Wisconsin 53744-4130
608/271-2233

SUB-ZERO ®

Model 590
Ice & Water Refrigerator-Freezer

Innovative Excellence

Sub-Zero has led the built-in home refrigeration industry for years with product enhancements which have set trends. Sub-Zero continues to redefine the art of built-in refrigeration for the 90's with the introduction of the distinctive Model 590 with its innovative version of ice and water through the refrigerator door.

The convenient placement and inconspicuous appearance of the ice and water dispenser and its controls were designed with you in mind.

And the ability to match your kitchen design has been assured with the Model 590. Like all Sub-Zero units, the Model 590 will fit flush with virtually all 24-inch cabinets and accept decorative side and front panels. Another exclusive feature of the Model 590 is the complementary color handle trim panels and glasswells which are offered at no charge.

Craftsmanship, a Sub-Zero trademark, is also built into each of these features:

•**Ice & Water Dispenser**– designed and practically placed for your convenience. A new industry feature, the water is constantly chilled within its huge 51 oz. reservoir.

•**Bulk Ice Dispenser**– conveniently located inside the refrigerator door when larger quantities are needed. This new industry feature is activated at the touch of a button.

•**Two Refrigeration Systems** – ensures independent, accurate freezer and refrigerator temperature control.

•**Decorative Door Panels** – front panels of virtually any material not exceeding 1/4" perimeter thickness are accommodated. Only color and stainless steel panels are available from the factory. (50# per door panel weight limit)

•**Automatic Defrosting** – freezer and refrigerator have own systems.

•**Adjustable Shelves** – cantilever type, easy to move and clean.

•**Spacious Crispers with Humidity Control** – four self-sealing crispers have clear view and individual controls.

•**Adjustable Door Shelves** – easy to adjust shelves provide complete flexibility on both doors.

•**Automatic Ice Maker** – an adequate supply of cresent-shaped ice is ensured.

•**Dairy Module** – a moveable, sealed environment for freshness.

•**Master Switch** – quick practical acc is offered to shut unit off.

•**Rollers** – provides easy installation.

•**Positive Sealing Doors** – magnetic gaskets guarantee a tight seal.

•**Brushed Satin Trim** – offers clean design so there's no distraction from beauty of your kitchen.

•**Portable Egg Containers** – easy acc and convenient storage.

•**Panel Grille** – 11" panel grille is standard. Other sizes from 10" to 15' available in one inch increments.

•**Solid Toe Plate** – allows custom finishing.

Ice & Water Dispenser with Night Light.

Refrigeration System Control and Bulk Ice Dispenser.

Model 590 shown with optional bright white handle trim panel and glasswell.

Sub-Zero 12 Year Protection Plan— full five-year (parts and labor) warranty and limited sixth through twelfth-year (parts) warranty on the sealed system, consisting of the compressor, condenser, evaporator, drier and all connecting tubing; a full two-year (parts and labor) warranty on the entire product from the date of installation. (Does not include installation. See warranty for other exceptions.)

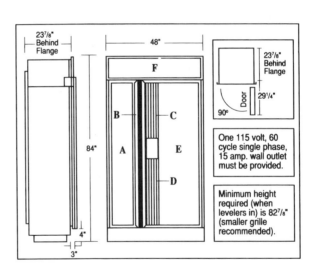

One 115 volt, 60 cycle single phase, 15 amp. wall outlet must be provided.

Minimum height required (when levelers in) is 82⁷/₈" (smaller grille recommended).

Beauty—our award-winning interior is beautiful to the eye, but more importantly it is spacious with nearly 30 cubic feet of flexible storage for all your needs.
Refrigerator – 18.2 cubic feet.
Freezer – 11.2 cubic feet.

Capacity: Refrigerator 18.2 cu. ft. Freezer 11.2 cu. ft.	Dimensions: Height 84" Width 48" Depth 24"
Two Compressors	Finished Roughed-in Dimensions: 47¹/₂ x 83³/₄
Weight: 598 lbs. crated	
Door Panel Dimensions: **A** 15 ¹/₈ w x 67 ¹¹/₁₆ h **B** 2 ⁹/₁₆ w x 67 ¹¹/₃₂ h **C** 6 ⁷/₈ w x 25 ⁷/₃₂ h	**D** 6 ⁷/₈ w x 31 ⁷/₃₂ h **E** 20 ⁹/₁₆ w x 67 ¹¹/₁₆ h Grille Panel Dimension: **F** 46 ³/₁₆ w x 9 ³/₁₆ h
B,C & D may not exceed .050" thickness	

Due to our continuous improvement program, models and specifications are subject to change without notice.

Color Selection Guide
for model 590 only

Complete Flexibility

Your Sub-Zero Model 590 will be shipped with handsome pin-striped pewter gray handle trim panels and glasswell. But an exclusive feature from Sub-Zero allows you to change this color scheme to accent your kitchen.

Model 590 shown with standard pin-striped pewter gray handle trim panels and glasswell.

Ask your local dealer about specific color combinations. The eight glasswell and laminate handle trim panel alternatives we offer at no charge are:

P1/G1 Bright White	**P2/G2** Almond Buff
P3/G3 Camel	**P4/G4** Adobe
P5/G5 Pewter Gray	**P6/G6** Smoke Gray
P7/G7 Charcoal	**P8/G8** Port Brown
	P9/G9 Black Slate

*The colors illustrated here are only meant to give you an idea of the shades available and you should contact your dealer for more accurate color combinations and shading.

Note: Metal handle trim panels to match Sub-Zero supplied metal door and side panels are also available in white, almond, avocado, coffee, harvest gold and stainless steel at no charge.

Sales

In addition to the Model 590, Sub-Zero features a full line of built-in home refrigeration units with side-by-side, over-and-under and undercounter models which vary in size from 4.5 to cubic feet of storage. For the dealer ne you look in the yellow pages or call Sub-Zero at **800/222-7820** for your nearest distributor.

Service

Sub-Zero has an extensive service network throughout the United States and Canada to meet your needs. You can find them in the yellow pages or c us at **800/356-5826.**

SUB-ZERO FREEZER CO., INC.
P.O. Box 44130
Madison, WI 53744 - 4130
(608) 271- 2233

It takes vision to create

a revolutionary new

system of refrigeration.

SUB-ZERO

▲ Spice cabinets. China
cabinets. Now Sub-Zero
introduces orange juice
and pork chop cabinets.

Ponder it, just for a mo

The convenience of st

your vegetables in a dr

by the sink. Fresh fis

Under the cooktop. N

the table. In the island.

the question isn't wh

can you put a refrigera

But rather, where can't y

another drawer near

cooktop. Milk, juice

last night's leftovers i

Tuck a freezer into the ▶
island and you'll never be
stranded there.

binet by the kitchen
ble. And a separate
ezer drawer near the
ck door for the kids.
e advantages of our
egrated refrigerators
nd freezers go well
eyond aesthetics.
asuring just 27 inches
, they allow you to put
frigeration in places
ver before possible.
ead of being limited to

a single, centralized
refrigerator, you can now
utilize several. (Hence,
when your teenager
complains there's nothing
good in the refrigerator,
you can reply, "Which
refrigerator?") With five
different configurations,
you can mix and match
our tall units with
additional base units.
Or use them to

supplement a 500 Series
Sub-Zero. (In fact, who
says you have to limit
them to the kitchen?
Imagine hiding a refrig-
erator in the living room,
bedroom or entertain-
ment area.) And rest
assured, each features
Sub-Zero's legendary,

uncompromising crafts-
manship. Which is why
we're confident enough
to back them with the
12-Year Sub-Zero
Protection Plan. So the
only unknown you will
ever face with our new
refrigerators is how many
places to put them.

▲ How's this for a reminder to
wash the fruits and vegetables?
Store them near the sink.

With its inconspicuous looks, you could misplace the refrigerator. But thanks to its brilliant halogen lighting,

Its advanced features are fresher than anything you are likely to put inside it.

you'll never misplace the food inside. All units also feature a microprocessor control panel that lets you program specific temperatures. In one tall refrigerator, for instance, you could store fresh meat at 30 degrees, while storing your vegetables at the optimal 32 degrees — and the milk and leftovers at 38 degrees. Leave any door or drawer ajar and an alarm will sound. (It can be disengaged for loading groceries.) And like all Sub-Zeros, our tall units offer the ultimate in adjustable, drip-proof shelving.

▲ A see-through, humidity controlled crisper cover provides easy access to fresh fruits and vegetables.

◄ The tall unit comes with spill-proof shelves and a deli drawer for handy storage.

▲ The microprocessor control panel uses "fuzzy logic," which helps save energy by continuously adapting to usage and climates.

All the doors and compartment shelves are adjustable, providing exceptional flexibility. ►

700TR-All Refrigerator

DIMENSIONS
H 80" W 27" D 24"
Door Swing Clearance: 25½"

ENERGY USAGE
553 kwh/$46/Annually*

STORAGE INFORMATION

Refrigerator:
15.0 cu. ft. of Storage
    9.8 cu. ft. upper cabinet
    5.2 cu. ft. combined drawers
3 Adjustable Glass Shelves
1 Stationary Glass Shelf
3 Adjustable Door Shelves
1 Adjustable Dairy Compartment
1 Adjustable Deli-Drawer
1 Removable Crisper Cover
2 Removable Drawer Dividers
1 Egg Tray

CRATED WEIGHT
360 pounds

700TC-Refrigerator/Freezer

DIMENSIONS
H 80" W 27" D 24"
Door Swing Clearance: 25½"

ENERGY USAGE
672 kwh/$56/Annually*

STORAGE INFORMATION

Refrigerator (Top Cabinet):
9.8 cu. ft. of Storage
3 Adjustable Glass Shelves
1 Stationary Glass Shelf
1 Adjustable Crisper/Deli Drawer
3 Adjustable Door Shelves
1 Adjustable Dairy Compartment

Freezer (Combined Drawers):
5.4 cu. ft. of Storage
2 Removable Drawer Dividers
(1 Removable Divider when Ice Maker ordered)
Ice Maker Optional (700TCI)

CRATED WEIGHT
360 pounds

700TF-All Freezer

DIMENSIONS
H 80" W 27" D 24"
Door Swing Clearance: 25½"

ENERGY USAGE
782 kwh/$65/Annually*

STORAGE INFORMATION

Freezer:
15.2 cu. ft. of Storage
    9.8 cu. ft. upper cabinet
    5.4 cu. ft. combined drawers
4 Adjustable Door Shelves
3 Adjustable Glass Shelves
1 Stationary Glass Shelf
2 Removable Drawer Dividers
(1 Removable Divider when Ice Maker ordered)
Ice Maker Optional (700TFI)

CRATED WEIGHT
360 pounds

700BR-All Refrigerator

DIMENSIONS
H 34½" W 27" D 24"
Drawer Clearance: 19½"

ENERGY USAGE
449 kwh/$37/Annually*

STORAGE INFORMATION

Refrigerator (Combined Drawers):
4.9 cu. ft. of Storage
2 Removable Drawer Dividers
1 Removable Crisper Cover

CRATED WEIGHT
190 pounds

700BF-All Freezer

DIMENSIONS
H 34½" W 27" D 24"
Drawer Clearance: 19½"

ENERGY USAGE
522 kwh/$43/Annually*

STORAGE INFORMATION

Freezer (Combined Drawers):
5.1 cu. ft. of Storage
2 Removable Drawer Dividers
(1 Removable Divider when Ice Maker ordered)
Ice Maker Optional (700BFI)

CRATED WEIGHT
190 pounds

*Annual energy costs are based on 8.3 cents per kilowatt hour.
Consultant: Jerome Caruso Design, Inc.

Our Integrated 700 Series offers five different configurations, to fit any lay-out. In addition to a tall refrigerator/freezer combination unit, we offer both the tall and base models in all-refrigerator or all-freezer models. You also have a choice of left or right-hand door swing, as well as an optional ice maker. And all units can accept most any style of cabinetry panels. Additional accessories, such as stainless steel fronts and handles, are also available. For more details, review our Planning and Installation Guide with your designer, architect or dealer.

**Sub-Zero Freezer
Company, Inc.**

Post Office Box 44130

Madison, Wisconsin
53744-4130

800-200-7820 or
608-271-2233

This book represents

Sub-Zero's Integrated

700 Series. To see our

full line, including our

classic 500 Series,

call us for the

dealer nearest you.

*L*ife's Perfect

Little Moments Deserve

a Perfect Backdrop

Kitchen and Bath
Styles from
Aristokraft

Construction

Superior hinge and door guide systems, state-of-the-art finishes, easy-clean interiors, are all part of Aristokraft's dedication to constructing the absolute best cabinets in the industry. Just take a look at what goes into our construction process.

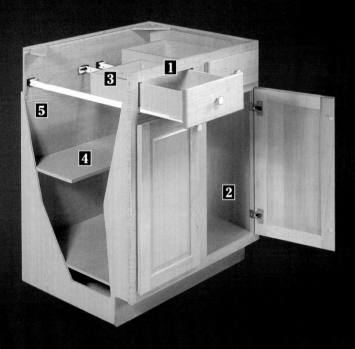

Traditional Cabinetry

1. Mortise and tenon jointed hardwood face frame construction

2. Easy-to-clean, durable Aristex® interior surface

3. Extra durable drawer construction with easy-rolling lifetime drawer guide system

4. Accommodating fixed half-shelf in base cabinets

5. Fully enclosed back on all wall and base cabinets

Adjustable full-depth shelves in wall cabinets (not shown).

Full Access Cabinetry

1. Sturdy construction using 5/8" industrial particleboard, doweled and glued

2. 3/8" fully-captured back panel

3. Secure rear mounted installation rail

4. 3/4" adjustable, full-depth shelf

5. Heavy-duty, four-sided drawer box with self-closing, easy rolling lifetime drawer guide system

6. No frame interference allows for better and easier accessibility

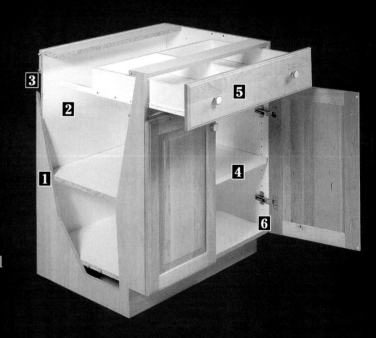

Select Choices

Aristokraft has designed and developed three construction methods for cabinetry. This allows you to choose the type of cabinets suitable to your lifestyle and budget. We call the construction methods Select Choices.

"Standard" Cabinets — Construction Method One

3/8" thick particleboard sides, which are the standard of the industry.

1/2" thick adjustable shelves for lifetime stability.

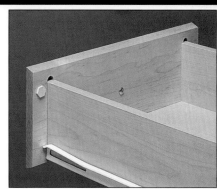

Heavy duty wood and particleboard drawers with rabbet joint construction.

"Select" Cabinets — Construction Method Two

3/8" thick particleboard sides, which are the standard of the industry.

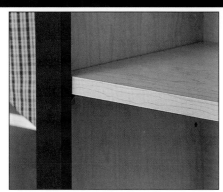

3/4" thick adjustable shelves enhance durability and handle the heaviest loads.

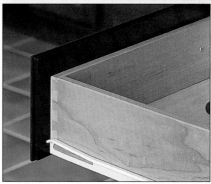

All-wood dovetailed drawers with a clear topcoat.

"Ply Select" Cabinets — Construction Method Three

3/8" thick 5-ply, plywood sides that ensure strength and dependability.

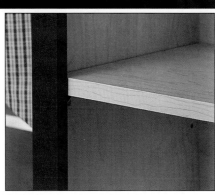

3/4" thick adjustable shelves that won't warp or sag.

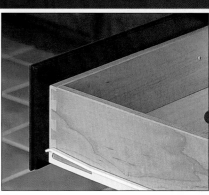

All-wood dovetailed drawers with a clear topcoat.

Door Style

Aristokraft offers eight different types of designs to appeal to — and accommodate — any taste. The choices are seemingly limitless. Choose from a wide variety of traditional and full access frameless styles.

Door Style Selection

Select from Square, Cathedral or Roman Arch door styles. Take your pick of recessed, raised or flat panel designs. When you add all the different finish colors that Aristokraft offers in each of these styles, the choices are almost endless.

Finish

Aristokraft offers an impressive array of styles in maple, oak, hickory, and laminate. There's a color to please — clean whites, sun-dappled neutrals, and rich, deep shades. Whatever style or color you choose, you can be sure that all our cabinetry is crafted with the attention to detail that epitomizes Aristokraft. When it comes to wood species, Aristokraft chooses only the finest materials available. While variations in color and grain are natural characteristics and add to the distinctive beauty of the cabinetry, all Aristokraft cabinet woods are stained to obtain as constant a tone as possible.

Aristokraft employs a multi-step finishing process on all cabinets. This process is designed to protect the wood and bring out its full luster, depth and beauty. For easy care and lasting beauty, Aristokraft covers interior surfaces of cabinet walls, backs and shelves with Aristex®, a urethane-coated laminate.

Aristokraft ▲

P.O. Box 420
Jasper, Indiana • 47547-0420
812-482-2527
http://www.aristokraft.com

Roman Arch Raised Panel

Cathedral Raised Panel

Cathedral Recessed Panel

Furniture Styled Square Raised Panel

Square Raised Panel

Square Recessed Panel

Square Mullion Recessed Panel

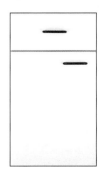
Square Flat Panel

Maple in Alpine

Natural

Autumn

Rouge

Oak in Opal

Natural

Wheat

Spice

Laminate in White

Natural

Antique

Hickory in Natural

Toffee

For complete specifications or additional information on any of the cabinetry or collections featured in this brochure, please contact your local Aristokraft distributor/dealer.

KraftMaid Cabinetry Has What's Important to You and Your Customers

You want a cabinetry company that offers

Industry-Surpassing Quality to Guarantee the Life of Your Cabinetry

Cabinetry Styles That Are on the Cutting Edge of Design Trends

Accessories and Finishes to Customize Any Project

A Selection to Satisfy You and Your Customers, Every Time

On-Time and Complete Delivery

CONSUMERS BEST BUY DIGEST

*KraftMaid
can customize
any cabinetry
project.*

*Personalize your
selection of
traditional,
contemporary and
universal designed
cabinetry styles,
available in oak,
hickory, cherry,
maple, pine, birch
and poplar woods
and white and ivory
laminates, with
designer
enhancements and
space-saving storage
options. Whether
creating
a kitchen, bath or
home office, the
flexibility of
KraftMaid cabinetry
and your
imagination
can produce a
customized design
in any room.*

KraftMaid

The Finishing Touches

As more daring approaches to finish combinations in kitchen and bath cabinetry gain popularity, consumers are incorporating accent colors with standard wood finishes. KraftMaid increases its depth of finish selections by offering premium finishes, such as taupe, porcelain and chocolate glazes, buttercream, platinum lustre, indigo and cypress, that provide furniture-quality custom looks and colorful options.

Entertainment Cabinetry from KraftMaid

Today's consumers demand quality premium cabinetry looks without premium prices. KraftMaid helps you make this possible by offering entertainment cabinetry that you can customize with moldings, finishes and decorative accessories to create an impressive design. And like all of KraftMaid's cabinetry, our entertainment cabinetry offers the same superior standard construction features.

USER TESTED

Universal Design Certified
By the Institute for Technology Development

Quality craftsmanship.

Impressive detailing.

Design versatility.

KraftMaid Cabinetry.

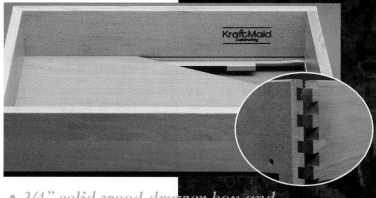

• *3/4" solid wood drawer box and concealed undermount suspension system are constructed to last a lifetime.*

• *Exclusive 14-step furniture finish process with DuraKraft catalyzed topcoat provides the industry's finest finish.*

• *3/4" shelving material is 20 - 50% thicker than industry standards, increases shelf load capacity and reduces sagging.*

• *Full-depth base shelves provide up to 50% more storage space.*

• *Exclusive PermaSet bumpers are pre-drilled to stay in place forever.*

• *KraftMaid is the only cabinetry company to offer a free care and cleaning kit, to protect your client's investment, with each kitchen cabinetry purchase.*

• *Multi-adjustment hinges feature corrosion-free performance.*

You require confidence in the products you use and expect your customers to be confident in the products they select for their homes. KraftMaid manufactures quality products built to last, with construction features that not only surpass industry requirements, but are also standard in all of KraftMaid's cabinetry. And as a Consumers Digest Best Buy, with lifetime warranted cabinetry,

unsurpassed construction features and an unrivaled finishing process, the look you and your customers choose is guaranteed to last.

KraftMaid
Cabinetry

Middlefield, OH 44062
440/632-5333
www.kraftmaid.com

WELLBORN CABINET, INC.

The Woodcraft Series

All Wood Cabinetry

Nothing Could Be More Natural

The Woodcraft Series

Matching Finished Veneer Exterior Plywood End Panels in Oak, Maple, Cherry or Hickory

1 Matching finished end panels eliminate the cost and labor of adding finished skins to cabinet ends, saving time and money during installation.

½" Thick Plywood End Panels

2 Plywood end panels provide a strong foundation for cabinetry construction and is the highest quality.

Lifetime limited *warranty*
• Solid Wood Drawers •
• Drawer Guides •
• Door Hinges •

¾" Thick Solid Wood Drawer Sides

3 Natural finished solid wood drawer sides, sub-front and back easily wipe clean and carry a Lifetime Warranty.

Dovetail Drawer Construction

4 Dovetail construction has always been recognized as the strongest, most durable method of assembly and creates a beautiful, long lasting drawer.

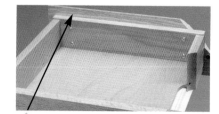

5 Undermount Drawer Guides

Epoxy coated captive self-closing drawer guides have positive stops to prevent spills and slide shut with just a slight touch. The drawer has a 75 lb. capacity and carries a Lifetime Warranty.

6 ¼" Thick Finished Plywood Drawer Bottom

The drawer bottom locks into the dadoed sides and are glued and stapled into place. The finished interior is easy to clean.

7 Adjustable Drawer Front

Four screws attach the drawer front to the drawer sub-front providing easy adjustment.

Than All Wood!

¾" Thick Plywood Hanging Rails **8**

Hanging rails are built-in at the top and bottom of wall and base cabinets to secure installation and add strength.

½" Thick Plywood Tops and Bottoms **9**

Tops and bottoms lock into the dadoed hanging rails and face frames and are glued and stapled into place for extra strength.

³⁄₁₆" Thick Plywood Backs **10**

Backs are locked into a step groove within the hanging rails and are glued and stapled into place.

¾" Thick Fully Adjustable Laminated & Edgebanded Furniture Board Shelves **11**

Cabinet shelves and interiors are covered in a natural colored wood grain laminate which easily wipes clean and is resistant to most household chemicals.

¾" Thick Solid Oak, Maple, Cherry or Hickory Face Frames **12**

All face frames joints are precisely aligned with blind mortise and tenon joints. The frames are then machined squared and glued and stapled at each joint to assure tightness.

¾" Thick Natural Finished Plywood Toe Space **13**

Captive toe space is fully enclosed featuring a rodent proof design.

¾" Thick Plywood Shipping Brace **14**

The shipping brace provides extra security to the end panels during shipping and handling.

WELLBORN
CABINET, INC.

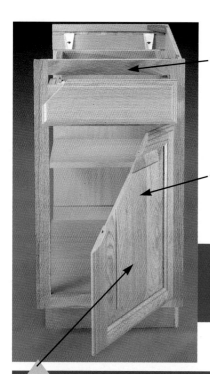

15 Solid Oak, Maple, Cherry or Hickory Drawer Fronts

Solid wood drawer fronts are attached to the hardwood sub-front with four screws for complete adjustability.

16 Solid Oak, Maple, Cherry or Hickory Doors

A large selection of door styles are constructed of solid wood. No wood substitutes are used.

Nothing Can Match Our Latest Technology!

18 WellGrip Corner Brace

High impact polystyrene material resists shock and is stapled to the cabinet to produce a strong corner brace. Pilot holes prevent splitting during countertop installation and the WellGrip Corner Brace features a smooth flat surface to provide a secure level bond to countertop surfaces. This material is proven stronger than wood.

17 WellGuard Finishing System

Combining Time Tested Finishing Techniques with today's technology has resulted in the 18 steps Wellborn uses to create the furniture-like luster that shines deep from within the wood. Hand sanding prepares surfaces, end grain sanding protects edges and hand rubbing stains deep into the wood grain produces the highest quality finish. Research has proven Wellborn's oven cured and melamine rich sealers and top coats to be strong and tough to last for years of beauty.

WellLock Shelf Clips 20

Positive locking shelf clips in a natural color blend with the interior. They lock shelves in place to prevent tipping and are simple to release to adjust shelf height.

19 Unique Step Down Groove Construction

End Panels are joined to the face frame with a step down groove for added strength.

22 WellLine Hinges

Hinges can be adjusted both vertically and horizontally to maintain perfect alignment and carry a Lifetime Warranty.

Natural Wood Grain Laminated Interior 21

Laminated interiors are easy-to-wipe clean and resistant to most household chemicals. Enjoy the natural wood grain interior look and eliminate shelf paper forever.

WELLBORN
CABINET, INC.

38669 Hwy 77 • P.O. Box 1210
Ashland, Alabama 36251
(205) 354-7151 • Fax (205) 354-7022

©Wellborn Cabinet, Inc. (4/97)

NATIONAL KITCHEN
NKBA
& BATH ASSOCIATION

KITCHEN CABINET
KCMA
MANUFACTURERS ASSOCIATION

One of the most dramatic shower scenes since "Psycho."

Peninsula/right angle shower enclosure
Total installation time: 1 hour 50 minutes

Economical, easy-installing glass block shower enclosures from

IBP glass block grid system™

WINDOWS | WALLS • SKYLIGHTS • FLOORS | DOORS | SHOWERS

Turn corners. Turn heads. All without mortar or costly labor.

Execute breathtaking shower designs with the IBP Glass Block Grid System™.

Glass block adds drama to any shower enclosure, but the difficulties of conventional mortared installation often add extra costs and occasional callbacks as well. Now for the first time, these exciting accents are as practical as they are beautiful—with IBP Glass Block Grid System Shower Enclosures.

The IBP shower enclosure system replaces mortar with a combination of three elements:

- a precision-engineered aluminum grid

- closed-cell foam tape around each block

- Dow Corning TradeMate™ silicone sealant

Together, these elements provide a degree of versatility, strength, and safety unmatched by other glass block installation methods. By eliminating the need for highly skilled trades, the system also saves builders money.

IBP technology has been proven in more than 45,000 window, wall, floor, door, and skylight installations. In adapting the grid system for shower enclosures, IBP's design team has developed a number of features that allow easy attachment to a standard shower curb (see back page) using standard construction methods:

Notice the dramatic difference that an IBP Shower Enclosure adds to the corner of a bath.

- **Aluminum corner extrusions in 22½° increments:** These corner pieces easily snap together with aluminum grid wall sections to produce a clean, symmetrical joint without mortar or grout. You can construct corners of 22½°, 45°, 67½°, and 90° with ease.

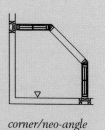

corner/neo-angle

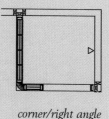

corner/radius

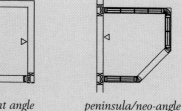

corner/right angle

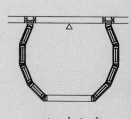

peninsula/neo-angle

peninsula/radius

Even for designs like the buttress-style enclosure pictured below, IBP shower installations are simple. They call only for common tools and conventional construction skills—which saves money and reduces the chance of callbacks.

- **Flush aluminum finishing pieces that encase the grid system:** This innovative feature allows for easy shower door attachment and simple installation to adjoining walls and shower bases.

- **Glass block door headers that eliminate the need for lintels:** Conventional glass block shower enclosures are typically designed without headers, which usually entails some trade-off between support and appearance. IBP's unique header design is self-supporting.

The result is a watertight, aesthetically pleasing, virtually callback-free installation—often accomplished in two hours or less.

Total installation time is approximately two hours. To complete your decorative scheme, IBP also offers matching glass block window grids.

Choose colors and patterns to complement any decor.

The grid system and corner extrusions are available in white, black, red, gold, and silver finishes. However, with six weeks' advance notice, IBP can custom-match your color sample.

A wide selection of glass block patterns and colors provides design choices to strike the perfect balance of ambiance and privacy.

Another benefit of the grid system is that you can easily view different combinations of glass block colors and patterns before siliconing the installation. Also, block can be removed and replaced in the future to fit remodeling color schemes or plans.

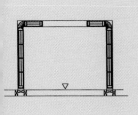

peninsula/right angle

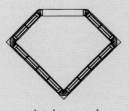

island neo-angle

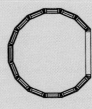

island/radius

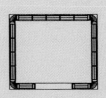

island/right angle

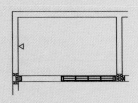

traditional in-line

Use IBP's technical assistance to multiply your design options.

Ten examples of typical shower installations are illustrated inside, but these are merely suggestions. The final design is literally up to you. IBP offers free design service for all Glass Block Grid System products. IBP detail drawings and installation details are also available in AutoCad® Release 12 format.

Other exciting IBP applications include skylights, windows, walls, floors, doors, and more. Simply call toll-free for additional information: **1-800-932-2263**. Add drama and economy to your next bath with the IBP Glass Block Grid System.

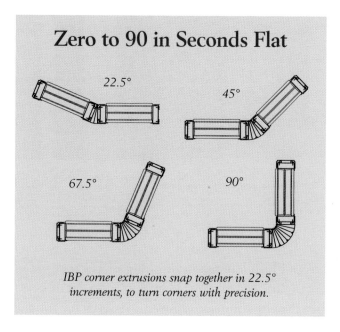

Zero to 90 in Seconds Flat

22.5°   45°

67.5°   90°

IBP corner extrusions snap together in 22.5° increments, to turn corners with precision.

Engineered for Trouble-Free Installation

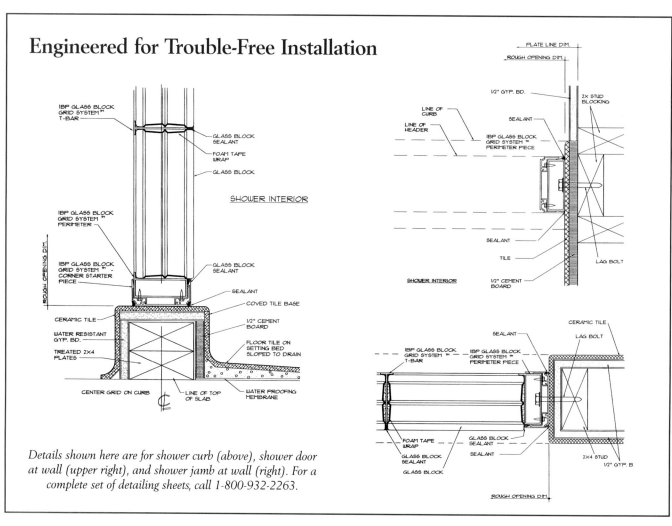

Details shown here are for shower curb (above), shower door at wall (upper right), and shower jamb at wall (right). For a complete set of detailing sheets, call 1-800-932-2263.

Since 1891

Acme Brick Company • P.O. Box 425 • Fort Worth, TX 76101 • 1-800-932-2263

IBP-SWR-A1-4/95

The most fun you can have without a barrel.

WHIRLPOOLS
AND SOAKERS

TUB/SHOWERS

SHOWER
MODULES

ASSISTED
CARE UNITS

Clarion

BATHWARE ////////////////////////////////////

Clearly A Difference

larion's whirlpool and soaker tub collection offers both acrylic and fiberglass models. President's Series acrylic models are vacuum formed from a one-piece solid sheet of cast acrylic to provide years of care free use. Each whirlpool is engineered and manufactured to meet the most demanding specifications. Clarion's acrylic is the tub of choice for many families. Clarion's gel-coated fiberglass whirlpools and soaker tubs are manufactured with the same exacting standards as our acrylic products.

Multiple laminates of fiberglass and 16-18 mills of gel-coat make our products among the strongest in the industry. All whirlpools are manufactured using custom formed PVC pipe, 3/4 H.P. motors with a 5 year warranty, and matching trim. The air control, suction outlet, and on/off switch are all factory installed. Clarion pressure water tests each whirlpool before it is delivered. A host of options such as 6 jets, brass or chrome trim, mood lites, and heaters are among some of the upgrades available for your new whirlpool.

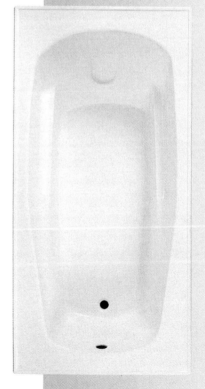

MODEL# AC6060SO
59^1/$_2$" x 59^1/$_2$" x 26^1/$_2$" x 26^1/$_2$" x 21^3/$_4$"H

VAN BUREN

ACRYLIC

MODEL# AC7236SO
71^1/$_2$"L x 36"W x 21^1/$_2$"H

BUCHANON

ACRYLIC

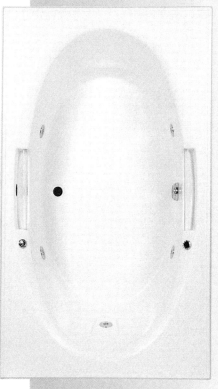

MODEL# AC7242SO
70³/₄"L x 41¹/₂"W x 21¹/₂"H

LINCOLN

ACRYLIC

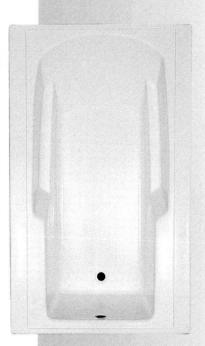

MODEL# AC6036SO
60¹/₂"L x 36"W x 21¹/₂"H

WASHINGTON I

ACRYLIC

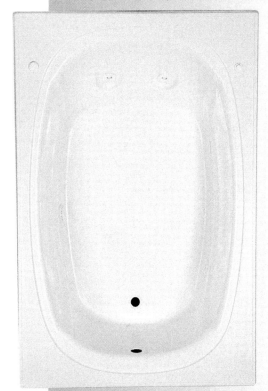

MODEL# AC7248SO
71³/₄"L x 47³/₄"W x 21¹/₂"H

TAFT

ACRYLIC

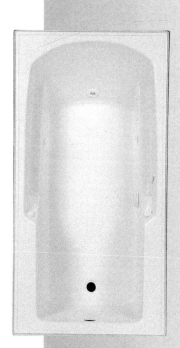

MODEL# AC6032SO
60"L x 31³/₄"W x 21¹/₂"H

WASHINGTON II

Lucite XL

Clarion Bathware uses LUCITE XL cast acrylic sheet in all of its acrylic modules. LUCITE XL is beautiful, durable and will not mildew and stain. It hard, non-porous surface is scratch resistant. Its rich colors go all the way through the thickness of the material to ensure color fastness and its high gloss finish wipes to a shine without scrubbing. LUCITE XL, easy to maintain with common household non-abrasive cleaning products, is your assurance of quality.

Freight Information

Clarion ships product on our own fleet of air-ride trailers with new tractors and company drivers. Assisted care products ship on Clarion's trucks or on any number of LTL companies contracted with CFM.

Limited Warranty

Clarion Bathware offers a Three-Year Limited Warranty against defects in material and workmanship on fiberglass and acrylic products. Whirlpool systems carry a Full Three-Year Limited Warranty.

For More Information

For sales information, service, technical support or ordering information call your Clarion Bathware distributor or the corporate office below.

CFM, Inc.

CORPORATE AND SALES OFFICE

Clarion Bathware

205 Amsler Avenue	Phone	814-226-5374
Shippenville, PA 16254	Fax	814-226-5568

MANUFACTURING PLANT

Clarion Bathware

Star Route Box 20	Phone	814-782-3011
Marble, PA 16334	Fax	814-782-3434

Strom Plumbing

■ ■ ■ ■ ■ ■ ■

P0150

P0146

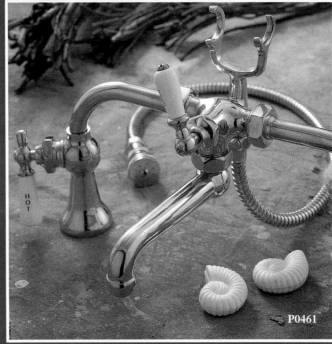

P0461

BY

Sign of 🦀 the Crab

Sign of the Crab, Ltd.
3756 Omec Circle, Dept. 214
Rancho Cordova, CA 95742

Telephone (916) 638-2722
FAX (916) 638-2725

SIGN OF THE CRAB specializes in solid brass plumbing and decorative accessories. Through years of product development, our products include authentic reproduction items and new, designer-oriented products. Also available is the service that is necessary to see your project through to completion. We have custom made many items to include stainless steel and brass products for the Sheraton Palace Hotel in San Francisco and the Beverly Wilshire Hotel in Beverly Hills.

Enclosed is a sampling of some of our items. Please write to us or call us for our complete catalog available at no charge to the trade. We welcome you to the world of STROM PLUMBING.

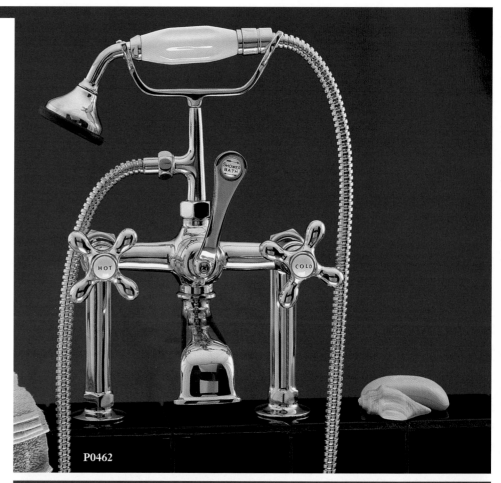

P0462

P0460

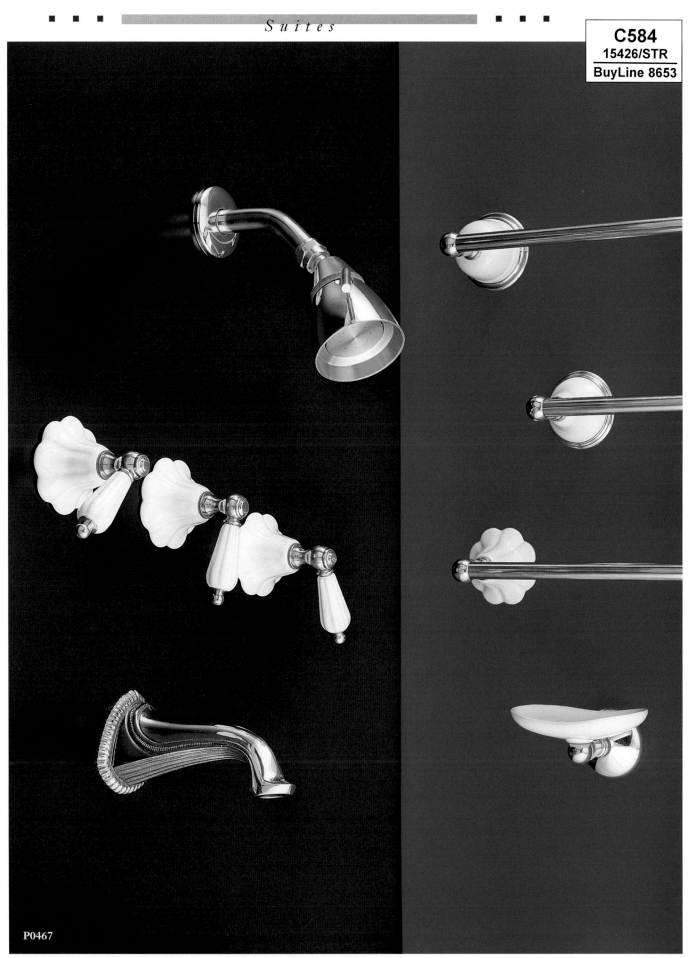

P0467

This photograph indicates how towel bars and other bath accessories can be modified with different escutcheons to create a bath "suite", thereby coordinating an entire room with matching faucets and accessories.

P0034 – Leg Tub Shower Enclosure Set.

Includes: P0006, P0008, P0009, P0010.

P0006 – Leg Tub Faucet with Diverter. Porcelain handles marked "Hot", "Cold" and "Shower", 33/8″ centers.

P0008 – Shower Enclosure with Adjustable Ceiling 36″ and Wall 12″ Braces. 5/8″ (1/4″ IPS) heavy gauge polished brass tubing, 45″ long, 25″ wide.

P0009 – Shower Riser (2 piece). 3/8″ brass pipe size, 5′ total height, 1/2″ iron pipe size shower head fitting extends 9″ from vertical.

P0010 – Shower Head. Polished brass, 47/8″ diameter, 1/2″ IPS connection.

All items may be purchased separately.

P0034P – Leg Tub Enclosure Set. Same as P0034, but with P0051 porcelain shower head instead of P0010.

P0008-1

P0087

P0051

GB0215

P0147

For gooseneck spout order P0400 faucet or P0403 enclosure set

P0008-1 – C Clamp only.

Extra braces include c-clamp, brace & escutcheon:

P0008 – 12
P0008 – 24
P0008 – 36
P0008 – 48

P0034 – Shower Enclosure
P0034P – Shower Enclosure with P0051 Porcelain Shower Head

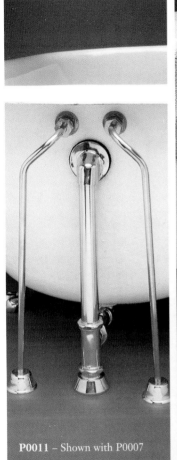

P0011 – Shown with P0007

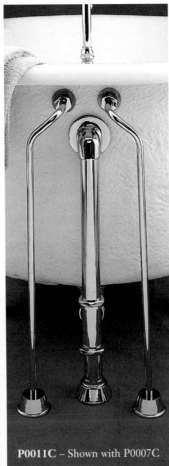

P0011C – Shown with P0007C

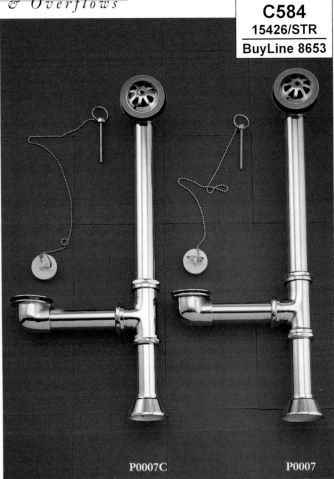

P0007C   **P0007**

P0149-1 and P0398   **P0398**   **P0146 and P0398**

P0140

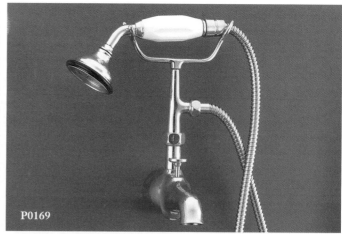

P0169

P0402

P0400C

P0499C

P0460

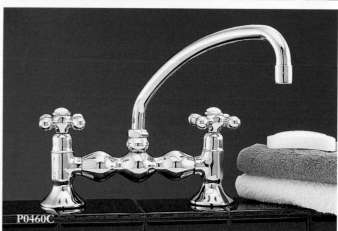

P0460C

P0353C

P0354C

P0355C

P0356C

P0357C

P0353C on P0081 Pedestal Lav

P0359C – Roman Tub Set
P0362C – Roman Spout Only

P0360C – Tub & Shower Set
P0408C – Tub Only Set
P0409C – Shower Only Set

P0188

P0188C

P0188X

P0188XC

P0317 – Tub & Shower Set
P0449 – Tub Only Set
P0450 – Shower Only Set

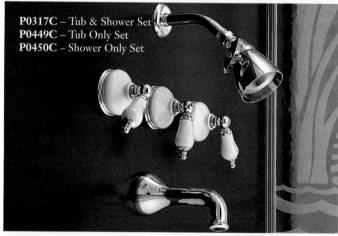

P0317C – Tub & Shower Set
P0449C – Tub Only Set
P0450C – Shower Only Set

P0444

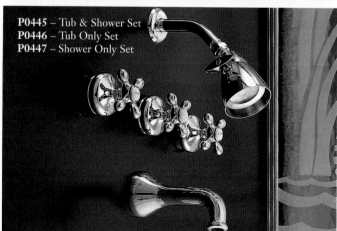

P0445 – Tub & Shower Set
P0446 – Tub Only Set
P0447 – Shower Only Set

Tri-View Medicine Cabinets with Light

MODEL LC-F3630SM-W SHOWN

These superbly crafted medicine cabinets are fabricated of heavy 20 gauge prime cold rolled steel. They are fabricated for <u>SURFACE</u> mounting. The tri-view doors are mounted with completely invisible European-style cabinet hinges. The cabinet body and doors are bonderized after forming to resist rust, spray painted with our special white color enamel paint, then baked at high temperature for durability.

Mirrors are 3/16" first quality plate glass and are available in FRAMELESS POLISHED edge or FRAMELESS BEVELED edge. Doors can be completely frameless or have bright stainless steel trim at the top & bottom.

Integral light fixture is bright chrome plated and accepts standard G25 base bulbs. The fixture is four (4") high and one (1") deep and the face of the fixture is flush with the face of the mirrored doors. The chrome light socket base projects and additional one (1") in front of the mirrors. Optional brass light fixture is also available substitute "LB" instead of "LC" at the beginning of the part number.

Overall Size w x h	Mirrored Area Size w x h	Polished Stainless Steel Trim	Frameless Polished Edges	Frameless Beveled Edges	Fixed Metal Shelves	Number Of Bulbs
24" x 28"	24" x 24"	LC-S2424SM-W	LC-F2424SM-W	LC-BV2424SM-W	2	4
24" X 34"	24" X 30"	LC-S2430SM-W	LC-F2430SM-W	LC-BV2430SM-W	3	4
30" X 28"	30" X 24"	LC-S3024SM-W	LC-F3024SM-W	LC-BV3024SM-W	2	5
30" X 34"	30" X 30"	LC-S3030SM-W	LC-F3030SM-W	LC-BV3030SM-W	3	5
36" X 34"	36" X 30"	LC-S3630SM-W	LC-F3630SM-W	LC-BV3630SM-W	3	5
36" X 40"	36" X 36"	LC-S3636SM-W	LC-F3636SM-W	LC-BV3636SM-W	4	5
48" X 34"	48" X 30"	LC-S4830SM-W	LC-F4830SM-W	LC-BV4830SM-W	3	6
48" X 40"	48" X 36"	LC-S4836SM-W	LC-F4836SM-W	LC-BV4836SM-W	4	6
54" X 40"	54" X 36"	LC-S5436SM-W	LC-F5436SM-W	LC-BV5436SM-W	4	6
60" X 40"	60" X 36"	LC-S6036SM-W	LC-F6036SM-W	LC-BV6036SM-W	4	8
72" X 40"*	72" X 36"	LC-S7236SM-W	LC-F7236SM-W	LC-BV7236SM-W	4	9

* STANDARD WITH 4 DOORS, 3 DOOR CABINET OPTIONAL

Bi-View Medicine Cabinets

These superbly crafted medicine cabinets are fabricated of heavy 20 gauge prime cold rolled steel. They are fabricated for surface mounting.

The bi-view doors are mounted with completely invisible European-style hinges. The cabinet body and doors are bonderized after forming to resist rust, spray painted with our special white enamel paint, then baked at high temperature for durability.

Mirrors are 3/16" first quality plate glass and are available in FRAMELESS POLISHED edge or FRAMELESS BEVELED edge. Doors can be completely frameless or have bright stainless steel trim at the top & bottom.

MODEL BV2030DD SHOWN

Width	Size Height	Depth	Polished Stainless Steel Trim	Frameless Polished Edges	Frameless Beveled Edges	Fixed Metal Shelves
24"	24"	5¼"	S2424DD-W	F2424DD-W	BV2424DD-W	2
20"	30"	5¼"	S2030DD-W	F2030DD-W	BV2030DD-W	3
24"	30"	5¼"	S2430DD-W	F2430DD-W	BV2430DD-W	3
24"	36"	5¼"	S2436DD-W	F2436DD-W	BV2436DD-W	4
24"	42"	5¼"	S2442DD-W	F2442DD-W	BV2442DD-W	4

Custom Sizes Available in Quantity

Corner Medicine Cabinet

BODY: 20 gauge prime sheets of cold rolled steel.
FINISH: Bonderized after forming to resist rust and sprayed with a special white color enamel, baked on at a high temperature for durability.
MIRRORS: 3/16" first quality plate glass
SHELVES: Adjustable glass shelves
DOOR STOP: Stop hinge-reversible swing door.
DOOR STYLES:　1. Polished brass frame
　　　　　　　　2. Polished stainless steel frame
　　　　　　　　3. Frameless polished edge mirror
　　　　　　　　4. Beveled frameless polished edge mirror

MODEL CR1436PE SHOWN

Polished Stainless Steel Frame	Polished Brass Frame	Frameless Polished Edge Mirror	Beveled Frameless Polished Edge Mirror	Overall Size W x H	Shelves
CR1430-W	CR1430PB-W	CR1430PE-W	CR1430BV-W	14" X 30"	2
CR1436-W	CR1436PB-W	CR1436PE-W	CR1436BV-W	14" X 36"	3
CR1442-W	CR1442PB-W	CR1442PE-W	CR1442BV-W	14" X 42"	4

SUGGESTED ARRANGEMENT FOR CORNER MEDICINE CABINET

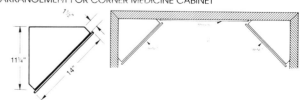

2

Tri-View Medicine Cabinets

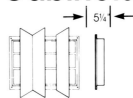

These superbly crafted medicine cabinets are fabricated of heavy 20 gauge prime cold rolled steel. They can be fabricated for both SURFACE and PARTIALLY RECESSED mounting. The tri-view doors are mounted with completely invisible European-style cabinet hinges. The cabinet body and doors are bonderized after forming to resist rust, spray painted with our special white color enamel paint, then baked at high temperature for durability.

Mirrors are 3/16" first quality plate glass and are available in FRAMELESS POLISHED edge or FRAMELESS BEVELED edge. Doors can be completely frameless or have bright stainless steel trim at the top & bottom.

Size w x h	Wall Opening w x h	Polished Stainless Steel Trim	Frameless Polished Edges	Frameless Beveled Edges	Fixed Metal Shelves
24" x 24"	23 ¾" x 23 ½"	S2424XX-W	F2424XX-W	BV2424XX-W	2
24" x 30"	23 ¾" x 29 ½"	S2430XX-W	F2430XX-W	BV2430XX-W	3
30" x 24"	29 ¾" x 23 ½"	S3024XX-W	F3024XX-W	BV3024XX-W	2
32" x 24"	30" x 20"	S3224PR-W	F3224PR-W	BV3224PR-W	2
30" x 30"	29 ¾" x 29 ½"	S3030XX-W	F3030XX-W	BV3030XX-W	3
36" x 30"	35 ¾" x 29 ½"	S3630XX-W	F3630XX-W	BV3630XX-W	3
36" x 36"	35 ¾" x 35 ½"	S3636XX-W	F3636XX-W	BV3636XX-W	4
48" x 30"	47 ¾" x 29 ½"	S4830XX-W	F4830XX-W	BV4830XX-W	3
48" x 36"	47 ¾" x 35 ½"	S4836XX-W	F4836XX-W	BV4836XX-W	4
54" x 36"	53 ¾" x 35 ½"	S5436XX-W	F5436XX-W	BV5436XX-W	4
60" x 36"	59 ¾" x 35 ½"	S6036XX-W	F6036XX-W	BV6036XX-W	4
72" x 36"**	71 ¾" x 35 ½"	S7236XX-W	F7236XX-W	BV7236XX-W	4

MODEL BV3630SM-W WITH LS-36 LIGHT FIXTURE SHOWN

"XX" SUBSTITUTE "SM" FOR SURFACE MOUNTED OPTION OR "PR" FOR PARTIALLY RECESSED OPTION. ALL PARTIALLY RECESSED CABINETS REQUIRE A WALL DEPTH OF 3". **STANDARD WITH 4 DOORS, 3 DOOR CABINET OPTIONAL.

Optional side mirror kits are available for surface mounted tri-views. Mirrors are 1/8" plate mirror, polished on all sides.

TRI-VIEW HEIGHT	MIRROR KIT MODEL NO.
24"	MKTV-24
30"	MKTV-30
36"	MKTV-36

Fully Recessed Tri-View Medicine Cabinets

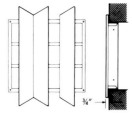

This tri-view cabinet is a FULLY RECESSED medicine cabinet which when mounted only protrudes from the wall a total of ¾". The doors are mounted with completely invisible European-style hinges which allows the door to sit flush against the wall. The body is heavy 20 gauge prime cold rolled steel bonderized to resist rust, sprayed with a special white color enamel then baked at high temperature for durability. Mirrors are 3/16" first quality plate glass and are available in FRAMELESS POLISHED edge or FRAMELESS BEVELED edge. Doors can be completely frameless or have bright stainless steel trim at the top & bottom.

Size w x h	Wall Opening w x h	Polished Stainless Steel Trim	Frameless Polished Edges	Frameless Beveled Edges	Fixed Metal Shelves	Optional Adjustable Glass Shelves
24" x 24"	21 ¾" x 22"	S2424FR-W	F2424FR-W	BV2424FR-W	2	2
24" x 30"	21 ¾" x 28"	S2430FR-W	F2430FR-W	BV2430FR-W	3	3
24" x 36"	21 ¾" x 34"	S2436FR-W	F2436FR-W	BV2436FR-W	4	4
30" x 24"	27 ¾" x 22"	S3024FR-W	F3024FR-W	BV3024FR-W	2	2
30" x 30"	27 ¾" x 28"	S3030FR-W	F3030FR-W	BV3030FR-W	3	3
36" x 30"	33 ¾" x 28"	S3630FR-W	F3630FR-W	BV3630FR-W	3	3
36" x 36"	33 ¾" x 34"	S3636FR-W	F3636FR-W	BV3636FR-W	4	4
48" x 30"	45 ¾" x 28"	S4830FR-W	F4830FR-W	BV4830FR-W	3	N/A
48" x 36"	45 ¾" x 34"	S4836FR-W	F4836FR-W	BV4836FR-W	4	N/A
54" x 36"	51 ¾" x 34"	S5436FR-W	F5436FR-W	BV5436FR-W	4	N/A
60" x 36"	57 ¾" x 34"	S6036FR-W	F6036FR-W	BV6036FR-W	4	N/A
72" x 36"**	69 ¾" x 34"	S7236FR-W	F7236FR-W	BV7236FR-W	4	N/A

MODEL S3630FR-W WITH G25B436 LIGHT SHOWN

Custom Sizes Available

ALL CABINETS REQUIRE A WALL DEPTH OF 3 ¼"

**Standard with 4 Doors, 3 Doors Cabinet Optional

3

Slim Line Surface Mounted With Light

This elegant medicine cabinet is fabricated with a very slim profile and projects only 3-1/2" from the wall. The cabinet is equipped with an integral beveled mirror light fixture with four candelabra base (G16) bulb sockets.

The body is heavy 20 gauge prime cold rolled steel bonderized to resist rust, sprayed with our special white enamel paint then baked at high temperature. Mirrors are first quality 3/16" plate glass with a 1/2" bevel around the perimeter of the mirror. Mirrors on sides of cabinet are 1/8" plate with polished edges on all sides.

The cabinet door is equipped with a spring-loaded touch latch and is hung on completely invisible European-Style hinges.

Model No.	Size
LM423BV-W	16"w x 26⅛"h
LM425BV-W	16"w x 30⅛"h
LM426BV-W	16"w x 34⅛"h
LM427BV-W	18"w x 28⅛"h
LM428BV-W	18"w x 34⅛"h
LM429BV-W	16"w x 40⅛"h
LM431BV-W	18"w x 40⅛"h

Slim Line Surface Mounted Medicine Cabinets

The new Slim Line surface mounted medicine cabinets are a very slim profile wall mounted cabinet that projects only 3 1/2". The cabinets are available with mirrored sides or with our traditional luxurious painted enamel sides. The cabinet door is equipped with a spring-loaded touch latch and is hung on completely invisible European-Style hinges.
The body is heavy 20 gauge prime cold rolled steel bonderized to resist rust, sprayed with our special white enamel then baked at high temperature for durability. Mirrors are first quality 3/16" plate glass and are available in four different door styles. Mirrors on sides of cabinet are first quality 1/8" plate with polished edges on all sides. See additional door styles on page 7.

Polished Stainless Steel Frame	Polished Brass Frame	Frameless Polished Edge Mirror	Beveled Frameless Polished Edge Mirror	Overall Size w x h	Glass Shelves
WM321-W	WM321PB-W	WM321PE-W	WM321BV-W	13½" X 36"	3
WM323-W	WM323PB-W	WM323PE-W	WM323BV-W	16" X 22"	2
WM325-W	WM325PB-W	WM325PE-W	WM325BV-W	16" X 26"	3
WM326-W	WM326PB-W	WM326PE-W	WM326BV-W	16" X 30"	3
WM327-W	WM327PB-W	WM327PE-W	WM327BV-W	18" X 24"	3
WM329-W	WM329PB-W	WM329PE-W	WM329BV-W	16" X 36"	4
WM331-W	WM331PB-W	WM331PE-W	WM331BV-W	18" X 36"	4
WM333-W	WM333PB-W	WM333PE-W	WM333BV-W	18" X 42"	5

MODEL NUMBERS ABOVE ARE FOR CABINET WITH PAINTED ENAMEL SIDES. ADD "MS" TO THE ABOVE MODEL NUMBERS FOR CABINETS WITH MIRRORED SIDES.

MODEL WM331PE-W-MS SHOWN

AVAILABLE WITHOUT MIRRORED SIDES - SEE TABLE AT RIGHT

Slim Line Recessed Medicine Cabinets

SLIM LINE medicine cabinets are the ideal cabinets for use in conjunction with wall mirrors or for side wall mounting where the side is exposed on entry to the bathroom. The SLIM LINE cabinet only protrudes from the wall 5/16", eliminating unsightly gaps between cabinet and wall mirror.

The cabinet door is equipped with a spring-loaded magnetic catch. Press gently and the catch releases opening the door. Close the door and the magnet holds it securely. The door is mounted with completely invisible European-style hinges which allow the door to sit flush against the wall.

The body is heavy 20 gauge prime cold rolled steel bonderized to resist rust, sprayed with our special white enamel then baked at high temperature for durability.

Mirrors are 3/16" first quality plate glass. See additional door styles on page 7.

Polished Stainless Steel Frame	Polished Edge Mirror	Beveled Edge Mirror	Wall Opening w x h x d	Overall Size w x h	Glass Shelves
FM321-W	FM321PE-W	FM321BV-W	12⅜ x 34¼ x 3¼	13½ x 36	3
FM323-W	FM323PE-W	FM323BV-W	14⅞ x 20¼ x 3¼	16 x 22	2
FM325-W	FM325PE-W	FM325BV-W	14⅞ x 24¼ x 3¼	16 x 26	3
FM326-W	FM326PE-W	FM326BV-W	14⅞ x 28¼ x 3¼	16 x 30	3
FM327-W	FM327PE-W	FM327BV-W	16⅞ x 22¼ x 3¼	18 x 24	3
FM329-W	FM329PE-W	FM329BV-W	14⅞ x 34¼ x 3¼	16 x 36	4
FM331-W	FM331PE-W	FM331BV-W	16⅞ x 34¼ x 3¼	18 x 36	4
FM333-W	FM333PE-W	FM333BV-W	16⅞ x 40¼ x 3¼	18 x 42	5
FM335-W	FM335PE-W	FM335BV-W	16⅞ x 50¼ x 3¼	18 x 52	5

Suggested Arrangements for Slim Line Medicine Cabinets

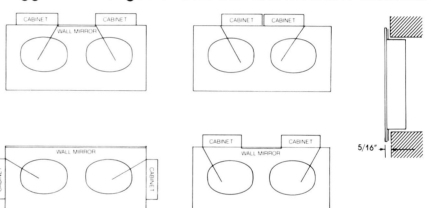

Slim Line Semi-Recessed Series Medicine Cabinets

The SR Series by BASCO is designed for recessing in very shallow walls. The cabinet only recesses into the wall 2" yet provides a fully 3" of storage depth.

The cabinet door is equipped with a magnetic touch latch and invisible European-style hinges. The body is heavy 20 gauge prime cold rolled steel bonderized to resist rust, spray painted with our special white enamel than baked at high temperature.

Mirrors are 3/16" first quality plate glass. See additional door styles on page 7.

Only 2" Wall Depth Required

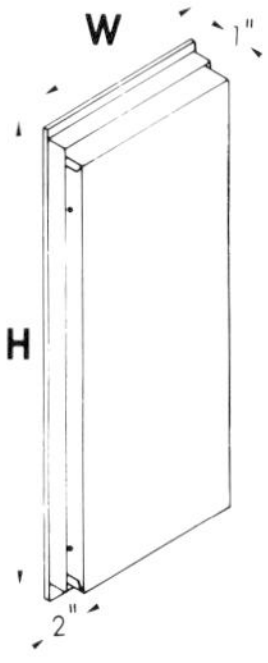

Polished Stainless Steel Frame	Polished Brass Frame	Frameless Polished Edge Mirror	Beveled Frameless Polished Edge Mirror	Wall Opening W x H x D	Overall Size W x H	Glass Shelves
SR321-W	SR321PB-W	SR321PE-W	SR321BV-W	12⅜" x 34¼" x 2	13½" x 36"	3
SR323-W	SR323PB-W	SR323PE-W	SR323BV-W	14⅞" x 20¼" x 2	16" x 22"	2
SR325-W	SR325PB-W	SR325PE-W	SR325BV-W	14⅞" x 24¼" x 2	16" x 26"	3
SR326-W	SR326PB-W	SR326PE-W	SR326BV-W	14⅞" x 28¼" x 2	16" x 30"	3
SR327-W	SR327PB-W	SR327PE-W	SR327BV-W	16⅞" x 22¼" x 2	18" x 24"	3
SR329-W	SR329PB-W	SR329PE-W	SR329BV-W	14⅞" x 34¼" x 2	16" x 36"	4
SR331-W	SR331PB-W	SR331PE-W	SR331BV-W	16⅞" x 34¼" x 2	18" x 36"	4
SR333-W	SR333PB-W	SR333PE-W	SR333BV-W	16⅞" x 40¼" x 2	18" x 42"	5

MODEL SR327BV-W SHOWN   REQUIRES ONLY 2" WALL DEPTH

Stainless Steel Framed Medicine Cabinets

MODEL 378P-W SHOWN

BODY: Heavy 20 gauge prime sheets of cold rolled steel.
DOOR: Heavy 20 gauge prime cold rolled steel. Equipped with magnetic catch(s) and rubber door silencers. Door mounted with a full length piano hinge and is field removeable & replaceable.
FINISH: Bonderized after forming to resist rust and sprayed with a special white color enamel, baked on at a high temperature for durability.
MIRRORS: First quality plate glass, with two coats of silver, then electrolytically copper clad as defined in U.S. Commercial Standard **CS-27-36**. Warranteed for 5 years against silvering defects.
SHELVES: Glass, adjustable 1/4" thick with polished front edge.
SHELF BRACKETS: Aluminum shelf brackets are removable and adjustable and lock in place.
DOOR STOP: Stop hinge-reversible swing door.

Recessed Model No.	Surface Model No.	Mirror Type	Wall Opening w x h x d	Overall w x h	Glass Shelves
360-W	SM360-W	⅛" Plate	12" x 18" x 3"	14⅛" x 20¼"	2
370-W	SM370-W	⅛" Plate	10" x 34" x 3"	12⅛" x 36¼"	4
371-W	SM371-W	⅛" Plate	14" x 18" x 3"	16⅛" x 22¼"	2
372P-W	SM372P-W	³⁄₁₆" Plate	14" x 20" x 3"	16⅛" x 22¼"	2
373P-W	SM373P-W	³⁄₁₆" Plate	14" x 28" x 3"	16⅛" x 30¼"	3
374P-W	SM374P-W	³⁄₁₆" Plate	16" x 22" x 3"	18⅛" x 24¼"	3
375P-W	SM375P-W	³⁄₁₆" Plate	14" x 24" x 3"	16⅛" x 26¼"	3
376P-W	SM376P-W	³⁄₁₆" Plate	18" x 24" x 3"	20⅛" x 26¼"	3
377P-W	SM377P-W	³⁄₁₆" Plate	14" x 34" x 3"	16⅛" x 36¼"	4
378P-W	SM378P-W	³⁄₁₆" Plate	16" x 34" x 3"	18⅛" x 36¼"	4
379P-W	SM379P-W	³⁄₁₆" Plate	16" x 40" x 3"	18⅛" x 42¼"	4
380P-W	SM380P-W	³⁄₁₆" Plate	16" x 58" x 3"	18⅛" x 60¼"	5
381P-W	SM381P-W	³⁄₁₆" Plate	16" x 28" x 3"	18⅛" x 30¼"	3
390P-W	SM390P-W	³⁄₁₆" Plate	22" x 28" x 3"	24⅛" x 30¼"	4
392P-W	SM392P-W	³⁄₁₆" Plate	22" x 34" x 3"	24⅛" x 36¼"	4

SURFACE CABINETS PROJECT 5" FROM WALL AND HAVE FULL SIZE STORAGE COMPARTMENT BEHIND DOOR.

Custom Sizes Available in Quantity

**POLISED BRASS FRAMES ARE AVAILABLE
ADD PREFIX "PB" TO ABOVE MODEL NUMBERS.**

Polished Edge and Beveled Edge Mirror Cabinet

MODEL BV378P-W SHOWN

BODY: Heavy 20 gauge prime sheets of cold rolled steel.
DOOR: Heavy 20 gauge prime cold rolled steel. Equipped with magnetic catch(s) and rubber door silencers. Door mounted with a full length piano hinge and is field removeable & replaceable.
FINISH: Bonderized after forming to resist rust and sprayed with a special white color enamel, baked on at a high temperature for durability.
MIRRORS: First quality plate glass, with two coats of silver, then electrolytically copper clad as defined in U.S. Commercial Standard **CS-27-36**. Warranteed for 5 years against silvering defects. Edges polished or polished with 1/2" bevel.
SHELVES: Glass, adjustable 1/4" thick with polished front edge.
SHELF BRACKETS: Aluminum shelf brackets are removable and adjustable and lock in place.
DOOR STOP: Stop hinge-reversible swing door.

Bevel Edge Model No.	Polished Edge Model No.	Wall Opening w x h x d	Overall w x h	Glass Shelves
BV370P-W	PE370-W	10" x 34" x 3"	12" x 36"	4
BV371P-W	PE371-W	14" x 18" x 3"	16" x 22"	2
BV372P-W	PE372P-W	14" x 20" x 3"	16" x 22"	2
BV374P-W	PE374P-W	16" x 22" x 3"	18" x 24"	3
BV375P-W	PE375P-W	14" x 24" x 3"	16" x 26"	3
BV376P-W	PE376P-W	18" x 24" x 3"	20" x 26"	3
BV377P-W	PE377P-W	14" x 34" x 3"	16" x 36"	4
BV378P-W	PE378P-W	16" x 34" x 3"	18" x 36"	4
BV379P-W	PE379P-W	16" x 40" x 3"	18" x 42"	4
BV380P-W	PE380P-W	16" x 58" x 3"	18" x 60"	5
BV390P-W	PE390P-W	22" x 28" x 3"	24" x 30"	4
BV392P-W	PE392P-W	22" x 34" x 3"	24" x 36"	4

ALSO AVAILABLE SURFACE MOUNTED, SPECIFY PREFIX "SM".

SURFACE CABINETS PROJECT 5" FROM WALL AND HAVE FULL SIZE STORAGE COMPARTMENT BEHIND DOOR.

Custom Sizes Available in Quantity

Medi-Lock Box

Securely stores medicines and personal items under lock and key. Installs into any BASCO medicine cabinet 14" or wider.

Fabricated of 20 gauge steel and finished in our special baked white enamel. Equipped with a tumbler lock and furnished with two keys.

MODEL MLB-4   SIZE: 13"w x 5"h x 4"d
MODEL MLB-3   SIZE: 13"w x 5"h x 3"d

Light Fixture With Bright Chrome or Polished Brass Finish

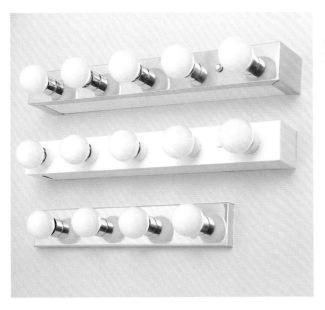

Basco's lighting fixtures are fabricated entirely of 20 gauge steel, chrome plated steel or brass plated steel. Heavy duty construction ensures durability and safety. All fixtures are U.L. approved. All fixtures use G25 lamps (Not Included). Optional convenience outlets available add suffix - CO to part numbers listed below.

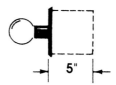

Length	Bright Chrome Model	Polished Brass Model	Size	Number of Bulbs
16"	LS-16	LS-16PB	3½" x 16" x 5" deep	3
18"	LS-18	LS-18PB	3½" x 18" x 5" deep	3
24"	LS-24	LS-24PB	3½" x 24" x 5" deep	4
30"	LS-30	LS-30PB	3½" x 30" x 5" deep	5
36"	LS-36	LS-36PB	3½" x 36" x 5" deep	5
48"	LS-48	LS-48PB	3½" x 48" x 5" deep	6
54"	LS-54	LS-54PB	3½" x 54" x 5" deep	7
60"	LS-60	LS-60PB	3½" x 60" x 5" deep	8
72"	LS-72	LS-72PB	3½" x 72" x 5" deep	9

Custom Sizes Available

Length	Bright Chrome Model	Polished Brass Model	Size	Number of Bulbs
13"	G25B413	G25B413PB	4" x 13" x 1" deep	2
16"	G25B416	G25B416PB	4" x 16" x 1" deep	3
18"	G25B418	G25B418PB	4" x 18" x 1" deep	3
20"	G25B420	G25B420PB	4" x 20" x 1" deep	4
24"	G25B424	G25B424PB	4" x 24" x 1" deep	4
30"	G25B430	G25B430PB	4" x 30" x 1" deep	5
36"	G25B436	G25B436PB	4" x 36" x 1" deep	5
48"	G25B448	G25B448PB	4" x 48" x 1" deep	6
54"	G25B454	G25B454PB	4" x 54" x 1" deep	7
60"	G25B460	G25B460PB	4" x 60" x 1" deep	8
72"	G25B472	G25B472PB	4" x 72" x 1" deep	9

Custom Sizes Available

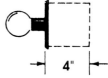

Length	White Enamel Model	Size	Number of Bulbs
16"	L4W-16	3½" x 16" x 4" deep	3
18"	L4W-18	3½" x 18" x 4" deep	3
24"	L4W-24	3½" x 24" x 4" deep	4
30"	L4W-30	3½" x 30" x 4" deep	5
36"	L4W-36	3½" x 36" x 4" deep	5
48"	L4W-48	3½" x 48" x 4" deep	6
54"	L4W-54	3½" x 54" x 4" deep	7
60"	L4W-60	3½" x 60" x 4" deep	8
72"	L4W-72	3½" x 72" x 4" deep	9

Basco Door Styles

The six basic door styles listed are available on all BASCO swing door medicine cabinets.

Many combinations are pictured in our catalog matching various door styles with different size cabinets and body styles.
Since we are a custom medicine cabinet manufacturer we can fabricate any combination of door style with any body style or size.

Your inquiries regarding custom combinations or custom sizes are welcomed.

DOOR STYLES:

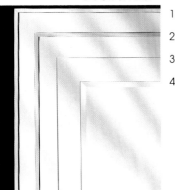

1.

2.

3.

4.

1. Polished brass frame
2. Polished stainless steel frame
3. Frameless polished edge mirror
4. Beveled frameless polished edge mirror
5. Plastic laminated door add "PL" to any Basco part number. PL door is fabricated of ½" thick medium density partical board finished with white melamine on the interior side. The front and edges are finished in Wilsonart Mica.
Standard color is Wilsonart Frosty White Matte #1573. Other Wilsonart colors are available as selected by architect. (not shown)
6. Solid wood door with high quality unfinished birch veneer on the front and edges. Interior side of door is finished in white mica. Add "WD" to any Basco part number.

DOOR STYLE #6

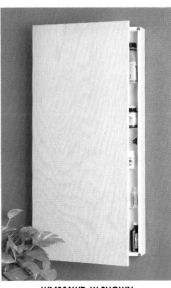

WM331WD-W SHOWN

7

Fixed Tilting Mirror

FIXED TILTING MIRROR

Basco's new design of fixed tilting mirror attempts to take the institutional look out of accessories for the handicapped. Mirrors are fabricated out of heavy 20 gauge prime cold rolled steel and painted a very appealing white enamel. Mirrors are 3/16" first quality plate mirror and are reinforced with a shock absorbing filler and a 20 gauge steel back. Mirrors project 4" from the wall at the top and 1" at the bottom. Mirrors are mounted on a concealed wall hanger fabricated of 20 gauge galvanized steel. Basco's L4W series light fixtures are especially made 4" deep to compliment the tilting mirrors and are also painted white to match the mirror.

Mirror	Size	Matching Light	Size	Bulbs
HTM-16x30-W	16" x 30"	L4W-16	16"w x 3½"h x 4"d	3
HTM-18x24-W	18" x 24"	L4W-18	18"w x 3½"h x 4"d	3
HTM-18x30-W	18" x 30"	L4W-18	18"w x 3½"h x 4"d	3
HTM-24x30-W	24" x 30"	L4W-24	24"w x 3½"h x 4"d	4
HTM-30x24-W	30" x 24"	L4W-30	30"w x 3½"h x 4"d	5
HTM-36x30-W	36" x 30"	L4W-36	36"w x 3½"h x 4"d	5
HTM-48x24-W	48" x 24"	L4W-48	48"w x 3½"h x 4"d	6
HTM-48x30-W	48" x 30"	L4W-48	48"w x 3½"h x 4"d	6

Other sizes available in quantity.

Medicine Cabinet With Tilting Mirror

This quality medicine cabinet is designed for the use by handicapped persons. The medicine cabinet mirror may be used in the upright position or tilted down to accommodate a seated person. The cabinet door is equipped with a latch to keep the door closed when mirror is tilted down. The tilted mirror is secured by an elbow hinge and a stainless steel piano hinge at the bottom.

BODY: 20 gauge prime sheets of cold rolled steel.
FINISH: Bonderized after forming to resist rust and sprayed with a special white enamel, baked on a high temperature for durability.
MIRRORS: First quality plate glass, with two coats of silver, then electrolytically copper clad as defined in U.S. Commercial Standard CS-27-36. Warranteed for 5 years against silvering defects.
FRAME: Stainless steel.
SHELVES: Glass, adjustable.
DOOR STOP: Stop hinge.

Model No.	Wall Opening	Overall Size	Glass Shelves
372P-ATM - W	14" x 20" x 3"	16⅛" x 22¼"	2
SM372P-ATM - W	SURFACED MTD.	16⅛" X 22¼" X 5¾"	2
374P-ATM - W	16" x 22" x 3"	18⅛" x 24¼"	3
SM374P-ATM - W	SURFACED MTD.	18⅛" X 24¼" X 5¾"	3
375P-ATM - W	14" x 24" x 3"	16⅛" x 26¼"	3
SM375P-ATM - W	SURFACED MTD.	16⅛" X 26¼" X 5¾"	3

Other sizes available in quantity.

MODEL TL-SM-373-W SHOWN

Surface Mount/Top Light

BODY: Heavy 20 gauge prime sheets of cold rolled steel.
DOOR: Heavy 20 gauge prime sheets of cold rolled steel. Equipped with magnetic catch(S) and rubber door silencers. Door mounted with a full length piano hinge and is field removable & replaceable.
FINISH: Bonderized after forming to resist rust and sprayed with a special white color enamel, baked on at a high temperature for durability.
MIRRORS: First quality 3/16" plate glass, with two coats of silver, then electrolytically copper clad as defined in

U.S. commercial standard CS-27-36. Warranteed for 5 years against silvering defects.
SHELVES: Glass, adjustable 1/4" thick with polished front edge.
SHELF BRACKETS: Locking aluminum shelf brackets removable and adjustable with tabs to prevent accidental removal of shelf.
DOOR STOP: Stop Hinge
LIGHT: (2) 60 watt incandescent bulbs (not include UL Approved

Surface Model No.	Overall Size	Mirror Size
TL-SM-371-W	16⅛" x 23½" x 7⅜"	16⅛" x 20¼"
TL-SM-373-W	16⅛" x 33½" x 7⅜"	16⅛" x 30¼"
TL-SM-378-W	18⅛" x 39½" x 7⅜"	18⅛" x 36¼"

Specifications: All grab bars are fabricated of heavy duty 18 gauge type 304 satin finish stainless steel tubing. Bars are heliarc welded to stainless steel flanges. Bars will withstand a force of 900 lbs. Flanges and cover plates are type 304 stainless steel with a satin finish. All bars have a 1½" wall clearance.

Construction: CONCEALED WITH SNAP-ON FLANGE
14 Gauge mounting flange 3" in diameter with 3 mounting holes.
20 Gauge type 304 stainless steel cover
CONCEALED WITH SET SCREWS
10 Gauge 4" deep 3" diameter flange with a minimum of 3 set screws 13 Gauge concealed mounting plate with 3 slotted mounting holes.
EXPOSED SCREW MOUNTING 10 Gauge mounting flange 3" in diameter with 3 mounting holes.

Optional Finishes: PEENED GRIPPING SURFACE:
ADD SUFFIX "P"
KNURLED GRIPPING SURFACE:
ADD SUFFIX "K"
BRIGHT POLISHED FINISH:
ADD SUFFIX "B"
BRASS WITH POLISHED FINISH:
ADD SUFFIX "BB"
BRASS WITH SATIN FINISH:
ADD SUFFIX "SB"

Specifying Instructions: When specifying grab bars insert the model numbers (SHAPES) into the double zeros at the end of the grab bar series number.

EXAMPLE: An exposed fastened 1½" grab bar 24" long is part number 8414H.

SNAP-ON CONCEALED MOUNTING
5100H SERIES 1" DIAMETER
5200H SERIES 1¼" DIAMETER
6200H SERIES 1½" DIAMETER

CONCEALED WITH SET SCREW
5800H SERIES 1" DIAMETER
5400H SERIES 1¼" DIAMETER
6400H SERIES 1½" DIAMETER

OPTIONAL PEENED FINISH

EXPOSED SCREW MOUNTING
5600H SERIES 1" DIAMETER
5000H SERIES 1¼" DIAMETER
8400H SERIES 1½" DIAMETER

OPTIONAL KNURLED FINISH

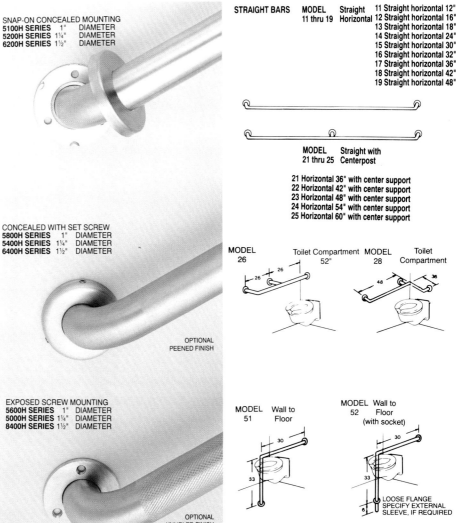

STRAIGHT BARS MODEL 11 thru 19 Straight Horizontal
11 Straight horizontal 12"
12 Straight horizontal 16"
13 Straight horizontal 18"
14 Straight horizontal 24"
15 Straight horizontal 30"
16 Straight horizontal 32"
17 Straight horizontal 36"
18 Straight horizontal 42"
19 Straight horizontal 48"

MODEL 21 thru 25 Straight with Centerpost

21 Horizontal 36" with center support
22 Horizontal 42" with center support
23 Horizontal 48" with center support
24 Horizontal 54" with center support
25 Horizontal 60" with center support

MODEL 26 Toilet Compartment 52"

MODEL 28 Toilet Compartment

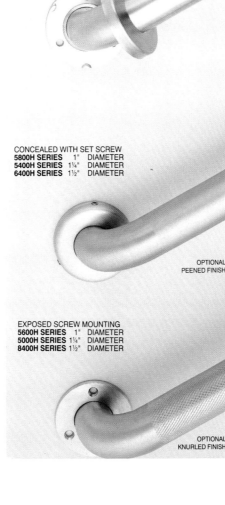

MODEL 80

Toilet Straddle

MODEL 84

SWINGS 90°
OR 26 ADJUSTABLE

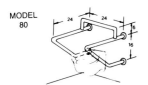

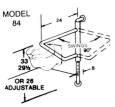

MODEL 51 Wall to Floor

MODEL 52 Wall to Floor (with socket)

LOOSE FLANGE SPECIFY EXTERNAL SLEEVE, IF REQUIRED

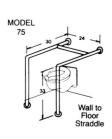

MODEL 33 90° Angle 16 x 32

LEFT HAND SHOWN

MODEL 32 90° ANGLE 16 X 32

RIGHT HAND SHOWN

MODEL 42 Shower Bar

RIGHT HAND SHOWN TWO PIECES, UNLESS OTHERWISE SPECIFIED

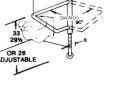

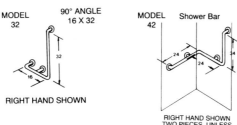

LEFT HAND SHOWN
MODEL 57 Wall to Floor with Outrigger

MODEL 75 Wall to Floor Straddle

MODEL 92 RIGHT HAND SHOWN

Tub and Shower Bar

MODEL 69

Shower Compartment Bar

MODEL 46

Inside Corner Angle Bar

MODEL 41 Inside Corner Angle Bar

MODEL 44 Tub and Shower Bar
RIGHT HAND SHOWN TWO PIECES, UNLESS OTHERWISE SPECIFIED

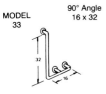

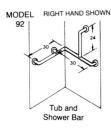

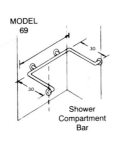

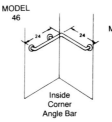

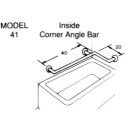

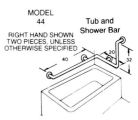

Europa Hotel Bath Accessories

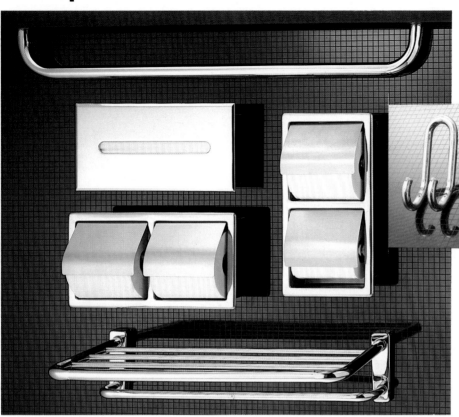

915P Towel Bar
Crafted of 1" diameter seamless 20 gauge type 304 stainless steel tubing polished to a bright finish. Concealed mounting hardware solid brass. Available in 18", 24", 30", 36", length. (Custom sizes available)

925P Towel Bar
Same as 915P except ¾" diameter.

7925C Recessed Facial Tissue Cabinet
Polished chrome panel with galvanized steel storage box. Overall size: 11¾" x 6". Wall opening required: 10¾" x 5" x 2⅝".

7987P Horizontal Dual Hooded Toilet Paper Holder
Fabricated in one piece of type 304 stainless steel polished to bright finish. Furnished with chrome plated roller. Overall size: 12⅜" x 6½". Wall opening required: 11⅝" x 5¾" x 3".

7988P Vertical Dual Hooded Toilet Paper Holder
Same specifications as Model 7987P. Overall size: 6½" x 12⅜". Wall Opening required: 5¾" x 11⅝" x 3".

1680P Towel Shelf with Towel Bar
Superbly crafted entirely of type 304 stainless steel tubing and then polished to a bright finish. Heavy duty concealed wall brackets are fabricated of 11 gauge (.119) cadmium plated steel. Unique mounting system insures secure attachment to wall.
Sizes: 18" x 9¼" x 4⅞"
                  20¾" x 9¼" x 4⅞"
                  24" x 9¼" x 4⅞"

1648P Chrome Robe Hook
Size: 2⅛" x 5½" x 2" Projection

All items available in polished brass finish. Add "PB" in front of part number.

Europa II Stainless Steel Bath Accessories

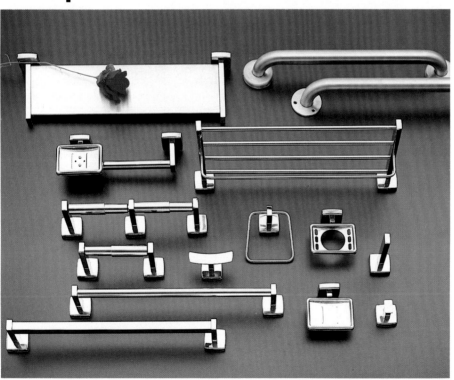

The Europa II series bath accessories are fabricated of type 304 stainless steel and are available in the following finishes:
Bright Polished - add suffix "P" to part number
Satin finish - add suffix "S" to part number
Bronze finish - add suffix "BZ" to part number
Polished Brass - add suffix "PB" to part number

1614*	Soap Dish and Bar with drain holes
1615*	Soap Dish without drain holes
1616*	Soap Dish with drain holes
1618*	Toothbrush Tumbler Holder
1626*	Shelf 6³⁄₁₆" deep - available in 18" and 24" lengths
1630*	Toilet Paper Holder - plastic roller
1631*	Toilet Paper Holder - chrome roller
1630D*	Dual Toilet Paper Holder - plastic roller
1631D*	Dual Toilet Paper Holder - chrome roller
1641*	Square Towel Bar ¾" diameter - available in 18", 24", 30" and 36" lengths
1642*	Round Towel Bar ¾" diameter - available in 18", 24", 30", and 36" lengths
1643*	Double Robe Hook 2" projection
1644*	Single Robe Hook 2" projection
1645*	Towel Pin 4¼" long
1646*	Single Robe Hook 4¼" high
1650*	Towel Ring 5" wide x 4½" high
1651*	Towel shelf 8" deep - available in 18" and 24" lengths
1652*	Towel Shelf w/drying rod 8" deep - available in 18" and 24" lengths

*Add finish code "P", "S", "BZ" or "PB"

THE CONCEALED-MOUNTING SYSTEM
Post is welded to mounting bracket and flange to form an integral unit. Post assembly mounts on stainless steel wall plate and is secured with set screw on bottom.

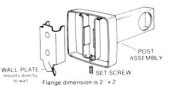

POST ASSEMBLY

WALL PLATE
mounts directly to wall

SET SCREW

Flange dimension is 2" x 2"

Contempo Chrome Bath Accessories

• FUNCTIONAL STYLING   • DELUXE EXPOSED SCREW DESIGN

The Contempo Series offers easy installation and modern design. BASCO makes these quality fixtures available to you at a price you're sure to enjoy. These triple chrome plated accessories are made of durable Zamac.

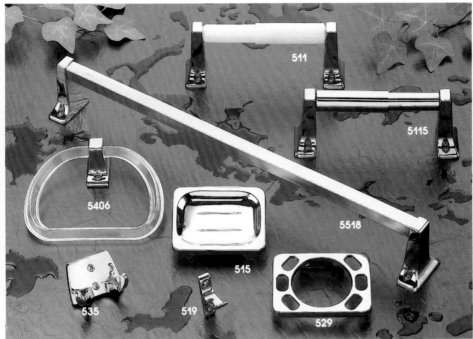

519	Robe Hook
5115	Paper Holder, Chrome Roller
511	Paper Holder, White Roller
535	Double Robe Hook
529	Chrome Toothbrush & Tumbler Holder
515	Chrome Soap Holder
5586	Soap Holder with 8" Grab Bar (not illustrated)
5406	Lucite Towel Ring
5406C	Chrome Towel Ring

⅝" Square Polished Stainless Steel Towel Bar Set

5518	18" Long
5524	24" Long
5530	30" Long
5536	36" Long

⅝" Square Aluminum Bar Towel Bar Set

5518A	18" Long
5524A	24" Long
5530A	30" Long
5536A	36" Long

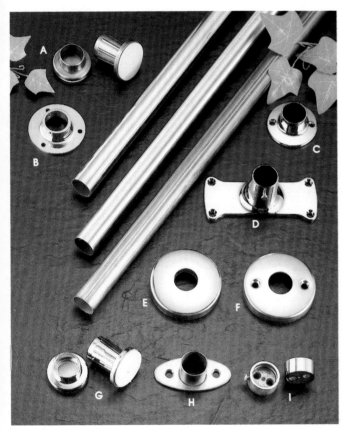

Basco Shower Rods & Flanges

Shower Rods - Available in 3, 5 & 6 Foot Lengths

MODEL NO.	MATERIAL & FINISH	DIAMETER	WALL THICKNESS
1210	Anodized Aluminum	1"	.022
1210AB	Anodized Alum., Antique Brass	1"	.022
1210PB	Anodized Alum., Polished Brass	1"	.022
1212	Polished Stainless Steel	1"	.015
1213B	Polished Type 304 St. Steel	1"	.035
1213PB	Polished Brass	1"	.042
1214B	Polished Type 304 St. Steel	1"	.049
1215B	Polished Type 304 St. Steel	1¼"	.049
1216B	Polished Type 304 St. Steel	1¼"	.035
1217B	Polished Type 304 St. Steel	1½"	.035
1218B	Polished Type 304 St. Steel	1½"	.049

SHOWER ROD END FLANGES

MODEL NO.	DESCRIPTION	DIAMETER	ILLUSTRATION NO.
1200B	Concealed Screw Stainless Steel	1"	E
1201	Adjustable Chrome Plated Cast Zinc	1"	G
1201AB	Adjustable Antique Brass Cast Zinc	1"	A
1201PB	Adjustable Polished Brass Cast Zinc	1"	(Not Shown)
1202	Extended Exposed Screw Stainless Steel	1"	H
1203	Exposed Screw Chrome Plated Cast Zinc	1"	C
1203PB	Exposed Screw Solid Polished Brass	1"	B
1204B	Exposed Screw Polished Stainless Steel	1"	F
1205B	Exposed Screw Polished Stainless Steel	1¼"	F
1208B	Concealled Screw Chrome Pltd. Brass	1"	I
1209B	Concealled Screw Chrome Pltd. Brass	1¼"	I
1230B	Concealled Screw Stainless Steel	1¼"	E
1235B	Jumbo Exposed Screw Chrome Pltd. Steel	1"	D

Classic Chrome Bath Accessories

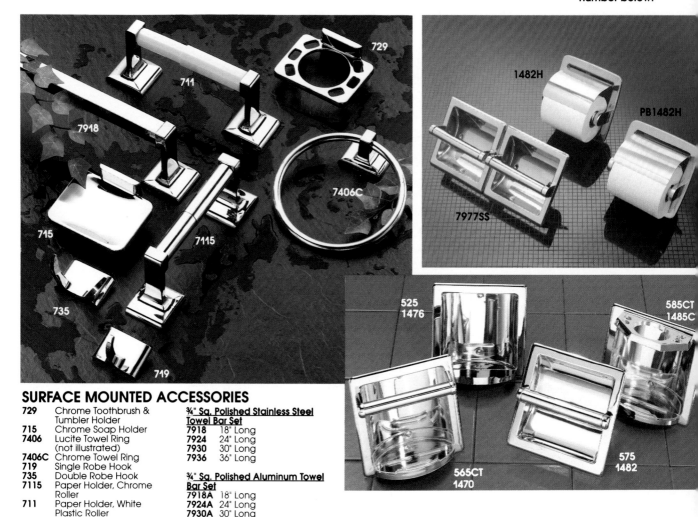

SURFACE MOUNTED ACCESSORIES

729	Chrome Toothbrush & Tumbler Holder	**¾" Sq. Polished Stainless Steel Towel Bar Set**	
715	Chrome Soap Holder	**7918**	18" Long
7406	Lucite Towel Ring (not illustrated)	**7924**	24" Long
		7930	30" Long
7406C	Chrome Towel Ring	**7936**	36" Long
719	Single Robe Hook		
735	Double Robe Hook	**¾" Sq. Polished Aluminum Towel Bar Set**	
7115	Paper Holder, Chrome Roller	**7918A**	18" Long
711	Paper Holder, White Plastic Roller	**7924A**	24" Long
		7930A	30" Long
		7936A	36" Long

BASCO'S very finest concealed screw accessories! The classic design of these chrome fixtures will supply you with a complete range of your bathroom needs. Made of durable Zamac, the quality craftsmanship of the Classic Series is unsurpassed. Available with ¾" square towel bars in stainless steel or aluminum. Our easy-to-install concealed screw fixtures are a must for any modern bathroom.

BASCO'S recessed accessories are crafted of solid brass and are luxuriously triple chrome plated, or made of highly polished stainless steel.

RECESSED MOUNTED ACCESSORIES

Standard Size
Chrome Plated Brass

Overall dimensions 6¼" x 6¼"
Wall Opening 5¼" x 5¼"

525	Soap Holder
565	Soap Holder & Grab Bar
575	Paper Holder with Chrome Roller
576	Paper Holder with Plastic Roller
525CT	Soap Holder with Protective Tray
565CT	Soap Holder & Grab Bar with Protective Tray
585CT	Toothbrush, Tumbler & Soap Holder with Protective Tray
PB1482	Recessed polished brass toilet paper holder. Overall Size: 6¼" x 6¼" Wall Opening: 5¼" x 5¼" x2"
PB1482H	Recessed polished brass toilet paper holder with hood. Overall Size: 6¼" x 6¼" Wall Opening: 5¼" x 5¼" x2"

Standard Size
Polished Stainless Steel

Overall Dimensions 6¼" x 6¼"
Wall Opening 5¼" x 5¼"

1470	Soap Holder and Grab Bar
1476	Soap Holder
1482	Paper Holder with Chrome Roller
1488	Paper Holder with White Plastic Roller
1485CT	Toothbrush, Tumbler & Soap Holder with Protective Tray
1482H	Recessed Polished stainless steel toilet paper holder with hood. Overall Size: 6¼" x 6¼" Wall Opening: 5¼" x 5¼" x 2"
7977SS	Recessed polished stainless steel dual toilet paper holder. Overall Size: 12⅝" x 6¼" Wall Opening: 11½" x 5¼" x 2"

Installation Clamp

For use with screw type recessed fixtures, this handy device simplifies installation by eliminating framework or setting in cement.

630	Installation Clamp with Retainer Spring
630LS	Installation Clamp, less Retainer Spring

Cement and Tile Installation

Add the suffix "L" to any model number. A special lug will be secured to the back of any recessed fixture ordered in this manner, permitting it to be set in cement.

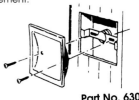

Part No. 630
Optional

BASCO

40 AERO ROAD, P.O. BOX 237, BOHEMIA, N.Y. 11716
(516) 567-4404 • FAX (516) 567-4815

1999 ZEFA GERMANY/ALL STOCK

(Printed in USA)

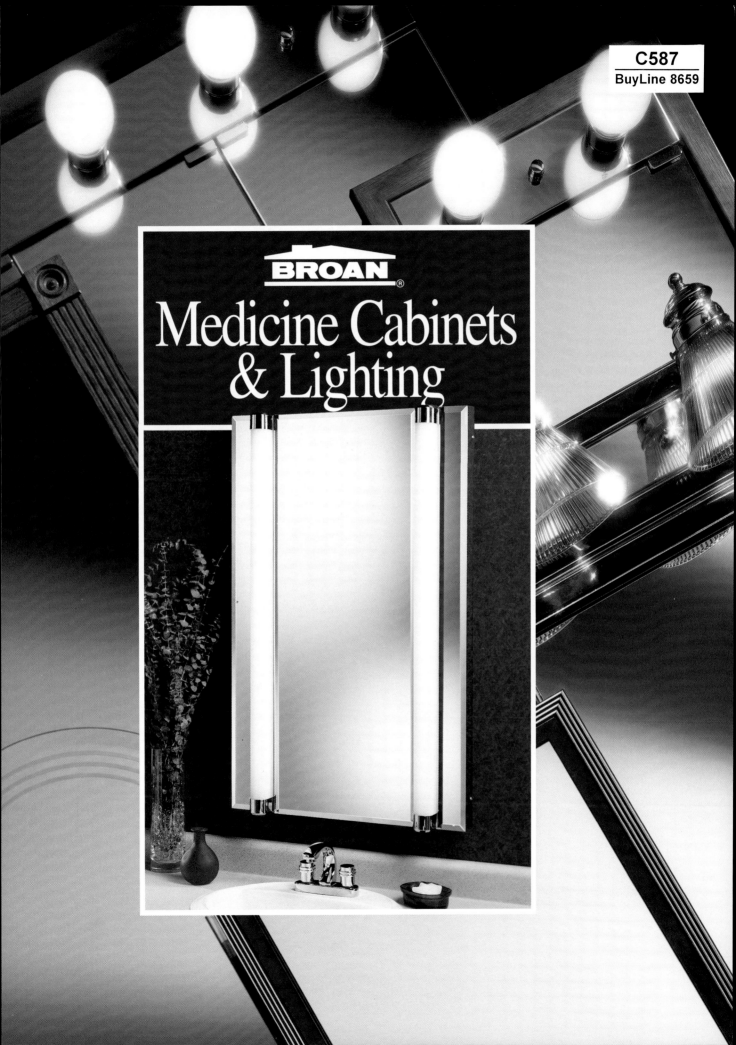

BROAN®
Medicine Cabinets & Lighting

Introducing
this streamlined, elegan
new look for your bath
from Broan...

Contents

*W*elcome to the world of Broan Medicine Cabinets and Lighting. This catalog includes a unique variety of lighting, mirrors and storage options for your bathroom. To help you review our large selection, we have divided the catalog into sections by product similarities, and included a detailed specification list at the back, making it easy for you to choose the right models to meet your individual needs.

Throughout our product line, Broan prides itself on quality and craftsmanship. From genuine oak frames to the jewel-like finish of our beveled-edge mirrors, no detail is overlooked. We use premium float glass mirrors for distortion-free viewing and all lighting products are UL listed so they can be installed with confidence. In each design and with all of our materials, we strive to balance timeless beauty with the decorative trends of today and the enduring quality construction that our customers demand.

Broan selection, quality and value... a nice reflection on you!

2

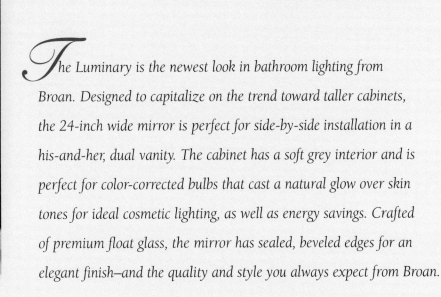

Luminary (See page 5)

The Luminary is the newest look in bathroom lighting from
Broan. Designed to capitalize on the trend toward taller cabinets,
the 24-inch wide mirror is perfect for side-by-side installation in a
his-and-her, dual vanity. The cabinet has a soft grey interior and is
perfect for color-corrected bulbs that cast a natural glow over skin
tones for ideal cosmetic lighting, as well as energy savings. Crafted
of premium float glass, the mirror has sealed, beveled edges for an
elegant finish—and the quality and style you always expect from Broan.

The Frameless group of cabinets offers the beauty of mirrored panels that multiply the available light for an increased sense of space.

Cabinet PRC1148; PRL1048 Soffit Light

Cabinet LBC10

PRIMEVÉRE *Expressions*

Tasteful design on a grand scale, our leader in luxury options features a polished-edge, clear tri-view mirror framed with beveled mirror trim in clear finish. The accompanying 8" diameter magnifying mirror can be mounted on the inside of the cabinet door at the height of your choice. Matching soffit light with mirror trim sold separately; features instant-on, warm-tone, color-correct fluorescent light (included). Parabolic diffuser softens the light for a decidedly elegant atmosphere.

Style	Model	Overall Size W H D	Wall Opening W H D
Tri-View Built-In Cabinets	PRC1148	48 x 37⅜	36⅞ x 32⅞ x 3⅞
	PRC1160	60 x 37⅜	48⅞ x 32⅞ x 3⅞
Tri-View Wall Mount Cabinets	PRC1148SM	48¼ x 37⅜	–
	PRC1160SM	60¼ x 37⅜	–
Matching Soffit Lights for Tri-View Wall Mount or Built-In Cabinets	PRL1048	48 x 4¼ x 5⅜	–
	PRL1060	60 x 4¼ x 5⅜	–

LE BACCARAT *Expressions*

Like fine cut crystal, Le Baccarat brings the bath to life with a rich kaleidoscope of light. This arched-top, beveled mirror is framed in clear finish mirror mosaic trim with a clear mirrored single-door in the center. Matching wall mirrors echo the arched motif and the mosaic beveled glass design. The accompanying 8" diameter magnifying mirror can be mounted on the inside of the cabinet door at the height of your choice.

Style	Model	Overall Size W H D	Wall Opening W H D
Single-Door Built-In Cabinet	LBC10	24 x 35⅜	16½ x 25¼ x 3⅞
Wall Mirror Only	LBM15	24 x 35⅜	–

Models on this page are handcrafted. Please allow time for these special orders.

For a contemporary look with an elegant note... the Luminary.

Cabinet 658BC

Cabinet 658BC

LUMINARY

Perfect for side-by-side installation, the Luminary is designed to capitalize on the trend toward taller cabinets. Color-corrected bulbs* offer energy saving, natural light, creating the perfect grooming environment. Premium float glass mirror and mirrored trim with sealed, 1/2" beveled edges; adjustable glass shelves; a soft gray interior; six-way adjustable hinges; a mirrored cabinet back wall and a convenient grounded electrical outlet complete this modular presentation.

Style	Model	Overall Size W H D	Wall Opening W H D
Single-Door Built-In Cabinet	658BC	24 x 37⅜	14¼ x 34¼ x 3½
Single-Door Wall Mount Cabinet	652BC	24 x 37⅜ x 7¼	–

*Bulbs not included.

Chrome lens caps available on request. Part # 90714216

See pages 31-35 for detailed specifications.

Cabinet 655236

SATURN

The distinctive look of the industry's first 1/2" beveled-edge, tri-view mirror designed for new warm-tone fluorescent light tubes (not included). These lights provide true-color reflections making them ideal for cosmetic lighting, while offering substantial energy savings over incandescent bulbs. Electrical outlets inside cabinet add convenience and glass shelves add elegance.

Style	Model	Overall Size W H D	Wall Opening W H D
Tri-View Built-In Cabinets	655036	36 x 30	33¾ x 24¾ x 3½
	655048	48 x 30	45¾ x 24¾ x 3½
Tri-View Wall Mount Cabinets	655236	36 x 30	–
	655248	48 x 30	–

Chrome lens caps available on request. Part # 90714216

TORINO

Beveled-edge and frosted cut-glass teardrop designs are ideal for use with a "his-n-hers" vanity or pedestal sinks. Matching side light fixtures feature beveled-edge mirror backplates and frosted glass shades.

Style	Model	Overall Size W H D	Wall Opening W H D
Single-Door Built-In Cabinets	5520	16½ x 34½	14 x 18 x 3½
	5528	16½ x 34½	14 x 24 x 3½
Side Lights for Single-Door Built-In Cabinets	73591*	5⅜ x 13¾ x 6½	–

*Packed in pairs.

Cabinet 5528; Lights 73591

See pages 31-35 for detailed specifications

Cabinet 1350

Cabinet 1454; Lights 73190

CAMEO OVAL BEVEL

This cabinet features the tailored elegance of a classic cameo oval mirrored door. Frameless, 1" beveled-edge float glass mirror is supported by heavy-gauge steel construction. Adjustable shelves. Reversible.

Style	Model	Overall Size W H D	Wall Opening W H D
Single-Door Built-In Cabinets	1350	21 x 31	14 x 18 x 3½
	1358	24 x 35	14 x 24 x 3½

MIRAGE

Faceted like a gemstone, this octagonal, 1/2" beveled-edge mirror cabinet teams nicely with side lights featuring beveled-edge mirror backplates and smoked glass shades.

Style	Model	Overall Size W H D	Wall Opening W H D
Single-Door Built-In Cabinets	1454	18 x 27	14 x 18 x 3½
	1456	17⅜ x 32	14 x 24 x 3½
Side Lights for Single-Door Built-In Cabinets	73190*	5 x 12 x 6½	–

*Packed in pairs.   (Globes are smoked glass and accommodate slim line 60w bulbs.)

SONATA

Graceful top and bottom curves on this 1/2" beveled-edge cabinet and lights make an elegant and unusual ensemble in a single-door design. Matching side light fixtures feature beveled-edge mirror backplate and distinctive frosted glass shades with grey accent and chrome-plated fittings.

Style	Model	Overall Size W H D	Wall Opening W H D
Single-Door Built-In Cabinet	258	16 x 32	14 x 24 x 3½
Side Lights for Single-Door Built-In Cabinet	72052*	5 x 17½ x 6⅛	–

*Packed in pairs.

Cabinet 258; Lights 72052

7

Cabinet 1420FL; Light 735FL

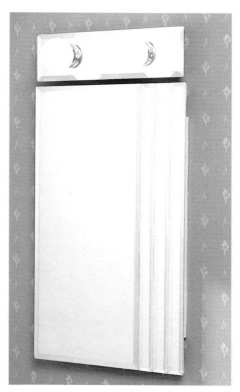

Cabinet 1418; Light 73290

DECORAH

Beveled-edge mirror with a soft gold-tone and soft white floral design lends a unique decorator touch that beautifully completes an overall floral motif.

Style	Model	Overall Size W H D	Wall Opening W H D
Single-Door Built-In Cabinet	1420FL	16 x 26	14 x 18 x 3½
Top Light for Single-Door Built-In Cabinet	735FL	16 x 4⅜ x 2	–

AURORA

Deep-cut, 1/2" beveled-edge design mirrors fill the bath with shimmering reflections, adding a new dimension to a classic style.

Style	Model	Overall Size W H D	Wall Opening W H D
Single-Door Built-In Cabinet	1418	16 x 26	14 x 24 x 3½
Top Light for Single-Door Built-In Cabinet	73290	16 x 4½ x 2	–

MIRROR-ON-MIRROR

Stunning 1/2" beveled-edge, mirror-on-mirror designs create a sophisticated, upscale look even in small-space environments. Each features a clear center mirror with contrasting grey smoke background mirror for an all-glass, picture-frame effect.

Style	Oval Model	Rectangular Model	Overall Size W H D	Wall Opening W H D
Single-Door Built-In Cabinets	1452 1457	1450BC 1458	16 x 26 16 x 26	14 x 18 x 3½ 14 x 24 x 3½
Top Light for Single-Door Built-In Models	73290	73290	16 x 4½ x 2	–
Side Lights for Single-Door Built-In Models	73190*	73190*	5 x 12 x 6½	–

*Packed in pairs. (Globes are smoked glass and accommodate slim line 60w bulbs.)

Cabinet 1450BC; Lights 73190

Cabinet 1452; Light 73290

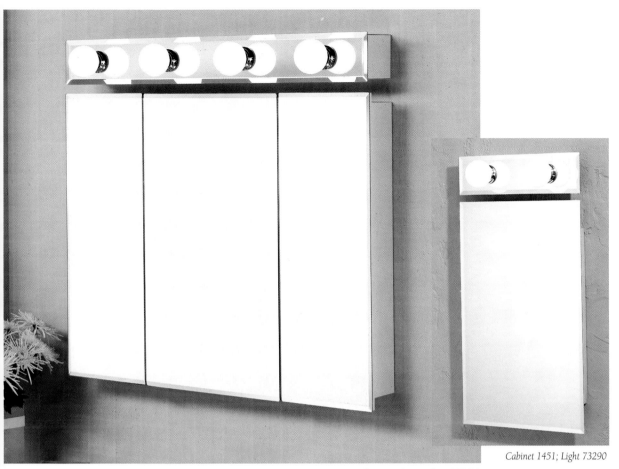

Cabinet 1451; Light 73290

Cabinet 255236; Light HO33690

HORIZON

Our most popular style, the Horizon features the understated elegance of beveled-edge design. A wide selection of tri-view and single-door models and optional matching light bars means this classic is right at home in any size bath.

Style	Model	Overall Size W H D	Wall Opening W H D
Tri-View Built-In Cabinets	255024	24 x 24	21¾ x 20⅞ x 3½
	255030	30 x 28¼	27¾ x 25⅛ x 3½
	255036	36 x 28¼	33¾ x 25⅛ x 3½
	255048	48 x 28¼	45¾ x 25⅛ x 3½
Tri-View Wall Mount Cabinets	255224	24 x 24 x 5¼	–
	255230	30 x 28¼ x 5¼	–
	255236	36 x 28¼ x 5¼	–
	255248	48 x 28¼ x 5¼	–
Top Lights for Tri-View Built-In Cabinets	HO42490	24 x 4½ x 2¼	–
	HO43090	30 x 4½ x 2¼	–
	HO43690	36 x 4½ x 2¼	–
	HO44890	48 x 4½ x 2¼	–
Top Lights for Tri-View Wall Mount Cabinet	HO32490	24 x 4½ x 5⅞	–
	HO33090	30 x 4½ x 5⅞	–
	HO33690	36 x 4½ x 5⅞	–
	HO34890	48 x 4½ x 5⅞	–
Single-Door Built-In Cabinets	1451	16 x 26	14 x 18 x 3½
	1459	16 x 26	14 x 24 x 3½
	1453†	16 x 20	14 x 18 x 2½
Side Lights for Built-In Cabinets	73190*	5 x 12 x 6½	
Top Light for Single-Door Built-In Cabinets	73290	16 x 4½ x 2	–

*Packed in pairs — See page 7 for picture.
†Molded body.
(See page 29 for stainless steel body cabinets.)

Cabinet 295230

FOCUS

Simple, clean polished-edge design enables this tri-view mirror with built-in top lights to complement a diverse range of decorating styles.

Style	Model	Overall Size W H D
Tri-View Wall Mount Cabinets	295224	24 x 30 x 5¼
	295230	30 x 34 x 5¼

See pages 31-35 for detailed specifications.

Cabinet 455248

QUANTUM

Beveled-edge elegance with a softened radius corner design. Quantum is ideal for the curvaceous, flowing lines of many of today's vanity tops and bath fixtures.

Style	Model	Overall Size W H D
Tri-View Wall	455230	30 x 36½ x 5¼
Mount Cabinets	455236	36 x 36½ x 5¼
	455248	48 x 36½ x 5¼

LAFAYETTE

A choice of beveled-edge mirror cabinets to suit your decorating tastes. Both square corner and radius corner styles feature built-in top lights.

Style	Model	Overall Size W H D
Single-Door Wall	1402	18⅛ x 32⅜ x 6
Mount Cabinets	1462	18⅛ x 28⅜ x 6

Cabinet 1462

Cabinet 1402

Broan's Metal Trimmed line is styled to emphasize a modern functionality with a flair all its own.

Cabinet 155130; Light SB23129

VIENNA

Our most economical steel body tri-view cabinet, the Vienna features contemporary elegance trimmed in polished chrome finish. Matching top light has polished stainless steel faceplate.

Style	Model	Overall Size W H D
Tri-View Wall Mount Cabinets	155124 155130	24 x 26 x 5½ 30 x 26 x 5½
Top Lights for Tri-View Wall Mount Cabinets	SB22529 SB23129	24 x 4 x 5½ 30 x 4 x 5½

STYLELINE 2

The Styleline 2 has stainless steel trim top and bottom, with polished vertical edges. Built-in top light features stainless steel faceplate.

Style	Model	Overall Size W H D
Single-Door Wall Mount Cabinet	565	18 x 28 x 6

Cabinet 565

Broan's Decorator Frames series offers unique patterns, designs and colors to accessorize your bath or powder room.

A duo with neo-classical timelessness, the Classico medicine cabinet and matching fixture are available in Honey Oak Burl with gold trim or Mahogany Burl with black trim.

Cabinet 3890; Light 715M

Cabinet 3870; Light 715K

CLASSICO

Smart, neo-classical styling adds flavor to bathroom decor. Available in two finishes: Honey Oak Burl with Gold Accent, or Mahogany Burl with Black Accent. Both have plate glass mirror and heavy gauge steel construction. Matching top light fixtures feature glass shades, brass fittings, brass faceplate and use standard 60 watt bulbs.

Style	Oak Model	Mahogany Model	Overall Size W H D	Wall Opening W H D
Single-Door Built-In Cabinets	3870	3890	18¹/₁₆ x 28¹/₁₆	14 x 18 x 3¹/₂
	3878	3898	18¹/₁₆ x 28¹/₁₆	14 x 24 x 3¹/₂
Single-Door Wall Mount Cabinets (almond body)	3872	3892	18¹/₁₆ x 28¹/₁₆	–
Top Lights for Single-Door Built-In Cabinet	715K	715M	18⅝ x 8 x 7	–
Top Lights for Single-Door Wall Mount Cabinet	716K	716M	18¹/₁₆ x 8 x 9¾	–

See pages 31-35 for detailed specification

Cabinet 3910; Light 711FG

Cabinet 6120; Light 761WH

With the exquisitely elegant look inspired by the artistry of Florentine craftsmen, the Florentine medicine cabinet and light fixture are the perfect addition to the classic bath.

The beauty of the flowering Hibiscus is captured in the Art Nouveau look of this distinctive cabinet and complementary light fixture.

FLORENTINE

With classic Italian-style details finished in simulated gold leaf for the traditional American home, this style has 3/4" beveled-edge float glass mirrors, and heavy gauge steel construction. Matching light fixture features glass shades, brass fittings, mirror faceplate, and uses standard 60 watt bulbs.

Style	Model	Overall Size W H D	Wall Opening W H D
Single-Door Built-In Cabinets	3910	17^{15}/$_{16}$ x 27^{15}/$_{16}$	14 x 18 x 3½
	3918	17^{15}/$_{16}$ x 27^{15}/$_{16}$	14 x 24 x 3½
Single-Door Wall Mount Cabinet (almond body)	3912	17^{15}/$_{16}$ x 27^{15}/$_{16}$	–
Top lights for Built-In Cabinet Light	711FG	17^{15}/$_{16}$ x 8 x 6^{15}/$_{16}$	–
Top Lights for Wall Mount Cabinet	712FG	17^{15}/$_{16}$ x 8 x 9^{15}/$_{16}$	–

HIBISCUS

Almond   Forest Green

Dramatic Art Nouveau styling accents matching cabinets and light fixtures with 3-dimensional floral carving. Available in 3 high-gloss lacquer finishes: White, Almond, and Forest Green. The white and almond models can be painted to further customize them to your bathroom color scheme. Float glass mirrors. Heavy-gauge steel storage cabinets. Light fixtures use G-25 bulbs.

Style	White Model	Almond* Model	Green* Model	Overall Size W H D	Wall Opening W H D
Single-Door Built-In Cabinets	6120	6130	6140	18½ x 27½	14 x 18 x 3½
Single-Door Wall Mount Cabinets	6122	6132	6142	18½ x 27½	–
Top Lights for Built-In Cabinets	761WH	761AL	761GR	18½ x 6¾ x 3	–
Top Lights for Wall Mount Cabinets	762WH	762AL	762GR	18½ x 6¾ x 5½	–

*Please allow extra time for customization.

Cabinet 350WH (3); Light 745WH (3)

SPECTRUM WITH MATCHING LIGHTING

Spectrum single door medicine cabinets feature a white "Enduro" frame with "hardshell" acrylic finish on a molded core which offers long life in the high moisture atmosphere of a bathroom. Matching top light fixtures feature bright chrome faceplate.

Style	Model	Overall Size W H D	Wall Opening W H D
Single-Door Built-In Cabinets	350WH	18 x 27½	14 x 18 x 3½
	358WH	18 x 27½	14 x 24 x 3½
Top Light for Single-Door Built-In Cabinets	745WH	18 x 6½ x 3	–

SPECTRUM TRI-VIEW

Tri-view cabinets with matching top light are available in gloss white and are constructed using the same Enduro frame material as other styles.

Style	Model	Overall Size W H D	Wall Opening W H D
Tri-View Wall Mount or Built-In Cabinets	3230WH	30 x 30 x 4½	27½ x 27 x 3½*
	3236WH	36 x 30 x 4½	33½ x 27 x 3½*
Top Lights for Tri-View Wall Mount Cabinets	SP132WH	30 x 6½ x 5¼	–
	SP133WH	36 x 6½ x 5¼	–

*Optional Wall Opening.

Cabinet 3236WH; Light SP133WH

SPECTRUM WITH BUILT-IN LIGHTING

This model, also in white, features a look similar to the other Spectrum models, but with a built-in light for a compact, space-saving look and easy installations.

Style	Model	Overall Size W H D	Wall Opening W H D
Tri-View Wall Mount or Built-In Cabinets w/Built-In Top Light	3330WH 3336WH	31 x 30⅜ x 5 37 x 30⅜ x 5	28¾ x 27½ x 3½* 34¾ x 27½ x 3½*
Single-Door Wall Mount or Built-In Cabinet w/Built-In Top Light	2009WH	19⅛ x 32¼ x 5	16¾ x 28¾ x 3½

*Optional Wall Opening.

Cabinet 3336WH

Cabinet 2009WH

VERONA

Reflective, glossy metallic-framed mirror in fixture-matching brass finish. Molded frame core is designed for the bath.

Style	Model	Overall Size W H D	Wall Opening W H D
Single-Door Built-In Cabinets	310BR 318BR 313BR†	17¼ x 27¼ 17¼ x 27¼ 16 x 20	14 x 18 x 3½ 14 x 24 x 3½ 14 x 18 x 2½
Top Light for Single-Door Built-In Cabinets	747BR	17¼ x 5½ x 3	

†Molded body.

Cabinet 318BR; Light 747BR

VICEROY

Bright brass metallic-look framing on a molded core complement today's bathroom accessories.

Style	Model	Overall Size W H D	Wall Opening W H D
Single-Door Wall Mount or Built-In Cabinet w/Built-In Top Light	2012BR	18 x 31 x 5	16¾ x 29 x 3½*

*Optional Wall Opening.

Cabinet 2012BR

See pages 31-35 for detailed specifications.

This Wood Frame series uses natural and painted hardwoods to achieve a warm look matching or complementing your bathroom decor.

Cabinet 820; Light 70323

Cabinet 870, Light 70373

BAKER STREET

Charming Victorian detail lends a distinctive period touch to practical bathroom storage. Choose from classic colonial white painted hardwood or warm, honey-finish solid oak frames. Matching light fixtures feature frosted glass shades and bright brass fittings.

Style	Colonial White Model	Honey Oak Model	Overall Size W H D	Wall Opening W H D
Tri-View Wall Mount	842230	–	30 x 28½ x 5½	–
Cabinets	842236	–	36 x 28½ x 5½	–
Top Lights for Tri-View	BS84023	–	30 x 6 x 6½	–
Wall Mount Cabinets	BS84623	–	36 x 6 x 6½	–
Single-Door Built-In	820	870	18 x 27	14 x 18 x 3½
Cabinets	828	878	18 x 27	14 x 24 x 3½
Single-Door Wall Mount Cabinets	822	872	18 x 27 x 5	–
Top Lights for Single-Door Built-In Cabinets	70323	70373	18 x 8 x 9	–
Top Lights for Single-Door Wall Mount Cabinets	70223	70273	18 x 8 x 13½	–

Cabinet 842236; Light BS8462

Cabinet 8570; Light 76378

CANTERBURY

This traditional cathedral arch design is available in solid oak with honey oak finish and matching finish sides. Matching top lights feature clear ribbed prismatic glass shades and bright brass fittings for a warm, inviting look.

Style	Model	Overall Size W H D	Wall Opening W H D
Single-Door Built-In Cabinet	8570	18¼ x 27¼	14 x 18 x 3½
Single-Door Wall Mount Cabinet	8572	18¼ x 27¼ x 5½	–
Top Light for Single-Door Built-In Cabinet	76378	18 x 8 x 8	–
Top Light for Single-Door Wall Mount Cabinet	76478	18 x 8 x 11½	–

See pages 31-35 for detailed specifications.

17

Cabinet 562230; Light WH53023

WHITE MARBLE

Solid oak frame with honey oak finish has white onyx cultured marble inlay. White accent brightens the room; oak frame blends with most wood vanities. Also looks great over a white pedestal sink. Matching wood-tone sides.

Style	Model	Overall Size W H D	Wall Opening W H D
Tri-View Wall Mount Cabinet	562230	30 x 28½ x 5¼	–
Top Light for Tri-View Wall Mount Cabinet	WH53023	30 x 7¼ x 12¼	–
Single-Door Wall Mount Cabinet	5622	17⅛ x 27⅛ x 5½	–
Top Light for Wall Mount Cabinet	708WH	17⅛ x 7¼ x 10⅛	–

Cabinet 5622; Light 708WH

18

PRAIRIE

Painted hardwood frame with traditional detailing is simply elegant in colonial white. Matching top light fixtures feature clear prismatic glass shades and bright brass finish fittings.

Style	Model	Overall Size W H D	Wall Opening W H D
Single-Door	8120	18 x 27½	14 x 18 x 3½
Built-In Cabinets	8128	18 x 27½	14 x 24 x 3½
Single-Door Wall Mount Cabinet	8122	18 x 27½ x 5	–
Top Light for Single-Door Built-In Cabinets	70928	18 x 8 x 8	–

Note: The Prairie can also be special ordered in two tri-view sizes featuring a blonde oak finish frame.

Style	Model	Overall Size W H D	Wall Opening W H D
Tri-View Wall Mount Cabinets	8199703	30 x 28⁵⁄₁₆	–
	8199704	36 x 28⁵⁄₁₆	–
Top Lights for Tri-View Wall Mount Cabinets	OK8199705	30 x 8 x 8	–
	OK8199706	36 x 8 x 8	–

Cabinet 8120; Light 70928

AUTUMN

Warm solid oak, honey finish frame with matching wood-tone sides. Canopy design shields bulbs and provides close-up make-up light, yet delivers plenty of subdued lighting for the whole bath.

Style	Model	Overall Size W H D	Wall Opening W H D
Tri-View Wall Mount or Built-In Cabinets	197230	30 x 29 x 5½	28¾ x 27½ x 3½*
	197236	36 x 29 x 5½	34¾ x 27½ x 3½*

*Optional Wall Opening.

Cabinet 197236

GRAND OAK II

Solid oak frame, honey finish tri-view cabinet for wall mounting or built-in installation. Top light has matching frame and oak finish faceplates.
Light is designed for use with wall mount cabinet.

Style	Model	Overall Size W H D	Wall Opening W H D
Tri-View Wall Mount or Built-In Cabinets	277924	24 x 25	22¼ x 23 x 3½*
	277930	29 x 28⅞	27½ x 27 x 3½*
	277936	35 x 28⅞	33½ x 27 x 3½*
	277948	47 x 28⅞	45½ x 27 x 3½*
Top Lights for Tri-View Wall Mount Cabinets	SG32479	24 x 5⅝ x 4¾	–
	SG33079	29 x 5⅝ x 4¾	–
	SG33679	35 x 5⅝ x 4¾	–
	SG34879	47 x 5⅝ x 4¾	–
Wood Tone Trim Kit for Wall Mount Application	97014099	–	–

*Optional Wall Opening.

Cabinet 277930; Light SG33079

GRANT

Solid oak, honey finish frame cabinet has top light with matching frame and oak finish faceplate.

Style	Model	Overall Size W H D	Wall Opening W H D
Single-Door Built-In Cabinets	8770	16¼ x 24¼	14 x 18 x 3½
	8778	16¼ x 26¼	14 x 24 x 3½
	8773†	16¼ x 22	14 x 18 x 2½
	973BC†	16 x 20	14 x 18 x 2½
Single-Door Wall Mount Cabinet	8772	16¼ x 24¼ x 5½	–
Top Light for Single-Door Built-In Cabinets	74279	16¼ x 5½ x 3	–

†Molded body.

Cabinet 8778; Light 74279

Cabinet 2072

OAKDALE

This cabinet, in solid oak with a honey oak finish, features attached lighting for one-step installation.

Style	Model	Overall Size W H D	Wall Opening W H D
Single-Door Wall Mount or Built-In Cabinet	2072	18 x 31 x 5½	16¾ x 28¾ x 3½*

*Optional Wall Opening.

Cabinet 1370

DUNHILL

Solid oak oval with honey finish frames your face in cameo style.

Style	Model	Overall Size W H D	Wall Opening W H D
Single-Door Built-In Cabinet	1370	21 x 31	14 x 18 x 3½

See pages 31-35 for detailed specifications.

Cabinet 8278

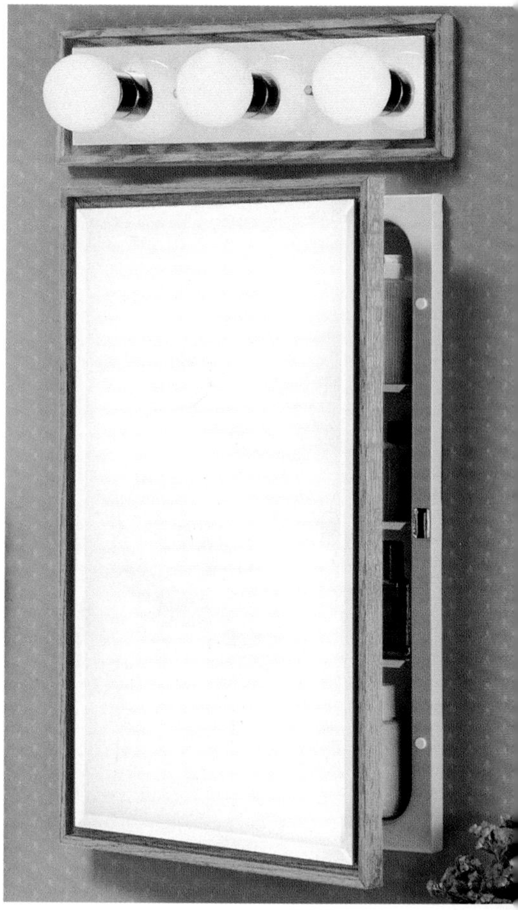

Cabinet 8378; Light 71829

CHAPEL HILL

Honey oak finish mirror frame has contemporary rounded-edge styling.

Style	Model	Overall Size W H D	Wall Opening W H D
Single-Door Built-In Cabinet	8278	17¼ x 27¼	14 x 24 x 3½

KINGSTON

Solid wood, honey oak mirror frame with beveled-edge mirror has a shadow box effect.

Style	Model	Overall Size W H D	Wall Opening W H D
Single-Door Built-In Cabinets	8370	16½ x 26½	14 x 18 x 3½
	8378	16½ x 26½	14 x 24 x 3½
Top Light for Single-Door Built-In Cabinets	71829	16½ x 5½ x 2¼	–

OAKHILL

Classically shaped edges on this solid oak, honey finish frame make it a traditional style. Attached top lights make wall mounting or built-in installation easier.

Style	Model	Overall Size W H D	Wall Opening W H D
Tri-View Wall Mount	177924	23¼ x 29⅝ x 4¼	22¾ x 27½ x 3½*
or Built-In Cabinets	177930	30 x 29⅝ x 4¼	28¾ x 27½ x 3½*
w/Built-In Top Lights	177936	36 x 29⅝ x 4¼	34¾ x 27½ x 3½*
	177948	48 x 29⅝ x 4¼	46¾ x 27½ x 3½*

*Optional Wall Opening.

Cabinet 177930

The Prestique Wood Body cabinets feature beautiful woods in a variety of classic designs with ample storage capacities.

Cabinet 907236; Light CR93679

Cabinet 902236; Lights CR93629

SOLID OAK OR WHITE FRAME

Our most popular wood body tri-view cabinet features solid oak or white painted hardwood frames with matching finish cabinet body. Matching top light for the oak model has brass finish faceplate and white model has bright chrome finish faceplate.

Style	Solid Oak Model	White Model	Overall Size W H D
Tri-View Wall	907224	902224	24 x 26 x 4¾
Mount Cabinets	907230	902230	30 x 30 x 4¾
	907236	902236	36 x 30 x 4¾
	907248	–	48 x 30 x 4¾
Top Lights for Tri-View	–	CR92429	24 x 5⅞ x 5½
Wall Mount Cabinets	CR93079	CR93029	30 x 5⅞ x 5½
	CR93679	CR93629	36 x 5⅞ x 5½
Bulk Pack			
Tri-View Cabinet			
(24 - bulk pack)	907224BP*	–	24 x 26 x 4¾
(20 - bulk pack)	907230BP*	–	30 x 30 x 4¾

*Bulk pack models have open face cartons with top and bottom banded carton caps.

Prestique
Bathroom Cabinets

Our Prestique Series features:
• Cabinet-maker wood box styling
• Sturdy glue-and-nail butt-joint construction
• Classic designs at affordable prices

Cabinet 905236; Light CR93690

FRAMELESS BEVELED-EDGE

This frameless, tri-view cabinet has beveled-edge glass mirrors and matching, mirrored light fixture.

Style	Model	Overall Size W H D
Tri-View Wall	905224	24 x 26 x 4¾
Mount Cabinets	905230	30 x 30 x 4¾
	905236	36 x 30 x 4¾
	905248	48 x 30 x 4¾
Top Lights for Tri-View	CR92490	24 x 5⅞ x 5½
Wall Mount Cabinets	CR93090	30 x 5⅞ x 5½
	CR93690	36 x 5⅞ x 5½
	CR94890	48 x 5⅞ x 5½

See pages 31-35 for detailed specifications.

WOOD FRAME WITH BUILT-IN TOP LIGHT

All-in-one frame style offers upscale look in a value-priced cabinet. Available in tri-view and single-door models in oak or white finish. Lights have bright chrome finish faceplate.

Style	Oak Model	White Model	Overall Size W H D
Tri-View	947224	942224	24 x 28⅞ x 4⅛
Wall Mount	947230	942230	30 x 28⅞ x 4⅛
Cabinets	947236	942236	36 x 28⅞ x 4⅛
Single-Door Wall Mount Cabinets	9472	9422BC	15¾ x 23⅝ x 4⅛

Cabinet 94723C

Cabinet 9472

PERFUME & MEDICINE CABINETS

Add color and variety to any bath with one of Broan's distinctive two-compartment cabinets. The narrow compartment features a clear, beveled-edge glass window with a delicate stenciled pattern and three shelves. It's perfect for displaying today's elegant designer fragrances and colorful health and beauty product packaging. The larger compartment has a framed, beveled-edge mirror door and two shelves.

Style	Oak Model	White Model	Overall Size W H D
2-Door Wall Mount Cabinets	977225	972225	25½ x 28 x 4¾

Cabinet 977225

Cabinet 972225

WOOD FRAME CABINETS

These value-priced, wood frame cabinets are standardized on a 25½" height and are available in oak or white finish.

Style	Oak Model	White Model	Overall Size W H D
Tri-View	967224	–	24 x 25½ x 4¾
Wall Mount	967230	–	30 x 25½ x 4¾
Cabinets	967236	–	36 x 25½ x 4¾
Single-Door Wall	902	902WH	16 x 20 x 4¾
Mount Cabinets	982	982WH	16 x 26 x 4¾
Bulk Pack (38 - bulk pack)	902BP	–	16 x 20 x 4¾

Cabinet 967224

Cabinet 902WH

Prestique *Bathroom Cabinets*

Our Prestique Series features:
• Cabinet-maker wood box styling
• Sturdy glue-and-nail butt-joint construction
• Classic designs at affordable prices

Cabinet 902

Broan's Specialty Cabinets offer unusual sizes and shapes specially designed to meet your unique needs.

Cabinet 629

ILLUSION

Auxiliary storage with frameless, polished, sealed-edge mirror doors, this special low-profile style (¹⁄₄" projection from wall) fits flush with adjacent ¹⁄₄" wall mirrors.*

Style	Model	Overall Size W H D	Wall Opening W H D
Built-In Cabinets	629	15 x 36	14 x 34 x 3½
	639BC	13 x 36	12 x 34 x 3½

*Surrounding mirrors not included.

Hide cabinet storage in a flat wall mirror area.

See pages 31-35 for detailed specifications.

AVANTI CORNER CABINET

Triangular shape ideal for 3-way viewing with a simple wall mirror makes small corner areas look larger.

Style	Model	Trim	Overall Size W H D
Wall Mount Corner Cabinet	631	Stainless Steel	13 x 36 x 7¼

Triangular Shaped

Cabinet 631 (2); Mirror PEM3636 (see pg. 30)

CENTERED CORNER CABINET

For use over a corner vanity, this corner cabinet is perfect for small spaces.

Style	Model	Trim	Overall Size W H D
Wall Mount Corner Cabinets	672	Oak	19½ x 33½ x 10½
	672SS	Stainless Steel	17¼ x 31 x 9⅞

Cabinet 672

BEL AIRE AUXILIARY

Ideal in combination with a wall mirror and light strips, this model provides extra storage and 3-way viewing. Stainless steel trim top and bottom with polished vertical mirror edges.

Style	Model	Overall Size W H D	Wall Opening W H D
Built-In Cabinet	625	13 x 36	11¼ x 33½
Wall Mount Cabinet	626	13 x 36 x 4¼	–

Cabinet 626 (2); Mirror PEM3036 (see pg. 30)

Cabinet 6

STAINLESS STEEL BODY

This easy to clean, rust-resistant single-door cabinet features high luster type 304 stainless steel with bright #4 satin finish and choice of two mirror styles. One-half inch beveled-edge mirror looks like Horizon Series on page 9. Stainless steel looks like Styleline on page 29.

Style	Model	Trim	Overall Size W H D	Wall Opening W H D
Built-In Cabinets	1448	Beveled-Edge	16 x 26	14 x 24 x 3½
	448BC	Stainless Steel Frame	16 x 26	14 x 24 x 3½

Cabinet 1448

MODULAR SHELF

Our unique cabinet design provides maximum storage capacity. Six modular half-shelves can be positioned in a number of configurations utilizing four snap-in center posts. This flexible design means shelves can quickly be adjusted without tools to accommodate various container sizes.

Style	Model	Trim	Overall Size W H D	Wall Opening W H D
Built-In Cabinet	468MOD	Stainless Steel Frame	16 x 26	14 x 24 x 3½

468MOD

FOCUS

Polished-edge mirror features simplicity and supreme functionality.

Style	Model	Overall Size W H D	Wall Opening W H D
Single-Door Built-In Cabinets	1430	16 x 22	14 x 18 x 3½
	1438	16 x 26	14 x 24 x 3½
	1433†	16 x 20	14 x 18 x 2½

†Molded body.

Cabinet 1430

OAK HOLLYWOOD

Solid, honey oak frame and matching wood-tone sides has built-in incandescent top light, grounded outlet, on-off switch and gold-tone door pulls.

Style	Model	Overall Size W H D
Wall Mount	2471IL	24¾ x 24½ x 9
Cabinets	2871IL	28¾ x 24½ x 9

Cabinet 2471IL

BEAUTY GLIDE

Stainless steel shadow box frame with chrome door pulls features grounded outlet and on-off switch. Models with built-in top light include fluorescent tube.

Style	Model	Overall Size W H D	Wall Opening W H D
Built-In Cabinets Unlighted	SD15	24 x 18¾	21½ x 17 x 3½
	SD41	27½ x 19¼	26¼ x 17¼ x 3½
Built-In Cabinet w/Top Light	SDL82	27½ x 22	26¼ x 18¼ x 3½

Cabinet SDL82

ENSIGN

Stainless steel trim with built-in incandescent light includes convenient grounded outlet and on-off switch.

Style	Model	Overall Size W H D
Wall Mount	124LP	24 x 23½ x 8¼
Cabinets	128LP	28 x 23½ x 8¼

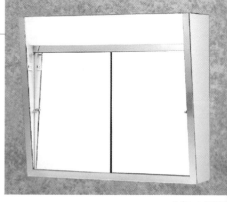

Cabinet 128LP

FLAIR

Our economy leader, this model has incandescent built-in top light, stainless steel trim and on-off switch.

Style	Model	Overall Size W H D
Wall Mount	323LP	24 x 19½ x 8
Cabinets	327LP	28 x 19½ x 8

Cabinet 323LF

CABINET 455FL

This one-piece steel storage cabinet has attached fluorescent side lights (tubes included), grounded outlet and on-off switch.

Style	Model	Overall Size W H D	Wall Opening W H D
Built-In Storage Cabinet	455FL	20⅜ x 22¼ x 7⅜	14 x 19 x 3½

Cabinet 455FL   *Cabinet 555IL*

CABINET 555IL

This surface mounted steel cabinet has a stainless steel frame and trim with built-in light, grounded outlet and on-off switch.

Style	Model	Overall Size W H D
Wall Mount Cabinet	555IL	16 x 24 x 8

STYLELINE

This classic, one-piece mirrored storage cabinet comes in a variety of sizes. Steel or molded body.

Style	Model	Overall Size W H D	Mirror Glass Thickness	Wall Opening W H D
Built-In Cabinets Molded	401ADJ† *New! '97*	16 x 20	³⁄₃₂	14 x 18 x 3½
	449BC†	16 x 22	³⁄₃₂	14 x 18 x 3½
	407ADJ† *New! '97*	16 x 22	³⁄₃₂	14 x 18 x 3½
Bulk Packs	405BP	(407BC in a 2-Pack)		
	405BP27	(407BC in a Bulk Pack of 30)		
Built-In Steel Cabinets	410BC	16 x 22	³⁄₃₂	14 x 18 x 3½
	420BC	16 x 22	¹⁄₁₆	14 x 20 x 3½
	421BC	16 x 22	⅛	14 x 20 x 3½
	458	16 x 26	⅛	14 x 24 x 3½
	468	16 x 26	³⁄₃₂	14 x 24 x 3½
	468MOD*	16 x 26	¹⁄₁₆	14 x 24 x 3½
	490	18 x 24	³⁄₁₆	16 x 21½ x 3½
	478FS**	16 x 26	⅛	14 x 24 x 3½
	495	20 x 30	³⁄₁₆	17¼ x 26¼ x 3½
Wall Mount Steel Cabinets	412SM	16 x 22 x 4¾	³⁄₃₂	–
	422SM	14 x 20 x 5	³⁄₃₂	–
	452SM	16 x 22 x 4¾	³⁄₃₂	–

†Molded body
*Modular storage. See page 27 for details.
**Meets Federal spec #WW-P-541/8B
(For stainless steel body cabinets see page 27.)
ADJ = Adjustable shelves.

Cabinet 407ADJ

WHITE FRAME

Molded polystyrene body with white finish molded frame.

Style	Model	Overall Size W H D	Wall Opening W H D
Built-In Cabinet	313WH	16 x 20	14 x 18 x 2½

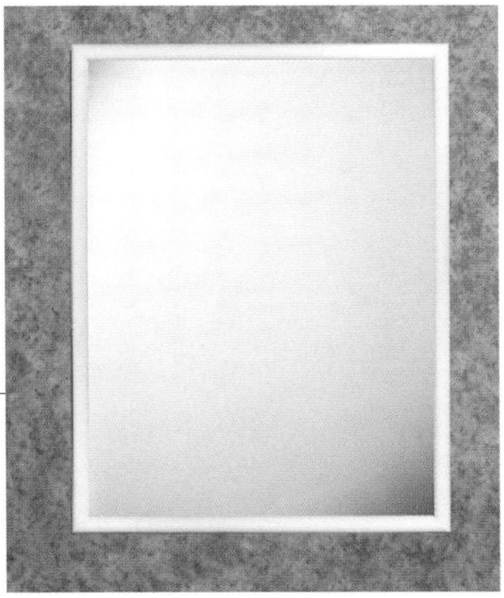

Cabinet 313WH

See pages 31-35 for detailed specifications.

Cabinet 62:

HIDEAWAY

Steel single-door can be wallpapered to blend with wall for hidden storage and is reversible for left- or right-hand opening. Door has tension latch.

Style	Model	Overall Size W H D	Wall Opening W H D
Single-Door Built-In Cabinet	622	17⅛ x 21½	14 x 18 x 3½

Combination VM230M

Light IL30; Mirror PEM3024; Cabinet V30

Cabinet 602   *Cabinet 603*

Cabinet 60

COMMODORE

Choose the convenient combination unit or match individual components to suit your needs. Components channeled for easy installation. Light fixture includes grounded outlet and switch. Mirrors feature polished edges and copper backing. Stainless steel trim.

Style	Model	Mirror Door Model	Styrene Door Model	Overall Size W H D
Combination Mirror & Cabinet	–	VM224M	VM224P	24¼ x 32 x 4⅛
	–	VM230M	VM230P	30¼ x 32 x 4⅛
	–	VM236M	VM236P	36¼ x 32 x 4⅛
Storage Cabinets	–	V24	–	24¼ x 8¾ x 4¼
	–	V30	–	30¼ x 8¾ x 4¼
	–	V36	–	36¼ x 8¾ x 4¼
	–	V48	–	48¼ x 8¾ x 4¼
Incandescent Light Fixtures	IL24	–	–	24 x 4 x 7½
	IL30	–	–	30 x 4 x 7½
Wall Mirrors	PEM2424	–	–	24 x 24
	PEM3024	–	–	30 x 24
	PEM3624	–	–	36 x 24
	PEM4824	–	–	48 x 24
	PEM3036	–	–	30 x 36
	PEM3636	–	–	36 x 36
	PEM4836	–	–	48 x 36
	PEM6036	–	–	60 x 36

LOUVER DOOR

Versatile auxiliary cabinets for added storage are available in white mold polystyrene or unfinished pine which can be painted or stained.

Style	Model	Overall Size W H D	Wall Opening W H D
Arch Top Door (Unfinished) Built-In Cabinets	602	16 x 24	14 x 18 x 3½
	605ADJ†	16 x 24	14 x 18 x 2½
Flat Top Door (Unfinished) Built-In Cabinets	606	16 x 22	14 x 18 x 3½
	609	16 x 26	14 x 24 x 3½
	607ADJ†	16 x 22	14 x 18 x 2½
White Molded Door Built-In Cabinet	603†	16 x 22¼	14 x 18 x 2½

†Molded body.

See pages 31-35 for detailed specificati

MEDICINE CABINET SPECIFICATIONS

…ge	Model No.	Style Name	Frame	Style T-Tri-View B-BiView S-Single SB-Slide-by L-Light WM-Wall Mirror	Overall Size W H D	Mount Type WM-Wall Mount B-Built-In B/WM-Built-In or Wall Mount M-Mirror	Wall Opening W H D	Hinge Type P-Piano C-Con. L-Leaf PN-Pin B-Butt	Single Door Hinge L-Left R-Right RV-Rev.	Cabinet Body S-Steel SS-Stainless P-Polystyrene W-Wood	Shelves			Matching Light Fixture	Recommended Bulbs Qty-Type
											Quantity *	G-Glass S-Steel P-Polystyrene AL-Aluminum	F-Fixed A-Adjustable		
8	124LP	Ensign	Stainless Steel Trim	SB	24x23½x8¼	WM	-	-	-	S	1	S	F	Built-In	4-60W Std. MB
8	128LP	Ensign	Stainless Steel Trim	SB	28x23½x8¼	WM	-	-	-	S	1	S	F	Built-In	4-60W Std. MB
7	1350	Cameo Oval Bevel	Frameless Bevel	S	21x31	B	14x18x3½	P	RV	S	2	P	A	-	-
7	1358	Cameo Oval Bevel	Frameless Bevel	S	24x35	B	14x24x3½	P	RV	S	3	P	A	-	-
1	1370	Dunhill	Solid Oak, Honey	S	21x31	B	14x18x3½	P	RV	S	2	P	A	-	-
0	1402	Lafayette	Frameless	S	18⅛x32⅜x6	WM	-	P	R	S	3	S	F	Built-In	3-60W G25/G40
3	1418	Aurora	Frameless	S	16x26	B	14x24x3½	P	RV	S	3	P	A	73290	-
3	1420FL	Decorah	Frameless	S	16x26	B	14x18x3½	P	RV	S	2	P	A	735FL	-
7	1430	Focus	Frameless	S	16x22	B	14x18x3½	P	RV	S	2	P	A	-	-
7	1433	Focus	Frameless	S	16x20	B	14x18x2½	P	RV	P	2	P	F	-	-
7	1438	Focus	Frameless	S	16x26	B	14x24x3½	P	RV	S	3	P	A	-	-
7	1448	Stainless Steel	Frameless	S	16x26	B	14x24x3½	P	RV	SS	2	G	A	-	-
3	1450BC	Mirror-on-Mirror	Frameless	S	16x26	B	14x18x3½	P	RV	S	2	P	A	See pg. 8	-
9	1451	Horizon	Frameless	S	16x26	B	14x18x3½	P	RV	S	2	P	A	73290	-
3	1452	Mirror-on-Mirror	Frameless	S	16x26	B	14x18x3½	P	RV	S	2	P	A	73290	-
9	1453	Horizon	Frameless	S	16x20	B	14x18x2½	P	RV	P	2	P	F	73290	-
7	1454	Mirage	Frameless	S	18x27	B	14x18x3½	P	RV	S	2	P	A	73190	-
7	1456	Mirage	Frameless	S	17⅜x32	B	14x24x3½	P	RV	S	3	P	A	73190	-
3	1457	Mirror-on-Mirror	Frameless	S	16x26	B	14x24x3½	P	RV	S	3	P	A	See pg. 8	-
3	1458	Mirror-on-Mirror	Frameless	S	16x26	B	14x24x3½	P	RV	S	3	P	A	See pg. 8	-
9	1459	Horizon	Frameless	S	16x26	B	14x24x3½	P	RV	S	3	P	A	73290	-
0	1462	Lafayette	Frameless	S	18⅛x28⅜x6	WM	-	P	R	S	3	S	F	Built-In	3-60W G25/G40
1	155124	Vienna	Chrome Finish Trim	T	24x26x5½	WM	-	L	-	S	2	S	F	SB22529	-
1	155130	Vienna	Chrome Finish Trim	T	30x26x5½	WM	-	L	-	S	2	S	F	SB23129	-
2	177924	Oakhill	Solid Oak, Honey	T	23¼x29⅝x4¼	B/WM	22¾x27½x3½	PN	-	S	2	S	F	Built-In	3-60W G25/G40
2	177930	Oakhill	Solid Oak, Honey	T	30x29⅝x4¼	B/WM	28¾x27½x3½	PN	-	S	2	S	F	Built-In	4-60W G25/G40
2	177936	Oakhill	Solid Oak, Honey	T	36x29⅝x4¼	B/WM	34¾x27½x3½	PN	-	S	2	S	F	Built-In	5-60W G25/G40
2	177948	Oakhill	Solid Oak, Honey	T	48x29⅝x4¼	B/WM	46¾x27½x3½	PN	-	S	2	S	F	Built-In	6-60W G25/G40
9	197230	Autumn	Solid Oak, Honey	T	30x29x5½	B/WM	28¾x27½x3½	PN	-	S	2	S	F	Built-In	4-60W Std. MB
9	197236	Autumn	Solid Oak, Honey	T	36x29x5½	B/WM	34¾x27½x3½	PN	-	S	2	S	F	Built-In	5-60W Std. MB
5	2009WH	Spectrum	Molded Acrylic Fin.	S	19⅛x32¼x5	B/WM	16¾x28¾x3½	PN	R	S	3	S	F	Built-In	3-60W G25/G40
5	2012BR	Viceroy	Molded Brass Finish	S	18x31x5	B/WM	16¾x29x3½	PN	R	S	3	S	F	Built-In	3-60W G25/G40
1	2072	Oakdale	Solid Oak, Honey	S	18x31x5½	B/WM	16¾x28¾x3½	PN	R	S	3	S	F	Built-In	3-60W G25/G40
8	2471IL	Oak Hollywood	Solid Oak, Honey	SB	24¾x24½x9	WM	-	-	-	S	1	S	F	Built-In	4-60W Std. MB
9	255024	Horizon	Frameless	T	24x24	B	21¾x20½x3½	C	-	S	2	S	A	H042490	-
9	255030	Horizon	Frameless	T	30x28¼	B	27¾x24¾x3½	C	-	S	2	S	A	H043090	-
9	255036	Horizon	Frameless	T	36x28¼	B	33¾x24¾x3½	C	-	S	2	S	A	H043690	-
9	255048	Horizon	Frameless	T	48x28¼	B	45¾x24¾x3½	C	-	S	2	S	A	H044890	-
9	255224	Horizon	Frameless	T	24x24x5¼	WM	-	C	-	S	2	S	F	H032490	-
[illegible]	255230	Horizon	Frameless	T	30x28¼x5¼	WM	-	C	-	S	2	S	F	H033090	-
[illegible]	255236	Horizon	Frameless	T	36x28¼x5¼	WM	-	C	-	S	2	S	F	H033690	-
[illegible]	255248	Horizon	Frameless	T	48x28¼x5¼	WM	-	C	-	S	2	S	F	H034890	-
7	258	Sonata	Frameless	S	16x32	B	14x24x3½	P	R	S	3	P	A	75052	-
0	277924	Grand Oak II	Solid Oak, Honey	T	24x25	B/WM	22¼x23x3½	PN	-	S	2	S	F	SG32479	-
0	277930	Grand Oak II	Solid Oak, Honey	T	29x28⅞	B/WM	27½x27x3½	PN	-	S	2	S	F	SG33079	-
0	277936	Grand Oak II	Solid Oak, Honey	T	35x28⅞	B/WM	33½x27x3½	PN	-	S	2	S	F	SG33679	-
0	277948	Grand Oak II	Solid Oak, Honey	T	47x28⅞	B/WM	45½x27x3½	PN	-	S	2	S	F	SG34879	-
3	2871IL	Oak Hollywood	Solid Oak, Honey	SB	28¾x24½x9	WM	-	-	-	S	1	S	F	Built-In	4-60W Std. MB
9	295224	Focus	Frameless	T	24x30x5¼	WM	-	C	-	S	2	S	F	Built-In	3-60W G25/G40
9	295230	Focus	Frameless	T	30x34x5¼	WM	-	C	-	S	2	S	F	Built-In	4-60W G25/G40
5	310BR	Verona	Brass Finish	S	17¼x27¼	B	14x18x3½	P	RV	S	2	P	A	747BR	-
5	313BR	Verona	Molded, Brass Finish	S	16x20	B	14x18x2½	B	RV	P	2	P	F	747BR	-
9	313WH	White Frame	Molded, White Finish	S	16x20	B	14x18x2½	B	RV	P	2	P	F	-	-
5	318BR	Verona	Molded, Brass Finish	S	17¼x27¼	B	14x24x3½	P	RV	S	2	P	A	747BR	-
8	323LP	Flair	Stainless Steel Trim	SB	24x19½x8	WM	-	-	-	S	1	S	F	Built-In	4-60W Std. MB
4	3230WH	Spectrum	Molded, Acrylic Fin.	T	30x30x4½	B/WM	27½x27x3½	PN	-	S	2	S	F	SP132WH	-

…abinet bottom always provides an additional storage level.
…ote: Unless so stated, bulbs not included.

**3 shelves in each side.

MEDICINE CABINET SPECIFICATIONS

Page	Model No.	Style Name	Frame	Style T-Tri-View B-BiView S-Single SB-Slide-by L-Light WM-Wall Mirror	Overall Size W H D	Mount Type WM-Wall Mount B-Built-In B/WM-Built-In or Wall Mount M-Mirror	Wall Opening W H D	Hinge Type P-Piano C-Con. L-Leaf PN-Pin B-Butt	Single Door Hinge L-Left R-Right RV-Rev.	Cabinet Body S-Steel SS-Stainless P-Polystyrene W-Wood	Shelves: Quantity *	Shelves: G-Glass S-Steel P-Polystyrene AL-Aluminum	Shelves: F-Fixed A-Adjustable	Matching Light Fixture	Recommended Bulbs Qty-Type
14	3236WH	Spectrum	Molded, Acrylic Fin.	T	36 13/16x30x4¼	B/WM	34⅝x27⅛x3½	PN	-	S	2	S	F	SP133WH	-
27	327LP	Flair	Stainless Steel Trim	SB	28x19½x8	WM	-	-	-	S	1	S	F	Built-In	4-60W Std. ME
15	3330WH	Spectrum	Molded, Acrylic Fin.	T	30 13/16x30x4¼	B/WM	28⅝x27⅛x3½	PN	-	S	2	S	A	Built-In	4-60W G25/G4
15	3336WH	Spectrum	Molded, Acrylic Fin.	T	36 13/16x30x4¼	B/WM	34⅝x27⅛x3½	PN	-	S	2	S	A	Built-In	5-60W G25/G4
14	350WH	Spectrum	Molded, Acrylic Fin.	S	18x27½	B	14⅛x18¼x3½	P	RV	S	2	P	A	745WH	-
14	358WH	Spectrum	Molded, Acrylic Fin.	S	18x27½	B	14x24x3½	P	RV	S	3	P	A	745WH	-
12	3870	Classico	Oak Burl	S	18 1/16x28 1/16	B	14⅛x18¼x3½	P	RV	S	2	P	A	715K	2-60W
12	3872	Classico	Oak Burl	S	18 1/16x28 1/16	WM	-	P	RV	S	3	P	F	716K	2-60W
12	3878	Classico	Oak Burl	S	18 1/16x28 1/16	B	14x24x3½	P	RV	S	3	P	A	715K	2-60W
12	3890	Classico	Mahogany	S	18 1/16x28 1/16	B	14⅛x18¼x3½	P	RV	S	2	P	A	715M	2-60W
12	3892	Classico	Mahogany	S	18 1/16x28 1/16	WM	-	P	RV	S	3	P	F	716M	2-60W
12	3898	Classico	Mahogany	S	18 1/16x28 1/16	B	14x24x3½	P	RV	S	3	P	A	715M	2-60W
13	3910	Florentine	Simulated Gold Leaf	S	18x28x2¼	B	14⅛x18¼x3½	P	RV	S	2	P	A	711FG	2-60W
13	3912	Florentine	Simulated Gold Leaf	S	17 15/16x27 15/16	WM	-	P	RV	S	3	P	F	712FG	2-60W
13	3918	Florentine	Simulated Gold Leaf	S	17 15/16x27 15/16	B	14x24x3½	P	RV	S	3	P	A	711FG	2-60W
28	401ADJ	Styleline	Stainless Steel	S	16x20	B	14x18x3½	B	RV	P	2	P	A	-	-
28	405BP	Styleline	Stainless Steel	S	16x22	B	14x18x2½	B	RV	P	2	P	A	-	-
28	405BP27	Styleline	Stainless Steel	S	16x22	B	14x18x2½	B	RV	P	2	P	A	-	-
28	407ADJ	Styleline	Stainless Steel	S	16x22	B	14x18x3½	B	RV	P	2	P	A	-	-
28	410BC	Styleline	Stainless Steel	S	16x22	B	14⅛x18¼x3½	B	RV	S	2	P	A	-	-
28	420BC	Styleline	Stainless Steel	S	16x22	B	14x20x3½	P	RV	S	3	S	A	-	-
28	421BC	Styleline	Stainless Steel	S	16x22	B	14x20x3½	P	RV	S	3	S	A	-	-
28	422SM	Styleline	Stainless Steel	S	14x20x5	WM	-	P	RV	S	2	P	F	-	-
26	448BC	Styleline	Stainless Steel	S	16x26	B	14x24x3½	P	RV	SS	3	SS	A	-	-
28	449BC	Styleline	Stainless Steel	S	16x22	B	14x18x3½	B	RV	P	2	P	F	-	-
28	452SM	Styleline	Stainless Steel	S	16x22x4¾	WM	-	P	RV	S	3	P	F	-	-
28	455FL	Cabinet 455FL	Stainless Steel	S	20⅜x22¼x3¾	B	14¼x18⅞x3½	P	R	S	2	P	A	Built-In	Fluorescent (inc
10	455230	Quantum	Frameless	T	30x36½x5¼	WM	-	C	-	S	2	S	F	Built-In	4-60W G25/G4
10	455236	Quantum	Frameless	T	36x36½x5¼	WM	-	C	-	S	2	S	F	Built-In	5-60W G25/G4
10	455248	Quantum	Frameless	T	48x36½x5¼	WM	-	C	-	S	2	S	F	Built-In	6-60W G25/G4
28	458	Styleline	Stainless Steel	S	16x26	B	14⅛x24x3½	P	RV	S	3	P	A	-	-
28	468	Styleline	Stainless Steel	S	16x26	B	14⅛x24x3½	P	RV	S	3	P	A	-	-
26, 28	468MOD	Modular Shelf	Stainless Steel	S	16x26	B	14x24x3½	P	RV	S	6†	P	A	-	-
28	478FS	Styleline	Stainless Steel •	S	16x26	B	14⅛x24x3½	P	RV	S	3	A	A	-	-
28	490	Styleline	Stainless Steel	S	18x24	B	16x21½x3½	P	RV	S	3	P	A	-	-
28	495	Styleline	Stainless Steel	S	20x30	B	17¼x26¼x3½	P	RV	S	3	P	A	-	-
6	5520	Torino	Frameless	S	16½x34½	B	14⅛x18¼x3½	P	R	S	2	P	A	73591	-
6	5528	Torino	Frameless	S	16½x34½	B	14⅛x24x3½	P	R	S	3	P	A	73591	-
28	555IL	Cabinet 555IL	Stainless Steel	S	16x24x8	WM	-	P	R	S	2	S	F	Built-In	2-60W
17	5622	White Marble	Solid Oak & White	S	17⅛x27⅛x5½	WM	-	P	RV	S	3	S	F	708WH	-
17	562230	White Marble	Solid Oak & White	T	30x28½x5¼	WM	-	L	-	S	2	S	F	WH53023	-
11	565	Styleline 2	Stainless Steel	S	18x28x6	WM	-	P	R	S	3	S	F	Built-In	3-60W G25/G4
29	602	Louver Door	Unfinished Pine	S	16x24	B	14⅛x18¼x3½	B	R	S	2	P	A	-	-
29	605ADJ	Louver Door	Unfinished Pine	S	16x24	B	14x18x2½	P	R	P	2	P	A	-	-
29	606	Louver Door	Unfinished Pine	S	16x22	B	14⅛x18¼x3½	B	RV	S	2	P	A	-	-
29	607ADJ	Louver Door	Unfinished Pine	S	16x22	B	14x18x2½	P	RV	P	3	P	A	-	-
29	609	Louver Door	Unfinished Pine	S	16x26	B	14x24x3½	P	RV	S	3	S	A	-	-
13	6120	Hibiscus	Floral, White	S	18½x27½	B	14⅛x18¼x3½	P	RV	S	2	P	A	761WH	2-G25
13	6122	Hibiscus	Floral, White	S	18½x27½	WM	-	P	RV	S	3	P	A	762WH	2-G25
13	6130	Hibiscus	Floral, Almond	S	18½x27½	B	14⅛x18¼x3½	P	RV	S	2	P	A	761AL	2-G25
13	6132	Hibiscus	Floral, Almond	S	18½x27½	WM	-	P	RV	S	3	P	A	762AL	2-G25
13	6140	Hibiscus	Floral, Green	S	18½x27½	B	14⅛x18¼x3½	P	RV	S	2	P	A	761GR	2-G25
13	6142	Hibiscus	Floral, Green	S	18½x27½	WM	-	P	RV	S	3	P	A	762GR	2-G25
29	622	Hideaway	Steel Door	S	17⅛x21½	B	14⅛x18¼x3½	P	RV	S	2	P	A	-	-
26	625	Bel Aire Auxiliary	Stainless Steel Trim	S	13x36	B	11¼x33¼x3½	P	RV	S	3	P	A	-	-
26	626	Bel Aire Auxiliary	Stainless Steel Trim	S	13x36x4¼	WM	-	P	RV	S	3	P	F	-	-

*Cabinet bottom always provides an additional storage level. † Modular half shelves. • Meets federal spec., see page 29.

Page	Model No.	Style Name	Frame	Style T-Tri-View B-BiView S-Single SB-Slide-by L-Light WM-Wall Mirror	Overall Size W H D	Mount Type WM-Wall Mount B-Built-In B/WM-Built-In or Wall Mount M-Mirror	Wall Opening W H D	Hinge Type P-Piano C-Con. L-Leaf PN-Pin B-Butt	Single Door Hinge L-Left R-Right RV-Rev.	Cabinet Body S-Steel SS-Stainless P-Polystyrene W-Wood	Shelves			Matching Light Fixture	Recommended Bulbs Qty-Type
											Quantity *	G-Glass S-Steel P-Polystyrene AL-Aluminum	F-Fixed A-Adjustable		
3	6142	Hibiscus	Floral, Green	S	18½x27½	WM	-	P	RV	S	3	P	A	762GR	2-G25
30	622	Hideaway	Steel Door	S	17⅛x21½	B	14x18x3½	P	RV	S	2	P	A	-	-
26	625	Bel Aire Auxiliary	Stainless Steel Trim	S	13x36	B	11¼x33¼x3½	P	RV	S	3	S	A	-	-
26	626	Bel Aire Auxiliary	Stainless Steel Trim	S	13x36x4¼	WM	-	P	RV	S	3	P	F	-	-
25	629	Illusion	Frameless	S	15x36	B	14x34x3½	C	RV	S	3	S	A	-	-
26	631	Avanti Corner	Stainless Steel Trim	S	13x36x7¼	WM	-	P	RV	S	3	G	F	-	-
25	639BC	Illusion	Frameless	S	13x36	B	12x34x3½	C	RV	S	3	S	A	-	-
5	652BC	Luminary	Frameless - ½" Bevel	S	24x37⅜x7¼	WM	-	C	-	S	3	G	A	Built-In	2-25W Fluor.
6	655036	Saturn	Frameless	T	36x30	B	33¾x24¾x3½	C	-	S	2	G	A	Built-In	2-17W Fluor.
6	655048	Saturn	Frameless	T	48x30	B	45¾x24¾x3½	C	-	S	2	G	A	Built-In	2-17W Fluor.
6	655236	Saturn	Frameless	T	36x30	WM	-	C	-	S	2	G	A	Built-In	2-17W Fluor.
6	655248	Saturn	Frameless	T	48x30	WM	-	C	-	S	2	G	A	Built-In	2-17W Fluor.
5	658BC	Luminary	Frameless - ½" Bevel	S	24x37⅜	B	14¼x34¼x3½	C	-	S	3	G	A	Built-In	2-25W Fluor.
26	672	Centered Corner	Solid Oak, Honey	S	19½x33½x10½	WM	-	PN	RV	S	3	S	F	-	-
26	672SS	Centered Corner	Stainless Steel	S	17¼x31x9⅞	WM	-	PN	RV	S	3	S	F	-	-
16	70223	Baker Street	Hardwood, White	L	18x8x13½	For WM Cab.	-	-	-	-	-	-	-	-	2-60W Std. MB
16	70273	Baker Street	Solid Oak, Honey	L	18x8x13½	For WM Cab.	-	-	-	-	-	-	-	-	2-60W Std. MB
6	70323	Baker Street	Hardwood, White	L	18x8x9	For B Cab.	-	-	-	-	-	-	-	-	2-60W Std. MB
6	70373	Baker Street	Solid Oak, Honey	L	18x8x9	For B Cab.	-	-	-	-	-	-	-	-	2-60W Std. MB
8	708WH	White Marble	Solid Oak & White	L	17⅛x7¼x10⅛	For WM Cab.	-	-	-	-	-	-	-	-	2-60W Std. MB
9	70928	Prairie	Hardwood, White	L	18x8x8	For B Cab.	-	-	-	-	-	-	-	-	2-60W Std. MB
3	711FG	Florentine	Gold Leaf	L	8x17 15/16x6 15/16	B	-	-	-	-	-	-	-	-	2-60W Std. MB
3	712FG	Florentine	Gold Leaf	L	8x17 15/16x9 15/16	WM	-	-	-	-	-	-	-	-	2-60W Std. MB
2	715K	Classico	Oak	L	18⅝x8x7	B	-	-	-	-	-	-	-	-	2-60W Std. MB
2	716K	Classico	Oak	L	18 1/16x8⅛x9¾	WM	-	-	-	-	-	-	-	-	2-60W Std. MB
2	715M	Classico	Mahogany	L	18⅝x8x7	B	-	-	-	-	-	-	-	-	2-60W Std. MB
2	716M	Classico	Mahogany	L	18 1/16x8⅛x9¾	WM	-	-	-	-	-	-	-	-	2-60W Std. MB
22	71829	Kingston	Solid Oak, Honey	L	16½x5½x2¼	For B Cab.	-	-	-	-	-	-	-	-	3-60W G25/G40
7	72052	Sonata	Frameless	L▲	5x17½x6⅛	For B Cab.	-	-	-	-	-	-	-	-	2-75W Std. MB
8,9	73190	Mirage	Frameless	L▲	5x12x6½	For B Cab.	-	-	-	-	-	-	-	-	2-60W Slim Line
,9	73290	Horizon	Frameless	L	16x4½x2	For B Cab.	-	-	-	-	-	-	-	-	2-60W Std. MB
6	73591	Torino	Frameless	L▲	5⅜x13¾x6½	For B Cab.	-	-	-	-	-	-	-	-	2-75W Std. MB
8	735FL	Decorah	Frameless	L	16x4⅜x2	For B Cab.	-	-	-	-	-	-	-	-	2-60W G25/G40
20	74279	Grant	Solid Oak, Honey	L	16¼x5½x3	For B Cab.	-	-	-	-	-	-	-	-	2-60W G25/G40
4	745WH	Spectrum	Molded, Acrylic Fin.	L	18x6½x3	For B Cab.	-	-	-	-	-	-	-	-	3-60W G25/40
15	747BR	Verona	Molded, Brass Fin.	L	17¼x5½x3	For B Cab.	-	-	-	-	-	-	-	-	3-60W G25/40
13	761WH	Hibiscus	Floral, White	L	18½x6¾x3	B	-	-	-	-	-	-	-	-	2-G25
3	761AL	Hibiscus	Floral, Almond	L	18½x6¾x3	B	-	-	-	-	-	-	-	-	2-G25
3	761GR	Hibiscus	Floral, Forest Green	L	18½x6¾x3	B	-	-	-	-	-	-	-	-	2-G25
13	762WH	Hibiscus	Floral, White	L	18½x6¾x5½	WM	-	-	-	-	-	-	-	-	2-G25
13	762AL	Hibiscus	Floral, Almond	L	18½x6¾x5½	WM	-	-	-	-	-	-	-	-	2-G25
13	762GR	Hibiscus	Floral, Forest Green	L	18½x6¾x5½	WM	-	-	-	-	-	-	-	-	2-G25
17	76378	Canterbury	Solid Oak, Honey	L	18x8x8	For WM Cab.	-	-	-	-	-	-	-	-	2-60W Std. MB
17	76478	Canterbury	Solid Oak, Honey	L	18x8x11½	For WM Cab.	-	-	-	-	-	-	-	-	2-60W Std. MB
19	8120	Prairie	Hardwood, White	S	18x27½	B	14x18x3½	P	RV	S	2	P	A	70928	-
19	8122	Prairie	Hardwood, White	S	18x27½x5	WM	-	P	RV	S	3	P	F	71028	-
19	8128	Prairie	Hardwood, White	S	18x27½	B	14x24x3½	P	RV	S	3	P	A	70928	-
19	8199703**	Prairie	Solid Oak, Blonde	T	30x28 5/16	WM	14x24x3½	P	RV	S	3	P	A	OK8199705	-
19	8199704**	Prairie	Solid Oak, Blonde	T	36x28 5/16	WM	14x24x3½	P	RV	S	3	P	A	OK8199706	-
16	820	Baker Street	Hardwood, White	S	18x27	B	14x18x3½	P	RV	S	2	P	A	See p. 16	-
16	822	Baker Street	Hardwood, White	S	18x27x5	WM	-	P	RV	S	3	P	F	See p. 16	-
22	8278	Chapel Hill	Solid Oak, Honey	S	17¼x27¼	B	14x24x3½	P	RV	S	3	S	F	75719	-
16	828	Baker Street	Hardwood, White	S	18x27	B	14x24x3½	P	RV	S	3	P	A	See p. 16	-
22	8370	Kingston	Solid Oak, Honey	S	16½x26½	B	14x18x3½	P	RV	S	2	S	A	71829	-
22	8378	Kingston	Solid Oak, Honey	S	16½x26½	B	14x24x3½	P	RV	S	3	S	A	71829	-
16	842230	Baker Street	Hardwood, White	T	30x28½x5½	WM	-	L	-	S	2	S	F	BS84023	-

abinet bottom always provides an additional storage level. ▲ Packed in pairs. **Special Order

MEDICINE CABINET SPECIFICATIONS

Page	Model No.	Style Name	Frame	Style T-Tri-View B-BiView S-Single SB-Slide-by L-Light WM-Wall Mirror	Overall Size W H D	Mount Type WM-Wall Mount B-Built-In B/WM-Built-In or Wall Mount M-Mirror	Wall Opening W H D	Hinge Type P-Piano C-Con. L-Leaf PN-Pin B-Butt	Single Door Hinge L-Left R-Right RV-Rev.	Cabinet Body S-Steel SS-Stainless P-Polystyrene W-Wood	Shelves: Quantity *	Shelves: G-Glass S-Steel P-Polystyrene AL-Aluminum	Shelves: F-Fixed A-Adjustable	Matching Light Fixture	Recommended Bulbs Qty-Type
16	842236	Baker Street	Hardwood, White	T	36x28½x5½	WM	-	L	-	S	2	S	F	BS84623	-
17	8570	Canterbury	Solid Oak, Honey	S	18¼x27¼	B	14x18x3½	P	R	S	2	P	A	76378	-
17	8572	Canterbury	Solid Oak, Honey	S	18¼x27¼x5½	WM	-	P	R	S	3	P	F	76478	-
16	870	Baker Street	Solid Oak, Honey	S	18x27	B	14x18x3½	P	RV	S	2	P	A	See p. 16	-
16	872	Baker Street	Solid Oak, Honey	S	18x27x5	WM	-	P	RV	S	3	P	F	See p. 16	-
20	8770	Grant	Solid Oak, Honey	S	16¼x24¼	B	14x18x3½	P	RV	S	2	P	A	74279	-
20	8772	Grant	Solid Oak, Honey	S	16¼x24¼x5½	WM	-	P	RV	S	2	P	F	-	-
20	8773	Grant	Solid Oak, Honey	S	16¼x22	B	14x18x2½	B	RV	P	2	P	F	74279	-
20	8778	Grant	Solid Oak, Honey	S	16¼x26¼	B	14x24x3½	P	RV	S	3	P	A	74279	-
16	878	Baker Street	Solid Oak, Honey	S	18x27	B	14x24x3½	P	RV	S	3	P	A	See p. 16	-
24	902	Prestique	Wood, Oak Finish	S	16x20x4¾	WM	-	B	RV	W	1	Wood	F	-	-
24	902BP	Prestique	Wood, Oak Finish	S	16x20x4¾	WM	-	B	RV	W	1	Wood	F	-	-
24	902WH	Prestique	Wood, White Finish	S	16x20x4¾	WM	-	B	RV	W	1	Wood	F	-	-
23	902224	Prestique	Hardwood, White	T	24x26x4¾	WM	-	L	-	W	2	Wood	F	CR92429	-
23	902230	Prestique	Hardwood, White	T	30x30x4¾	WM	-	L	-	W	2	Wood	F	CR93029	-
23	902236	Prestique	Hardwood, White	T	36x30x4¾	WM	-	L	-	W	2	Wood	F	CR93629	-
23	905224	Prestique	Frameless	T	24x26x4¾	WM	-	C	-	W	2	Wood	F	CR92490	-
23	905230	Prestique	Frameless	T	30x30x4¾	WM	-	C	-	W	2	Wood	F	CR93090	-
23	905236	Prestique	Frameless	T	36x30x4¾	WM	-	C	-	W	2	Wood	F	CR93690	-
23	905248	Prestique	Frameless	T	48x30x4¾	WM	-	C	-	W	2	Wood	F	CR94890	-
23	907224	Prestique	Solid Oak, Honey	T	24x26x4¾	WM	-	L	-	W	2	Wood	F	-	-
23	907224BP	Prestique	Solid Oak, Honey	T	24x26x4¾	WM	-	L	-	W	2	Wood	F	-	-
23	907230	Prestique	Solid Oak, Honey	T	30x30x4¾	WM	-	L	-	W	2	Wood	F	CR93079	-
23	907230BP	Prestique	Solid Oak, Honey	T	30x30x4¾	WM	-	L	-	W	2	Wood	F	CR93079	-
23	907236	Prestique	Solid Oak, Honey	T	36x30x4¾	WM	-	L	-	W	2	Wood	F	CR93679	-
23	907248	Prestique	Solid Oak, Honey	T	48x30x4¾	WM	-	L	-	W	2	Wood	F	CR94879	-
24	942224	Prestique	Wood, White Finish	T	24x28⅞x4⅛	WM	-	PN	-	W	2	Wood	F	Built-In	3-60W G25/G40
24	9422BC	Prestique	Wood, White Finish	T	15¾x23⅝x4⅛	WM	-	PN	R	W	2	Wood	F	Built-In	2-60W G25/G40
24	942230	Prestique	Wood, White Finish	T	30x28⅞x4⅛	WM	-	PN	-	W	2	Wood	F	Built-In	4-60W G25/G40
24	942236	Prestique	Wood, White Finish	T	36x28⅞x4⅛	WM	-	PN	-	W	2	Wood	F	Built-In	5-60W G25/G40
24	9472	Prestique	Wood, Oak Finish	S	15¾x23⅝x4⅛	WM	-	PN	R	W	2	Wood	F	Built-In	2-60W G25/G40
24	947224	Prestique	Wood, Oak Finish	T	24x28⅞x4⅛	WM	-	PN	-	W	2	Wood	F	Built-In	3-60W G25/G40
24	947230	Prestique	Wood, Oak Finish	T	30x28⅞x4⅛	WM	-	PN	-	W	2	Wood	F	Built-In	4-60W G25/G40
24	947236	Prestique	Wood, Oak Finish	T	36x28⅞x4⅛	WM	-	PN	-	W	2	Wood	F	Built-In	5-60W G25/G40
24	967224	Prestique	Wood, Oak Finish	T	24x25½x4¾	WM	-	L	-	W	2	Wood	F	-	-
24	967230	Prestique	Wood, Oak Finish	T	30x25½x4¾	WM	-	L	-	W	2	Wood	F	-	-
24	967236	Prestique	Wood, Oak Finish	T	36x25½x4¾	WM	-	L	-	W	2	Wood	F	-	-
20	97014099	Grand Oak II	Trim Kit for 2779 Series				-	-	-	-	-	-	-	-	-
24	972225	Prestique	Wood, White Finish	2-Door	25½x28x4¾	WM	-	**	RV	W	5	Wood	F	-	-
20	973BC	Grant	Solid Oak, Honey	S	16x20	-	14x18x2½	B	RV	P	2	P	F	74279	-
24	977225	Prestique	Wood, Oak Finish	2-Door	25½x28x4¾	WM	-	**	RV	W	5	Wood	F	-	-
24	982	Prestique	Wood, Oak Finish	S	16x26x4¾	WM	-	B	RV	W	2	Wood	F	-	-
24	982WH	Prestique	Wood, White Finish	S	16x26x4¾	WM	-	B	RV	W	2	Wood	F	-	-
16	BS84023	Baker Street	Hardwood Wh. Paint	L	30x6x6½	For WM Cab.	-	-	-	-	-	-	-	-	3-60W Std. MB
16	BS84623	Baker Street	Hardwood Wh. Paint	L	36x6x6½	For WM Cab.	-	-	-	-	-	-	-	-	4-60W Std. MB
23	CR92429	Prestique	Hardwood, White	L	24x5⅞x5½	For WM Cab.	-	-	-	-	-	-	-	-	3-60W G25/G40
23	CR92490	Prestique	Frameless	L	24x5⅞x5½	For WM Cab.	-	-	-	-	-	-	-	-	3-60W G25/G40
23	CR93029	Prestique	Hardwood, White	L	30x5⅞x5½	For WM Cab.	-	-	-	-	-	-	-	-	4-60W G25/G40
23	CR93079	Prestique	Solid Oak, Honey	L	30x5⅞x5½	For WM Cab.	-	-	-	-	-	-	-	-	4-60W G25/G40
23	CR93090	Prestique	Frameless	L	30x5⅞x5½	For WM Cab.	-	-	-	-	-	-	-	-	4-60W G25/G40
23	CR93629	Prestique	Hardwood, White	L	36x5⅞x5½	For WM Cab.	-	-	-	-	-	-	-	-	5-60W G25/G40
23	CR93679	Prestique	Solid Oak, Honey	L	36x5⅞x5½	For WM Cab.	-	-	-	-	-	-	-	-	5-60W G25/G40
23	CR93690	Prestique	Frameless	L	36x5⅞x5½	For WM Cab.	-	-	-	-	-	-	-	-	4-60W G25/G40
23	CR94890	Prestique	Frameless	L	48x5⅞x5½	For WM Cab.	-	-	-	-	-	-	-	-	6-60W G25/G40
9	HO32490	Horizon	Frameless	L	24x4½x5⅞	For WM Cab.	-	-	-	-	-	-	-	-	3-60W G25/G40
9	HO33090	Horizon	Frameless	L	30x4¼x5⅞	For WM Cab.	-	-	-	-	-	-	-	-	4-60W G25/G40

*Cabinet bottom always provides an additional storage level.
**Semi concealed, self closing hinge.

age	Model No.	Style Name	Frame	Style T-Tri-View B-BiView S-Single SB-Slide-by L-Light WM-Wall Mirror	Overall Size W H D	Mount Type WM-Wall Mount B-Built-In B/WM-Built-In or Wall Mount M-Mirror	Wall Opening W H D	Hinge Type P-Piano C-Con. L-Leaf PN-Pin B-Butt	Single Door Hinge L-Left R-Right RV-Rev.	Cabinet Body S-Steel SS-Stainless P-Polystyrene W-Wood	Shelves Quantity *	G-Glass S-Steel P-Polystyrene AL-Aluminum	F-Fixed A-Adjustable	Matching Light Fixture	Recommended Bulbs Qty-Type
9	HO33690	Horizon	Frameless	L	36x4¼x5⅞	For WM Cab.	-	-	-	-	-	-	-	-	4-60W G25/G40
9	HO34890	Horizon	Frameless	L	48x4½x5⅞	For WM Cab.	-	-	-	-	-	-	-	-	5-60W G25/G40
9	HO42490	Horizon	Frameless	L	24x4½x2¼	For B Cab.	-	-	-	-	-	-	-	-	3-60W G25/G40
9	HO43090	Horizon	Frameless	L	30x4½x2¼	For B Cab.	-	-	-	-	-	-	-	-	4-60W G25/G40
9	HO43690	Horizon	Frameless	L	36x4½x2¼	For B Cab.	-	-	-	-	-	-	-	-	4-60W G25/G40
9	HO44890	Horizon	Frameless	L	48x4½x2¼	For B Cab.	-	-	-	-	-	-	-	-	5-60W G25/G40
30	IL24	Commodore	Stainless Steel Trim	L	24x4x7½	ForWM Cab.	-	-	-	-	-	-	-	-	4-60W MB
30	IL30	Commodore	Stainless Steel Trim	L	30x4x7½	ForWM Cab.	-	-	-	-	-	-	-	-	4-60W MB
4	LBC10	Le Baccarat	Frameless	S	24x35⅜	B	16½x25¼x3⅞	C	R	SS	3	G	A	-	-
4	LBM15	Le Baccarat	Frameless	WM	24x35⅜	M	-	-	-	-	-	-	-	-	-
9	OK8199705**	Prairie	Solid Oak, Blonde	L	30x8x11	ForWM Cab.	-	-	-	-	-	-	-	-	3-60W Std. MB
9	OK8199706**	Prairie	Solid Oak, Blonde	L	36x8x11	ForWM Cab.	-	-	-	-	-	-	-	-	4-60W Std. MB
30	PEM2424	Commodore	Frameless	WM	24x24	WM	-	-	-	-	-	-	-	-	IL24
30	PEM3024	Commodore	Frameless	WM	30x24	WM	-	-	-	-	-	-	-	-	IL30
30	PEM3036	Commodore	Frameless	WM	30x36	WM	-	-	-	-	-	-	-	-	IL30
30	PEM3624	Commodore	Frameless	WM	36x24	WM	-	-	-	-	-	-	-	-	-
30	PEM3636	Commodore	Frameless	WM	36x36	WM	-	-	-	-	-	-	-	-	-
30	PEM4824	Commodore	Frameless	WM	48x24	WM	-	-	-	-	-	-	-	-	-
30	PEM4836	Commodore	Frameless	WM	48x36	WM	-	-	-	-	-	-	-	-	-
30	PEM6036	Commodore	Frameless	WM	60x36	WM	-	-	-	-	-	-	-	-	-
4	PRC1148	Primevère	Frameless	T	48x37⅜	B	36⅞x32⅞x3⅞	C	-	SS	3	G	A	PRL1048	-
4	PRC1148SM	Primevère	Clear Mirror	T	48¼x37⅜	WM	-	C	-	SS	3	G	F	PRL1048	-
4	PRC1160	Primevère	Clear Mirror	T	60x37⅜	B	48⅞x32⅞x3⅞	C	-	SS	3	G	A	PRL1060	-
4	PRC1160SM	Primevère	Clear Mirror	T	60¼x37⅜	WM	-	C	-	SS	3	G	F	PRL1060	-
4	PRL1048	Primevère	Clear Mirror	L	48x4¼x5⅜	For B/WMCab.	-	-	-	S	-	-	-	-	Fluorescent (Incl.)
4	PRL1060	Primevère	Clear Mirror	L	60x4¼x5⅜	For B/WMCab.	-	-	-	S	-	-	-	-	Fluorescent (Incl.)
1	SB22529	Vienna	Chrome Trim	L	24x4x5½	ForWM Cab.	-	-	-	-	-	-	-	-	3-60W G25/G40
1	SB23129	Vienna	Chrome Trim	L	30x4x5½	ForWM Cab.	-	-	-	-	-	-	-	-	4-60W G25/G40
28	SD15	Beauty Glide	Stainless Steel Trim	SB	24x18¾	B	21½x17x3½	-	-	S	1	S	A	-	-
28	SD41	Beauty Glide	Stainless Steel Trim	SB	27½x19¼	B	26¼x17¼x3½	-	-	S	1	S	A	-	-
28	SDL82	Beauty Glide	Stainless Steel Trim	SB	27½x22	B	26½x18¼x3½	-	-	S	1	S	A	Built-In	Fluorescent (Incl.)
20	SG32479	Grand Oak II	Solid Oak, Honey	L	24x5⅝x4¾	For B/WMCab.	-	-	-	-	-	-	-	-	3-60W G25/G40
20	SG33079	Grand Oak II	Solid Oak, Honey	L	29x5⅝x4¾	For B/WMCab.	-	-	-	-	-	-	-	-	4-60W G25/G40
20	SG33679	Grand Oak II	Solid Oak, Honey	L	35x5⅝x4¾	For B/WMCab.	-	-	-	-	-	-	-	-	5-60W G25/G40
20	SG34879	Grand Oak II	Solid Oak, Honey	L	47x5⅝x4¾	For B/WMCab.	-	-	-	-	-	-	-	-	6-60W G25/G40
14	SP132WH	Spectrum	Molded, Acrylic Fin.	L	30x6½x5¼	For B/WMCab.	-	-	-	-	-	-	-	-	4-60W G25/G40
14	SP133WH	Spectrum	Molded, Acrylic Fin.	L	36x6½x5¼	For B/WMCab.	-	-	-	-	-	-	-	-	5-60W G25/G40
30	V24	Commodore	Stainless Steel Trim	SB	24¼x8¾x4¼	WM	-	-	-	Cosmetic Box, Mirrored Door					
30	V30	Commodore	Stainless Steel Trim	SB	30¼x8¾x4¼	WM	-	-	-	Cosmetic Box, Mirrored Door					
30	V36	Commodore	Stainless Steel Trim	SB	36¼x8¾x4¼	WM	-	-	-	Cosmetic Box, Mirrored Door					
30	V48	Commodore	Stainless Steel Trim	SB	48¼x8¾x4¼	WM	-	-	-	Cosmetic Box, Mirrored Door					
30	VM224M	Commodore	Stainless Steel Trim	SB	24¼x32x4⅛	WM	-	-	-	Cosmetic Box & Mirror, Mirrored Door					
30	VM224P	Commodore	Stainless Steel Trim	SB	24¼x32x4⅛	WM	-	-	-	Cosmetic Box & Mirror, Styrene Door					
30	VM230M	Commodore	Stainless Steel Trim	SB	30¼x32x4⅛	WM	-	-	-	Cosmetic Box & Mirror, Mirrored Door					
30	VM230P	Commodore	Stainless Steel Trim	SB	30¼x32x4⅛	WM	-	-	-	Cosmetic Box & Mirror, Styrene Door					
30	VM236M	Commodore	Stainless Steel Trim	SB	36¼x32x4⅛	WM	-	-	-	Cosmetic Box & Mirror, Mirrored Door					
30	VM236P	Commodore	Stainless Steel Trim	SB	36¼x32x4⅛	WM	-	-	-	Cosmetic Box & Mirror, Styrene Door					
18	WH53023	White Marble	Solid Oak & White	L	30x7¼x12¼	ForWM Cab.	-	-	-	-	-	-	-	-	3-60W MB

abinet bottom always provides an additional storage level.

**Special Order

$\mathcal{T}$OWEL WARMERS

THE COMPLETE RANGE

MYSON
TOWEL WARMERS
www.MysonInc.com

MYSON'S QUALITY CONTROL, AND CRAFTSMANSHIP ensure that the highest

standards are maintained. *Elegant and stylish…* Myson Towel Warmers enhance the appearance of bathroom, entryway, spa or hotel suites. *Economical and efficient…* Myson Towel Warmers add to the comfort of the room and keep towels warm and dry. Myson offers a wide range of standard models, either UL approved electric or hydronic (warm water), or you can have one custom designed in your choice of colour, size or finish.

PREMIER TOWEL WARMERS

PREMIER ELECTRIC ⓊL

Model Type	V/HZ	Watts	Amps	Overall Height	Overall Width Including Flanges	Overall Width Including Electric Box	Width C/C Vertical Tubes	Center of Right Rail to Wiring Connection	Floor to Center of Electric Box	Overall Projection	Tube Diameter	Shipping Weight
EB24/4	110V/60Hz	140	1.10	37-5/8	27-1/4	29-5/8	24	2-5/8	15	5-5/8	1-1/4	37 lbs.
EB26/1	110V/60Hz	165	1.30	36	27-1/4	29-5/8	24	2-5/8	12	*	1-1/4	44 lbs.
EB29	110V/60Hz	165	1.30	41	27-1/4	30	24	3	N/A	4-7/8	1-1/4	62 lbs
EB31/2	110V/60Hz	165	1.30	33-1/4	33-1/4	36	30	3	N/A	5-5/8	1-1/4	52 lbs.
EB34/5	110V/60Hz	100	.76	27-1/4	27-1/4	30	24	3	N/A	5-5/8	1-1/4	55 lbs.

* Depends on Wall Stays

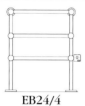

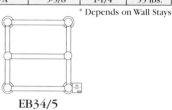

EB24/4 EB26/1 EB29 EB31/2 EB34/5

PREMIER HYDRONIC

Model Type	Btu/hr at 100° F Temp. Difference	Overall Height	Overall Width Including Flanges	Width C/C Vertical Tubes	Center to Center Connection	Floor to Center Connection	Overall Projection	Tube Diameter	Shipping Weight
B24/1	634	37-1/2	27	24	18	4-1/4	5-1/8	1	25 lbs.
B24/2	710	37-1/2	33	30	24	4-1/4	5-1/8	1	25 lbs.
B24/3	790	37-1/2	39	36	30	4-1/4	5-1/8	1	25 lbs.
B24/4	750	37-5/8	27-1/4	24	18	4-1/4	5-3/8	1-1/4	30 lbs.
B24/5	850	37-5/8	33-1/4	30	24	4-1/4	5-3/8	1-1/4	30 lbs.
B24/6	940	37-5/8	39-1/4	36	30	4-1/4	5-3/8	1-1/4	30 lbs.
B26/1	1,350	36-7/8	27-1/4	24	18	4-1/4	Depends on Wall Stays	1-1/4	25 lbs.
B26/2	1,440	36-7/8	33-1/4	30	24	4-1/4		1-1/4	25 lbs.
B26/3	1,530	36-7/8	39-1/4	36	30	4-1/4		1-1/4	25 lbs.
B26/4	1,620	36-7/8	45-1/4	42	36	4-1/4		1-1/4	25 lbs.
B29	1,650	41	27-1/4	24	24	N/A	4-7/8	1-1/4	30 lbs.
B30	1,500	39	27-1/4	24	18	4-1/4	8-3/4	1-1/4	30 lbs.
B31/1	1,594	27-1/4	26-1/4	24	18	N/A	6-7/8	1-1/4	25 lbs.
B31/2	1,669	33-1/4	33-1/4	30	24	N/A	6-7/8	1-1/4	25 lbs.
B31/3	1,747	33-1/4	39-1/4	36	30	N/A	6-7/8	1-1/4	25 lbs.
B31/4	1,795	33-1/4	45-1/4	42	36	N/A	6-7/8	1-1/4	30 lbs.
B34/1	1,429	27	27	24	18	N/A	6-5/8	1	25 lbs.
B34/2	1,547	27	33	30	24	N/A	6-5/8	1	25 lbs.
B34/3	1,702	27	39	36	30	N/A	6-5/8	1	25 lbs.
B34/4	1,802	33	39	36	30	N/A	6-5/8	1	25 lbs.
B34/5	713	27-1/4	27-1/4	24	18	N/A	6-7/8	1-1/4	30 lbs.
B34/6	805	27-1/4	33-1/4	30	24	N/A	6-7/8	1-1/4	30 lbs.
B34/7	894	27-1/4	39-1/4	36	30	N/A	6-7/8	1-1/4	30 lbs.
B34/8	952	33-1/4	39-1/4	36	30	N/A	6-7/8	1-1/4	30 lbs.

B24 B26 B29 B30 B31 B34

All dimensions are in inches

◣◣ May be custom ordered in electric version, call Myson for details

MYSON - For more information: call 800-698-9690 or online www.MysonInc.com

CLASSIC TOWEL WARMERS

CLASSIC ELECTRIC ⓊⓁ

Model Type	V/HZ	Watts	Amps	Overall Height	Overall Width Including Electric Box	Width C/C Vertical Tubes	Center of Right Rail to Wiring Connection	Floor to Center of Electric Box	Overall Projection	Shipping Weight
EMR750	110V/60Hz	300	2.50	29-7/8	22-3/8	18-1/2	2	N/A	3-5/8	40 lbs.

Model Type	V/HZ	Watts	Amps	Overall Height	Overall Width Including Flanges	Center of Flange to Wiring Connection	Bottom Rail to Center of Flange	Overall Projection	Tube Diameter	Panel Insert Height x of Sections	Shipping Weight
EO100	110V/60Hz	100	.76	24-1/4*	23	23	13-7/8	4	1	N/A	37 lbs.
EO140	110V/60Hz	140	1.10	33-1/2*	23	23	23-1/8	4	1	N/A	44 lbs.
EO165	110V/60Hz	165	1.26	33-1/2*	33	33	20-1/4	4	1	N/A	62 lbs.
EO350	110V/60Hz	200	1.75	33-1/2*	25-1/4	25-1/4	26	41/2	1	15" x 9"	52 lbs.

*add 3-1/2 inches for portable appliances

Type	V/HZ	Watts	Amps	Overall Height	Overall Width Including Flanges	Overall Width Including Electric Box	Width C/C Vertical Tubes	Center of Right Rail to Wiring Connection	Floor to Center of Electric Box	Overall Projection	Tube Dia.	Shipping Weight
ES40/1	110V/60Hz	100	.76	6-3/4	18-1/4	21-5/8	17	2-5/8	N/A	12	1-1/4	33 lbs.
ES40/2	110V/60Hz	140	1.10	6-3/4	24-1/4	27-5/8	23	2-5/8	N/A	12	1-1/4	33 lbs.

EMR750

EO100 Portable

EO140

EO100 & EO165

EO350

ES40

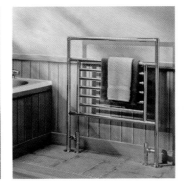

CLASSIC HYDRONIC

Model Type	Btu/hr at 100° F Temp. Difference	Overall Height	Overall Width Including Flanges	Width C/C Vertical Tubes	Center to Center Connection	Floor to Center Connection	Overall Projection	Tube Diameter	Shipping Weight
S6/1	1,350	36-5/8	27-1/4	24	17-1/2	4-1/4	Depends on Wall Stays	1-1/4	25 lbs.
S6/2	1,440	36-5/8	33-1/4	30	23-1/2	4-1/4		1-1/4	25 lbs.
S6/3	1,530	36-5/8	39-1/4	36	29-1/2	4-1/4		1-1/4	25 lbs.
S6/4	1,620	36-5/8	45-1/4	42	35-1/2	4-1/4		1-1/4	30 lbs.
S11/1	1,429	27-1/4	27-1/4	24	17-1/2	N/A	6-1/2	1-1/4	25 lbs.
S11/2	1,547	33-1/4	33-1/4	30	23-1/2	N/A	6-1/2	1-1/4	25 lbs.
S11/3	1,702	33-1/4	39-1/4	36	29-1/2	N/A	6-1/2	1-1/4	25 lbs.
S11/4	1,802	33-1/4	45-1/4	42	35-1/2	N/A	6-1/2	1-1/4	30 lbs.
S14/1	594	27	27	24	17-3/4	N/A	6-1/2	1	20 lbs.
S14/2	669	27	33	30	23-3/4	N/A	6-1/2	1	20 lbs.
S14/3	747	27	39	36	29-3/4	N/A	6-1/2	1	20 lbs.
S14/4	795	33	39	36	29-3/4	N/A	6-1/2	1	20 lbs.
CYG14/1	369	27	27	24	17-3/4	N/A	5-1/2	1	20 lbs.
CYG14/2	433	27	33	30	23-3/4	N/A	5-1/2	1	20 lbs.
CYG14/3	495	27	39	36	29-3/4	N/A	5-1/2	1	20 lbs.
CYG14/4	536	33	39	36	29-3/4	N/A	5-1/2	1	20 lbs.

S6   **S11**

S14   **CYG14**

All dimensions are in inches

〰 May be custom ordered in electric version, call Myson for details

MYSON - For more information: call 800-698-9690 or online www.MysonInc.com

MULTIRAIL HYDRONIC

Model Type	Btu/hr at 100° F Temp. Difference	Optional Additional Towel Rail	Overall Height	Overall Width Including Flanges	Width C/C Vertical Tubes	Center to Center Connection	Floor to Center Connection	Overall Projection	Tube Dia.	Shipping Weight
MRR1	1,605	MRAC 1	29-7/8	19-3/4	18-1/2	18-1/2	N/A	3-7/8		25 lbs.
MRR2	1,904	MRAC 2	29-7/8	23-5/8	22-1/2	22-1/2	N/A	3-7/8		30 lbs.
MRR3	2,351	MRAC 3	29-7/8	29-1/2	28-1/4	28-1/4	N/A	3-7/8		35 lbs.
MRR4	2,341	MRAC 1	46-7/8	19-3/4	18-1/2	18-1/2	N/A	3-7/8	1.25 Vertical Tubes 1.00 Round Cross Tubes	40 lbs.
MRR5	2,797	MRAC 2	46-7/8	23-5/8	22-1/2	22-1/2	N/A	3-7/8		45 lbs.
MRR6	3,483	MRAC 3	46-7/8	29-1/2	28-1/4	28-1/4	N/A	3-7/8		50 lbs.
MRR7	3,524	MRAC 1	70-7/8	19-3/4	18-1/2	18-1/2	N/A	3-7/8		55 lbs.
MRR8	4,204	MRAC 2	70-7/8	23-5/8	22-1/2	22-1/2	N/A	3-7/8		65 lbs.
MRR9	5,222	MRAC 3	70-7/8	29-1/2	28-1/4	28-1/4	N/A	3-7/8		75 lbs.

MMR1

All dimensions are in inches

MYSON TOWEL WARMER FEATURES

Myson Model	UL Approved	Back Lit Switch	Wall Model	Floor Model	Portable Model	Available in More Than 5 Finishes	Matching Installation Accessories	De-Zine Brass Tubing	Custom Sizes	Suitable for Central Heating or Hot Water	Custom UL Electric Version Available	Additional Towel Rail
Premier Electric	✗	✗	✗	✗		✗	✗		✗			
Premier Hydronic			✗	✗		✗	✗	✗	✗	✗	✗	
Classic Electric	✗	✗	✗		✗	✗	✗		✗			
Classic Hydronic			✗	✗		✗	✗	✗	✗	✗	✗	
Multirail Hydronic			✗			✗	✗	✗	✗	✗		✗

MYSON TOWEL WARMER FINISHES AVAILABLE

Myson Model	Chrome Plate	Nickel Plate	Satin Nickel Plate	Traditional Gold Plate	Regal Brass Plate	Custom Colors	Combination Finishes
Premier Electric	✗	✗	✗	✗	✗	✗	✗
Premier Hydronic	✗	✗	✗	✗	✗	✗	✗
Classic Electric	✗	✗	✗	✗	✗	✗	
Classic Hydronic	✗	✗	✗	✗	✗	✗	
Multirail Hydronic	✗	✗	✗	✗	✗	✗	

5 YEAR WARRANTY

Innovations in Unique Heating Products

MYSON, INC.
49 Hercules Drive
Colchester, VT 05446

For more information:
Phone: 800-698-9690
Fax: 802-654-7022
www.MysonInc.com

Century Shower Door
Full Line Catalog

C593
10824/CEN
BuyLine 7554

Glasstec GP-1631-B

CENTURY

Century Design Options are endless and our quality is second to none. Create beautifully clear barriers with Glasstec enclosures in solid brass or aluminum and a myriad of handle styles. With Brassline you can choose from four styles, many handle designs and nine metal finishes, all in solid brass. Centec is the most unique frameless unit available. Century also offers two lines of framed enclosures, Lucette and Crest, to match any design, color scheme or budget.

Custom Applications Are Our Specialty And Our Guarantee is Watertight. Creating custom enclosures to your exacting specifications is an important part of our business. We are the only manufacturer with full-time product designers to answer questions and solve problems, guaranteeing the best possible service and fit for your enclosure. We stock a multi-million dollar inventory of extrusions and glass options for immediate delivery to meet virtually any need. Century enclosures come with a guarantee that is as watertight as our products.

Glasstec Frameless Series is clearly the most innovative enclosure available. Featuring a completely frameless construction, heavy-duty tempered glass and a patented pivot system, each enclosure is crafted to match specific customer needs.

Lucette Series With a spectrum of colors, finish, glass options and detailing, these deluxe framed enclosures offer design options limited only by your imagination.

2

Brassline Series Solid innovation and elegant design in a superior hand-crafted enclosure. Brassline quality, strength and good looks are truly one of a kind.

Centec Series The clean, open, contemporary look in a top-quality frameless enclosure. Select the color, finish, and other options to make it the perfect fit in your home.

Trimline Series With originality of design, quality construction, style and affordability coordinating today's look with Krystal Flute, Rain or Clear glass. Chrome, brass or 14 painted finishes to complete your bath.

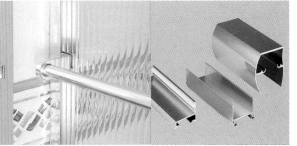

Glasstec
The beauty of frameless glass

Glasstec frameless enclosures are constructed of ⅜" or ½" tempered glass with a beveled edge design that seals tight to eliminate the need for channels. The hinge, header and hardware is available in solid brass or aluminum and the full Century range of finishes, each individually crafted to customer specifications. Glasstec handles are available in a wide range of styles.

Glasstec GP-1632B Cameo Cream & Clear Glass

4   **Glasstec GP-1669BB 24K Gold & Clear Glass**   **Glasstec GP-1632B Brass Finish & Clear Glass**

Glasstec **GP-1669BB** Brass Finish & Clear Glass

Glasstec **GP-1629** Durabrass Finish & Clear Glass

Glasstec **GAPW-1631B** Gold Anodized Finish & Clear Glass

Glasstec **GP-1669-B** Brass Finish & Custom Etched Glass

Any design, any opening, Glasstec enclosures are the finest all glass and brass enclosures in the industry. And now these same header and hinge designs are also available in aluminum. Our unique offset pivot design offers benefits not found else-where, like mitered glass and tight wall clearances to eliminate the need for jambs and provide superior performance in steam units. The hinges are adjustable to facilitate out of square openings and easy installation. With the most unique selection of handles and towel bar options, Century also provides the perfect finishing touch.

5

Glasstec
The ultimate frameless system

Glasstec GP-1669 Nickel Finish & Clear Glass

Glasstec GAPW-1627 Gold Anodized Aluminum Finish & Clear Glass with optional C-pull handle

Glasstec Specifications

MANUFACTURER

Manufacture: To establish a standard of quality, design and function desired, Drawings and specifications have been based on Century Shower Door Inc., 250 Lackawanna Avenue, West Paterson NJ 07424, (973) 785-4290, Product: "Glasstec," no substitution will be accepted.

COMPONENTS

A. Header, trim and hardware: Extruded Architectural Bronze, copper alloy number 385 or extruded Aluminum, alloy 6463-TS.

B. Glass: [select one of the following]
1. Clear tempered and Star Fire glass: 3/8 or 1/2 inch thick safety glass, ASTM C 1048 FT, complying with Class 1 clear, quality q3 glazing select, conforming to ANSI Z97.1.
2. Custom glazing: [Optional grey tinted, bronze tinted, sandblasted, or etched glass is available, contact Century Shower Door for more information.]

C. Hinge: Adjustable pivot hinge, solid brass or aluminum matching selected frame finish. Hinge shall allow glass to come within 1/32 inch from sidewall, and be capable of 1/4 inch side to side adjustment and 3/16 inch front to back adjustment.

FACTORY FINISH

Header, trim and hardware:
1. Polished Brass, US 3 finish (Bright brass, clear coated).
2. Satin Brass, US 4 finish (Satin brass, clear coating).
3. Antique Brass, US 5 finish (Satin brass blackened).
4. Polished Chrome plate, US 26 finish (Bright chromium plated)
5. Satin Chrome plate, US 26D finish (Satin chromium plated).
6. Polished Nickel plate, US 14 finish (Bright nickel plated).
7. Satin Nickel plate, US 15 finish (Satin nickel plated).
   Custom 24 K gold plate.
8. Bright Copper finish.   9. Satin Copper finish.
10. Polished Gold (24K) finish.   11. Satin Gold (24K) finish.
12. Bright aluminum finish: Highly specular bright finish, clear anodized; Aluminum Association AAC31A21.
13. Bright gold finish: Highly specular bright finish, colored anodized; Aluminum Association AAC31A21.
14. Colored finish: Sprayed-applied thermo-set colored finish in manufacturers standard or custom color as directed by the Architect.

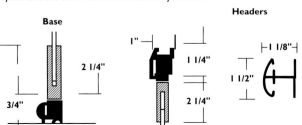

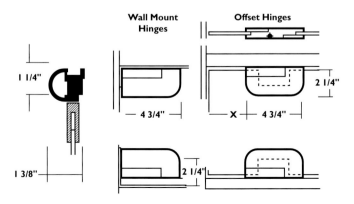

Options

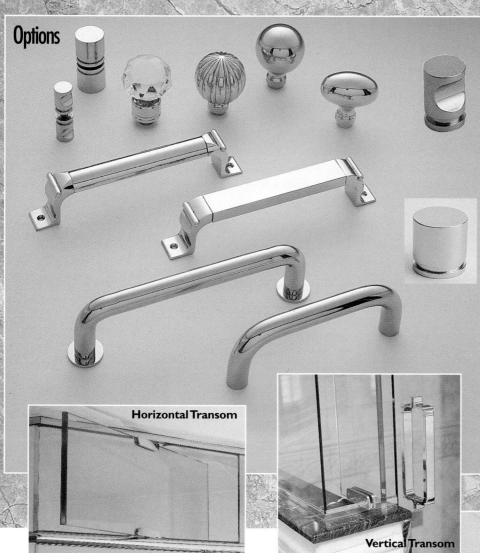

Our hinge system features a spring closure that guarantees a watertight fit year after year. It can be mounted glass to glass, directly to the wall, with or without a header in any finish you choose.

Horizontal Transom

Vertical Transom

Glasstec **GP-1631B** Brass Finish & Clear Glass
with Vertical Transom

Glasstec **GP-1669** Chrome Finish & Clear Glass
with Horizontal Transom

Brassline
The richness of solid brass

Brassline enclosures are heavy gauge solid brass, in 1" or 1¼" frame. Four different hinged, framed & frameless. Nine different finish options are available including polished, satin, and antique brass, polished and satin chrome, polished and satin nickel & 24K gold. Century offers the most extensive brass line available and the Century Guarantee.

Brassline B-1628B Chrome Finish & Clear Glass

Brassline B1631-B Brass Finish & Clear Glass

Brassline Specifications

MANUFACTURER

    Manufacture: To establish a standard of quality, design and function desired, Drawings and specifications have been based on Century Shower Door Inc., 250 Lackawanna Avenue, West Paterson NJ 07424, (973) 785-4290, Product: "Brassline," no substitution will be accepted.

COMPONENTS

A.   Frame and hardware: Extruded Architectural Bronze, copper alloy number 385.

B.   Glass: *[select one of the following]*

    1.   Clear safety glass: conforming to ANSI Z97.1 and certified by Safety Glazing Certification Council.

    2.   Custom glazing: *[Optional glass types include obscure, clear, mirror, bronze striped, grey striped, bronze tint, grey tint, rain, krystal flute, and other custom glass types are available, contact Century Shower Door for more information.]*

C.   Hinge: Adjustable continuous piano hinge or pivot, as required.

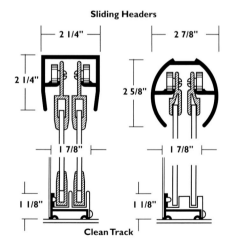

Sliding Headers

2 1/4"   2 7/8"

2 1/4"   2 5/8"

1 7/8"   1 7/8"

1 1/8"   1 1/8"

Clean Track

FACTORY FINISH

    Frame and hardware: *[select one of the following]*

1.   Polished brass, US 3 finish (Bright brass, clear coated).

2.   Satin Brass, US 4 finish (Satin brass, clear coating).

3.   Antique Brass, US 5 finish (Satin brass blackened).

4.   Polished Chrome plate, US 26 finish (Bright chromium plated)

5.   Satin Chrome plate, US 26D finish (Satin chromium plated).

6.   Polished Nickel plate, US 14 finish (Bright nickel plated).

7.   Satin Nickel plate, US 15 finish (Satin nickel plated).

8.   Bright Copper finish.   9. Satin Copper finish.

10. Polished Gold (24K) finish. 11. Satin Gold (24K) finish.

...tury Brassline & Glasstec frames and hardware are ...lable in the following finishes: Polished Brass, Satin ...ss, Antique Brass, Polished Chrome, Satin Chrome, ...shed Nickel, Satin Nickel and 24K Gold.

Brassline B-1669 Chrome Finish & Clear Glass

Brassline BCT-5 Brass Finish & Clear Glass

Hinged Headers

1"
1 1/4"
1 1/4"
1 1/4"
1 3/8"

Door to panel connection

1 1/4"
1 1/4"
3/4"

Brassline B-636-B 1¼" Chrome Finish & Clear Glass

Centec
The unique design

Centec frameless enclosures feature a unique rounded header design constructed of heavy gauge anodized aluminum with ¼" or ⅜" (by-pass only) tempered glass doors. Finishes include: polished aluminum, gold anodized, fourteen standard painted finishes, and custom-matched colors. Centec features pass-through towel bars in traditional or contemporary styles and an easy to clean bottom track.

Centec CS-5 Gold Anodized Finish & Antique Glass with Traditional Towel Bars

Centec CH-1627 Pearl White Finish & Clear Glass
with optional 6" C-Pull Handle

10

Centec Specifications

MANUFACTURER

Manufacture: To establish a standard of quality, design and function desired, Drawings and specifications have been based on Century Shower Door Inc., 250 Lackawanna Avenue, West Paterson NJ 07424, (973) 785-4290, Product: "Centec," no substitution will be accepted.

COMPONENTS

A. Perimeter frame: Extruded aluminum, alloy 6463-T5. *[Optional Brass-Centec is available with solid brass perimeter framing, contact Century Shower Door for more information.].*

B. Glass: *[select one of the following]*
1. Clear or antique tempered glass: 1/4 inch thick safety glass, ASTM C 1048 FT, fully tempered, complying with Class 1 clear, quality q3 glazing select, conforming to ANSI Z97.1. *[Brass Centec is available with 1/4 or 3/8 inch thick tempered glass].*
2. Special order glazing: *[Optional 1/4" "v-groove," grey tinted or bronze tinted glass is available, additionally, sandblasted glass or etched glass is available with Brass Centec.]*

FACTORY FINISH

Frame and hardware: *[select one of the following]*
1. Bright aluminum finish: Highly specular bright finish, clear anodized; Aluminum Association AAC31A21.
2. Bright gold finish: Highly specular bright finish, colored anodized; Aluminum Association AAC31A21.
3. Colored finish: Sprayed-applied thermo-set colored finish in manufacturers standard or custom color as directed by the Architect.
4. Brass Finishes *[Same finishes are available as Brassline enclosures, with optional solid brass framing.].*

Centec CT-5 Brass Finish & Clear Glass with Towel Bar & Knob

Centec CT-5 Custom Paint & Clear Glass

ow available in by- pass and hinged
closures. Select the color, finish
d other options to make it the
rfect fit for any home.

Centec CH-1669 Silver Anodized Finish & Clear Glass with optional 6" C-Pull Handle

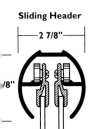

Sliding Header
2 7/8"

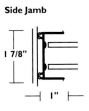

Side Jamb
1 7/8"
1"

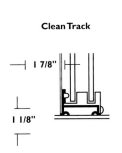

Clean Track
1 7/8"
1 1/8"

Header
1 1/4"
1 1/8"

Base
7/8"
3/4"

Swing Direction
1"

11/16"
1 5/16"
1 5/8"
1/2"
9/16"

Centec
The unique design

CT-636-B Silver Anodized Finish & Clear Glass
with V-Groove & Traditional Towel Bars

CH-1631-B Gold Anodized Finish & Clear Glass
with Clamp on Handle

CH-1628-B Gold Anodized Finish & Antique Glass
with optional 6" C-Pull Handle

CH-1627 Silver Anodized Finish & Obscure Glass
with Clamp on Handle

Trimtec
The unique design & innovation

Trimtec frameless aluminum enclosures combine beauty and functionality along with a superior design. This unique enclosure features a reversible round or flat header, self sealing side jambs and adjustable jamb bumpers. Decorative glass options include 3/16" Krystal Flute, Rain or Clear glass. Standard or deluxe towel bar in chrome, gold anodized or 14 painted finishes complete your bath.

Trimtec TSD-4 Chrome Finish & Clear Glass with Deluxe Towel Bar

Trimtec TT-5 Brass Finish & Rain Glass with Standard Towel Bar

Trimtec Specifications

Deluxe Towel Bar

MANUFACTURER
Manufacture: To establish a standard of quality, design and function desired, Drawings and specifications have been based on Century Shower Door Inc., 250 Lackawanna Avenue, West Paterson NJ 07424, (973) 785-4290, Product: "Trimtec," no substitution will be accepted.

COMPONENTS
A. Perimeter Frame: Extruded aluminum, alloy number 6463-T5.
B. Glass: [select one of the following]
    1. Clear 3/16" safety glass: Conforming to ANSI Z97.1 and certified by Safety Glazing Certification Council.
    2. Rain glass: pattern safety glass, nominal 3/16 inch thick, conforming to ANSI Z97.1.
    3. Krystal Flute: pattern safety glass, nominal 3/16 inch thick, conforming to ANSI Z97.1.
    4. Custom glazing: Flax pattern safety glass, nominal 3/16 inch thick, conforming to ANSI Z97.1.

FACTORY FINISH
Perimeter Frame and hardware: [select one of the following]
1. Bright aluminum finish: Highly specular bright finish, clear anodized; Aluminum Association AAC31A21.
2. Bright gold finish: Highly specular bright finish, colored anodized; Aluminum Association AAC31A21.
3. Colored finish: Sprayed-applied thermo-set colored finish in manufacturers standard or custom color as directed by the Architect.

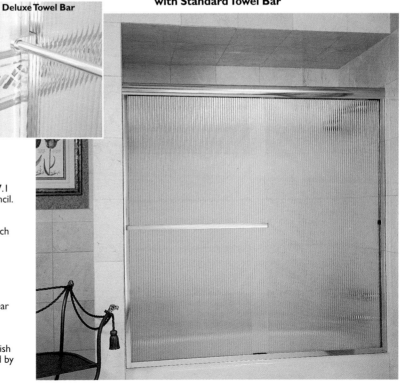

Trimtec TT-5 Brass Finish & Krystal Flute Glass with Standard Towel Bar

13

Lucette
The flexibility of Lucette

Lucette framed aluminum enclosures have been designed as a system to fit all standard formats and virtually any custom configuration you can dream up. Finishes include: polished aluminum, gold anodized, fourteen standard painted finishes or custom colors, and the widest range of glass and sizes available. A system of over 72 extrusions provides angles & sizes to meet any need.

L-636B Gold Anodized Finish & Clear Glass

L-1627 with Hinged Transom For Steam
Gold Anodized Finish & Clear Glass

Header
2"
2 1/4"

Side Jamb
1 3/4"
1 1/8"

1 7/8"

1 1/8"

Clean Track

Lucette Specifications

MANUFACTURER
Manufacture: To establish a standard of quality, design and function desired, Drawings and specifications have been based on Century Shower Door Inc., 250 Lackawanna Avenue, West Paterson NJ 07424, (973)-785-4290, Product: "Lucette", no substitution will be accepted.

COMPONENTS
A. Frame: Extruded aluminum, alloy number 6463-T5.
B. Glass: *[select one of the following]*
   1. Obscure glass: Patterned safety glass, nominal 5/32 inch thick, conforming to ANSI Z97.1.
   2. Clear safety glass: conforming to ANSI Z97.1 and certified by Safety Glazing Certification Council. *[Antique glass is available.]*
   3. Custom glazing: *[Optional glass types include obscure, clear, mirror, bronze striped, grey striped, bronze tint, grey tint, rain, krystal flute, and other custom glass types are available, contact Century Shower Door for more information.]*
C. Hinge *[with hinged doors]*: Continuous aluminum piano hinge, matching selected frame finish.
D. Track *[with sliding doors]*: Extruded aluminum, matching frame finish. Provide doors with adjustable rollers with ball bearings and nylon tires.

FACTORY FINISH
Frame: *[select one of the following]*
   1. Bright aluminum finish: Highly specular bright finish, clear anodized; Aluminum Association AAC31A21.
   2. Bright gold finish: Highly specular bright finish, colored anodized; Aluminum Association AAC31A23.
   3. Colored finish: Sprayed-applied thermo-set colored finish in manufacturers standard or custom color as directed by the Architect.

| Dusty Rose |
| Teal Green |
| Bronze Tone |
| Cobalt Blue |
| Royal Red |
| Almond Tone |
| Cameo Cream |
| Caramel |
| Linen White |
| Platinum Grey |
| Powder Grey |
| Black |
| Silver Anodized |
| Gold Anodized |
| Pearl White |
| Biscuit |

L-1669 Black Painted Finish & Clear Glass

L-1629 Silver Anodized Finish & Clear Glass

L-1631-B Silver Anodized Finish & Clear Glass
with optional 6" C-Pull Handle

L-158 Gold Anodized Finish & Clear Designer Glass
with White Stripe

15

General Specifications

SUMMARY

This Section consists of standard and custom fabricated shower and tub enclosures.

SUBMITTALS

A. Literature: Manufacturer's catalog cuts, detail sectional drawings and installation instructions.

B. Shop drawings: Plan and elevations, bearing dimensions of actual measurements taken at the project.

C. Selection samples: Sample card indicating Manufacturer's full range of finishes available for selection by Architect.

D. Verification samples:
   1. Samples of special order glass type.
   2. Sectional samples, illustrating metal finishes.

DELIVERY, STORAGE & HANDLING

Deliver, store, and handle enclosure components following manufacturer's recommended procedures.

FIELD MEASUREMENTS

Take field measurements before preparation of shop drawings and fabrication, to ensure proper fit.

INSTALLATION

Install shower and tub enclosures in accordance with shop drawings and manufacturer's instructions. Install plumb and level, securely and rigidly anchored, with doors operating freely and smoothly.

Options	Brassline	Glasstec	Centec	Lucette	Crest	Trimtec
Sliding	■	■	■	■	■	■
Hinged	■	■	■	■	■	
Standard Sizes	■	■	■	■	■	■
Custom Sizes	■	■	■	■	■	■
Finishes						
Bright Aluminum		■	■	■	■	■
Anodized Gold		■	■	■		■
Century Colors	■		■	■		■
Brass Finishes (9)	■	■	■			
24K Gold	■	■	■			
Glass						
¼" Clear Laminated	■			■	■	
¼" Opal Laminated	■			■	■	
Obscure	■		■*	■	■	■
Clear	■	■	■	■	■	■
Rain	■		■*	■	■	■
Antique	■		■	■		
Krystal Flute	■			■	■	■
Pattern 62	■		■*	■	■	■
Star Fire	■	■	■	■		
Mirror	■			■	■	
Bronze Tint	■	■	■	■	■	■
Grey Tint	■	■	■	■	■	■
Clear Stripe	■			■	■	
Bronze Striped	■			■	■	
Grey Striped	■			■	■	
V-groove			■			
Custom Glass	■	■	■	■	■	■
⅜" ½" Tempered		■	■			
Transoms						
Steam Transom	■	■		■		
Grille	■			■	■	

*Available on Centec hinged doors only

Century Shower Door, Inc.

250 Lackawanna Avenue ■ West Paterson, NJ 07424
973 785 4290 ■ 800 524 2578 ■ Fax: 973 785 0777

Printed in the U.S.A.

Unmistakably Powerful *even before you turn it on.*

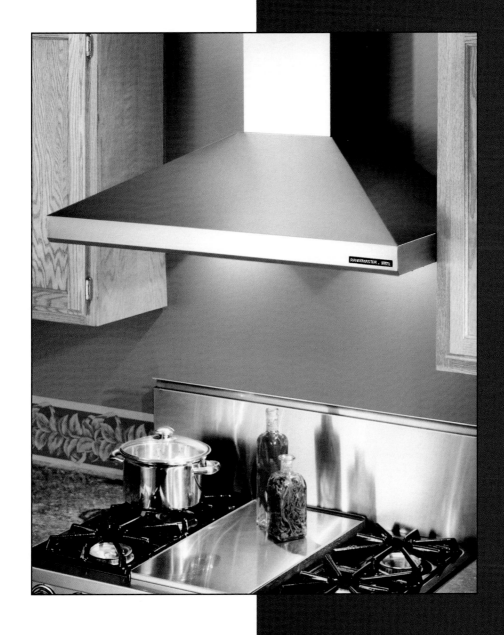

Rangemaster® **by Broan** *the leader in home ventilation.*

Ballista™

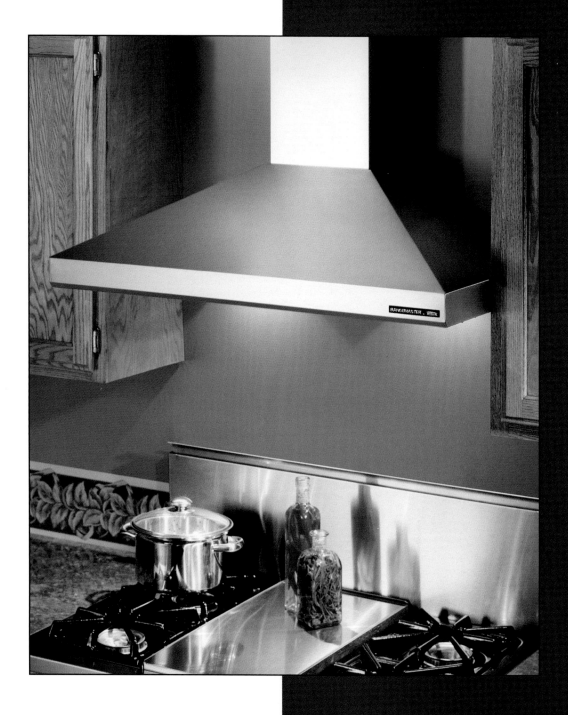

450cfm centrifugal blower

3-speed slide control

two 20-watt halogen lights

Stainless steel.

Seamless corners for easy cleaning.

Telescopic flue fits 8' to 10' ceilings.

A flawless look. A lasting impression.

450cfm centrifugal blower

touch controls

two 20-watt halogen lights

Seamless underside with recessed lighting.

Easy-clean, seamless corner design.

Telescopic flue fits 8' to 10' ceilings.

Dramatically unites stainless steel and hand-blown glass.

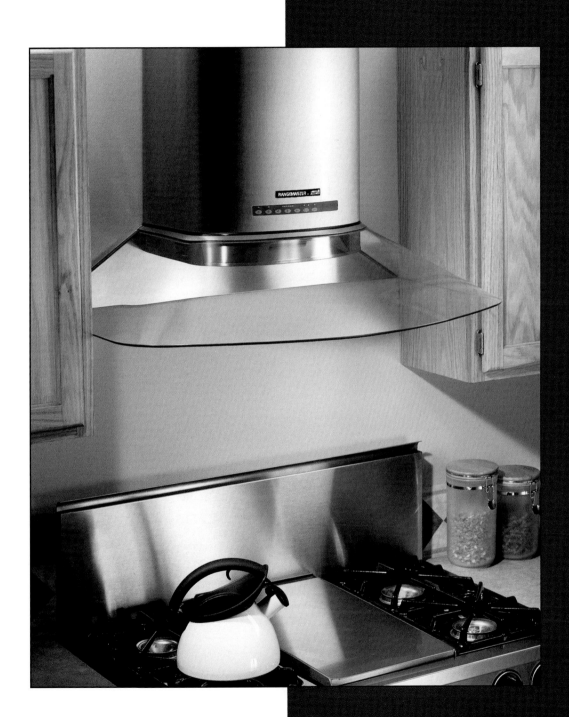

Mirage™

Provisa™

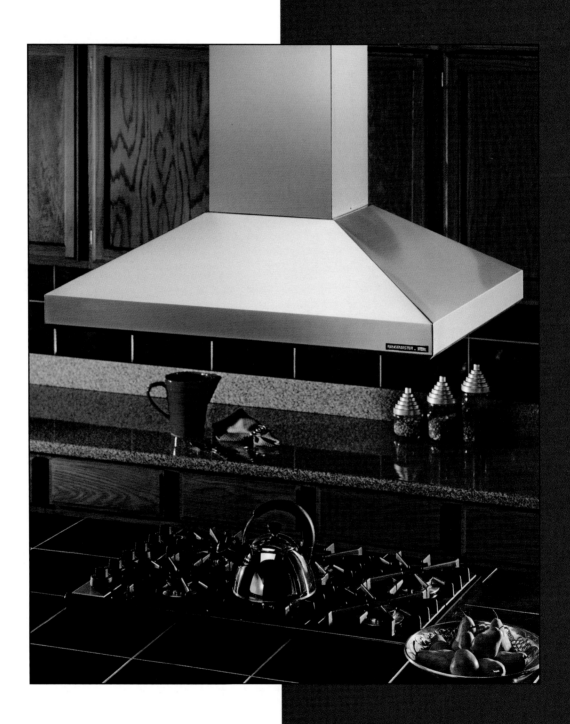

900 cfm centrifugal blower

3-speed control

four 20-watt halogen lights

Stainless steel.

Seamless corners for easy cleaning.

Telescopic flue fits 8' to 10' ceilings.

Designed to draw the eye from every vantage point.

600 or 900cfm external blower

600 or 1200cfm internal blower

infinite speed control

Available in stainless, white or black.

Twin infrared food-warming lamps.

Three 20-watt halogen lights.

The design says professional, the detail pure perfection.

Rangemaster
Original™

Rangemaster Original™ 60000

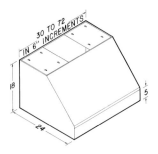
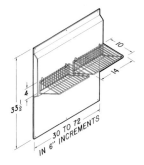

Ballista™ 61000

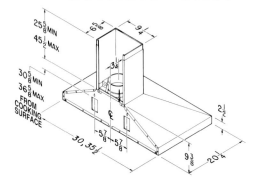

Mirage™ 62000

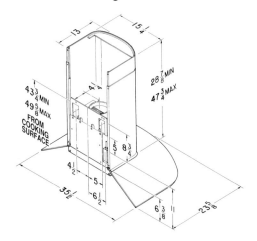

Provisa™ 63000

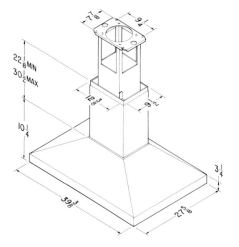

99850531A Printed in the U.S.A.

Model	Available Widths
Rangemaster Original 60000	30"/36"/42"/48"/54"/60"/66"/72"
Ballista 61000	30" or 90cm (35⁷⁄₁₆")
Mirage 62000	90cm (35⁷⁄₁₆")
Provisa 63000	70cm x 100cm (27⁹⁄₁₆" x 39³⁄₈")

Options for Rangemaster Original

Model	Description
325	600 cfm Internal Blower
326	1200 cfm Internal Blower
331	600 cfm External Roof or Wall Mount Blower Requires 332K rough-in kit.
332	900 cfm External Roof or Wall Mount Blower Requires 332K rough-in kit.
RN	Soffit Chimney for 60000–12" high
RP	Backsplash with fold down shelves. Can be used with all Rangemaster Hoods.

Rangemaster range hoods

are a perfect combination of power

and style for your professional-look

kitchen. Ask about matching

stainless steel backsplashes,

which are available as options,

to complete your wall-mounted

Rangemaster ensemble.

BROAN
A NORTEK COMPANY ®

C949
16500/ROB
Buyline 4899

roberts step-lite systems®

1999

Roberts Step-Lite System is a patented lighting system designed to provide an aesthetic solution to the problem of lighting interior and exterior steps, handrails and cove moulding for commercial, as well as residential applications.

Since 1973, architects around the world have specified Roberts Step-Lite Systems and have enjoyed complete freedom in design because the system is custom manufactured to exact dimensions.

You have a choice of five, ten or twenty-five footcandles of continuous uninterrupted light from a concealed source in lengths up to twenty feet in a single fixture. And by grouping various lengths, you can form any continuous lighting effect required.

The Lite fixture fits into polyvinyl extrusions which have been designed to be cast in place for concrete surfaces or siliconed into routed recesses in all other materials. Limitless configurations are possible since the system can be installed on any radius, and the light source can be totally concealed with extrusions and fixtures as small as one-half inch in width and seven-sixteenths of an inch tall.

With a lamp life in excess of fifty years, you virtually have a maintenance-free system. The light source is protected by a limited warranty for 36 months.

Energy efficient, the system operates on either a 12 or 24 volt power supply, but is wired for 24 volts unless specified for 12 volts. Transformers are furnished with the system.

The Lite fixtures are clear Lexan® tubing with clear lamps and are manufactured to exact dimensions since they cannot be modified at the job site. Stock lengths are available for QUICK SHIP if custom field measurements are not available.

Mounting clips or clear rubber silicone is used to adhere the Lite fixture into the extrusion, and for damp area applications, the fixture is moisture-proofed. However, the Lite fixtures should not be submerged in water.

For applications where the maximum length of run requires more than a single fixture, two fixtures can be powered from the same power point. Leads from both ends are provided for angle connections.

And when even lower light levels are desired, low voltage dimmers may be used in conjunction with the system.

This system is used to help prevent accidents and reduce vandalism, while adding aesthetic beauty to any installation.

Installation is quick and simple and all maintenance is virtually eliminated.

With a lamp life that is rated in years, Roberts Step-Lite Systems are easily installed in concrete, brick or hardwood surfaces and meet owners' responsibilities to provide safety lighting for public step and walkway areas.

Series A

roberts step-lite systems®

Roberts' low-voltage lighting systems have become so popular with architects, designers and contractors that nine totally different systems are now available. Each one is specifically designed to help you enhance the beauty of your project and add the extra safety lighting provided by these concealed lighting systems.

The smallest of Roberts' nine different Step-Lite systems is the A-Series. This is also the easiest system to conceal and the most flexible to use. The A-Series Step-Lite is perfect for handrail applications due to its small size.

For surface mounted or recessed applications, the A-Series is 1/2" wide by 7/16" deep, and may be used indoors or outdoors with either STD or EB Lite fixtures and with Superflex tubing.

On step applications, a nosing overhang of one inch is required. In curved applications, small cuts through all but the inside wall of the extrusion material may be required to ease curving of the extrusion. This process is called "kerfing."

Roberts supplies a clear rubber silicone sealant to be used to apply the extrusion to clean and level surfaces. This silicone will stretch to three times its original size and will adhere in sub-zero or extremely high temperatures.

Except for long lengths, Roberts Lite fixtures are shipped mounted into the extrusion, ready for installation.

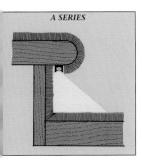

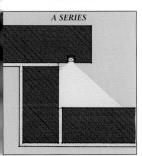

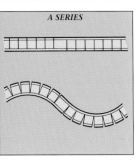

(UL)
SUITABLE FOR
WET LOCATIONS

❸

roberts step-lite systems®

Designed for convenience in applications of cove lighting, Roberts' B-Series and S-Series extrusions are the perfect solution for highlighting those ceiling mouldings whose beauty may not be enhanced by normal lighting.

Both these series feature six lamps per foot with 2" on center spacing and your choice of .9 watt lamps (15,000+ hrs.) or 1.8 watt lamps (10,000+ hrs.).

Also featuring re-lamp capacity for years of continual service, Roberts' low temperature lamps do not have to be turned off during re-lamping.

The fixtures are available in custom lengths or may be field cut. The maximum length is 20' at an economical 24 volts. 4', 6', 8', and 10' lengths are available for QUICK SHIP.

Whether installed in a horizontal or vertical position, the B and S-Series provide a widespread light distribution and can be used outdoors where not exposed to direct moisture.

With the lamps wired in parallel and mounted in polyvinyl extrusion, they are delivered ready for installation. For extra long runs, two 20' lengths can be center fed.

The lamps can be dimmed on the primary side of a step-down transformer.

Mounting holes are pre-drilled for screw or nail attachment and factory kerfing for radius applications is available (possibly additional cost).

Any visible surfaces of the extrusion may be painted to match or become a part of the moulding design.

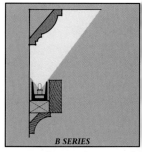

B SERIES

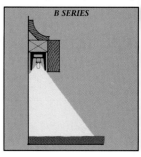

B SERIES

S SERIES

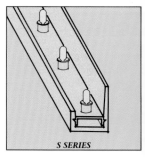

S SERIES

roberts step-lite systems®

With the V-Series cast-in-place lighting by Roberts Step-Lite Systems, you have an opportunity to provide your clients with virtually a vandal-proof lighting system.

For any application where the extrusion can be cast into the step material, such as concrete, terrazzo, Bomanite®, etc., the Roberts V-Series extrusion can be used, indoors or outdoors.

The V-Series, 1-5/16" wide by 3/4" deep extrusion is cast into place as the surface material is poured, and is held in place on wood or styrofoam forms with mechanical tape during the pouring process.

Also prior to pouring, the conduit must be in place to provide the raceway from the Power Point to the transformer for electrical hookup (The "Power Point" is the term applied to the end of the power line from the secondary side of the transformer to the location of the Lite fixture).

The white Polyvinylchloride extrusion may require kerfing on curved applications.

The V-Series extrusion is shipped immediately upon receipt of order so that it may be cast in place. Exact field measurements are then taken after the forms have been removed so that the Lite fixtures can be fabricated to the required dimensions.

All light tubing, whether STD, EB, or Superflex, may be used as required in V-Series extrusions.

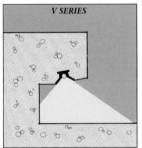

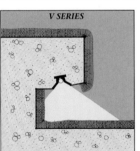

SUITABLE FOR
WET LOCATIONS

roberts step-lite systems®

Roberts' R-Series Step-Lite is the "ultimate" solution for aesthetic lighting on existing steps when remodeling or renovating commercial or institutional projects.

This system is designed to conceal the light source on steps, and direct the light source where it is most functional, while eliminating all glare.

Mounted to the step surface by screws, construction adhesive, or floor tile adhesive, the R-Series aluminum extrusion is 2-1/2" x 1-3/16" x 1-9/16" and can be used indoors or outdoors.

The bronze-tone color is attractive and provides an aesthetic solution for problem steps.

With pre-drilled holes 1/2" from the ends for power wire hook-up, the R-Series is easy to install.

This Step-Lite system is perfect for eliminating the wear on carpet nosing and bull nose wear. It is also perfect for illuminating the shallow risers that cause hazardous falls.

The R-Series is filling the need for retrofitting safety lighting to areas that are known problems.

Roberts' E-Series Step-Lite is designed to safely outline and define a step edge. The Step-Lite is mounted so that the steps will be safely highlighted, even in the darkest environment.

This system can be mounted on any bare step surface, such as concrete, brick, tile or any other flat step surface. The E-Series step extrusion is available in either natural aluminum or bronze color finish, and is secured to the step by a construction adhesive for aluminum bonding.

Stock or custom E-Series light lengths are available up to a maximum of 20 feet, with the maximum length of the aluminum extrusion being 10 feet. Each step light comes complete with 18 inches of lead wire on one end.

Lamps are spaced every 3 inches on center and mounted inside clear Lexan tubing for years of trouble-free service. They are available in 12 or 24 volt capacities, and come with low voltage transformers.

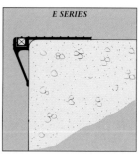

Series Series
C   K

roberts step-lite systems®

Roberts' C-Series Step-Lite is designed to conceal safety lighting and extrusion for carpeted steps and provide a dramatic effect in low light areas by isolating special areas of attention.

With these lights, areas requiring lighted steps, such as auditorium and civic center applications, can have both the luxury of carpeting and the accident prevention that public areas require.

The maximum length of single stock aluminum extrusion is 10', and an STD (2.4 watts per foot) or EB (4.8 watts per foot) 24 volt light system can be used. Both stock and custom lengths are available. Field measurements are required before manufacture.

End caps are supplied to close ends for carpet overhang installation and each Step-Lite is complete with an 18" lead wire on one end, for low voltage electrical hook-up.

Because each project is different, actual stub-thru conduit wire must be located and drilled at the job site. With each order, Roberts supplies a special adhesive for bonding aluminum to concrete. The set-up time for the adhesive is approximately 10-12 hours.

Designed to safely outline and illuminate carpeted steps, Roberts' K Series Step-Lite utilizes a bullnose aluminum extrusion to eliminate worn and frayed carpet at the step nose. Carpet is aesthetically finished under the extrusion, which is available in natural aluminum or bronze coat finish color.

K Series light lengths are available up to a maximum of 20 feet, and extrusions are available up to a maximum 10 feet. The aluminum extrusion is secured to the step by a construction adhesive for aluminum bonding, which is supplied by Roberts Step-Lite Systems with all orders.

Clear Lexan tubing contains the low voltage lamps, spaced every 3 inches on center, for years of trouble-free service. Lamps are available in either 12 or 24 volt, and include low voltage transformers. Each Step-Lite comes complete with 18 inches of lead wire on one end.

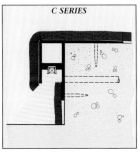

C SERIES

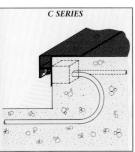

C SERIES

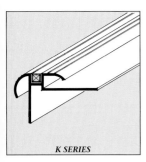

K SERIES

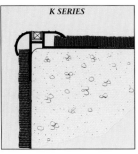

K SERIES

roberts step-lite systems®

Roberts' M-Series Mould-Lite is designed for wall mounting to direct soft, low-voltage lighting up toward the ceiling, or down toward the floor.

When it is desired to highlight and enhance the beauty of a particular style of moulding, or to provide perimeter lighting for a special effect, the M-Series Mould-Lite is the perfect solution.

The 3/4" wide by 1-1/4" deep by 10' long M-Series extrusion is designed to fit most standard trim mouldings.

For ceiling mould applications, EB Lites are suggested, while STD Lites may be used for other applications.

Careful measurements must be made from existing walls and provided to Roberts prior to fabrication of the Lite fixtures. And for more critical applications, accurate field measurements should be taken after extrusion is mounted in place.

The M-Series extrusion can be mounted to the moulding before mitering, or may be nailed directly to the wall prior to securing the moulding.

Curved applications may require kerfing to ease the curving of the extrusion.

Any visible surfaces of the extrusion may be painted to match the moulding.

M SERIES

M SERIES

HOW TO SPECIFY

SPECIFYING INFORMATION:

SPECIFICATION	A-V-R-M-C SERIES STD	EB	K-E STD
Watts per foot	2.4	4.8	1.6
Footcandles, six inches from Lite fixture	5	10	
Lamp spacing	2" o.c. 6 lamps per/ft.	1" o.c. 12 lamps per/ft.	3" o.c. 4 lamps per/ft.
Maximum single Lite fixture	20 linear feet	20 linear feet	20 linear feet

B or S SERIES LAMP CHOICES

SPECIFICATION	.9w Lamp	1.8w Lamp	2.4w Lamp
Watts per foot	5.4	10.8	14.4
Lamp spacing	2" o.c.	2" o.c.	2" o.c.
Maximum single Lite fixture	20 linear feet	20 linear feet	10 linear feet

T SERIES
Clear Tube Retainer

SAMPLE SPECIFICATION:

Lighting System for _(location)_ shall be _(Type A,B,V, etc.)_ Series with _(STD or EB)_ brightness, as manufactured by...

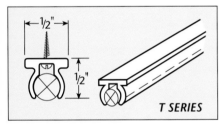

T SERIES

(UL)
SUITABLE FOR
WET LOCATIONS

---

roberts step-lite systems®

8413 Mantle Avenue • Oklahoma City, OK 73132
405-728-4895 • 1-800-654-8268
FAX: 405-728-4878

LITE FIXTURES

Roberts Step-Lite Systems' Lite fixtures are available in two light intensities, STD (Standard) and EB (Extra Bright).

For specifying, use the photometrics on next page to determine which Lite fixture will best suit your clients' needs.

LAMPS

All lamps are designed exclusively for Roberts Step-Lite Systems, Inc. to our specifications. For the Series A, V, R, C, M, K and E, each 5 volt, .15mscp .115 amp lamp is selected to within +-1% of the rated current to ensure conformance through all of our lighting fixtures. The approximate lamp life is 100,000 hours. For Series B and S, 1.8 watt, 75Mamp, 24 volt extra bright lamps are rated at 10,000+ hours, while the .9 watt, 37Mamp, 24 volt standard brightness lamp is rated at 15,000+ hours. Lamps are warm to the touch and can be re-lamped while the fixture is on. Each lamp is mounted to a base plug for socket insertion for quick installation. All B and S-Series fixtures come pre-lamped, ready to install.

TUBING

All of the rigid tubing used by Roberts Step-Lite Systems, Inc. is 1/32" thick, clear poly-carbonate "Lexan® 103" or equivalent, UL inflammability rating 94 V-2 on the resin, UV stabilized. Our Superflex tubing is clear polyvinyl, UL rating 94 V-1.

Each Step-Lite is sealed to make it the natural choice for "wet location" requirements.

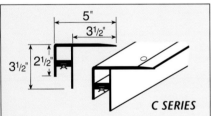

C SERIES

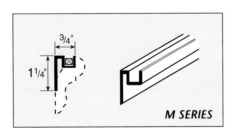

M SERIES

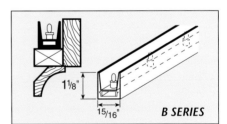

B SERIES

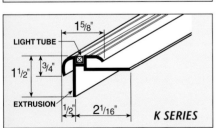

K SERIES

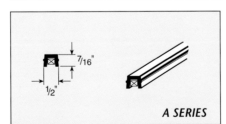

A SERIES

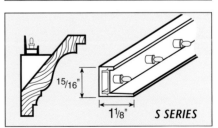

S SERIES

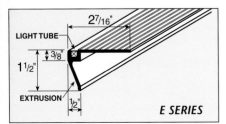

E SERIES

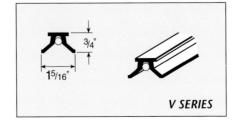

V SERIES

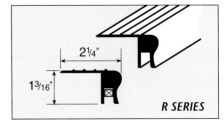

R SERIES

LISTED

TRANSFORMERS

All Roberts Step-Lite Systems lights are powered by a Class II or other UL Listed type transformer furnished by the manufacturer.

The Weatherproof type transformers are 120/240v-12/24v, which means you have the choice of primary voltage of standard 120 or 240 volt. The secondary voltage can be 12 or 24 volt with either 120 or 240 voltage. Unless requested differently, all lighting fixtures are 24 volt.

To figure the size of the transformer required for Series A,V,M,R and C-Series lights in Standard Brightness, multiply 3 watts per foot times total footage per transformer, per area. For transformer size with Extra Bright type lamps, multiply 5 watts per foot times total footage per transformer, per area.

To figure the size of the transformer for Series B and S with Standard Brightness lamps, multiply 6 watts per foot times total footage per transformer, per area. For transformer size with the Extra Bright lamps, multiply 12 watts per foot times total footage per transformer, per area.

To figure the size of the transformer for Series K and E, multiply 2 watts per foot times total footage per transformer, per area.

Many light fixtures may be fed from one transformer as long as the combined total load does not exceed the rating of the transformer. Weatherproof enclosure type transformers have a temperature rise of 131° F. to 240° F. inside the enclosure, depending on the KVA rating. The transformer manufacturer recommends that a thermal device, circuit breaker or fuse be used on the secondary side of the Weatherproof type transformers.

DIMENSIONS IN INCHES

KVA	HOUSING	HT.	WTH.	DTH.	WEIGHT IN LBS.
.040	Indoor Only	3-1/4	2-1/2	2	2
.050	Weatherproof	6-1/2	5-1/4	3-1/4	5
.100	Weatherproof	6-1/2	5-1/4	3-1/4	6
.150	Weatherproof	7-1/2	6-1/4	4-1/4	12
.250	Weatherproof	7-1/2	6-1/4	4-1/4	12
.500	Weatherproof	8-1/2	7	5	16
.750	Weatherproof	9-1/2	8	5-1/2	23
1.000	Weatherproof	9-1/2	8	5-1/2	27
.100	Indoor/Damp (fuse)	8.5	4.13	3.5	6
.150	Indoor/Damp (fuse)	8.5	4.13	3.5	8
.250	Indoor/Damp (fuse)	8.5	4.13	3.5	10
.500	Indoor/Damp (fuse)	10	4.13	3.5	13
.750	Indoor/Damp (fuse)	11.7	4.7	4.6	23
1.000	Indoor/Damp (fuse)	11.9	5.4	5.2	27

Larger sizes available on request.

roberts step-lite systems ®

PHOTOMETRICS

NOTES:
(1) Lighted width to point footcandle level falls to 10% of maximum.
(2) Average footcandles over lighted width.
(3) Footcandles directly below light fixture.
 • Average riser reflectance is 30%
 • For standard brightness Step-Lite (6 lamps/ft.), multiply all values by 0.50

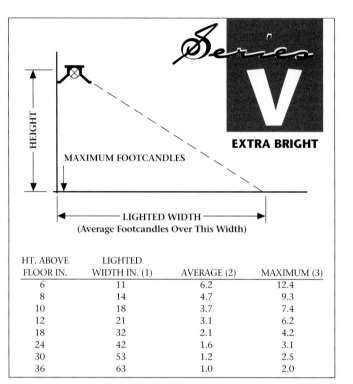

Series V — EXTRA BRIGHT

HT. ABOVE FLOOR IN.	LIGHTED WIDTH IN. (1)	AVERAGE (2)	MAXIMUM (3)
6	11	6.2	12.4
8	14	4.7	9.3
10	18	3.7	7.4
12	21	3.1	6.2
18	32	2.1	4.2
24	42	1.6	3.1
30	53	1.2	2.5
36	63	1.0	2.0

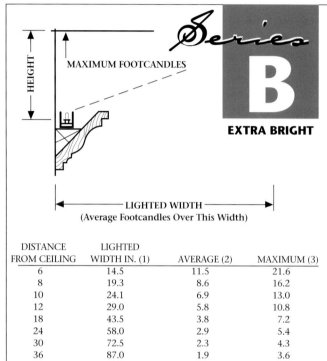

Series B — EXTRA BRIGHT

DISTANCE FROM CEILING	LIGHTED WIDTH IN. (1)	AVERAGE (2)	MAXIMUM (3)
6	14.5	11.5	21.6
8	19.3	8.6	16.2
10	24.1	6.9	13.0
12	29.0	5.8	10.8
18	43.5	3.8	7.2
24	58.0	2.9	5.4
30	72.5	2.3	4.3
36	87.0	1.9	3.6

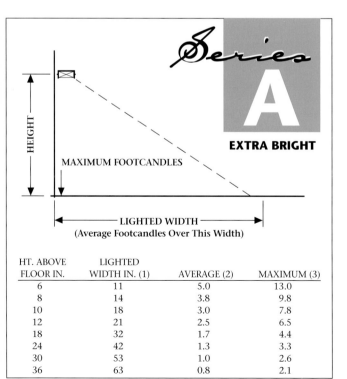

Series A — EXTRA BRIGHT

HT. ABOVE FLOOR IN.	LIGHTED WIDTH IN. (1)	AVERAGE (2)	MAXIMUM (3)
6	11	5.0	13.0
8	14	3.8	9.8
10	18	3.0	7.8
12	21	2.5	6.5
18	32	1.7	4.4
24	42	1.3	3.3
30	53	1.0	2.6
36	63	0.8	2.1

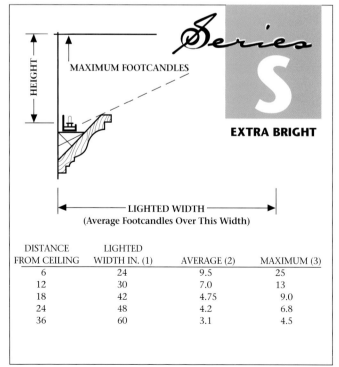

Series S — EXTRA BRIGHT

DISTANCE FROM CEILING	LIGHTED WIDTH IN. (1)	AVERAGE (2)	MAXIMUM (3)
6	24	9.5	25
12	30	7.0	13
18	42	4.75	9.0
24	48	4.2	6.8
36	60	3.1	4.5

AVAILABILITY

• Roberts Step-Lite Systems requires a minimum lead time of three weeks for custom Lite lengths.

• Roberts Step-Lites should be ordered through Manufacturer's Representatives or distributors in your area. Call 1-800-654-8268 for the representative nearest you.

• To insure delivery when needed on large projects, plan should be furnished to Roberts Step-Lite for layout of system in time for approval and field measurements to be taken.

• Manufacturer welcomes inquiries concerning unusual applications of the system and technical clarification.

WARRANTY

• If any Lite fixture should fail to light properly within a period of 36 months from shipping date, and this failure is, in the opinion of the Manufacturer, not a result of a faulty installation or mistreatment after installation, a duplicate Lite fixture will be provided by Manufacturer at no cost upon the return of the faulty Lite fixture. Warranty covers replacement of Lite fixture only. Date of sale and invoice number must accompany return.

• Under no circumstances will a Lite fixture connected to line voltage be covered by this warranty.

• Any faulty Lite fixtures covered under warranty should be completely cooled before removing from installation and shipping back to factory.

• Roberts Step-Lite Systems will not cover any expenses incurred for labor to remove or reinstall replacement Lite fixtures.

• The accuracy of field dimensions to manufacture Lite fixtures is the responsibility of the customer.

• Transformers are covered by a one year warranty from date of installation. Any faulty transformers should be returned to Manufacturer for replacement with date and invoice number of original sale.

ROBERTS STEP LITES ARE EVERYWHERE

Roberts Step-Lite Systems have become "The Ultimate Solution" worldwide in all types and sizes of commercial, institutional and residential facilities. Here are just a few:

Allied Signal Corp.
Morristown, New Jersey
Catch A Rising Star Comedy Club
New York, New York
Children's Hospital
Columbus, Ohio
Dale Earnhardt Residence
Alpharetta, Georgia
Disney Cruise Ship
Buena Vista Theatre
Disney Imagineering Corp. Headquarters
Glendale, California
Indo China Beach Hotel
Danang, Vietnam
Kraft Foods
Glenview, Illinois
MGM Lion Entry
Las Vegas, Nevada
Zoo - Imax Theatre
Kansas City, Missouri
Oklahoma Governor's Mansion
Oklahoma City, Oklahoma

Owens - Corning World Headquarters
Toledo, Ohio
Pennsylvania State Museum
Pennsylvania
Queenshouse Greenwich Maritime Museum
Greenwich, England
Raytheon Electrics
Bedford, Massachusetts
Sheraton Hotel
Bangkok, Thailand
Texas Motor Speedway
Fort Worth, Texas
University Of Miami School Of Medicine
Miami, Florida
Sherwin Williams Corporate Headquarters
Cleveland, Ohio
Langley Air Force Base
Portsmouth, Virginia

roberts step-lite systems®

8413 Mantle Avenue • Oklahoma City, OK 73132
405-728-4895 • 1-800-654-8268
FAX: 405-728-4878